ALL CORVETTES ARE RED

THE REBIRTH OF AN AMERICAN LEGEND

JAMES SCHEFTER

SIMON & SCHUSTER

SIMON & SCHUSTER
Rockefeller Center
1230 Avenue of the Americas
New York, NY 10020

Designed by Karolina Harris

Manufactured in the United States of America

1   2   3   4   5   6   7   8   9   10

Library of Congress Cataloging-in-Publication Data
Schefter, James L.
All corvettes are red : the rebirth of an American legend / James Schefter.
p.   cm.
1. Corvette automobile.   I. Title.
TL215.C6S34   1997
629.222'2—dc21   96-37167   CIP
ISBN 0-684-80854-4

Unless otherwise noted, all photographs appear
courtesy of General Motors Corporation.

ACKNOWLEDGMENTS

In a thirty-month project that lasted more than eight years, there are too many people to thank. But I must try.

Bob Stempel, for the wisdom to let me in and the courage to give me freedom.

Cardy Davis, Joe Spielman, John Cafaro, Russ McLean, and Dave Hill, for trusting me with their careers and giving so many hours of one-on-one time early in the morning and late at night.

Every person in every meeting—and there were hundreds of each—who first wondered about this fellow taking notes on his laptop, then accepted me without reservation.

The guys at lunch and in the cubicles who joked and guided and gave me insights. You know who you are and I'll never tell.

My agent, Dominick Abel, who stopped taking his cut when the money was running out.

Doug Williams and Beverly Gail, whose support, emotional and otherwise, got me through interesting times.

And the guys who took my words, offered a shaping here, a shading there, a cut from this chapter and a clarification in that one, all to make the story flow. Are there better editors than Bob Bender and his colleague-by-the-Sound Leonard Mayhew? Maybe. But I haven't met them.

For my sons, Mike, Will, and Drew,

boys who became men while I chased that red Corvette.

The one-millionth Corvette would be built in the next year or so and be painted in the old shop. At an earlier meeting, a discussion of paint quality and paint colors for future years of Corvette had dragged on so long that John Heinricy, then leading Corvette's development group of test drivers, couldn't take it any longer. "Why are we even having this discussion?" he asked. "All Corvettes are red. The rest are mistakes."

The price of progress is trouble.

—CHARLES F. ''BOSS'' KETTERING,

PIONEER GM INVENTOR AND ENGINEER

PREFACE

This is the story of secrets and intrigue in a corporate world as hidden from outsiders as the inner sanctum of the Central Intelligence Agency. The automobile industry intensely guards its workings, particularly its design studios and engineering rooms. General Motors may be the most secure of all.

Outsiders, even suppliers, are closely escorted when they are allowed in buildings at all. They often meet with their GM counterparts in lobbies, where they sit on vinyl couches or in uncomfortable chairs showing plans or sample parts to GM engineers.

Even insiders have limited access, or none at all, to the most secret rooms. Badges have both a photo and a magnetic strip coded to allow or deny entry through locked doors to buildings, or parts of buildings. Guards search briefcases at the end of the day looking for information that should not leave the premises. Cameras and tape recorders are banned. Laptop computers are logged in and out. An unfamiliar face in a hallway is scrutinized and the person's badge is given a quick confirmatory look.

I roamed those halls and entered the secret rooms for eight years. I expected to spend only half that time at GM but, as the book explains, the years stretched on as I found myself in the middle of GM's worst corporate crisis in decades. Originally called "the book guy" by GM employees, I was eventually known as "the paleontologist."

In my other life—the part away from General Motors—I was bound to a monk's silence. I came to understand the spy mentality. I had friends, divorced a wife, saw my youngest son grow from fifth grade to college. But outside of family, I couldn't tell anyone what I was really doing. I was a guy who sneaked off to Detroit for four or five days at a time and entered a secret world. By agreement with GM, I had to keep my mouth shut.

It started with an insight. In my position as West Coast Editor of *Popular Science* magazine, I was meeting automobile designers. Over a glass of wine or a beer, they'd tell stories about the traumas and the thrills of their jobs.

"We designed a such-and-such for the car and management vetoed it," they'd say morosely. "Too much money."

Or gleefully, "We had this idea five years ago and there it is on the car. What do you think?"

Slowly it dawned on me that creating a new car was not what I thought. It didn't happen on a computer screen, with techies connecting dots with curved lines. It didn't happen in boardrooms, with the suits voting on Proposition A versus Proposition B.

Instead it happened down in a pit, where passions erupted and every emotion from anger to euphoria played its part. Creating a car, I began to see, was a wonderful, frustrating, gut-wrenching, soaring, and terrible process. It mixed artists with engineers, financiers with bureaucrats, regulators with environmentalists. It threw people with opposing views into that pit where they fought it out until a winner climbed into the light.

Creating a car was a fit subject for a book. But what company would be foolish enough, or enlightened enough, to let me do it?

I knew two things for certain. Such a book would have to be approved by the president of the company. And if I made my approach through channels—through the public relations department—the idea would die. So I started with the president.

I lay in wait for Bob Stempel, president of General Motors, at a reception in Los Angeles. We'd met a few times, strictly business. He didn't travel with an entourage and was approachable. I caught him between conversations and we began to talk. The book wouldn't be about hardware, I said, so much as about people. Doing a car was an insane process. It should be a people story.

"It is insane," Stempel said. His eyes were beginning to glitter. "Especially at Design Staff. All those people are crazy. Put it on paper. Send me a letter."

That was in May 1988. The summer went by in silence. By September I was convinced that another great idea had disappeared into a corporate Black Hole.

Then I heard from Bob Stempel. "Come to Detroit," he said. "We're going to do it."

They had a car picked out. Artists were sketching the first preliminary lines. Engineers were debating performance. Managers were gathering budget numbers.

I was sworn to secrecy, introduced to a few key people, and turned loose into a world of brilliant confusion. In the years ahead I would fly more than a million miles, sleep more than 900 nights in motels, go through two laptop computers and pray that the third held up, take more than 20,000 pages of double-spaced notes, and fill several hundred file folders with documents, memos, and news clippings. I went everywhere inside General Motors, even into buildings where my badge was accepted, but the vice president with me required an escort. "If he's with you, it's okay," the guards told me. I saw and experienced and chronicled a world that most veteran GM employees only know in part and that the rest of the world knows not at all.

This is the story of that world. And the car it produced.

1

GENERAL Motors was dying. That was the message in the newspapers and magazines as business writers honed their obituary skills. The smell of corporate demise left a cold fear in the hallways of GM buildings in Detroit and its suburbs. Downsized, battered, and adrift in a tattered economy, the world's largest corporation staggered under new blows. Wall Street had cut the giant's credit rating. Its stock price was plummeting. And its cars weren't selling.

If money were blood, the company would already be dead. It was hemorrhaging by the billions. Its top management was in disarray. A "car guy," an engineer who'd come up through the ranks, was in the chairman's seat for the first time in decades, and he'd been overcome by crisis. It was a crisis he'd inherited more than made, but it was his to resolve. He hadn't succeeded.

Now, in the autumn of 1992, chairman of the board Robert C. Stempel retreated behind the barricades and brooded. As the worst year in General Motors history groped toward winter, the man charged with producing miracles withdrew into executive paralysis. He couldn't bring himself to decide which plants to close or which new car programs to fund. He ignored interview requests from the media and let mail go unanswered. People close to him found him remote and distracted.

When he looked out the executive windows on the fourteenth floor of the General Motors headquarters on West Grand Boulevard in Detroit, Stempel could see a grim vision of the future. General Motors' headquarters, once a symbol of the American dream, was surrounded by a slum. Stempel could see burned and gutted houses and apartments, or vacant lots where charred debris had been cleared away, or claptrap homes where some of Detroit's most dismal poor existed in dreary poverty. A sea of misery surrounded the island of the General Motors Building. It mirrored the condition of Stempel's company.

Inside his office, and inside his head, Bob Stempel felt surrounded. The national economy had escaped from recession and had been slowly improving for more than eighteen months. But General Motors was losing money, losing market share, losing respect, and losing its way. Nothing

Bob Stempel did seemed to work. Too often he did nothing. The day after Stempel ascended to the throne in 1990, Saddam Hussein invaded Kuwait and in the uncertainty of wartime psychology, automobile sales dried up.

Then, faced with having to lay off thousands of assembly-line workers and close an unknown number of plants, Stempel agreed to pay laid-off union people 90 percent of their take-home pay for up to three years. Billions of dollars would be drained from the company's coffers to let folks stay home and be 100 percent nonproductive. When plants did need workers, Stempel couldn't transfer UAW members who lived more than fifty miles from the assembly line. The shackles Stempel accepted in dealing with the union almost killed GM. An editorial cartoon given wide national play even portrayed the chairman of the board as a crash dummy.

It was as bad or worse for others in GM's senior ranks. The foppish dandy pushed into the company presidency by Stempel, over the objections of some board members, had failed, too. Lloyd E. Reuss had fulfilled the dire forecasts about his management style and ability. He finally suffered a rude demotion by the board of directors in a spring 1992 rebellion. When Reuss fell as president, he took the chief financial officer with him, and triggered another of the bewildering reorganizations that cascaded over GM with every slip in market share, leaving the rank and file shaking their heads in bewilderment.

Now it was happening again. The events of spring 1992 were leading to an autumn coup.

At the General Motors Technical Center in Warren, Michigan, an industrial Detroit suburb a few miles northeast of GM's headquarters, the rumors of Stempel's impending demise flew freely. A new president, Jack Smith, had been in power for barely six months. There were signs that he knew what he was doing, but the confusion and frustration at the working level remained. Smith had given unprecedented power to a Strategy Board composed of about eighteen senior executives from GM's North American Operations (NAO), the biggest and most important piece of the international GM empire. NAO, the core automotive business—the cars, the trucks, and the parts that go into them—of the company, would reportedly lose more than *$10 billion* in 1992.

Everything bad that happened at the top flowed quickly down to the car programs, where General Motors met the real world. New-car programs were being hit with delay after delay. A new Chevrolet Camaro intended to be a 1992 model wouldn't reach dealers until late 1993. And a new Corvette, intended to be introduced as a '93, had been hammered with so many budget cuts and executive-ordered delays that it was barely alive as a 1997 model.

The story of Corvette mirrored the story of General Motors. A new Corvette was long overdue. The model on the road, introduced in 1983, was a moneymaker. But its $100 million or so in annual profit was puny by GM standards. Teams of artists and engineers had been working secretly on a new design since 1988. They lived a roller-coaster existence. The budget for doing the new Corvette, up to $250 million, had been granted, trimmed, partly restored, cut again, even wiped completely from the books. As GM sank into its sea of red ink, the ripple effect on Corvette was like a tidal wave. On a Monday morning in mid-October, 1992, the tidal wave made landfall.

Like the company itself, Corvette was dying.

General Motors was all but out of control, managed by rumor, innuendo, press leak, and reflex. Nobody was fully in charge. Bob Stempel collapsed at a meeting in Washington and was hospitalized. Two months later he underwent open-heart surgery.

The press had a field day—weeks of field days—as tasty bits of inside information that could only have come from the board of directors were leaked to reporters at the *Washington Post* and then blazed from headlines and anchor desks across the country. The board members' treachery was known. Stempel's personal advisers warned him that directors J. Willard Marriott and Anne McLaughlin, both of them rich and with little feel for the automotive business, were feeding the *Post*. Stempel did nothing to stop them.

At lower levels in the company, people tried to cope. Corvette program manager Russ McLean—the man charged with producing the current Corvette and with developing its replacement—gathered a dozen of his key people in his office shortly after 8 A.M. on Monday, October 19.

"I want everybody to take a deep breath," McLean told them. "The Strategy Board met all weekend. There'll be an announcement about another reorganization in the next day or two.

"But the impact for us . . . well, all programs after '96 have been put on hold or canceled. Since we were a 1997, all I can say is for you to clear your calendars, stop everything, and go into a holding pattern. Right now, things are pretty confused. . . ."

Automotive News, the most influential publication in the industry, called the General Motors shake-up one of the one hundred most significant events in the history of the automobile. To Corvette, it ranked in the top ten.

A midlevel Corvette manager, Pete Liccardello, replayed McLean's words again and again, looking for salvation. As a key engineering and administrative manager for the 1997 Corvette, he knew that they were on the brink of disaster. If the Corvette team couldn't deliver a new car for 1997, it was almost certain that General Motors and Chevrolet would have no Corvettes at all. The current car, dubbed C4 because it was the fourth-generation

Corvette, was first sketched out in design studios in 1979, engineered in the early eighties, and produced continuously since late 1983. But it was an old-looking car for the nineties. Its future was limited. Though it turned a profit for GM and was still popular among Corvette lovers, it wouldn't meet the federal government's increasingly strict safety standards about broadside crashes effective with 1997 models.

The choice for General Motors was either to deliver an all-new fifth-generation Corvette, a C5 engineered from the ground up, or to spend millions of dollars to change the old Corvette. With the new car already overdue, the coming side-impact standards signed the death warrant for C4. The last of the fourth generation would be produced in the spring of 1996. There were two possible scenarios for the day after the assembly line stopped: Either the Corvette plant in Bowling Green, Kentucky, would shut down and the legend would die, or the plant would switch over to a new-model Corvette and the legend would live.

Some of the basic engineering for C5 was done. Decisions made two and three years earlier, when the goal was simply to produce a world-class sports car that would beat the competition in performance and quality, made the Corvette team look prescient. Their design exceeded the new crash standards. But that might not matter. Liccardello thought that a total shutdown looked likely. Corvette could die. But he found some hope in Russ McLean's closing words an hour ago.

"Maybe we'll know more when Joe Spielman has time to sort things out," McLean said. "He came out of this pretty good. A lot bigger chunk of North American Operations is his. . . ."

Spielman ran a massive engineering and manufacturing organization that was juggled and jimmied in 1992 until it finally took shape as the Midsize Car Division. When the dust settled enough in late October to see who'd won and who'd lost, more than 40 percent of GM's North American auto production, including Corvette, belonged to Joe Spielman.

So where do we fit? Liccardello wondered. *Spielman is a Corvette fanatic. But we're a little piece of a big business.*

For now, no one had a clue about the future of either Corvette or General Motors. A car that was an American legend could be facing an ignominious end. Liccardello called up a file on his computer and updated the four-year chronology he kept of C5's fits and starts. He posted the revised version outside his cubicle.

The new line read: "October 19, 1992..Chaos"

2

JOHN Cafaro's secret room opened in August 1988. It was a dingy place in the basement of the ultrasecure Design building at the General Motors Technical Center in Warren, Michigan, about twelve miles north of downtown Detroit. Behind locked and guarded doors, in a building more than thirty years old, General Motors housed its artists and designers, some of the most talented and creative people in the car business. It housed them shabbily.

The aging studios on the first and second floors were spartan. Fostering artistic genius through colorful, comfortable quarters and diversions like an occasional free pizza and video games was alien to the General Motors culture. But the twenty-odd design studios in the building were elegant compared to Cafaro's secret room in the basement. It was coated with faded green paint. Dusty white plaster flaked from the walls. Exposed pipes formed an irregular grid across the ceiling. In winter, the pipes clanked and wheezed. In summer, they sweated. Scuffed and cracked floor tiles added to the secret room's worked-over look. It was not a place where laymen would expect to find creativity. In this room, every expense had been spared.

John Cafaro didn't care. The room in the basement housed a dream. He felt torn between staying in his full-time studio on the second floor, called Chevy 3, and hanging out with the artists in the basement working on Corvette. In mid-December 1988, he looked pensively through the high north-facing windows of Chevy 3 and watched a pair of late-leaving swans swimming in circles near the warm-water outfall of a large reflecting pool. At thirty-four, Cafaro was the youngest production studio chief at the GM Design Staff. If artists like Cafaro touched the right nerve, their works achieved enduring beauty. If not, they faced derision and even ridicule in the automotive marketplace and in the critical press. Cafaro's career kept him walking a tightrope. He loved it.

Each of the studios in the building was locked to keep prying eyes from designs for cars still two, three, or four years from production. Behind those doors, corporate spies could find the future of General Motors. There was plenty to see in the production studios. Chevrolet had four of them. There were three more for Pontiac. Oldsmobile and Buick each had two studios. Cadillac had just one. So did Saturn. Two more studios were devoted to trucks. Two studios did nothing but interiors for whichever cars were being revised or replaced. Those were the production studios.

The other studios lived in the future. Four studios did the advanced designs, show cars, experimental vehicles, and impressionistic peeks at where current cars such as Corvette or Cadillac might go. Another created advanced interiors, trying out concepts like video instrument panels and heads-up displays where the instruments seem to float outside the car over the hood.

Two of Chevy's four studios worked on bread-and-butter sedans, and another concentrated on compacts and subcompacts. But Cafaro's Chevy 3 was unique. It did the hot Chevrolets. A full-size clay model of the flashy 1992 Camaro was behind his back, attended by a single artisan scraping away thin shards of tan-colored clay to refine the curve of a fender. It was barely a month from being handed over to the engineers and manufacturing types who would turn it from sculpted clay into fire-breathing metal and glass, and put it on the road.

The secret room could only be reached by a long, circuitous walk through dimly lit hallways. The room's glow came through cracks around the edges of its door, throwing slivers of light into the dead-end hall. Inside, fluorescent lights in egg-carton frames mixed unnatural yellows into the two hundred or more sketches of futuristic cars tacked to head-high portable partitions. The grim light soaked into a rough-hewn reddish brown clay sculpture that dominated the room's grubby center leaving no hint of shadow or grace. The psychology of creation blossomed in the room only by chance and by force of human will, not by design. And it did blossom. The room crackled with energy. Creativity and excitement gleamed in the eyes of the half-dozen artists and sculptors lucky enough, and good enough, to be sent there. They were a mixed lot, from a couple of young designers who couldn't believe their luck to a twenty-five-year veteran whose spare-time graphics adorned famous Indy cars and stock cars on America's racing circuits.

The secret room's location was ordered by the man who controlled all of General Motors' automotive styling. Charles M. Jordan, vice president for design, was called, but never to his face, the Chrome Cobra. He earned the sobriquet honestly. Jordan could be acerbic when he critiqued designs and capricious in dealing with real or imagined offenses. Artists or sculptors might begin their day working on a new production sedan or van and find themselves banished to another studio by midafternoon. Jordan was five years from retiring and the Corvette taking form in the basement was to be his crowning achievement. At this early stage, he wanted it kept secret.

Sculptors carved at the eight hundred pounds of clay packed over a wood and foam core. One knelt at the forward end, cutting and scraping with a long curved knife to match the lines roughly to the multicolored sketch leaning lazily on a tripod. Another pulled along the slab-sided length of clay with a broad serrated trowel, leaving parallel lines gouged into the surface and ribbons of half-moist clay trailing on the floor. A third sculptor leaned over the top, cutting away huge chunks to bring the height down to approximate size. Later all of them would use the finest tools of their craft, slim blades and keen-edged scrapers and pointed tines, to hone the emerging clay beast to its final shape.

John Cafaro couldn't stay away. He spent hours every day in the dismal basement, looking over shoulders, commenting and guiding, often sitting down to a table with pencil in hand to sketch feline curves and shapes that might miraculously touch the core of sensuous strength he sought for his car. To Cafaro, to Chevrolet, and to General Motors, the clay car in the basement was the crown jewel of the corporation. He wanted it to be the jewel in his own crown, too.

3 CAFARO walked purposefully from his upstairs studio, took the slow-moving elevator to the basement, and made the long corridor stroll to the secret room. Yellow light poured through the broad double doors when he pulled them open. His eyes lit up and his grin broadened when he stepped inside. Then he adjusted a sign held by a tall tripod just inside the room. It showed an aggressive pantherlike beast in hunting crouch glaring at anyone who would dare enter. The beast's claws were exposed over a futuristic car shape and flanked by a bow-tie-and-checkered-flag emblem recognized only a little less around the world than the logo for Coca-Cola.

Only three words were on the sign: Corvette Skunk Works.

"This place sucks!"

John Cafaro's loud announcement turned heads in the Skunk Works as he walked into the grubby room. Grins spread on the half-dozen faces. Cafaro was young in years and young at heart, and he knew how to get along with his guys. What he didn't do well was get along with his boss, Chuck Jordan. It was less Cafaro's fault than Jordan's. Jordan treated the young designer only a bit more harshly than he treated almost everyone else in the Design building, that is, with unconcealed animosity. His sarcasm and his outbursts frequently left Cafaro on edge. Cafaro's design genius was almost equaled by the way he displayed his own emotions. He was maturing and getting them under control. But the urge to parody a boss that many in the building considered mean-spirited was sometimes too much.

"How can you guys work in this place?" Cafaro asked. "It smells like old steam down here."

The grins widened. Cafaro's face twisted into a pinched caricature and his voice turned whiny and sharp as he imitated Chuck Jordan.

"I don't like that," he snapped, pointing to an exquisite rendering of a futuristic Corvette tacked to a display board. "It doesn't have enough reach."

He whirled to confront Randy Wittine, who at fifty had been in the Chevy 3 studio for twenty-five years. Wittine was working with a sculptor on a three-eighths-scale clay model, using a technique called a clown suit—half of the advanced Corvette in clay, the other half reflected in a mirror. "The rear end's too wide," Cafaro snarled. "This is supposed to bubble-up, not bubble-butt."

The room cracked up. Gary Clark, a modeler with tousled gray-blond hair and crinkly blue eyes, laughed at Cafaro's unerring parody. "Yes, sir, Mr. Jordan, sir, we'll fix that right up, sir."

"Well, see that you do," Cafaro whined. "Otherwise there's an opening over in trucks. You guys want to do Corvettes or trucks?"

He shifted gears without waiting for an answer and turned back to the six-man Skunk Works crew. "What d'ya got for me? We've been down here three months and Charlie's still not happy. Show me something."

That was the challenge. The new 1993 Corvette couldn't be merely good. It had to be great. From its first appearance in 1953, Corvette was an enthusiast's success. New body styles came along periodically, either as part of a Corvette that was virtually all new or as part of a reskinning to put a fresh face on an aging chassis-and-engine combination. New interiors also appeared now and then to give Corvette a grip on sales that might be slipping slightly. By 1988, it was a $30,000 sports car of legendary stature.

But there was competition. Car buyers were jumping to Nissan's 300ZX or Toyota's Supra, both priced almost $10,000 less than Corvette. (They would catch and pass Corvette's sticker price in the next few years.) Lower on the price scale were fun toys, the hot Mazda RX-7 and Toyota's spiffy MR-2. While American car companies seemed to be stuck in an interval between new cars that had somehow stretched out to ten years, the Japanese were bringing out new sports car models every five years.

None of the Japanese sports cars had Corvette's mystique or performance. Survey after survey showed that huge numbers of Americans remembered the first time they saw a Corvette. In uncounted minds, owning a Corvette was the ultimate symbol of success. But still, the image and the sales numbers were being slowly eroded.

Nissan was due to introduce a brand-new 300ZX in 1989, priced right up there with the fourth-generation Corvette. Toyota had a new car not far behind. Spy photos and drawings of a racy Mitsubishi and even a sleek, sporty Dodge built on the same chassis were showing up in the automotive press. Mazda was rumored to be moving up to the Corvette class in 1991 or 1992. The newcomers had sweeping macho lines and the GM team knew that they'd start biting into Corvette's sales in mid-1990.

Competition came from another front, too. The Japanese luxury cars Lexus and Infiniti were just arriving, to rave reviews, and would take away some Corvette sales as traditional, well-to-do sports car buyers opted for luxury sedans instead. Down the road there were rumors of a Nissan or perhaps Infiniti mid-engine sports car evolved from the Mid-4 show car that was the darling of recent Tokyo motor shows, and Honda was leaking word that it would have a $50,000-plus sports model in 1990.

Against that constellation of Japanese competition, it was time, and past time, to begin working on Corvette's future. True, there were changes coming in the current Corvette. The ZR-1 model to be put into production in 1990 would have a unique engine that could rip the car from zero to sixty in 4.1 seconds, go from zero to one hundred and back to zero in 15 seconds, and still get around twenty-six miles per gallon when driven at legal speeds. A modest face-lift for the regular Corvette's body was coming in 1991, to keep sales at the profitable 20,000 unit level or higher for another year or two. After that, continuing profits demanded a new car.

In the unmanageable mass of GM, Corvette was all too easy to ignore. Corvette's profit was a trifle against GM's billions on the bottom line. But even so, the giant company was stirring with the recognition that a new Corvette was overdue. The chosen year was 1993, Corvette's fortieth anniversary. If 1993 was a few years later than the marketplace demanded, the C5 Corvette would still be a success. Corvette may have been a footnote in the ledger books, but it put the final gloss on the corporation's public image. Whatever else GM did wrong, it did Corvette right. In some years, Corvette generated as many news clippings—almost all favorable—as the rest of the company's cars, financial clippings, and personnel announcements combined. Corvette's aura brought people into Chevrolet showrooms and sent many of them home in less expensive, less awesome new cars. "There's a little Corvette in every Chevrolet," Chevrolet's incoming general manager Jim Perkins liked to say. A lot of buyers agreed.

The tentative budget for the new Corvette—design, engineering, and plant conversion costs—was set at $250 million, a relatively modest sum. But to Jerry Palmer, head of advanced studio operations at Design Staff, and the man who designed the C4 Corvette, it was plenty.

"We can do a helluva Corvette for that," Palmer told his boss, Chuck Jordan. "We can do it right."

"It has to be better than right," Jordan snapped. "It has to be great."

If they stayed on schedule, the new '93 Corvette would roll off the assembly line in August 1992. Two months later, Chuck Jordan would retire. This Corvette would be his legacy. It could also make Jerry Palmer the obvious man to succeed him as GM's design czar.

"It'll be great," Palmer said, grinning his leprechaun grin. "It'll be magnificent."

But it wasn't there yet. Under the guidance of Jerry Palmer, John Cafaro had free choice of any designer in the building for temporary assignment to the Skunk Works. He'd cycled a half-dozen through the place since October, always keeping a core of his own Chevy 3 people there. To be chosen for this project could be the making or breaking of a career. "People would kill to get through that door," one of the young designers said, "if they knew what we're doing."

GM called this stage of design "bubble-up." Its goal was to let the creative juices flow, to play with ideas, to draft, draw, or doodle, trying this and that, getting wild with sketches and clay models. Working alone at a sloped desk, or talking in hushed tones with two or three peers, designers were supposed to unlock their minds, let out ideas, free up bizarre thoughts to be discussed, debated, even derided. If it worked, the designers would purge their minds of awkward or uninspiring concepts and slowly focus on a few sketches or models that could be refined and turned into full-size clay Corvettes. They'd find a theme for the new car that artists and engineers could take into the next phase of development and refine into something that could be put on the road.

Hundreds, maybe thousands of pencil and chalk sketches had gone into the burn bin in the past ninety days. Many of them had the quality of a star, setting hearts racing and imaginations twirling at the thought of parking that Corvette, or *that one,* or *that one,* in the garage. A dozen clay models had been ripped apart and started over, taking their lines from new sketches. Two or three of them might have made Corvette into the Car of the Year for 1993, if the engineering and performance matched the raw beauty of the exterior styling. Artists at General Motors often went through hundreds of designs looking for the one that would make Chuck Jordan smile.

So far he hated them all.

John Cafaro studied the newest sketches on the boards and thought about the mix of talent in the noisy, steamy Skunk Works. Each of the four designers, two from Cafaro's Chevy 3 studio, two on loan from other studios, had been letting his imagination stretch. Each did it differently. Randy Wittine, whose studio nickname was Mr. Corvette, spent a part of each day reading the papers, both the *Detroit News* and *Detroit Free Press*. His routine was well known: Talk little, stick to yourself, ignore the politics of the building. His designs had contributed to every Corvette, Camaro, and Beretta in the past quarter century and his reputation was so solid that nobody said a word when he freelanced designs for racing teams on company time. Roger Mears relied on Wittine exclusively for his racing colors, and Wittine paint schemes had flashed around the nation's tracks on cars driven by Mario Andretti, Danny Sullivan, A. J. Foyt, and others.

"Designers need to get out and breathe fresh air," Cafaro said now and then. "One of the things we do wrong is not sending guys out where they can experience the world, get a different perspective. We're all breathing the same stale Detroit air here."

The only concession Chuck Jordan made to spiritual exploration was to assign designers to spend anywhere from six months to several years at GM's Advanced Concepts Center near Los Angeles or at the Opel Design Studio in Germany. The Advanced Concepts Center did wild things, hoping to capture some elusive California flavor that could be brought back to Detroit. Opel did production cars in the European tradition. Few artists were lucky enough to get those assignments.

Cafaro naturally favored his own artists in the Skunk Works. The floor around Kirk Bennion's table was littered with sketches, crumpled and tossed away in disgust. He did dozens in a day. Some were keepers. His display board usually had fifteen or twenty sketches up for viewing. Several other sketches were posted over a clay model that was taking shape under the knife of a skilled sculptor. The torpedo-like model was the second clown suit in the room and it was so smooth and aerodynamic that it cast a shadow that either flowed like an "S" or darted like an arrow, depending on where a watcher stood.

The old guy from the Advanced 4 studio, George Camp, watched Cafaro move around the room. Camp drew methodically, finding inspiration in aviation magazines and in photos of limited-production European sports cars like Lamborghinis and Ferraris.

Clay Dean was the fourth designer and had a limited track record. Dean sent so many letters to Design Staff that one midlevel manager finally agreed to meet with him. The manager liked what he saw and set up a meeting in Las Vegas with Jerry Palmer. Dean drove four hundred miles from Provo, Utah, to grab his chance.

Palmer was impressed. He offered financial and consulting support for Brigham Young University's automotive design program and arranged for Dean to intern between his junior and senior years under another talented GM designer at the Advanced Concepts Center studio in California. John Schinella was running ACC after winning acclaim for the Fiero sports car designed in his old studio, Pontiac 2. Schinella's grasp of futuristic design concepts, and his ability to communicate with his temperamental charges, convinced young Clay Dean that his future lay with GM's Design Staff. Shortly after Dean reported to Detroit for full-time work in mid-1988, Cafaro put him to work on tomorrow's Corvette.

"I can't believe it," Dean marveled. "My first assignment is the Y-car!"

"Y" is the General Motors designation for the Corvette platform. A platform in automotive industry lingo is the basic car—chassis, various engines and transmission, and general specifications such as wheelbase and interior dimensions. Several car models are combined in a platform. At GM, the A-car was a Buick Century or an Oldsmobile Cutlass Ciera. The F-car was a Chevy Camaro or a Pontiac Firebird. A W-car could be a Buick Regal, a Chevy Lumina, an Olds Cutlass Supreme, or a Pontiac Grand Prix. Other letter designations covered various Cadillacs, Buicks, vans, and the rest.

There was only one platform at GM that was devoted to a single car. The Y-car was pure Corvette.

A design studio took the basic car and dressed it with a skin and interior. The process often led to quarrels with engineers on the platform team who had to change *their* designs to accommodate the styling variations that Chuck Jordan's people wanted. "Those prima donnas at Design Staff throw their styling over the wall and we're supposed to figure out how to manufacture it" was a frequent complaint from engineers on every platform.

The Y-car group that Clay Dean joined was eager and excited. Cafaro changed the mix every three or four weeks, keeping Wittine and Dean but sending other designers back to their studios sworn to secrecy. Two of the designers would be in their twenties, dreaming of hot-thunder cars like Corvettes, feeling the awe of working in the grubby, magical Skunk Works. The other two would be middle-aged, veterans of GM design wars with notches on their paintbrushes for the production cars they'd fretted over. In Cafaro's eyes, middle age was no constraint. And youth was a definite plus in the Skunk Works. They were designing a car that might someday soften their own midlife crisis, or let thousands of other well-to-do dreamers enjoy a toy in some upscale second childhood. But most of all, every man in the dingy basement room wanted to give the massive international Corvette cult a worthy successor to forty years of great cars.

"This is good," Cafaro said, bending at the waist to look down the side of Kirk Bennion's clay clown suit. "It's got the feel of Corvette. But the upper . . . it doesn't quite flow. I want to see a faster windshield, more sloped. Can you rake it a bit more into the roofline?"

"Sure," Bennion said. "What about the wraparound?"

Cafaro stepped back, studying the model and the sketches being used to sculpt it. *This one has possibilities,* Cafaro thought. He examined the model with a critical eye. The maybe-Corvette's nose came to a dramatically rounded point, with its hood sloping down steep from the windshield. The car had the feeling of a hungry jungle cat ready to pounce, rising dramatically from its front bumper to a high point just behind the driver's head. The windshield was "fast," raked long into the hood, but Cafaro wanted it even more dramatic. It wrapped around the sides much more than current 'Vettes, and Cafaro approved.

He nodded appreciatively at Bennion's idea for concealed headlights, buried under sharply rectangular covers with their long axis flowing up the clamshell hood. *Nice idea,* he thought. *I wonder if the engineers can make it work.* A parabolic air scoop molded into the hood cast an imaginary line back to upper door cuts, then seemed to blend seamlessly with the lines of the rear window and deck. Another inverted bubble, a modified three-dimensional parabola, was molded into each door, running from the door's leading edge, under the driver's or passenger's shoulder, and on to the door's trailing edge, where it flared out to help shape the rear wheel well. Cafaro ran his hand along the model's side. *Feels as good as it looks,* he thought.

The rear deck flattened briefly behind the hatch window before chopping off dramatically into rounded, compound curves that flowed left to right as well as top to bottom. The taillight design was missing.

"Nice work, Kirk," Cafaro said. "Try something different on the upper, make the windshield a little faster, and let me see some ideas for the rear end. When you come up behind this car at a stoplight, you have to know it's a Corvette."

The studio chief glanced around the room and grinned. "I see lots of great stuff here," he said. "But Charlie's been on a rampage. We gotta find a way to make him happy."

There were nods in the room and smiles faded. Every man there had lived through a Chuck Jordan tongue-lashing. It was a bitter and humiliating experience, always done in public, always ugly.

"I gotta get upstairs," Cafaro said. "Don't let the bastards get you down."

It was a slow trek back. No matter how many times he made the journey, Cafaro couldn't walk the hallways of the building called Design without stopping to look, without turning into an alcove or a side hall for a quick glance or a lingering inspection. There were cars everywhere.

In the halls, cars sat on display under artistically focused floodlights, placed strategically for inspection by the building's artists, by engineers and executives and marketers in for a meeting, or by the few outsiders allowed in the place, closely accompanied by a guardian to make sure they didn't wander into a studio where prying eyes weren't welcome. Other cars were on dollies, being moved from place to place in the building. Still more cars filled big white-walled rooms in the basement, jammed so tightly together that it was a chore to get them out.

Cafaro wore his artist's emotions openly. He knew he was looking at cars that didn't exist. The halls and the storerooms were filled with dreams and guesses and glimpses of the future. Dozens of cars. Scores of cars. Show cars. Concept cars. What-if cars. Maybe-someday cars. Probably-never cars. Their skins glistened with high-tech foil instead of paint. The windows, too, were foil, some matte black, some silver, all appealing. Their plastic tires flattened slightly against the granite floor. Badging and graphics and a strip of faux chrome, decals and foil instead of the real thing, perfected the illusions. From close up or afar, Cafaro saw cars to make pulses quicken and send true believers into ecstasy.

In a most real sense, however, none of them were cars at all. They were ideas in three dimensions.

These ideas were clay, artfully and lovingly sculpted. Back to clay is where most would go. Only a few were mock-ups of fiberglass and wood. On those few, doors opened and the glass was real. Even fewer were almost completely real. One magnificently futuristic car with a red and black fiberglass body was being moved toward a shipping dock. This one had an engine and actually ran on a night-darkened test track. It was an imaginary Camaro, designed and built in California, and scheduled for unveiling at the January 1989 auto shows. It was the closest thing to reality that the Advanced Concepts Center had ever produced. John Cafaro watched it disappear around a corner and shook his head. The California Camaro was a show car, unlike the real Camaro upstairs in Chevy 3.

But it was real enough and it was destined to bring frightful and wondrous havoc to all who touched it. Including John Cafaro.

4 H A L F a mile across the sprawling General Motors Technical Center, another piece of the Corvette bubble-up process was taking shape in late 1988. The business and product-engineering people were building a case for development money.

That part of the team was the real core of Corvette. The people on the business and engineering team—the *platform* team—carried the car throughout its life cycle.

The platform team would take the styling from John Cafaro and turn it into a real machine. Platform people were responsible for designing and engineering the chassis, the engine, the transmission—all the vital pieces that are under the pretty skin and behind the dazzling instruments. They included the business people who were involved with purchasing the individual parts and maintaining Corvette's account books, the engineers who oversaw quality and worked to improve the car with each passing year, and the administrative folks who kept all the paperwork straight.

The platform had to handle the problems, too. Engineers took the phone calls from owners, irate or overjoyed, and from the fanatics in the Corvette clubs who worship the car. Long after John Cafaro and his artists had gone on to other assignments, or were spending their days designing cosmetic changes to the existing Corvette, the platform people would be living with the car and figuring ways to make it better.

In 1988, Corvette's platform or program manager—the terms were used interchangeably—was Carlisle V. Davis. Cardy Davis was the only manager in his division to run two platforms simultaneously. His other job was directing midsize family sedans such as the Oldsmobile Cutlass and Buick Century. He spent about half his time with each platform. For Cardy Davis, that meant dividing up a sixty-hour week. His primary Corvette effort in the fading months of 1988 was to narrow the engineering alternatives and develop preliminary financial numbers for the fifth-generation Corvette, the C5. That was the platform contribution to the bubble-up process.

Davis and his Corvette team had five or six months to prepare their case before an executive review board early the next spring. But while the platform side of Corvette was doing its engineering and financial homework, angry words were changing the course of the program at Design Staff.

A professionally lettered sign appeared on the wall of the Chevy 3 studio overnight.

> *Lonesome?*
>
> *Like to meet new people?*
>
> *Need a change?*
>
> *Like excitement?*
>
> *Like a new job?*
>
> *Just screw up one more time.*

Chuck Jordan didn't notice it when he let himself in with his master key. People with frequent business in a studio either knew the three-digit punch code that unlocked the door or rang the doorbell. The savviest visitors noticed that the cleaning people carefully penciled the punch code on the grout between wall tiles somewhere near each locked door. Now and then, the security staff erased the codes, but they always reappeared within days.

Chuck Jordan didn't concern himself with such trivia. He had a key that opened every door in the building and he was still pocketing it when he strode across the Chevy 3 studio floor.

"Where's Cafaro?" His tone was typically high-pitched, almost fretful. Nine times out of ten, those were the first words out of his mouth when he strode into Chevy 3, even when John Cafaro was standing plainly visible in the middle of the huge room.

"Right here, Chuck!"

It was January 16, 1989, a day that would be known in Chevy 3 as Black Monday.

Jordan was on a rampage. Almost a year earlier Jordan called John Schinella at the Advanced Concepts Center in California. "You've got some wild talent out there," he told Schinella. "Turn it loose and give me a California Camaro. Give me a Camaro that would sell in California. Oh yeah, don't talk about it back here. I'm not spreading the word around."

It was a typical Jordan tactic, setting one studio against another without letting some of the participants know that a competition was under way. So while John Cafaro's Chevy 3 studio was carving clay and proceeding with a mainline Camaro, John Schinella had the budget to do a running car, one with a fiberglass body, a real interior, and a complete engine and drivetrain. The ACC car could zip around on private GM streets and test tracks while the Camaro in Chevy 3 could only sit like a nicely sculpted lump of clay.

Schinella's young designers produced a masterpiece. The little California Camaro had a low-slung fiberglass body, a dipping and curvaceous nose that came to a racer's point, and plenty of glass to give its interior a greenhouse effect. The overall look was of some space-age boy racer. But it wasn't intended to be a production car. Its front was too low to meet street clearance standards. It lacked bumpers that would withstand even a slight impact. It was unlikely that a real car based on the California Camaro could survive any of the rigorous crash tests GM inflicted on its vehicles. The compound curves of its body panels were designed for a one-of-a-kind handmade car and would be a nightmare to engineer and assemble in mass production.

But the little car was beautiful. It had energy and vitality, and it was displayed in the January auto shows to put a high gloss on GM's artistic talents. The California Camaro had the press and the general public agog.

That created a problem. John Cafaro and his Chevy 3 team had been working on a new 1992 Camaro for more than a year. In automaker scheduling, a '92 model should begin production in August 1991. The Chevy studio's part of the new Camaro was quickly winding down.

With a new Camaro all but in the bag, Cafaro's people were pumping up adrenaline to get on with the '93 Corvette. The new Corvette program had begun to move upstairs from the Skunk Works, taking over parts of the eighty-by-thirty-two-foot Chevy 3 studio. The west wall and several display boards glistened with breathtaking sketches and concepts for the next-generation Y-car. A handful of GM's best designers, working at broad, slanted tables placed sideways against the long, high-windowed north wall, furtively sketched their daily dreams. Over-the-shoulder snooping wasn't encouraged, but once a sketch met its creator's artistic standards, it was posted for comment and criticism. One color rendering was actual-size, stretched along the wall allowing people to pace off its length or stand next to it to gauge its height in relation to their own. It was a flaring, exotic design that caught the eye of everyone who visited the studio.

The full-size Camaro clay model still took up the center of the studio. It was sleek, modern, and a significant departure from the Camaro that had been on the road since the early eighties. It had passed scores of reviews. Release was only a week away, seven days until the surface of the 1992 Camaro was locked up and the studio's work was largely done. Release meant turning over the car to the platform engineers, who would shepherd the design through to production. After release, Chevy 3's job would be to handle the minor problems that always cropped up when a prototype of a new car went through extensive testing before it was approved for mass production.

But that would be routine. The studio's real work in the next year would be to come up with an eye-stopping design for an all-new 1993 Corvette. It was supposed to be a year of fun and excitement. Then reality intruded.

In January 1989, General Motors was on a roll, about to report record profits, $4.86 billion, for the previous year. Chairman Roger Smith was nearing the end of his reign. The reorganizations, management changes, plant modernizations and closings, and new-car initiatives he put into effect seemed to have GM back on a competitive track with its American rivals and, more important, with those naggingly efficient Japanese. But there were ominous signs in Smith's tea leaves. New-car sales were dropping sharply and the 1989 forecast, while still showing a multibillion-dollar profit across the giant corporation, hinted that profits from the mighty North American auto business would be down. Most ominous, the heart of GM's auto-making and sales business could actually lose money in 1990. That wasn't a message that Roger Smith wanted leaked to the public. Even many members of the company's board of directors didn't know that 1990 might bring trouble.

One reason for the glum long-term outlook was the suspicion that the new W-cars might never show a profit. The midsize W-cars, family sedans aimed squarely at such competition as the Ford Taurus, were set for introduction in the spring of 1989 under a variety of badges: Chevrolet Lumina, Pontiac Grand Prix, Buick Regal, and Oldsmobile Cutlass Supreme. In GM's grand old tradition, the cars were all too similar in exterior styling. Even worse, with four separate GM divisions marketing the cars, the company was more in competition with itself than with Ford. And GM planners had yet to catch up with real-world America. Planned production of two-door models was highest at just the time that baby boomers were settling down with their growing families and looking for four-door automobiles.

But the biggest blunder of all was in Roger Smith's vision of superefficient, roboticized assembly plants. They were single-car plants. GM converted plants to produce incredible numbers of cars, but the plants could not manufacture cars from multiple platforms. If W-cars weren't needed, the plants could only slow down and furlough workers.

Smith called his vision the "reindustrialization of General Motors." On his watch as chairman, he spent $78 billion on reindustrialization, pouring much of it into single-car plants.

Publicly Smith was optimistic: "General Motors has turned the corner and is developing new momentum in the increasingly competitive global marketplace . . . ," he said in his chairman's statement at the end of 1988. "We continue to be number one in the world in vehicle sales. We are experiencing a strong recovery in earnings. . . . As we look ahead, we see continued progress. A favorable economy should propel 1989 calendar-year U.S. vehicle sales to the vicinity of fifteen million units for the first consecutive year. And we intend that GM will get its fair share of those sales. . . ."

It never happened.

Chairman Smith and the man favored to be his successor, GM president Robert Stempel, did see some hope ahead. New models were in the pipeline, spaced prudently to give General Motors something fresh to show and sell in each of the coming years. One of them was the new 1992 Camaro and another was the 1993 Corvette. Beyond that, Bob Stempel looked ahead to 1994 as a pivotal year. Roger Smith would hit mandatory retirement on August 1, 1990, but Stempel figured that it would take much longer for the full impact of Smith's tenure to be felt. "Ninety-four," he said, "that's the year you'll know whether all these changes of the eighties really worked."

By 1994, any credit for success would be Stempel's. He couldn't know how many things would go wrong, starting with the '92 Camaro and that Black Monday in January 1989, when Chuck Jordan walked into the Chevy 3 studio.

"Right here, Chuck!" John Cafaro called.

When Jordan entered a studio, there was silence. As if on command, the studio artists, engineers, and sculptors formed an open-ended cone with Jordan at its focal point. The studio chief fell in beside him, with the chief engineer and deputy design chief close at hand. As Jordan moved through the studio, the cone followed. His voice didn't carry, unless he was yelling, and everyone strained to hear his words.

This cold January day was no exception. Jordan walked slowly around the full-size clay model of the Camaro. "Do something with the front," he snapped. "It doesn't have enough reach."

"We're a week from release, Chuck," Cafaro said.

"I don't care. The rear end, it's too awkward. You saw what Schinella did with the California Camaro. I want more of that flavor in this car." Jordan was just getting wound up. After more than a year of critiquing and compli-menting the styling work on the Camaro, he suddenly didn't like any of it. "Look at this roofline. It doesn't do anything for me. This car has to flow, it has to make a statement. I don't see a statement here."

He turned to face Cafaro, letting his eyes sweep over the people standing aghast in a rough semicircle. His nasal tone took on a grating quality. "I want this car redone, and I want it redone right. Use the California Camaro. That's what I want to see here. You guys didn't do the job on this one. Now get to work and do it right."

"In a week?" Cafaro asked.

"Yeah, do it in a week!" Jordan spun around and strode toward the door. Suddenly he turned and waved at the magnificent Corvette sketches and renderings on the wall.

"All that stuff is crap!" he said. "If you people can't design a Y-car, we'll do that in California, too! They'll by-god give me what I want!"

Jordan disappeared out the door. Five minutes later, he was on the phone to John Schinella in California. "Do me a California Corvette," he ordered, "a running model like you did the Camaro. You're in a head-to-head com-petition with the people back here, so make it good!"

Almost as an afterthought, Jordan walked downstairs to the Advanced 4 studio headed by a freethinking young designer named Tom Peters. "Drop whatever you're doing and get started on a Corvette," Jordan told the surprised Peters. "We're going to get a competition going on around here!" He didn't tell Cafaro what was happening.

"Jesus Christ!" Cafaro snorted in the Chrome Cobra's wake. "We've been working on this Camaro for a year. Goddamn Charlie, anyway, he sees a hot shape from California and he's like a teenager in heat. All he cares about is trying something new."

Cafaro stalked around the Camaro, coffee mug in hand. His Chuck Jordan impression was in high gear.

"You call this a car?" he snarled. "That's not a car! It's a piece of shit!"

Cafaro smashed his mug to the floor, sending a spray of coffee and ceramic shards in all directions. "Hey, it's like the godfather." He smiled grimly. "Remember when he throws the dinner plates?" It was twenty min-utes to quitting time, but Cafaro didn't wait. He grabbed his overcoat and stalked from the building.

5 CORVETTE was a rarity. It came along in the fifties, rather late in General Motors history. Only three hundred Corvettes were built in 1953. John Wayne bought one of them. In 1992, the one-millionth Corvette rolled off the assembly line and was promptly donated to the National Corvette Museum which would open in 1994.

By 1996, almost 1,100,000 Corvettes had been built and close to a million of them were still on the road, or at least actively registered by their owners each year. Many of those people are fanatics. Chevrolet's Fred Gallasch, assigned to monitor and assist the Corvette program, liked to tell the story of a friend who bought a twenty-year-old Corvette from the original owner. The car came with the original paperwork, the original price sticker painstakingly steamed from the window, original brochures from the dealer, and complete records of all maintenance.

As the new owner was about to drive away, the seller ran from his garage carrying a cardboard box. Inside were the original oil and air filters, the ones that came from the factory, carefully preserved in plastic bags. The fellow loved that car. He sold it only because his wife said that five Corvettes was too many, and he wanted to buy a new 1993. So the old '73 had to go.

People like that join Corvette clubs. There are nearly 300 clubs in the United States, with more than 12,000 members. There are another 100 or more clubs overseas, including several in Japan. Every continent except Antarctica has Corvette clubs.

Corvette people read Corvette magazines. There are half a dozen in the United States devoted only to Corvette, and more in Europe and Asia. Their monthly or quarterly circulations total more than all the Corvettes ever built.

Corvette fanatics take care of their cars. Catalogs of Corvette parts, clothing, and aftermarket goodies arrive in their mailboxes. The biggest of them comes from Mid-America Designs, which has made a rich business out of supplying Corvette lovers with whatever they need. And whatever they want.

When they aren't reading magazines, poring over catalogs, or working on their cars, Corvette lovers are driving in local parades, holding rallies, or going off to truly massive annual gatherings. More than fifty thousand of them convene in central Illinois each June for an event called Bloomington Gold, where Corvettes are shown, judged, traded, bought, and sold. Thirty thousand Corvette lovers, many but not all of them veterans of Bloomington, show up each July in Spearfish, South Dakota, for a similar event in the Black Hills. And when the National Corvette Museum in Bowling Green, Kentucky, opened on Labor Day weekend in 1994, more than four thousand Corvettes from every state, including Alaska and Hawaii, converged on the town. In three days, 118,000 people went through the museum's turnstiles and the museum's gift shop did $1 million in business.

Why? Something in Corvette's character caught on. The first cars were beautiful but not very good. They had underpowered six-cylinder engines, steered heavy, and rode rough. But then along came a V-8 engine, better suspension, and even more beautiful bodies. Many boys and a few girls, too, saw Corvettes in their teens and were imprinted with the desire to own one. That still happens. The average Corvette owner isn't rich, though sticker prices are into the forties. Corvette owners are everybody, the salt of American society. Supreme Court justice Clarence Thomas's black ZR-1 carries the license plate *Res Ipsa,* "It speaks for itself." Johnny Carson drives a white Corvette. Mailmen, mechanics, movie stars, and millionaire athletes own the car. When they're driving their Corvettes, they're all equal. The friendly wave that they call the Corvette salute is a greeting that few ignore when another of their kind passes by. "Save the wave," they tell each other on the Internet and at weekend rallies.

Corvette is the true American sports car. Over the years, it became an American icon.

The miracle is that it happened inside the maw of General Motors. Because inside General Motors, little things like Corvette often get swept aside.

General Motors' size, not just in the United States, but around the world, and the variety and complexity of its interests make it at least as bewildering as any government bureaucracy. No one, from its chairman or members of its eclectic and correct board of directors, to the wisest and most veteran industry analyst, can claim to understand it fully.

General Motors is beyond comprehension.

In 1988, this hulking giant made more money in a single year than any corporation in history. Just two years later it claimed the red ink record, too, losing $2 billion. And that was nothing compared to 1992, when it reported a staggering $24.2 billion loss—$4 billion in cash and $20.2 billion written off to pay future retirement obligations.

General Motors has history in its people. The old GM names are lustrous.

Durant. Sloan. Kettering. Other names that merged into the company brought their own aura. REO Speedwagon was not just a seventies rock group. R. E. O. was Ransom E. Olds and the Speedwagon was one of his later creations under the Reo Company. But much earlier, in 1897, he founded the Olds Motor Vehicle Company, to which General Motors traces its earliest ancestry. Henry Leland was only five years behind, building the first Cadillacs in 1902. David Dunbar Buick built his first car in 1903 but had to be rescued from financial disaster by William Durant. Edward M. Murphy started building Oaklands in 1907. The Oakland car name is lost in history, changed a few decades later to Pontiac.

It was a time of automotive derring-do. Auto companies came and went, some leaving no trace of their passing. Billy Durant, the buggy and bicycle maker and self-made millionaire who had saved Buick from the ash heap, masterminded the creation of the General Motors Company in 1908. He immediately sold his controlling interest in Buick to GM, then used his sway over the three-man board of directors to buy Olds Motor Works and Oakland Motors. Durant followed by buying a passel of other companies— parts manufacturers, a truck builder, and almost any other company involved in the young auto business. He brought Henry Leland's profitable Cadillac line into GM in 1909.

The apple pie of all American cars, the Chevrolet, was the last to arrive. Louis Chevrolet started the company in 1911, the same year that C. F. Kettering developed the self-starter for Cadillac. By that time, Durant had been thrown out of GM by financiers uncomfortable with his wheeling and dealing, so he poured his personal money and efforts into Chevrolet. Louis Chevrolet was the name up front, but Billy Durant was pulling the strings backstage. The instantly successful car springboarded Durant back to real industrial power in 1918, when he merged Chevy into the now-giant General Motors Corporation. But it didn't last and the GM board threw him out again.

When GM president Charlie Wilson went to Washington to become Dwight Eisenhower's secretary of defense in 1953, GM dominated the auto industry and much of American life. So it is understandable that the press misquoted Wilson then and continues to flog the misquote decades later. Wilson didn't say, "What's good for GM is good for the country." What he told the U.S. Senate was ". . . I thought what was good for our country was good for General Motors—and vice versa. The difference did not exist. Our company is too big. It goes with the welfare of the country."

Our company is too big.

General Motors' real estate holdings make it larger in acreage than the state of Connecticut. It has enough employees and retirees to match the populations of North and South Dakota combined. It spends more than $5 billion a year on health care for its people, which adds almost $1,200 to the sticker price of every car, truck, and van it sells.

It has designed and built some of the finest vehicles in the world, including Corvette. It has built other cars, mostly in the seventies and eighties, so ugly and shoddy that their mere presence on this earth puts an acid-etch tarnish on the company.

Great things lie forgotten beneath that tarnish. General Motors founded its own university, General Motors Institute in Flint, Michigan, one of the world's premier engineering schools. Outside of its field, it is virtually unknown.

General Motors was the first auto company to devote engineering attention to safety. It invented the auto test track, opening its Milford Proving Ground northwest of Detroit in 1924. It invented many other things, too, like those concrete barriers with flared bottoms on freeways or at construction sites, crash dummies, and robots with vision to distinguish one part from another.

Some of its innovations fell into the realm of finance and corporate structure. The company formed the General Motors Acceptance Corporation in 1919. The next year, 2 million cars were sold on time-payment plans and by 1925, 75 percent of all car buyers in the United States made monthly payments. The plan opened the road to millions of Americans whose horizon had been held to the county line. More than the horse, more than the transcontinental railroad, the installment plan for cars put the American Dream within reach of America's people. Ford and the rest quickly jumped on that bandwagon.

General Motors went to war. During World War II, something of its design or manufacture went into almost every weapon or war machine, from sidearms and rifles to sixteen-inch guns on battleships. It manufactured one-fourth of all airplane engines used by U.S. fighting forces, and two-thirds of the heavy military trucks that carried American men and supplies into combat.

That kind of industrial might is dwarfed by the General Motors of the late twentieth century. The company is too big. It may well be unmanageable, an out-of-control train in an age of semiconductors. At the top, it's a company populated by brilliant, articulate, farsighted people who face obstacles that are frequently insurmountable. In the rest of the company, where the work gets done, General Motors is dappled with pockets of genius, resiliency, and driven desire where anything is possible. The people there are often awesome. They bob and weave and finagle the system.

Sometimes they produce something wonderful.

Harley Earl broke new ground in automotive looks. He grew up in Los Angeles, the next-door neighbor to movie director Cecil B. DeMille, and he

made a name designing one-of-a-kind bodies for movie stars' cars. Alfred
B. Sloan enticed him to General Motors in Detroit, where his first car was
the rich and spectacular 1927 Cadillac LaSalle. With that success, Sloan let
him put together the industry's first Art and Color Section. It made car
design, *styling,* a factor in the industry. Styling wielded influence. Earl
introduced modeling clay to the art of car design and was the first to put
curved glass on a car. He didn't have real power compared to the engineering side, which decided most issues on what a car would be. Still, Earl
was the first design czar in the car business and his influence grew.

Real power came after he and Ed Cole of Cadillac put the first tail fins on
the 1948 Caddys. They did it because executives from the fourteenth floor
miles away in the General Motors Building mandated that Cadillac use the
existing rear doors from a Buick in designing the new car. Harley Earl was
a headstrong man, a fundamental trait in auto *stylists.* He acquiesced to the
bosses, then set to work on the tail fins with the connivance of the legendary Cole, who would move on to take over GM's largest division, Chevrolet,
and would one day become president of the whole company. Between
them, Earl and Cole made certain that their Cadillac was not, after all, just
some upscale Buick.

The gamble paid off. It made the top man in GM *styling* a man to be
courted. Harley Earl used his power to create an entirely new car. He'd
been watching a kind of car that GIs brought back from Europe after World
War II. The vehicles were something called sports cars and they were not
just transportation. They were fun to drive. Amateur owners raced them on
weekends. So did professionals. The most famous were the MG and the
Jaguar, both two-seaters that looked good and made drivers feel special.
Detroit made nothing like them.

Earl convinced the bosses to let him build an American sports car to
show at the 1953 Motorama, GM's traveling auto show. Their only caveat
was that he had to use standard GM parts underneath its body. Earl and Ed
Cole, now at Chevrolet, cribbed lines from the Jaguar, but only a little. They
decided to make the body from fiberglass to keep the car light. Finding the
car's name was a challenge. Earl discarded almost three hundred suggestions before he found one he liked. It was a name attached to a kind of fast
fighting ship in the old British navy. Corvette.

The original Corvette team worked in secret, but word leaked out. When
Motorama opened in New York City at the Waldorf-Astoria Hotel in January
1953, long lines of eager car buffs waited to get a peek.

Corvette was a hit. The bosses put it into production and the first salable
vehicle rolled out into the sunlight on June 30, 1953. It wasn't an easy car
to build. It had come along so fast that its body panels were all handmade

and each car was assembled as if it was a unique machine. All three hundred were polo white convertibles, with red interiors.

Corvettes were beautiful. They just weren't very good sports cars. The '53 and '54 Corvettes had 150-horsepower six-cylinder engines and two-speed automatic transmissions. They had bad suspensions that made for rough rides. Base price was $3,498. The only options were a heater for $91.40 and an AM radio for $145.15.

Nobody knows exactly how many of the original 300 are still around. Some say 290. Others say 120. Most are in private collections and it could take $100,000 to pry one away.

Yet in 1954, when thirty-six hundred Corvettes were produced, almost half were unsold. It still wasn't a good sports car.

Zora Arkus-Duntov fixed it. He'd made his own reputation as a racer on the European circuit and as an engine man who could get power and efficiency where others had failed. He loved the looks of the Corvette. When he sent a letter to Ed Cole outlining a way to salvage Corvette, Cole put him to work. He immediately put a V-8 into 1955 Corvettes. Only seven hundred cars were built in 1955, but they sold. Duntov went on to become Corvette's first chief engineer.

It didn't hurt that Ford had introduced the two-seater Thunderbird in 1955. General Motors executives were loath to kill Corvette in the face of competition from those boys across town. Nor did it hurt Corvette years later when a young fellow at Ford named Lee Iacocca changed the Thunderbird to a four-seat touring car and effectively removed it as any threat to Corvette.

Harley Earl was already redesigning the Corvette's body and interior—not a complete makeover, but a refinement to spruce up the car for the rest of the decade—when Duntov showed up. With Earl's styling and the 210-horsepower Chevy V-8 engine that Duntov got from Ed Cole, Corvette caught fire. Duntov replaced the old automatic transmission with a three-speed manual and pushed through options for bigger engines and better automatic transmissions. The '56 Corvette was a hot car. Owners raced them against Jags and other European sports cars and won. It was the first American car to hit 150 miles per hour at Daytona. A television show about Corvette, *Route 66,* added to the mystique.

So Corvette caught on and stuck around. By all precedents, it should have lost favor with General Motors management and been dropped. Two-seater sports cars have never been in favor in a company that concentrates on sedans and trucks. In the eighties and nineties alone, GM started, then abandoned, three sports cars—the wonderful little Pontiac Fiero, the innovative Buick Reata, and the upscale Cadillac Allante. Like Corvette, each of them was imperfect in the beginning. But each of them got better and better, until just as they reached something like real quality, and in the case of Fiero, had a genuine following, they were killed.

Killing cars is a General Motors tradition. Corvette people didn't know it in 1988, but the sports car they revered was soon to be lined up in the corporate crosshairs.

6 J O H N Cafaro leaned back in his chrome and black leather swivel chair, holding forth angrily to a handful of his studio troops. Less than thirty minutes after he got to work he heard that Chuck Jordan had carried out his threat to have the Advanced Concepts Center in California start work on a Corvette. He was still digesting that news when Tom Peters called to say that his Advanced 4 studio was in the race, too.

"Charlie really is a Chrome Cobra," Cafaro grunted. "He's old school, motivation through fear. Hell, I don't know if we're still on Corvette or not. I don't know whether to close up the Skunk Works or keep it going. He goes around pitting studio against studio instead of having us work together."

He slapped his hand on his glass desk. "Damn it! We're the Camaro studio. But we had a clay model and ACC comes in with a running car. You guys know release is . . . the moment we work for. Now we're one week from Camaro release and instead of being with us, that snake is telling us we did a shitty job and he wants a new car!"

"So what are we going to do?" one of the studio engineers asked.

Cafaro's volatile emotions usually ran hot. His New Jersey Italian father met and married his Japanese mother during the Korean War. The Italian genes won out. Except for a faint cast to his skin that glowed like a year-round tan, Cafaro was Italian in looks and temperament. By heritage and training, he was one of the most talented designers in the building.

John Cafaro was seven when he fell in love with cars. A cherished photo in his study at home shows him as a child in a soapbox push car, surrounded by his friends. The expression on his face can't be mistaken. "Let's go!" it says. "Faster! Faster!" He graduated from art school and went straight to General Motors. He worked for John Schinella in a Pontiac studio, helping design the feisty little Fiero sports car. Then he caught Jerry Palmer's eye.

Palmer was running the Chevy 3 studio and carving the lines for a new

Corvette in the early eighties. His first Corvettes were show cars in 1969, working under the tutelage of Bill Mitchell, then GM's vice president for design. No matter who held the title of studio chief in Chevy 3, Mitchell alone dictated Corvette's styling after he succeeded Harley Earl, just as Zora Arkus-Duntov controlled the engineering side of Corvette from 1955 on. Mitchell kept tight control over the car's distinctive looks until he retired in 1977.

Palmer's first design input to a production Corvette was with the '73 model. The next year Mitchell made him chief of the studio. In 1977, Palmer came into his own. That was the year they began sketching out an all-new Corvette. This car would have new chiefs all around. Palmer in Chevy 3 and Dave McLellan at the platform, who succeeded the retiring Zora Arkus-Duntov as only the second chief engineer in Corvette's history.

The division between designers and engineers at General Motors was part clear, part murky. Too often, they were at odds. Artists worked in a semivacuum of information, styling a new car with little input from the engineers. Chuck Jordan encouraged their independence after he took over as vice president for design in 1986. At one point, he deliberately angered platform managers and senior executives at the car divisions when he told a reporter for *Automotive News* that he didn't much care what those people thought. "We tell them what their cars are going to look like," he said bluntly. "They don't tell us."

The problem was complicated by the way General Motors divided up responsibility. Dave McLellan was chief engineer for Corvette, the number two man in Corvette because he worked for the platform manager. With a large complement of engineers reporting to him, McLellan oversaw the myriad of details that went into creating a car. He and his people decided on the engine and transmission, the chassis, the electrical system with all its switches and wiring harnesses. They designed and tested the suspension. They did the engineering drawings and specifications for every part, from the fenders and fascias designed in Chevy 3, to the nuts, bolts, screws, and fasteners that were buried deep inside a Corvette.

Once a design was released from the studio, McLellan's people managed the building of test cars, then drove them mercilessly on test tracks and in deserts, mountains, and Arctic snows. They destroyed some cars by crash-testing them into barriers. They worked with GM Powertrain engineers to run engines on test stands until they failed. They oversaw production of the tools and dies and stamping machines that made all the parts, and they worked inside the assembly plant to coordinate the system that would put the car together.

But what Dave McLellan couldn't do was put his engineers in the design studio. When he visited Chevy 3, he was a guest and not always a welcome one. Design Staff had its own engineers, three or four in each studio, and a separate team in the basement next to the Corvette Skunk Works. They were not production engineers. Their job was internal to Design Staff, to advise the stylists and keep them from going too far with a car design that couldn't be built. When McLellan's people made a decision, for instance, on the size of the engine, the data came through to the studio engineers, who worked with the stylists to make sure that this particular engine would fit under the hood. It was a cumbersome system that sometimes didn't work. The most valuable service provided by the studio engineers came at studio release. They'd run their measuring devices over the clay model, "picking points" by the thousands and recording them in three dimensions. The resulting data package defined the car's surface for McLellan's engineers.

With both Jerry Palmer and Dave McLellan settling into their new positions, GM's long-term plan called for a completely redesigned Corvette to be on the road by 1983. It would be the fourth generation of Corvettes to go into production since those first few cars stunned and enthralled the public in 1953. But things went wrong. Engineering and production problems slipped the schedule a full year and because the assembly plant had torn down the old lines to put in the new, there was no 1983 Corvette. When the '84 Corvette finally arrived, it replaced a car whose body style was a full fifteen years old. In the excitement of production, nobody realized that they were setting a precedent by nearly tripling the life span of a Corvette generation.

Design Staff loved working on Corvette. A permanent transfer to the Chevy 3 studio was worn like a badge of honor. Only the elite made it, finally allowed to design Corvettes and Camaros. Other studios looked at the Chevy 3 artisans with mixed emotions. Those people were good and everyone knew it, but their exalted status bred envy and resentment. When Jerry Palmer reached into the Pontiac studio in the early eighties and asked for John Schinella's deputy as his own, there was a brief tug-of-war. But Palmer got his way.

That left Schinella with no deputy. He looked around his studio and made a fateful decision. He moved young John Cafaro up to the deputy's job in the Pontiac studio. The brash and talented designer suddenly found himself in management. It was a toehold that he was determined to make grow. Sometimes his mouth got in the way.

John Cafaro was one of the few people at Design Staff who almost always said what he thought. It made him popular with the troops, less so with the bosses. And though he was still a rising star in Pontiac, Palmer took him into his own inner circle and the pair developed a relationship that went beyond mentor and protégé. They became friends. Their families sometimes vacationed together. Cafaro and Palmer shared a love of cars, but their fascination with styling and design reached out to boats and trains as well. Palmer's model train collection kept them entertained for hours and Cafaro sometimes claimed that Palmer would be happiest if he could design a train for the next generation.

Palmer counseled Cafaro and covered for him, telling people that John was young and he'd be more politic as he matured. His extraordinary talent at putting the right lines into the right car at the right time more than compensated for his occasional lapses. Palmer believed his predictions about Cafaro's future and backed them with action. When Chuck Jordan ascended to the vice presidency of design in 1986, Palmer moved up as well. Jordan named three of his longtime associates to a design hierarchy. Significantly he did not name a new design director to take over his own old position.

He thus ended the tradition that called for a design director to handle most of the creative aspects of the building while the vice president took care of administration, and only dabbled with the studios. Chuck Jordan had no intention of relinquishing creative control over the studios.

Instead he named one senior man to oversee the Chevy, Pontiac, Olds-mobile, and truck studios and another to handle the Buick and Cadillac studios. Jerry Palmer became executive director of Advanced Design, with those far-thinking studios reporting to him. The new Saturn studio would report directly to Chuck Jordan.

Jordan didn't need to work. He grew up in Whittier, California, in a family that made its fortune in oranges. He had talent, though, and the drive to succeed. Without both, he would never have risen in the intensely competi-tive design arena at General Motors. What Chuck Jordan didn't have was the common touch. He was tough without much compassion. He was artistic without grace. His fertile mind conceived those classic fins on late-fifties Cadillacs but seldom recognized the hurt in the eyes of a subordinate whom he'd just chastised in public.

Being wealthy allowed Jordan to be insensitive. His talent carried him to the top of his profession. But he wore thousand-dollar suits to work, with tailored and monogrammed shirts. Subordinates whispered that his shoes cost more than a typical studio chief's best Sunday suit. He didn't need to be nice to people. So he wasn't. And while his ego forced him to work long hours, often six and seven days a week, it combined with his money to let him thumb his nose at General Motors by collecting Ferraris. It wasn't the collecting that offended people. Car people collected cars. If they could afford to collect expensive cars, they did so. But Chuck Jordan carried it a step too far. He drove a Ferrari to work. He parked it indoors, in his executive parking spot, where it was washed by GM employees, gassed up with GM gas, and given the same pampering that went to GM cars driven by other executives. The difference was that Jordan drove an *Italian* car.

When he ascended to the pinnacle, Jordan faced certain questions. One was obvious. Who would get Chevy 3? It was the premier studio in the building. Palmer had Chuck Jordan's ear and he lobbied hard. He worked on the silver-haired vice president until he wore him down. When the announcement was made, shock waves rippled through Design Staff.

The young guy, John Cafaro, was the new chief of Chevy 3.

The turn of events held powerful lessons for Cafaro. He knew what Palmer had done and he knew that Chuck Jordan handed him the studio reluctantly. So he made up his mind to be a manager who worked with people, not against them. "If I had a hotshot in my studio, he was either going to get great assignments from me or if we were in a slow period, I'd find him a slot somewhere else so he could grow," Cafaro said in later years. "People did that for me; hell, Jerry Palmer did it for me and so did John Schinella, and I was damned sure that I was going to pass it on."

The downside of the promotion was that it hardened John Cafaro's penchant for lipping off. When Chuck Jordan sent a video crew around the building to tape key people talking about their design philosophies—"Be honest," Jordan said. "Don't hold back good ideas."—Cafaro went on record saying that he disagreed with almost everything Chuck Jordan wanted. Jordan was livid but to his credit allowed the tape to be shown uncensored. Cafaro's peers quietly applauded his honesty.

In a meeting of Design Staff management, Cafaro was asked to sum up the thinking of his working group. He looked straight at Chuck Jordan and began with words that would be quoted in the building for years to come. "Well, Chuck," he said, "we decided that when it comes to management philosophies, shit runs downhill. . . ."

Palmer urged the obstreperous Cafaro to tone down his caustic remarks. "Be politic," he said more than once. "I tell Charlie that you're the kind of guy he needs, who won't shut up when he should, but that won't work forever."

Cafaro would lay low for a while. Then something would set him off again. When Jordan rambled on in a meeting about the need for "reach" in designing new cars and asked for comments, Cafaro had one ready. "You preach to us about it, Chuck," Cafaro said, "but you never tell us what you mean. We don't know what you want because you use words like *reach* without giving us any context. The only guidance we get is that you'll know it when you see it."

• • •

"So what are we going to do?"

The question snapped Cafaro out of his reverie. He didn't know if his studio still had the Corvette. Even worse, there was the impossible job of remaking the Camaro in a California image. It couldn't be done in a week, or a month, or even six months. And redoing the Camaro while simultaneously doing a new Corvette? Now that was a challenge!

"I'm gonna talk to Palmer," Cafaro said. "Jerry's like a snake charmer with Chuck. He knows how to handle him.

"Look out there! We've got hundreds of Corvette sketches. If Chuck was smart, he'd look at them and pick out what he likes or doesn't like. He'd say, okay, I like this, do this to it, or do that, or take this piece from over here and work on it. But he doesn't do any of that. He comes in and tells us everything is shit and he's gonna get a car from California!

"I don't need this stuff. I've got a nice wife and a nice house and I've got my own Ferrari. I'm just smart enough not to drive it to work."

He set off in search of Jerry Palmer.

By early afternoon, the building was flooded with rumors. Jerry Palmer and Stan Wilen had been in to see Jordan in his lavish corner office, the traditional seat of power in this building. Pacing in front of a couch, Jordan explained his plan.

"I told Schinella, do me a California Corvette. They're doing lots of things out there, but they're set up, they're self-contained. They're doing that electric car and some other things, so maybe I'm overloading them. They'll have to slow something down to do the Corvette, but that's what I want, to keep the pressure on."

"What about Chevy 3 and the Skunk Works?"

"They didn't come through with the right ideas here," Jordan said, "so I'm going to do what I did on the Camaro. They'll do a running car out there in California and a clay here. Then I'm gonna bring that car here and blend 'em. I'm going to put 'em together and we'll have a Corvette that's a dream car."

They set a meeting in the basement to explain it to Cafaro.

The Skunk Works was a mess. It was a shrunk works. The designers' tables were shoved hard against the row of head-high partitions. Two of the three Corvette clown suit stands—six mirrored model halves in all— were pushed to the back of the room. The third clown suit was out in the hallway. The six small Corvette models had drawn appreciative comments only days earlier. The Skunk Works designers had been convinced they had something that could become a 1993 Corvette, something that would take the sports car world by storm. Now the artists and sculptors were upstairs salvaging Camaro. Their Skunk Works creations had been cast aside. The secret room was a design graveyard. Hissing steam and water gurgled through exposed overhead pipes. A sudden *thunka-chunka-boom-boom-boom* sounded from somewhere in the ceiling. Cafaro thought he might be attending a pipe fitter's wake.

Concept Corvettes, pencil sketches and pastel renderings, covered the partitions. Chuck Jordan stalked through the dismal room, looking at the displays and comparing them with a new Corvette show car, an advanced design called the Corvette Indy. The first Corvette Indy was done in 1986 as a possible pace car for the Indianapolis 500. A newer version was nearing completion at Lotus in England and would be displayed at the Detroit International Auto Show in 1990.

"If you saw the new Indy car next January and we told you that there'd be a new Corvette coming, you'd expect a lot more than the Indy car you're looking at," Jordan growled. "Well, there's nothin' here that's better. So I'm asking, what are you going to do?"

John Cafaro opened his mouth, but Jerry Palmer's wave shut it again. The Skunk Works was staffed by Palmer's people and Cafaro's jointly, so failure here would be Palmer's personal failure. "Here's what we're going to do," Palmer said without hesitation. "We're going back into sketches. Nothing in clay. I want to get Randy Wittine down tomorrow. I want George Camp back down here. John and I are going to be a lot more involved."

He looked at Cafaro, who nodded.

"Then I'm going to do a scale model in another room. We're going to get it right." Palmer stopped. Nobody picked up, not for a second anyway, that Palmer said no clay in one sentence, then threw in a scale model a few sentences later. Maybe Chuck Jordan would miss it. He didn't.

"Models. We've got models and they're no good," Jordan said caustically. Palmer held his tongue. Jordan was silent for a moment, then he turned to the two model stands at the back of the room. He dismissed a sleek three-eighths-scale Corvette finished off in shiny black Di-Nok, a colored foil that can be laid over clay like a tight-fitting skin. "This one's timid," Jordan said. "It doesn't say anything. I want this car to say something."

Palmer knew better than to argue. He pointed to a model skinned in shiny red foil. "This one's closer. It's got a statement to make."

Jordan looked in silence. Then he agreed. "I like the front a little," he conceded. "The rear isn't bad. It's closer to what I'm looking for."

The tension in the steamy room ratcheted down a notch. In the momentary quiet, somebody started hammering, three or four loud strokes, just beyond the partitions. Jordan looked up in irritation. The silence stretched on uncomfortably while he made up his mind.

"Get rid of all the models," he snapped suddenly. "No, keep the red model. But not this front. I want a different front. More speed, more reach."

"We can do it, Chuck," Cafaro said. "The engine's far enough back."

Jordan grunted and turned toward the sketches. Palmer pointed to two of them, both with fender lines and panels swept aerodynamically in toward the passenger compartment. "These I like," Palmer said. "They're stealthy. They're future."

Jordan jumped on the word and claimed it for his own. "Stealth. That's what I want. I want a stealthy Corvette." He turned back and pointed. "The smell's right on the red car. I want to see some of it in the next set of sketches."

Cafaro grinned. "Store's open, Chuck," he said.

"Store's *back* open," Jordan snapped.

7 CARDY Davis learned about the Corvette design competition through the rumor mill.

But at the moment, Carlisle V. Davis, the only man in the Chevrolet-Pontiac-Canada organization to manage two car platforms simultaneously, had more immediate concerns. His midsize A-car platform, the basic unit for the Pontiac 6000, Buick Century, and Oldsmobile Cutlass Ciera, was a cash cow for General Motors. It generated hundreds of millions of dollars in profit and since Cardy Davis took over, its quality was steadily improving. His Y-car platform, the prestigious Corvette, was a cash calf despite nagging flaws. It turned about $100 million profit annually through many of its midlife years, selling out its small production of around twenty-five thousand cars and leaving Corvette lovers hungry for next year's model.

Production Corvettes were test beds for new electronics, new suspensions, new chassis fabrication techniques, new fiberglass or plastic materials for body parts. It was a given in General Motors that Corvette most often got first crack at something new, and would work out the bugs for the rest of the company.

The Corvette platform thrived on the challenge. While designers in the Chevy 3 studio popped sweat beads in search of artistic inspiration, the platform engineers set performance goals for their car. Corvette had to be fast; if it wasn't the fastest production car in zero to sixty runs, fastest in the quarter mile, fastest in top speed, something was wrong. Corvette had to handle like a dream, letting average drivers take high-speed corners without scaring themselves silly and letting skilled drivers take those same corners easily at another twenty or thirty miles per hour. Corvette had to have superior brakes. Stopping on a dime was more than a cliché to Corvette engineers. Yet Corvette had to do all that while meeting or exceeding environmental and fuel economy standards. One rule for Corvette was sacrosanct: No gas-guzzler tax, a federal penalty on cars that fell too far below the corporate average fuel economy (CAFE) regulation.

What Corvette didn't have to be was soft and plush. It was a sports car, not a touring car like Ford's Thunderbird, or a heavy-handling highway chomper like the Toyota Supra, or a semisports car like the four-seat versions of Nissan's 300ZX. Corvette wasn't *uncomfortable*. The uniframe chassis on the Corvette designed and engineered by Dave McLellan's team did have a high step-over that took some effort to slip into the driver's seat. Women in tight skirts hated it. Men bruised their shins on the protruding instrument panel until they mastered the technique of entry and egress. Once in the car, it took some contortions to fasten the lap and shoulder belts. The seats could be adjusted to fit almost any body, but under way, driver and passenger in the tightly suspended two-seater felt the road until Corvette added an adjustable suspension that could be changed by setting a switch on the center console. In the *sport* setting, they still felt every bump and burble passing under the wide tires.

All of that combined to make the fourth-generation Corvette a car with many flaws. The car's styling made it tough to assemble and finicky buyers sometimes complained about gaps between panels. Its removable hardtop —making it a "targa" model in sportscar vernacular—was prone to rattles. The body itself was fiberglass and plastic, materials that helped keep Corvette's weight down and resisted many of the dings and dents accumulated by metal panels in parking lots. But the panels didn't like paint. Getting the paint just right was a long-standing Corvette problem and a solution was nowhere in sight. So while Corvette sold out almost every year, and while Corvette clubs around the world filled with people who worshiped the car and lusted after each new model that appeared, it was not a perfect machine. But to those who adored the car, imperfection was a small price to pay for its performance and character.

Cardy Davis was determined to make it better. In the early months of 1989, Davis and his Y-car platform team concentrated on *their* impending milestone. In the newly invented Four-Phase process of car development being debugged within General Motors, the official start of a new program was a specific event called Concept Initiation, or CI. Getting to CI took work.

Four-Phase was supposed to provide a step-by-step road map for doing a new car. The idea was that it is possible to define the specific steps in the birth and life of a car, from the first rough sketches to the thousands of cars rolling off the assembly line. Once those steps were defined, every program could simply follow them. It was never that easy.

At every car company in the world, developing a new car from scratch is extraordinarily difficult. At GM, it is a long, terrible, frustrating, joyous, detailed, and (maybe) rewarding process. Four-Phase added as much to the agonies as it did to the ecstasies. In attempting to map a journey of a million steps, it defined simplicity by creating complexity.

Four-Phase had five phases. The last of them was Phase Three. First came bubble-up.

Bubble-up might also be called "winging it." The secret Skunk Works in the basement of the Design building was part of the process. So was Dave McLellan's engineering team, laying out the basic specifications for performance and under-the-skin systems like chassis and engine. Marketing people got into the act by sampling opinions and developing the Voice of the Customer. Finally the business and financial people had to lay out a skeletal business plan that outlined how the new car would be budgeted and what kind of profit it would make. All that led up to the formal review by GM executives that was called Concept Initiation. If the plans passed muster, the program moved to Phase Zero.

In Phase Zero—the phases were numbered by someone with an absurd mind-set—the car would be precisely defined. Engineers would describe every aspect of the car in a document called the VTS, vehicle technical specifications. Stylists at Design Staff would settle on the car's appearance, both interior and exterior. The two camps had to work closely in Phase Zero because whatever the engineers did had to fit inside the skin being crafted by the design studio. Phase Zero didn't take into account the attitude of aloofness and independence fostered by Chuck Jordan. He never quite accepted the idea that people like Dave McLellan and Cardy Davis were supposed to influence a car's design.

By the end of Phase Zero, a new car was to have a firm budget and business plan, a stylish interior and exterior, and many of its parts designed by engineers. Those parts would be on order from suppliers, at least in an early form. Just as important, the skin and interior had to be released from the studio. The artists' work would be largely done.

Phase One was more fun for the engineers. The biggest jobs involved getting all the parts on order, at the best price, and early parts delivered. Then they'd build an early set of cars and test them. A few of the crude Corvettes would be driven for thousands of miles as engineers looked for trouble. Some would go north to subzero cold in the winter and south to the desert for testing under the extremes that future owners would expect them to survive. Invariably the development engineers would find trouble, fix it, and test again to see if it worked. Much of that testing was done on the next level of test cars, which more closely approximated the final designs. At the same time, manufacturing and industrial engineers would work out plans for modifying the assembly plant. If new machines were needed, they'd be found somewhere in GM's vast inventory, ordered from suppliers, or built from scratch. The United Auto Workers also got into the act. A new car would assemble in different ways and union jobs were on the line, to be either gained or lost.

In Phase Two, final prototype cars would be built and driven to their limits. They'd be perfected, inside and out. The assembly plant(s) would stop making the old car and be refitted to build the new car. One day a bell would ring and a few days later the first salable cars, called pilot cars, would begin to roll out the door. Their number would increase daily but never without glitches to be faced and fixed. Finally, after a few months of getting the assembly line up to speed, full-scale production would be declared.

Phase Three was called "continuous production and improvement." That's where the money was.

Along the way in all the phases, there would be formal meetings and reviews. The Four-Phase writers called them gates. A program had to go through many gates, especially to advance between phases. In the seldom-realized ideal scheme of things at General Motors, it would take forty-eight months from the beginning of Phase Zero to the end of Phase Two.

While the stylists bubbled-up artsy concepts for Corvette's new look, the platform team used the bubble-up months to research and prepare a profitable business case and to make key engineering decisions. At Concept Initiation, they would present their findings to a board of senior General Motors executives. Jordan's stylists were expected to show a theme, not necessarily the exact lines and shadows of the car, but a general direction that would be refined and perfected in the next year. Dave McLellan's platform engineers had to propose basic pieces of the car, its engine and drivetrain, its chassis, its wheelbase and overall dimensions inside and out. All this was called the *package,* and in a perfect world, the designers in Chevy 3 would "drape-to-shape," or fit a sleekly beautiful body over the package. Chuck Jordan hated the idea of drape-to-shape.

Cardy Davis insisted that the CI presentation include plans for sharply reducing the number of defects and complaints on Corvette. He was driving quality on his A-cars to new heights and he wanted the same for Corvette. In other areas, Corvette was already superior. Its performance goals were to be mapped out and explained to the executives. No one ever questioned that any new car would meet or exceed safety, environmental, and fuel economy standards. And no one questioned that the new car would make money for the company. If your business case didn't show a profit, you didn't go to CI. The job at CI was not to say that you'd make a profit, but to say *how* you would make a profit.

Profit was the tough part. Cardy Davis had finance people on his plat-forms, and they knew their numbers. He had purchasing people, tough negotiators who knew the cost of every part that went into a Corvette down to the penny. His manufacturing experts could design an assembly line and would use the latest ideas in synchronous manufacturing and just-in-time delivery to bring the Corvette plant in Bowling Green, Kentucky, to peak efficiency. In the months of bubble-up, he'd been given a target budget of

$250 million, then $80 million, then back to $210 million. That wasn't a big budget for creating an all-new car.

"At two-ten, I can do a car that's mostly new, but not the interior, and it will make money," Davis told Mike Mutchler, group vice president and head of the Chevrolet-Pontiac-Canada group to which Corvette belonged. But the money wouldn't begin to flow until CI, and then only if the review board approved. Cardy Davis's calendar had the day marked in red: March 23, 1989.

Cardy Davis was a car guy. He also was a minority at General Motors: In a company mostly populated by short to midsize people, he was tall, or at six-one, at least moderately so. His thick, wavy graying hair bounced when he walked and he had a hard time sitting through meetings without getting up and moving around.

Born in 1935, in Richmond, Virginia, the oldest of three children in a banker's family, he never knew poverty, or anything close to it, but his father instilled a work ethic into Cardy that he embraced. It helped that he came from a long line of achievers. His father's father was born in Virginia to Welsh immigrants, successful shopkeepers, just before the Civil War broke out. His mother's people, the Floyds, came from England, landing on the eastern shore of Virginia in their own ship around 1700. There were four brothers aboard and each made his mark in the colonies. The son of one of the original Floyds even signed the Declaration of Independence.

"I was always interested in mechanical things, building them or taking them apart," Cardy remembered. "So when it was time for college, I decided on engineering. Actually, I decided a long time before that to go to Virginia Polytechnic Institute at Blacksburg because my father took me there so often on business."

He graduated in the top 2 percent of his class and after culling through a half-dozen job offers, from tobacco, oil, and automobile companies, he looked at the money being promised. Ford, Chrysler, and General Motors each offered him $485 a month. The oil and tobacco companies offered more, but his heart was with cars. "I got advance warnings not to work for Ford or Chrysler," he said, "but nobody said anything bad about General Motors." He took GM's offer and found himself in Flint, Michigan, as an engineer working on Buick's automatic transmissions. His career moved steadily, if not spectacularly, upward and he told people along the way that he never had a job he didn't like.

The coming years at General Motors would test that liking to its limits.

John Cafaro's Skunk Works was humming again. With Concept Initiation only a few weeks off, he had to deliver a theme for the new Corvette to

Chuck Jordan. Jordan would change it later, often on a whim, but at this point it was mandatory to have models and sketches that would dazzle the executive review board.

Upstairs in Chevy 3, Cafaro's people had already pulled off one miracle. In barely a month, they reshaped the Camaro and brought it more or less to release. Cafaro had shifted just enough of the car's lines to give the illusion of change without really doing much that would impact Camaro's engineers. Then GM's executive vice president, Lloyd Reuss, dropped a bomb during a February design review. The company's forecasts beyond 1989 had turned sharply south in the past month and though they weren't saying so in public, top managers were looking for ways to reduce spending in 1990. Camaro suddenly fell into that category. It was already behind schedule by a month and that made it vulnerable. Reuss didn't hesitate to slip it further. He shifted it a full six months further into the future, from a 1992 model to a '92 and a half. The slowdown would save badly needed capital in 1990, even though it meant dealers wouldn't see the new Camaro until the spring of 1992. The money for tooling and plant conversion would still be spent, but at a slower pace. As the corporate financial crunch got worse, Camaro slipped all the way to 1993.

A month earlier, a released Camaro might have avoided that delay and given GM something to brag about when the car magazines reviewed it in late 1991. But February 1989 was a cusp month for General Motors. Its prospects as seen from the fourteenth floor at GM headquarters went from so-so to so-long. It was the month when the company reported that record $4.86 billion profit for 1988. It was a month when Chairman Roger Smith convinced the board of directors to declare a two-for-one stock split and to increase the quarterly dividend by 20 percent, to $1.50. It was a month when Smith and President Bob Stempel issued a joint statement saying, "The Corporation's turnaround—which began some time ago in terms of product quality, customer service, manufacturing efficiencies, and other key elements of GM's reindustrialization and strategic redirection—is beginning to show increasingly on the bottom line. With its accelerating momentum, GM is well positioned to achieve its ultimate objective of strong profitability today and industry leadership into the 21st Century." And it was a month when Smith and Stempel and Reuss and a few others at the tip of GM's management pyramid knew that things were about to go terribly wrong.

Still, the brass hoped they were misreading the tea leaves and if they fretted in private, they smiled in public.

Camaro was the first GM car to feel the pinch. The pinch would turn into a crisis and Camaro would one day be considered lucky because, if it didn't meet the original or even the thrice-revised production dates, it did finally make it to the streets.

Meanwhile, Corvette marched to its original schedule. With two weeks to go before the Concept Initiation review, Jordan called for a show of all Corvette designs being generated by Cafaro's crew. He looked over the Skunk Works sketches and clown suits, picked two, and ordered full-size clay models sculpted. Twenty-six-year-old Kirk Bennion's clown suit was dressed in shiny maroon foil. Its lines trapped light and shadows in a racy Z shape flowing along its sides. Bennion kept it close to the package mandated by Dave McLellan. He draped-to-shape brilliantly.

George Camp's car was longer and more traditionally Corvette. He went for the fast windshield but kept his lines more like the current car. A bulge in the hood reflected the power underneath and in Camp's sharpest departure from tradition, the nose of his model was not pointed at all, carrying its broad, smooth curve from fender to fender.

Jordan was satisfied, at least for now. Two days later, he and Jerry Palmer took GM chairman Roger Smith on an after-hours tour of the Skunk Works. Smith showed up alone, without entourage, just another company chairman driving himself home after work. He wandered from model to model, nodding appreciatively at the two Jordan had picked for full-size renditions. He looked at sketches, commenting now and then. "Yes, I like that . . . The rear end on that one isn't right, is it? . . . This one's good."

Then he stopped and dropped one of those offhanded comments that have far-reaching and unintended impact when they come from on high.

"We've got to be out front with the next Corvette," Roger Smith said. "It has to be the best Corvette we've ever done and for my money, it has to be radical. I like what I see here, but it doesn't reach out far enough. I want you to tell your people to take the Corvette design as far south as they can go, and then go one step more."

In a few sentences, Roger Smith gave Chuck Jordan a ticket to ride. Cautious, conservative Roger Smith wanted a radical Corvette. Jordan and Palmer looked at each other. If it had been polite, they would have licked their lips in anticipation.

Two months later, Palmer would say at a weekly design review: "Roger Smith's visit threw us into a lot of activity. It was like a license to steal. He had us going off and looking at mid-engines and at all sorts of far-out stuff that really doesn't apply at all. We wasted a lot of time looking at things that we'll never, ever do. That's what a few comments by the chairman of the board can do."

8 MARCH 23, 1989, came too soon, then went by with anticlimactic haste. The next day was Good Friday, the start of a four-day holiday weekend for General Motors employees.

Cardy Davis had the Corvette platform primed and ready. They rehearsed their Concept Initiation presentation until it was flawless, and prayed that none of the executives on the board would ask an off-the-wall question.

Chuck Jordan ignored the coming milestone, spending much of the previous week in California critiquing the work under way at the Advanced Concepts Center. He sent Jerry Palmer to CI, armed with drawings and with confidence that Design Staff's bubble-up gave them enough of a theme to move into Phase Zero. The theme was wordless, expressed in a series of Corvette sketches that showed a new car with more aerodynamic lines than the current models, sleeker, lower, and bulging with curves at front and rear fenders that hinted, more than hinted, at unbridled strength.

Palmer and everybody else knew that the final design would look nothing like the sketches. But it was a start. It was a theme.

Concept Initiation for the 1993 Corvette began promptly at 3 P.M. in a paneled conference room at Chevrolet's headquarters at the GM Technical Center in Warren, Michigan. Fourteen people sat at a horseshoe-shaped table. The most important of them was Lloyd Reuss, GM's executive vice president and the man responsible for building cars in North America. Mike Mutchler, head of the Chevrolet-Pontiac-Canada group, was there, along with Bob Burger, who was retiring as general manager and vice president for Chevrolet. Every vote around the table was equal, but the votes of Reuss, Mutchler, and Burger were more equal than the rest, and Reuss's vote was the most equal of all.

Reuss dominated the table despite his short height. He concealed his slender frame under a suit coat that flared out at the waist, giving him the appearance of more bulk. His black hair was traced with silver, evenly distributed and not nearly enough to show from any distance. What counted was the power he packed into his five-seven body. There was a joke around Design Staff and the platforms that you could do anything you wanted if you had an LRS. "What's an LRS?" neophytes asked. "Lloyd Reuss Says . . . !"

The name of the game at Concept Initiation was to get an LRS.

Cardy Davis didn't have a vote. Neither did Dave McLellan or Jerry Palmer. They were among the twenty-three people sitting or standing along the walls. Some of them were presenters, ready to make the case for the '93 Corvette. The rest were senior people in the program and each of them was ready to answer questions in his area of expertise.

Cardy Davis knew that the corporation was under financial stress. Something had to be done to stem the cash outflow in coming years. The Camaro delay had already pushed some costs for the new F-car into future years. Would Corvette be invited to the dismal dance? Davis hoped not, but he knew that most of the money for the new Corvette would come out of the coffers in 1990 through 1992. Mike Mutchler kept Cardy informed. "Future programs are on thin ice," he said, and Cardy knew that meant Corvette.

What he didn't know was that General Motors was getting ready to eat its children.

Cardy Davis had to remain confident. Corvette was an important car to GM, but in its best years, it was a flea on the elephant's back. Still, this was no time for timidity.

Despite Mike Mutchler's concern that $250 million was too much, despite his tacit instructions to hold off the $40 million for a new interior until the third or fourth year of the new car, Davis thought he could slip the whole program through in the next two hours. He started with one of those overhead slides that sets the goals for the meeting. "Here's what we want to do today," he told the group, putting up a slide listing a first priority of getting the okay to begin Phase Zero.

He aimed his next comment directly at Mike Mutchler. "We're asking for two hundred ten million dollars," he said. "Design Staff agrees, but they also want to do a new interior. That'll add another forty million." He paused.

Mutchler bristled. "Maybe we can delay that, Cardy, make it a downline improvement."

Cardy nodded. He'd spoken directly to Mutchler, but he'd planted the seed where it counted, with Lloyd Reuss. It was time to let the presentations roll on. For the next ninety minutes, the review board heard much that it already knew.

"Corvette is the ultimate expression of Chevrolet character."

"Corvette buyers are upscale. They're looking for excitement and they can afford it. Today's regular Corvette costs between thirty and forty thousand dollars. We have to hold that line on the new car."

"Our competition used to be Porsche. The Japanese were priced well below us. Now the world has changed. The new Nissan 300ZX jumps up in class from a twenty-thousand-dollar car to a thirty-thousand-dollar car. Toyota's next Supra will be in our price range. Mitsubishi will hit us with their new 3000GT and the top-of-the-line Dodge Stealth will be there, too. The Acura NS-X is stickered above fifty, but it'll take away some buyers from the Corvette ZR-1, which is around sixty. And Porsche doesn't count anymore. You can't touch one for under sixty thousand and their sales show it. They've almost dropped off the charts."

Speakers from Chevrolet marketing reviewed the results of extensive surveys they call the Voice of the Customer. The unanimous conclusion: Customers wanted a hot, new Corvette. Another conclusion was equally obvious: Corvette's competition was all Japanese and C5 had to be good enough to maintain or improve its 30 percent market share in the high-sports marketing segment.

"These sketches give you the flavor of where we're going." That was Jerry Palmer. "This next Corvette may have to last until the year 2000. We think it will be a style setter."

The business case presentation went flawlessly. Cardy Davis showed it with and without a new interior. The numbers looked best when the car was simultaneously new inside and out. It would cost more up front, but payback for the $250 million investment was less than three years. After that, Corvette would continue to generate its $100 million–plus profit year in and year out, at least until the car was middle-aged or older.

Occasional questions and comments from the table interrupted the presenters. When Alan Czarnomski of Chevy marketing flashed a slide showing the new Corvette on the streets in late 1992, Reuss quipped: "We'd better get it out there pretty quick or I'll be too old."

"I don't know how old you are," Czarnomski shot back, "but there's a Corvette for every age!" Reuss laughed and clapped.

Corvette interiors came up repeatedly, according to Cardy Davis's plan. The review board heard a glowing tribute to the interior of the new Nissan 300ZX, just then reaching dealers across the United States and already basking in glowing reviews from magazines like *Motor Trend* and *Car and Driver.* Some of the men at the table had already experienced a few driving days in the 300ZX. A few of them had heard the story of how Nissan created the car.

In May 1986, Nissan began its own competition to design an all-new 300ZX. Japanese designers outside Tokyo made up one team. Americans at Nissan Design International in La Jolla, California, headed by ex-GM designer Jerry Hirschberg, were the second team. An Italian studio was hired to produce a third design. Within a month, Nissan executives looked at the three preliminary designs and summarily fired the Italians. By early

September, they ordered Hirschberg's Americans to ship their full-size clay model to Japan for a month-long shoot-out with the Japanese team.

On October 1, 1986, the Japanese team won. Their new 300ZX, borrowing heavily in chassis and underbody from the secret new luxury car to be called the Infiniti, began a pell-mell rush to production. Just thirty months later the car was being sold to eager buyers. It would give Corvette heavy competition. And the fact that it had been done in under three years sent shivers through the Corvette team.

Their CI presentations wound toward an end, leaving time for more questions and discussion. Cardy Davis summed it up. "What we want is this," he said. "We recognize that we have more competition out there now, and probably more coming down the road. Some of it is going to be better than we are today. On the next Corvette, we intend to reclaim best-in-class performance and styling.

"And we're going to attain best-in-class handling. We can do it."

Reuss nodded. "I agree. Corvette is the technology test bed for all of General Motors and that's more important now than ever. If you can't do it in the Corvette, make it best-in-class, you're lost."

Concept Initiation was approaching its climax. There had not been a word of challenge about the styling, about performance, about upgrading engines to get ever higher accelerations and top speeds. That was expected in Corvette. The fifth-generation Corvette had to be faster than C4, or why bother?

What it boiled down to now was money. Lloyd Reuss took charge of the meeting. "Is there anybody here who doesn't agree that they've met the business case?"

No one argued.

"Is there anybody who objects to a Corvette that looks great and goes fast?"

That one brought smiles to every face in the room.

"Is there anybody here who disagrees with me that the interior and exterior should be done together?"

Mike Mutchler's eyebrows raised momentarily, then his face went expressionless. He kept his mouth shut, but he saw Cardy Davis smiling.

"Okay, Cardy, you passed Concept Initiation," Reuss said. "Tell your people that you've got a two-hundred-fifty-million-dollar program.

"I want the first production car off the line."

9 B E F O R E Corvette could become a production car, it had to survive a long gestation and birthing process at the General Motors Technical Center. Life at the Tech Center is a mix of art and science, engineering and finance, politics and intrigue.

Railroad tracks neatly bisect the mile-square Tech Center. The east side belongs to the working stiffs. Its plain vanilla buildings offer shelter and warmth for the engineers doing the day-to-day toil of designing parts for cars or engines. One building has noisy instrumented rooms where engines can be fired up on test stands and be run until they either break or survive the equivalent of two or three lifetimes of hard use. The same building houses laboratories for the people who design the wiring and program the chips and figure out which sound system best fits their car. It has labs for engineers who find the limits of their metal chassis or steering knuckles. And it has labs for engineers working on exhaust systems or shock absorbers. The building has a lot of labs.

Another building is a combination factory, drafting palace, analytical mecca, and administration hall. Several labs run endurance tests, hooking up automatic equipment that opens and closes doors and trunks tens of thousands of times to see if anything breaks. There's an assembly line inside the big building, small but effective. Side by side with GM engineers, UAW men and women build prototype cars on the line, then send them out to be tried and tested and sometimes to be driven until they break.

Before any prototype car can be built, its plans and drawings pass through one or more of the immense dark rooms filled with computer tubes where the drafters—they call them *designers*—draw every part of the car in detail and label each with dimensions and specifications.

Before the drafters get their crack at drawing parts, the math whizzes run their analytical equations to predict stresses and strains, and to offer suggestions about beefing up this piece or narrowing the gauge of that one. Some of the computer runs are done on high-powered work stations. Others take days of time on a Cray supercomputer.

The giant building also has offices for the managers, planners, accountants, and other administrative people. And it houses Corvette.

There are a few other buildings east of the tracks. Chevrolet has its headquarters in one of them. Cadillac is in the building next door. There are buildings for training classes and for GM maintenance specialists.

The central feature on the east side of the tracks is a large reflecting pool. It's not as nice as the pool on the west side.

The railroad tracks are lined with high fences and barbed wire, ostensibly to keep people safe. But the practical impact is to prevent people assigned to the east side of the tracks from wandering over to the west, where a more artistic and elite cadre of General Motors people spends its days. Access is by driving through a tunnel under the tracks or by leaving the Tech Center and returning through one of the guarded gates. It helps to have an invitation, or at least to be expected, when visiting over there.

The west side of the General Motors Technical Center is beautiful. It has a two-mile test track laid out along the railway with interesting curves and banks. The buildings are more colorful and intriguing. Outside walls are tiled in shiny shades of red and blue, or in brilliant yellow or orange. There are wide landscaped lawns and benches for taking the sun on a pleasant day. The reflecting pond on the west side has fountains that throw water high into the air, creating miniature rainbows. The buildings themselves have names like Advanced Engineering and Advanced Manufacturing, implying that the people in those buildings are doing something special. And frequently they are.

Isolation is part of being on the west side of the tracks. The forward-thinking people doing "advanced" work have peripheral impact on car design and production. They live in the far future. When they come up with something, maybe a new chip-driven controller module, special lights for instruments, or a whole new way to build a chassis, those products become available across the board. Some creations are intended for a specific model, like Corvette. Corvette is a favorite test bed for tricky technology, followed by Cadillac. Those leaps into the future often find their way into dozens of GM cars.

The General Motors Research Laboratory is across the street, fronting directly onto the north end of the reflecting pool. It is much more advanced than Advanced Engineering or Advanced Manufacturing. General Motors researchers are chemists, physicists, computer whizzes, robotic experts, and engineers with a variety of unusual skills. They work with polymers, electrons, and concepts. Many of the researchers have multiple degrees. The General Motors Research Laboratory is where science happens at General Motors.

At the other end of the reflecting pool is the Design building, home to John Cafaro and the Chevy 3 studio. It has its own small pond for added effect. Design was conceived by Harley Earl and he had a large hand in its architecture. When it opened in 1955, people wondered about the wide steps with the suspiciously low rise that led up from the lobby. The answer was that Harley Earl not only had big influence, he had big feet. He wanted steps he could ascend and descend comfortably. Harley Earl's big feet just fit on the wide steps.

The building called Design is one of the most secure in all of General Motors. While C5 was being designed, the building held twenty-one locked studios and within their walls was the future of General Motors. The studio configuration began to change in 1995, but that had nothing to do with Corvette.

The Patio is just outside Design's west end. At General Motors, there is only one Patio. Anyone who says "I saw such-and-such a car on the Patio" is one of the favored few at GM and expects listeners to know exactly what and where the Patio is.

It's a large area protected by high walls and its surface is covered with hexagonal tiles. Studios bring their full-size clay cars out to the Patio to see them in natural light. The clay almost always is covered with Di-Nok foil, so from even a few feet away, the cars look real. The windows are black or silver. The skin is red or whatever color the studio chief thinks will show off best. Authentic badges identify the car by division and model, and wheels and tires, sometimes real, sometimes fake, are fitted into the proper places. Two turntables set flush into the tiles allow a car to be turned slowly before the eyes of the invited few.

The Patio was another Harley Earl innovation.

Off the end of the Patio is a large silvered dome.

The Dome is visible to traffic on nearby Mound Road and, along with a shiny silver three-legged water tower that looks like a chubby flying saucer on stilts, to airplanes overhead. It is one of the Technical Center's (west-side) landmarks. The Dome was Harley Earl's final innovation.

Under the Dome, General Motors has shows. Sometimes the shows are cars, when a car program manager puts on a show of the past, the present, and the future for senior executives. Sometimes the shows are new technology, with GM suppliers—say, electronics or lighting companies—displaying their current and future wares for the Design Staff artisans and perhaps a few invited engineers. Sometimes the shows are private. GM's top executives meet now and then under the Dome to discuss the future of a product, or of the company.

The Dome roof can be opened, like an astronomical observatory, to let in the light. Nobody remembers the last time that happened at a show or meeting.

The last building on the west side of the Tech Center is the General Motors wind tunnel, where studios bring their model cars to check their aerodynamics. Air flow over a car is more important than ever because it affects not just handling and general performance, but fuel economy and top speed. Designers and engineers want their new cars to be slippery through the air. They want the coefficient of drag, c/D, as low as possible. A c/D of 0.35 is okay for a sedan. Most sports cars come in around 0.33. The new Corvette aimed for much better and models from John Cafaro's studio would be hauled over the wind tunnel time and time again before they got it down to a minimum.

One last feature distinguishes the west side of the Tech Center from the east. It isn't something visible to the casual observer and few people have the necessary security badge codes to make use of all its intricacies. But for those with even limited access, the maze of underground tunnels that connects all the buildings on the west is a godsend on cold winter days, or when it is necessary to move something secretly from one building to another. The west side has its secrets.

Even the fowl seem to know the differences between east and west. On the east side, the reflecting pool is populated by ducks. On the west side, under the fountains and rainbows, the birds are geese and swans. Now and then a duck will invade the west. But few geese and no swan has been seen on the east side.

So when Corvette's platform people, the business experts and engineers who finance and build the car, and the marketing people from Chevrolet who would sell it, drove through the car tunnel from their offices on the east side to visit John Cafaro's Corvette studio on the west, they passed into a different place. They were the working ducks, off to visit the swans.

10 WHAT a difference a month made.

With Concept Initiation safely behind, Cardy Davis made direct overtures for more face-to-face contact between the platform and Design Staff. Jerry Palmer and John Cafaro agreed, Cafaro more eagerly, and Wednesday morning meetings in a Design Staff conference room went onto everybody's calendar. The meetings gave Davis as platform manager and Dave McLellan as Corvette's chief engineer, along with all of their key subordinates, routine access to the Design building. Davis reasoned that it wouldn't take long for their faces to be so familiar in the halls that nobody would question whether platform people were making inroads into territory that had never been quite forbidden, but was never quite open, either.

The early meetings were spirited. Adrenaline flowed and both sides of Corvette buckled down to meet the Four-Phase deadlines that would lead to a 1993 car. The next big milestone was scheduled for December 1989, an event called Concept Alternative Selection. One of several Corvette designs would be picked by agreement among Chuck Jordan, Cardy Davis's platform team, and a Chevrolet squad headed by Jim Perkins, Chevy's new VP and general manager. Perkins was a good old Texas boy who'd been on the rise at GM, then went to Toyota for several years before being courted back into the fold. He could be counted on to have intense interest in a new Corvette.

The favorite car at the moment was Kirk Bennion's flashy design. Cafaro was throwing manpower at it, bringing it up to a full-size clay model. Five modelers swarmed over its surface in the basement Skunk Works, shaping, paring, carving, and scraping it with loving care. Bennion hovered over it all the while, supervising the details, particularly the undulating curves at the leading edge of the doors.

"We gotta get this car in shape quick," Cafaro told the early morning meeting on a Wednesday in mid-April. "Kirk's being promoted to assistant chief in the Chevy 1 studio." True to his own philosophy, Cafaro refused to stand in the way of talent on the way up. Behind the scenes, he lobbied to help Bennion get the job. "It's great for him, but it leaves me in a hole,"

Cafaro told Cardy Davis and his engineering and business staff. "I'd hate to replace him with somebody who has less talent, so I guess I have to run short-staffed for a while."

There was other work going on, too. Jerry Palmer kept some of the Skunk Works designers looking at futuristic designs. If the designers in the basement could come up with something fantastic, there was still time to get Roger Smith into the loop and push it into the competition. Smith's offhand remarks a few months earlier had caused talent to be drained into the side avenue of an alternative Corvette design. Models were taking shape in Tom Peters's Advanced 4 studio, too. After three months, there was nothing there to make a complete Corvette, but pieces of this one and pieces of that one caught Chuck Jordan's eye. At the same time, Chuck Jordan was traveling to California every week or two to track the designs flowing through John Schinella's Advanced Concepts Center. He wanted a running car ready by summer, while it could still influence the artistry in Cafaro's studio. And he wasn't counting out the possibility that Advanced 4 would produce a breakout design.

All that was about to come to a sudden stop. Cardy Davis felt a knot in his stomach when he got a copy of a memo written March 31, just eight days after CI, by Joe Pascucci, a young Lloyd Reuss aide. The memo was addressed to a midlevel Chevrolet-Pontiac-Canada planner and didn't reach Davis until mid-April.

> . . . I talked with Lloyd about the meeting and what his intentions were.
>
> He responded to me that he was not satisfied that the "fence" has been drawn around the appropriate competition and that he needs a better understanding of what the Level 1 Specs are. He stated, "I don't even know whether the body will still be plastic, or how they plan to get 350 and 450 HP from the engines." He also said, "I suppose you could say that I gave them concept initiation approval, but I did not give approval to any level of investment spending. I asked to see the program again in six (6) weeks. . . ."
>
> His emphasis was again to focus on "what it takes to do the car right (what is right for the product, and what it will take in terms of resources and dollars)." As I stated previously, I still believe that he intends that CPC will then have to fit the program within its current existing capital targets. I also think the program management team would be remiss not to include the engine investment required to execute the Level 1 engine power specs and the Paint Shop investment they think will be needed to achieve a world class finish since they (and Lloyd) believe that these items would be required to "do the car right."
>
> He closed the conversation by saying that the meeting in six weeks needs to be shorter and conducted with a much smaller audience.

Davis was aghast. *What the hell is going on here?* he thought. People walked away from the CI review grinning and shaking hands, confident that Reuss had given his approval and had verbally authorized the $250 million investment. Most of the items in the Pascucci/Reuss memo had been discussed. Some of them hadn't, but only because they were not required at the time. Concept Initiation was day one of Phase Zero, and a key goal of Phase Zero was to develop and refine so-called Level 1 specifications.

"Lloyd doesn't understand Four-Phase," Davis complained. "If this memo is right, he's asking for things to be completed in bubble-up that we aren't even supposed to start looking at until Phase Zero."

Davis was right in his complaints. Reuss was asking the wrong questions and he *had* approved both CI and the $250 million investment. Davis asked for guidance from Mike Mutchler. Keep going on the program, he was told. Mutchler didn't add that a full-scale review of CPC's capital budgets was under way.

Something was in the wind. When GM reported quarterly profits of $1.6 billion on April 20, the accompanying quotes from Roger Smith and Bob Stempel were slightly restrained. "The Corporation's long-term reindustrialization strategy continues to have an increasingly *pronounced* impact on product quality and profitability," the GM executives said. The choice of the word *pronounced* over the word *positive* was significant. A more accurate word would have been *negative*. But no one in the business press picked up on the sleight of tongue.

Late in the news release came another caveat: "No one is more aware of today's intensely competitive automotive marketplace than General Motors." But the final sentence seemed upbeat: "In the coming years General Motors will become increasingly stronger, more productive and more competitive." The word not used in listing things that would increase was the most significant word of all: *profit*.

A couple of Tuesdays later, Mike Mutchler summoned Cardy Davis to his office late in the afternoon. There was good news and bad news. The good news was that Cardy didn't have to worry about a rereview with Lloyd Reuss. The bad news was simply terrible. Just before quitting time, Cardy called Jeff Banasczynski, who set up the meetings at Design Staff and usually ran them. Then he went home to kick the cat.

When John Cafaro walked into the conference room at eight o'clock the next morning for the weekly Design Staff/platform meeting, he saw it immediately.

"Oh, shit!" he said. Banasczynski had changed headings on all the wall charts. The new charts read "1994 Mainstream Design."

"We've been slipped a year," Cardy Davis told the group. "Mutchler had to make some tough decisions and we were one of them. We're losing most of our engineering budget for this year, so on our side, we have to slow down. The big budget is still intact. Mutchler said that we can't exceed the investment target; we're just moving back a year." He looked directly at John Cafaro. "He also said that any mid-engine or transaxle designs are not to be pursued, except at a very low level. The mainstream Corvette is just what it has always been, front-engine, rear-drive."

Cafaro winced, thinking about the mid-engine designs that Jerry Palmer was pursuing in the Skunk Works.

Davis went on. "But I want you guys to keep going with what you're doing. I'll talk to Chuck Jordan today. This is a chance for you guys to really refine your design. It's free time and I hope you'll use it."

Cafaro nodded. Maybe he could keep up a head of steam, not have to go back to square one with another prolonged bubble-up. Still, this was a blow. "The Japanese can take a design today and have a car out in twenty-four months," he moaned, "and we're still more than three years away. We just can't do things that fast. Why? Why can't we speed up development? I wish I knew."

So did everybody else in the room. Part of the answer was GM's ponderous system for designing and developing a new car. A typical new GM car took more than five years to develop. Cafaro knew that he was exaggerating about the Japanese getting a car from paper to product in two years. But they'd already proven with the 300ZX that three years was possible. His frustration simmered. "Six months from start of design to release!" he said to Jerry Palmer later. "That's what Nissan did. We spent longer than that in bubble-up and now we're being told to back off!"

Palmer shrugged. That was just GM.

The reason for delaying Corvette from 1993 to 1994 was honestly stated within GM, if not in public. "The company is facing some lean times," Cardy Davis said. "We're being asked, no, we're being *told*, to give at the office."

It wouldn't be the last time.

Summer came hot and humid. The discomfort outside carried over into the Design studios with mounting pressure on John Cafaro's artists. They had to produce a Corvette skin that Chuck Jordan would like better than whatever John Schinella's team came up with out in California. Everyone knew that Schinella's left coasters would deliver a car that was striking, even breathtaking, but not very practical. At the Advanced Concepts Center, designers were not encouraged to be practical. Their mission was to soar and provoke. John Cafaro was in no mood to be provoked.

He was getting added pressure at home, too, from Tom Peters in the studio downstairs. The two studio chiefs respected each other and were friends at work and away. Peters understood that his role was to push and prod, to act as a catalyst. "We're just going to look out at the limits," Peters told Cafaro. "You'll always be the production studio for Corvette." Cafaro felt okay with that. Maybe Peters could provide a theme that could be incorporated into Cafaro's own designs.

Then the Chrome Cobra struck again. With July heat suffocating the Detroit area, he stalked through Cafaro's studio looking at three-eighths-scale clay models and scores of sketches. He didn't like any of them. With characteristic abruptness, Chuck Jordan pulled the future Corvette from Cafaro altogether. Prime responsibility went to Tom Peters downstairs. Cafaro and his people were ordered to finish up the last post-release work on the new Camaro and to get ready to do another production car. They'd have plenty of time. General Motors management ordered Corvette slipped to 1995. It was the second year-long delay ordered in barely three months. Cafaro was outspokenly angry.

"I'm really pissed," he told his team. "I thought we really had something going downstairs with Tom and me. Then Chuck comes in and doesn't like anything and shuts us down again." To John Cafaro, it was a personal affront.

At the same time, Jordan stretched John Schinella's deadline in California from midsummer to November 3, in line with the company-wide slowdown on virtually everything. Even that was optimistic.

More disasters hit General Motors. The new W-cars, the family sedans, bombed. When General Motors introduced its look-alike Chevrolet Lumina and Pontiac Grand Prix, followed soon by a Buick Regal, and Oldsmobile Cutlass Supreme, Lloyd Reuss predicted that they would push GM's share of the passenger-car market up a point and half to 37 percent. Advance fleet orders for 20,000 Luminas alone were in hand and the production schedule called for building 25,000–30,000 cars a month.

By the end of July, Reuss, Stempel, and Smith knew they had big trouble. In three months, Chevrolet dealers had delivered only eighteen thousand Luminas beyond the fleet sales. They had an enormous eighty-two-day supply of Luminas on their lots. Meanwhile, GM's assembly plants, those single-car plants of Roger Smith's dreams, were pumping out cars that had nowhere to go but into huge outdoor storage lots. W-cars badged to Buick and Oldsmobile reported even worse numbers.

In mid-1989, U.S. sales for every car company were down. Some people at GM cited the tax code revisions of 1986 as part of the problem, along with new and expensive government regulations taking effect. "It took this long for car buyers to wake up to the fact that interest on their car loans won't be deductible anymore," a senior GM executive lamented. "Don't tell them that they got a rate cut three years ago, because that's history. What matters is the twelve hundred dollars or two thousand dollars in interest that comes out of next year's paycheck, and the paychecks for three or four years after that. On top of that, the feds require air bags or some other passive restraint like an automatic seat belt on every 1990 car. So before you even factor in a normal four or five percent price hike for inflation, you have to add an extra seven hundred fifty to one thousand dollars to the sticker price on *every* car. You add seven hundred fifty dollars to a small car that ought to sticker for seventy-five hundred dollars and you've just upped the price by ten percent, *just for one new federal rule.* Between the interest problem and sticker shock, it's no wonder that car sales are in the dumper."

Even with sales down, GM had a cushion. It continued to report billion-dollar quarterly profits, but almost all of that came from its European division and from its financial arms like GMAC. The W-car family sedan fiasco threatened to wash a coat of red ink over North American Operations and even hefty rebates wouldn't help. Rebates would increase sales, but GM was losing up to $5,000 on every W-car already. Somehow the program managers had either missed or concealed data during development that showed they were spending too much on tooling, too much on single-car assembly plant conversions, and too much for parts. Then the company's sales forecasts far exceeded reality and even forecasts revised downward were proving to be too optimistic.

"Somebody lied," Cardy Davis said bitterly in one meeting. "And he probably got promoted."

"Watch what you say in public," one of his deputies chided. "At GM, people who complain about problems usually get the job of fixing them." It was a joke and everyone laughed. Later it was no joke at all.

Whether or not somebody deliberately misled top executives like Reuss, Stempel, and Smith, the result was the same. Everybody paid. Some programs paid more than others.

More bad news landed in Cardy Davis's lap in mid-October at GM's annual executive conference in Traverse City, Michigan. The gathering was a way to get GM's leaders together once a year for meetings, speeches, golf, and lavish spreads of food. After 1989, the conference was deemed too expensive and was never again held. Cardy Davis remembers with bitterness the moment when Bob Stempel stood before his top one thousand executives and outlined the new series of cutbacks he was ordering. Davis felt an electric shock when Stempel got to the line, *"The Corvette development program is now on indefinite status."*

Davis and a half-dozen other Corvette and Chevrolet people snapped their heads around, seeking each other in the crowd. One of the first Davis spotted was Corvette's chief engineer, Dave McLellan, sitting there stricken and pale. Neither of them knew that Corvette was falling under another ax.

Bob Stempel hadn't bothered to tell them what was coming. After the meeting, Davis sought out Stempel and asked for an explanation. He was given a small measure of hope, but even that wasn't very satisfying. "Everybody is taking pain," Stempel said. "Corvette's no exception." He apologized for the gaffe in not giving Cardy a heads up on what was coming. "But . . ." Stempel shrugged and walked away. If Stempel knew that even tougher times lay ahead, he didn't mention that either.

Dave McLellan brought Cardy's report to the weekly Corvette design review meeting early the next Wednesday. "Cardy talked to Stempel and the key statement he got was to move Corvette to indefinite status, but to still keep working on it as a '95." How to resolve the conflict between working and not working was something nobody understood.

A few weeks before the announcement in Traverse City, Roger Smith and Bob Stempel briefed Wall Street analysts on the company's prospects. They weren't overly optimistic, but neither did they give any hint of what was to come. Smith closed the session by saying that General Motors had "instilled a new discipline into the way it develops its products and motivates and rewards its managers."

Nothing was further from the truth.

In less than seven months, from the end of March to early October 1989, the hidden financial morass being faced by GM had slipped the C5 Corvette from 1993 to '94 to '95 to indefinite. It wasn't a big and expensive program by any measure. Corvette's budget was dwarfed against the billion-dollar-plus budgets of the family cars. A few years later, Ford would leave executives at other companies shaking their heads when it spent a reported $2.8 billion on a revamped but hardly all-new Taurus. That was more than eleven times what GM would spend on the Corvette. But instead of pushing ahead on a relatively inexpensive 1993 Corvette, and at least having one shiny new glamour car to show off in the dismal years ahead, Smith and Stempel swept everything away. If there was discipline involved, it was apparent to no one. They cut arbitrarily and across the board. Motivation and reward had ceased to exist, except for the motivation to survive. Even Corvette's heritage couldn't save it from the clumsy ax.

McLellan was as unhappy as he'd ever been when he finished his comments at the regular Wednesday meeting. "[Stempel] told Cardy that when we get back to them with a new business case that meets the corporate hurdles, we'll get a firm date for production."

There was only one sure way to wring more profit out of a revised business case and that was to increase sales. With a car like Corvette, there was only one way to increase sales: Lower the price. It was catch-22 at its meanest. The silver-haired McLellan let himself get wound up.

"The real question is, why were we among the lambs being led to the slaughter?" he railed. "I think Roger Smith is in a very precarious position and wants to make his last year a very profitable one, even over the dead bodies of future programs. He wants to make short-term stockholder profit as high as possible.

"Somebody should tell Roger," McLellan said, "that cutting back on product is a hard way to find success."

But he knew that nobody would. Nobody could tell Roger Smith anything. So Cardy Davis the platform manager and Dave McLellan the chief engineer did the one thing that they knew would keep the next generation Corvette alive.

They went into hiding.

11

KEEPING the C5 Corvette off the General Motors funeral bier was Cardy Davis's first priority. At Design Staff, it was easy. Chuck Jordan's budget was not part of the Corvette bookkeeping, except for roughly $10 million charged each year against some Corvette master account for Design Staff services. Jordan could justify a trickle of future Corvette designs because looking to the future was part of his charter. Not much was happening in Tom Peters's Advanced 4 studio, as Jordan cooled on even that design effort. But he kept hands off the ACC budget in southern California. The Advanced Concept Center under John Schinella had dubbed its futuristic Corvette the Stingray III. It would be a running car with severe speed and handling restrictions, but people would be able to get into the driver's seat and take a short spin. Any Corvette design in Detroit would be no more than foil-covered clay.

Technically Cardy Davis had no money for engineering development on C5. Through Dave McLellan, however, he still owned a full Corvette engineering staff. Its job was to improve the existing C4 Corvette from model year to model year, blending additions, changes, and fixes into the car in the never-ending effort to make it better. At the same time, many of McLellan's engineers had been doing double duty, planning new systems or components for C5.

Davis and McLellan recognized an opportunity. The engineers would be paid no matter what they were doing. So with Cardy Davis's approval, Dave McLellan kept most of them doing exactly what they had been doing before Bob Stempel put C5 on hold. It was just a matter of bookkeeping.

Tom Krejcar was Corvette's financial manager. He showed them how easy it was. Charge numbers for C5 simply ceased to exist. No matter what an engineer was really doing, he logged his time against C4. It was true that there was no money to do the usual thing and bring in outside suppliers to help design tricky parts, then to build and deliver the first samples for evaluation. Nor was there money to build mules, those running cars that looked cobbled and rough and gave engineers their first chance to put miles on their parts to see how they held up.

But the engineers could get their groundwork done. The big decisions about C5 could be made and the basic architecture could be locked in. A start could be made on establishing the all-important VTS document— vehicle technical specifications. The VTS is a car's bible at General Motors. Somewhere in its hundreds of pages lurks a definition for everything from zero-to-sixty acceleration times to the comfort of seats, the field of view in outside mirrors, and the size of the glove compartment. The VTS defines the car in microscopic detail.

A financial manager like Tom Krejcar was supposed to know what was going on in his domain and to keep work from being billed to the wrong account. But Krejcar was typical of people assigned to the Corvette program. He had a passionate love affair with the car and if it took bending the rules to keep C5 moving forward, he told Cardy Davis, "then, by god, we'll hide the work and hope we don't get caught."

Davis nodded his approval and Krejcar went away to make it happen. That left Davis with one remaining problem.

His name was Dave McLellan.

Corvette was thirty-six years old in 1989 and McLellan was only its second chief engineer. He followed Zora Arkus-Duntov, a Belgian-born Russian and an authentic legend in both automotive and Corvette circles. Duntov's cars included the Corvette that traveled the western United States on the *Route 66* television show, the 1963 split-window coupe, the Mako Shark, and the big-block racers. Duntov Corvettes have sold for $70,000 and more at auction.

Dave McLellan became a legend, too. He was a superior engineer and may have been the best outside man General Motors ever had. His hair quickly turned into a distinguished silvery mane, he dressed in style, and at an inch or so under six feet, he carried himself with charismatic confidence. McLellan was a darling of the automotive press, interviewed and quoted and invited to speak at Corvette functions across the country and even across the oceans. He told stories with flair and was the walking repository of Corvette history. He was also frequently gone from Detroit, leaving day-to-day engineering work to his subordinates.

When he was in Detroit, McLellan was the magnificent idea man that every corporation needs. He pushed the limits and tested the theories and expanded the envelope of what can be done. McLellan could throw out a hundred ideas, scattering them like wildflower seeds, then press them into the fertile loam two and three and four levels down in the Corvette engineering organization. Ninety-nine of those ideas would wither and die, after taking days or weeks of time by a junior engineer, who sometimes had been told to put his real work aside and not tell his own supervisor that he was doing a "McLellan Special." But the one-hundredth idea would bloom and add luster to Dave McLellan's reputation.

The problem with Dave McLellan was a closely guarded secret: He was not interested in the details of management. He too often responded to questions and concerns from his engineers with the phrase that became his internal motto: "Just do it." But sometimes it couldn't be done, at least not within budget and not on time. Or at all.

Dave McLellan's first new Corvette was late. There was no 1983 Corvette because engineering problems with the new C4 overwhelmed the schedule. He didn't focus on assigning people to fix problems like squeaks and rattles, or water leaks. He emphasized performance. C4 was a mean machine that delivered speed and handling, and, for a brute sports car, high levels of safety and fuel economy. Some owners hated C4 for its flaws and quickly moved on to other high-performance automobiles. But many more loved it and there were more C4 Corvettes on the world's roads than any other sports car.

The successes of Corvette under Dave McLellan couldn't obscure the facts that many senior executives knew and lamented. No one doubted McLellan's passion for all things Corvette. But they did doubt his engineering management. For all his pluses, McLellan was not the chief engineer they wanted. But he had a rabbi who made him untouchable, Lloyd Reuss.

In the early seventies, when McLellan was a young engineer, Reuss briefly headed the Corvette program. They struck up a friendship that lasted. McLellan could get through to Reuss and wrangle an LRS—Lloyd Reuss Says—or an LSD (Lloyd Says Do-it) over the objections of mere mortals like Cardy Davis. But Davis suspected that McLellan wouldn't focus on the narrow issues of doing C5 and keeping it secret. He was afraid that McLellan would see the new Corvette as a candy store and would begin tossing ideas hither and yon, diverting scarce resources from the treacherous path of doing C5 while not appearing to do C5.

If McLellan was untouchable, Davis knew others who weren't. So he reached out and touched someone.

12 EARL Werner was grinning from ear to ear. It was late in 1989, nobody yet knew when the new Corvette would get a green light, and General Motors itself was sinking deeper into financial turmoil. But Werner was happy. He'd been tapped by Cardy Davis, an old and respected acquaintance, for a very special job. It was the sum of all of Earl Werner's dreams: assistant to Dave McLellan with a shot at eventually becoming Corvette's chief engineer himself.

The job, and its partly covert nature, had the approval of executives up the line. Arvin Mueller, director of engineering for the Chevrolet-Pontiac-Canada group, had even called Werner into his office to make sure that there were no misunderstandings. Mueller applauded McLellan for his accomplishments. But he admitted that McLellan was first a figurehead, an important public person who played well to Corvette's devoted following. The day-to-day work, Werner remembers Mueller saying, was not holding up as well. Werner's job was to become de facto chief engineer, supporting and complementing Dave McLellan behind the scenes.

At the same time, it was an unwritten part of his job that he keep Cardy Davis informed about the true state of Corvette engineering and about what "special" projects McLellan might be trying to keep from view. If Werner couldn't keep the program on track, and provide the engineering management that McLellan didn't, he could call on Davis, who would put the brakes on McLellan's excursions. It was an assignment that could be thankless. When Werner kept the engineering side of Corvette from straying, McLellan reaped the credit. But in the end, Werner believed, he would be groomed and in position to be the heir apparent.

Werner came to the job with engineering credentials and with a passion for two American icons, Corvette and Harley-Davidson. As an adult, he'd owned a motorcycle shop and worked at a car dealership. But he was a kid when he was imprinted with a love for Corvettes. Werner worked a teenage summer at a racetrack near his southern Ontario home selling hamburgers and cold drinks. When a Corvette driver with radiator problems approached him for water, young Earl made a deal: "Trade you ice water from the soft drink box for a lap around the track."

The driver got his water and bellowed into second place only yards behind a screaming D-type Jaguar. Werner was enthralled. When the Corvette driver made good on the lap and Werner felt the thrill of speed and roaring engine, he was hooked for life. "Right then I started thinking about engineering," he remembered with a far-off glaze in his eyes. "I was so struck by the speed of that fiberglass V-8 sports car tearing around Harewood Acres that I eventually applied to General Motors Institute. I wanted a job that would lead me to Corvettes."

It took nearly thirty years. After graduating from GMI, he worked a variety of journeyman engineering jobs at General Motors, spent time outside the company selling motorcycles and cars, and came back to become chief of chassis technology at the GM Tech Center. Chassis work at GM was high profile. A car's structure, and the components that go into it, affect virtually every aspect of car development. Werner earned a reputation as an innovative and highly competent engineer, as well as an astute manager. When Cardy Davis asked him to bring those skills to Corvette, it was the chance of a lifetime.

Before Werner could report to work, Cardy Davis and Dave McLellan took critical steps that would keep C5 alive and moving forward, however slowly. They'd already agreed to let Corvette engineers look at an all-wheel drive (AWD) variation of the future Corvette and to approve a study by the Tech Center's Advanced Vehicle Engineering organization of a new idea for the car's structure. Called variously a "ladder" structure or a "backbone," the concept envisioned a chassis made from one-piece side rails, with a massive central tunnel running most of the length of the car, and cross members to hold it all together. When the engine, drivetrain, and components such as suspension bars, shock absorbers, and wheels were added, it became a drivable chassis much like a race car. Racing was very much in Corvette's tradition.

The idea of providing power to all four of Corvette's wheels, instead of just the rear two, was intriguing but doomed. "All-wheel drive is a natural kind of thing the competition may do," Davis said. "It exists on a number of cars and the Japanese and Germans talk about doing it all the time. Corvette engineers are really innovative and looking to do the ultimate in a sports car. But at the same time, we have to make sure that we don't end up with a vehicle that's so costly that we only sell two thousand to three thousand a year. Those are vehicles that we don't make any money on. They create a positive image, but we still have to make money."

So while Davis and McLellan gave their engineers the freedom to explore the concept, and encouraged the artists at Design Staff to play with stylish bodies that might cover an AWD chassis, both men knew that it was an exercise rather than a program direction.

The backbone concept was another story. At first blush, it looked like a solution to the flaws in the current Corvette structure. Getting into the car required stepping high over a doorsill—actually the side rail of a "birdcage" structure that integrated chassis and passenger compartment—then squeezing and lowering yourself into the seat. Men and women alike found it awkward, at least until they mastered the slip-and-slide maneuver of getting into the car.

Corvette's birdcage structure had other drawbacks. It vibrated and shivered in early models, requiring a never-ending series of fixes that never quite tamed it. Dimensional control was a nightmare; a few-thousandths-of-an-inch variation from car to car could create new rattles and cause the water leaks for which C4 was infamous. The structure added weight to Corvette in a time when government fuel economy rules demanded lighter cars. When the top was removed to make the convertible model, the vibrations got worse and handling deteriorated. It was still excellent. It just didn't meet the standards demanded by Corvette engineers or Corvette owners.

In theory, the backbone might be a cure-all. With the right kind of thin-walled steel construction, it could reduce the mass of the car. When the body was installed over the chassis, the car could sit lower to the ground. The high step-over would disappear. The side rails and cross members would make the car stiffer, absorbing or eliminating vibrations and shake. The central tunnel, which would contain a long driveshaft going back to a transmission or transaxle in the rear, added stiffness, too.

A backbone C5 could be everything that the birdcage C4 was not, giving the driver better control of the car at all speeds, providing a solid and comfortable ride for driver and passenger, even letting engineers eliminate water leaks by designing body panels with that in mind.

That was the theory. The problem was how to manufacture a side rail that might be fifteen feet long with numerous bends and twists, as a single seamless tube of steel. The Advanced Vehicle Engineering group, with a charter to explore new technology on behalf of the entire corporation, took on the challenge.

When Jerry Palmer heard about the backbone, he was upset. Design Staff had its own captive engineers and at the direction of Palmer and Chuck Jordan, they were moving in a different direction. Communications between Design Staff and the Corvette program had never been good. The weekly meeting between the stylists of Design Staff and the engineers and business people from the program already had been reduced to every other Wednesday. Cardy Davis on the platform side and John Cafaro in the studio tried to make a difference by getting better acquainted. But too often, almost nobody from Design showed up for meetings, even when the meeting was in their building.

Palmer did show up in October 1989, after the backbone idea was floated. "We ought to be working together on a daily basis instead of getting together every two weeks and springing things," he complained. "The doors are open. We want to participate in the packaging and putting together a new vehicle."

Davis swallowed the impulse to say that Design Staff people would be better informed if they came to meetings. "Okay," he said instead. "We probably shouldn't show anything new here that Design Staff doesn't already know about."

But it was seemingly okay, Davis grumbled sarcastically, for the Design Staff engineering department to be studying an offbeat Corvette design without telling either him or Dave McLellan. That study was for a radical departure from the tradition of Corvette. Instead of a front-engine, rear-drive sports car, Chuck Jordan and Jerry Palmer had asked their internal engineers to look at a mid-engine car. In mid-engine designs, the motor is mounted over the car's center of gravity, in other words, behind the driver.

That changes all the proportions of the car. It can be shorter and lower to the ground. With no engine compartment up front, the hood can slope more steeply forward. The rear of the car must accommodate an engine, but might also have a small trunk. Automotive artists like mid-engine cars. They have more freedom to play with body styles, more chance to imprint their own talent in a mid-engine car's sweeps and curves. Palmer let it be known inside Design Staff that he favored changing the future Y-car to a mid-engine and there were artists who agreed with him.

Cardy Davis and Dave McLellan disagreed strongly. They were powerless to stop Design Staff from pursuing a dream.

"GM doesn't really know how to handle an indefinite status," McLellan complained to the group of senior managers who made up the Corvette business team. "It creates problems with the rest of the corporation." Indefinite, he said, means you don't exist, so nobody has to help you.

Earl Werner, barely on board and still the new guy, was beginning to make his presence felt. He understood the pressures that bosses up the line were feeling as GM foundered. "We have to be aware that management, particularly Mike Mutchler, will look at any budget for a new Corvette with an eye to making it zero."

McLellan nodded. "It really means that we have to make our business case." The only path to the future, he said, was in showing the corporation that Corvette would make money. "Whether or not we've got heavy-duty design activity going on in the next few months, we've got to keep the fires burning."

The team agreed, but Werner tossed out a note of caution: "Roger [Smith] is trying to posture himself for financial success in the short term," reminding the group that Smith was barely nine months from retiring as chairman of the board and that his successor still hadn't been named. "But also we've got to face the posturing of the heirs apparent. Their politics are apt to screw up some thinking, too."

The corporate confusion created a vacuum around Corvette. Chuck Jordan and Jerry Palmer moved swiftly to fill it. By late November, they were pushing hard on a mid-engine car. The mood when Cardy Davis arrived for one bi-Wednesday meeting at Design Staff was confrontational.

After listening to Jeff Banasczynski, the manager who served as liaison between the artists and the platform, extol the mid-engine designs, Davis erupted. "I'll tell you this, my bosses Mike Mutchler and Lloyd Reuss are not sanctioning any money or any time on a mid-engine. You guys are on your own on this one. You're not getting any direction from the platform or any sanctioning. If Mutchler finds out that one minute of time is being spent on a mid-engine version, he'll come unglued."

Banasczynski snapped back. "We're your design consultant and our management thinks it's important to look at the alternatives. We've done the front-engine version and we've come up short. And if we come up with something that's viable, we need to present it to you."

A transverse package, with the rear engine mounted sideways, was looking good, he said.

Davis shook his head in disgust, silver-gray hair flopping over his forehead. "My boss told me, 'Under no circumstances, waste one minute on something as ridiculous as that.' Quote, unquote."

But Design Staff held all the cards and Davis knew it. Chuck Jordan and his people could do whatever they pleased, with or without his consent. After a moment, Davis relented. "Just don't let Mutchler know you're doing it."

Banasczynski accepted victory with gracious humor. "And don't let him know that Cardy knows," he laughed.

When GM shut down for its traditional Christmas holiday, five scale-model Corvettes were sitting on display stands in Tom Peters's Advanced 4 studio. Two of them were mid-engine machines.

Upstairs in John Cafaro's production studio, sexy Chevys were a temporary memory. Cafaro was still responsible for annual changes in the C4 Corvette. But his new assignment was a real comedown. The mighty Corvette studio was doing a new subcompact sedan, the Chevy Cavalier.

13

THE hounds of belt-tightening were loose across the length and breadth of General Motors.

Car and light truck sales were down 7.5 percent for 1989, yet the company would soon report a $4.2 billion net profit on record sales and revenues of $126.9 billion. That $4.2 billion sounded like a lot of money. But capital spending planned for 1990 was $7 billion (quickly reduced to $6.4 billion).

The profit came mostly from overseas operations and from GM's financial unit. The company lost money in its key North American business. The Chevrolet-Pontiac-Canada group that included Corvette lost more than $1 billion in 1989 and was projecting a $2.6 billion loss for 1990.

Cardy Davis warned his people that little money would be available for working on the 1995 Corvette and that they'd have to find ways to take money out of the current car as well. One of those changes already was mandated by Mike Mutchler, head of CPC.

"We have to change the T-handle on the transmission fluid dipstick to a loop handle," Davis told his team. "That saves fifteen cents per car."

It didn't sound like much, Davis said, but fifteen cents times the million-plus cars manufactured by CPC was significant money. "However," he added with a small grin, "it doesn't make sense for Corvette."

The engineering-change paperwork alone would cost $4,500, more than they'd save on a low-volume car like Corvette. And they'd also have to change the owner's manual.

"So we just won't do it," Davis said, "and if anybody wants to yell at me, so be it."

It was a decision of the kind that earned Cardy Davis the respect of his people. He was willing to stand up for Corvette to keep work on the future car moving, however slowly, by diverting C4 money to C5, and even to fight Chuck Jordan and Design Staff when he thought they were moving in the wrong direction.

But some things were beyond his control. Completely fending off the merciless wave of internal cost-cutting was one. When that $4.2 billion profit was announced in February, President Bob Stempel and Chairman

Roger Smith put on smiling faces. "We are pleased with General Motors' strong overall performance in 1989," they said in a statement attributed to both. "Although profitability of GM's North American automotive operations declined due to lower volume and higher selling expense, they made significant progress in terms of both product competitiveness and improved operating efficiencies."

That wasn't quite true. By their internal actions, Stempel and Smith had shown that they were highly displeased with GM's 1989 performance. Only a month before their upbeat public statements, Stempel issued detailed orders intended to cut costs company-wide. Cardy Davis showed the document to his people without comment.

1990 QUICK START PROGRAM

Addendum 3

1. A six-month stop on all work on non-approved product programs.
2. Cancel existing orders and issue no new engineering materials orders for delayed programs.
3. Defer all capital spending three months.
4. Stop all program expenditures until reapproved by a Group Executive on a project-by-project basis.
5. Cease all office renovations and all new furniture/fixture purchases.
6. Cut media expenses 25% in the first and second quarters.
7. Cut motorsport participations by 20% from the 1990 plan, to be accomplished by the end of the first quarter.
8. Immediate salaried and hourly hiring freeze, except for hiring 500 new college graduates between January 1 and June 30, 1990.
9. Reduce temporary and contract employment by 10% by Feb. 1.
10. Allow completion of the 1989 salaried employee merit program.
11. Eliminate all overtime except overtime approved by a Group Executive. Employees performing authorized overtime may take compensatory time in lieu of pay.
12. Reduce Corporate travel, entertainment, offsite, etc. by a minimum of 30% and communications expenses by a minimum of 10% and do it in the first quarter.
13. Postpone all non-contractual training programs not essential to new products or processes.
14. Reduce/eliminate outside consulting expenses to a maximum of 50% of 1989, reduction to occur in the first quarter of 1990.
15. Reduce outside legal fees by 15% and do it in the first quarter of 1990.
16. Any other Group actions that would assist in meeting our goals.

The first three items amounted to temporarily shutting down General Motors in terms of new product development. It was called "Quick Start," but it was really a quick stop.

"Keep this very quiet," Davis said. "They are absolutely paranoid about it getting out to the *[Detroit] Free Press* or *Wall Street Journal.*"

When Corvette's financial manager, Tom Krejcar, announced that Mutchler wanted to cut more from Corvette's 1990 engineering budget, Dave McLellan had had enough.

"Corvette is a pocket of profitability," McLellan said, "and it's being used as a cash cow to fund other programs instead of being allowed to use the money to fund our own destiny. A cash cow stops giving cash if money isn't put back into it."

Cardy Davis agreed. "My guess is that 1990 will be the most traumatic year any of us has ever lived through in the automobile industry." He laid out a plan for keeping C4 alive and vital, particularly in its 1993 fortieth-anniversary year. But when it came to C5, he had little to offer except to keep working and look for any help possible from other parts of GM and from outside suppliers. He did not mention Design Staff.

"We're going through a cycle in the history of the corporation," Davis said, "where all decisions are financial decisions and that's because of the background of the guy running the company. So we're dead in the water for the next six months [and] everything we do in the next two months is cash flow related."

He tried to end on a positive note, telling the Corvette team about a meeting a day earlier. "Advanced Vehicle Engineering has a list of forty-seven things already funded with people working on them," he said. "The Corvette backbone was among the first four in importance."

Davis had made sure that somebody out there still cared.

14

A s fast as General Motors tried to shut itself down, the small Corvette team found ways to keep going on an all-new car for 1995. Mike Mutchler, who had had Cardy Davis's job eight years earlier and was now head of the Chevrolet-Pontiac-Canada group, agreed to listen to a pitch for more money by the Corvette team at the end of January 1990.

"No promises," he told Davis, "but I'll listen." That alone was like a blank check for the team to spend much of January focusing on C5 and what the car should be.

It wasn't so easy at Design Staff. Chuck Jordan's engineers had three separate studies going. They were trying to sort out the problems of packaging a mid-engine Corvette over a backbone structure (without worrying yet about how the backbone itself would be built), a front-engine Corvette with all-wheel drive over a backbone, and the same combination shoehorned into the current Corvette birdcage structure.

None of the three fit with the car envisioned by Cardy Davis and Dave McLellan. But in the vacuum of early 1990, Design Staff went its own way. Scale-model bodies for the various concepts were being clay-sculpted by artists in Tom Peters's studio. Upstairs in the Design building, an unhappy John Cafaro had slipped back into the fray, telling Randy Wittine, his most senior Corvette designer, to temporarily forget about the Cavalier and spend his days sketching the future.

In a matter of weeks, Jerry Palmer felt confident enough about the work to schedule a show of designs for Chevrolet and Corvette platform executives. Then he got nervous. "Jerry canceled the Corvette body show for tomorrow," Jeff Banasczynski told Cardy Davis and the Y-car business team. "All engineering work on packages has stopped and he's saying that no program exists, so any models will be out of date when we restart in a year."

Banasczynski suggested that the bi-Wednesday meetings between Design Staff and the platform be suspended. Cardy Davis folded his hands over his stomach and noted the brief smile on Dave McLellan's face. Since no one on the platform was happy about the directions that Design was going, that was just fine. The meetings could be resumed when everybody was back in synch.

A week later, Mike Mutchler walked into an engineering conference room to hear what the Corvette team had to say. Davis had put his people through two rehearsals and was firm in what they were to do. "Our stated purpose is to bring Mutchler up-to-date on the state of Corvette," he stressed. "The underlying intent is to get the new car back on track."

Introductions and job titles went around the room. Twenty-four people gave their names and job descriptions. Mutchler, a slender six-footer with graying hair and a craggy, somber face, was last. "Mike Mutchler," the executive vice president said. "Car salesman." Then he smiled at the sight of tense faces and shoulders relaxing. It wasn't going to be adversarial after all.

Davis and the others launched into their pitch. They were producing more than 20,000 Corvettes a year at the Bowling Green assembly plant and making money. Break-even was 16,500 units and the team thought that C4 could sell up to 25,000 cars a year with the improvements already planned. Among these was making traction control standard on the car beginning in 1992 and producing a special Fortieth-Anniversary Edition in 1993.

One of the speakers was Harry Turner, newly assigned by Chevrolet as liaison to both the Corvette and Camaro platforms—the "sporty cars" in Chevy-speak. He told Mutchler that traction control, which gives drivers more control of a car on slippery roads, and ABS, or antilock brake system, which prevents wheels from locking up in heavy braking, would be on the car in 1992 at less cost than ABS alone in 1989. Mutchler nodded agreement and accepted that the current Corvette still had a few profitable years remaining. So far, so good.

It was Dave McLellan's turn. "The 1995 program has no budget," he said. "We're managing and leveraging resources from other organizations to keep it alive."

Despite that, McLellan said that his people were pushing studies to give a C5 convertible more structural integrity, to improve entry/egress and roominess, and to reduce both the mass and the cost of the car.

"But we are really shut down on the '95 program in terms of moving ahead," McLellan said.

"That's where I expected you'd be," Mutchler responded with a heavy sigh.

But McLellan wasn't done. He walked to the back of the room and unveiled a series of displays showing the intense competition Corvette faced from Japan. Mutchler stood and followed. When another team member pointed out that "they're taking on this market on every possible front,"

Mutchler shoved his hands into his pockets and nodded dejectedly. The Japanese had been late coming to the sports cars market. Now they threatened to dominate it.

Turner, McLellan, and others took turns hammering Mutchler with the Japanese threat and the need to meet it head-on with a new Corvette. High quality was the Japanese automakers' strength, but they'd also begun making cars like the Nissan 300ZX, the Toyota Supra, and the Mazda RX-7 nimble and fast. They were cars that were fun to drive.

"How do you meet that?" Mutchler asked. "Will you face compromises?"

No, McLellan said. Corvette's heritage was power, performance, and styling. There would be no compromises in C5, only improvements.

"For instance, we have to have more baggage space, someplace to put golf clubs," McLellan said. "If the car doesn't have some utility in addition to being sporty, it's out of the hunt."

Mutchler laughed. "On the current car, you've got to leave either your clubs or your wife at home. That's why I'm not a golfer."

Then he asked the right question. "If I can reinstate something for you, what do you want the most?"

Nobody answered. It wasn't a question they expected. He filled in the silence with his own priority: "My number one is a new paint shop in Bowling Green." Paint quality had been a Corvette problem. The one-millionth Corvette would be built in the next year or so and be painted in the old shop. At an earlier meeting, a discussion of paint quality and paint colors for future years of Corvette had dragged on so long that John Heinricy, then heading Corvette's development group of test drivers, couldn't take it any longer. "Why are we even having this discussion?" he asked. "All Corvettes are red. The rest are mistakes."

A priority list would be on Mutchler's desk in a few days, Cardy Davis promised. After the paint shop, Davis's list would cite the need for an engineering budget to get C5 restarted. Again.

"You're doing it right," Mutchler said. "I, too, want a new Corvette, but I'd say that '95 is realistically the time."

It wasn't a guarantee, or even much of a victory. But Cardy Davis, Dave McLellan, and the rest left the meeting with new hope. C5 might be on life support, but it was still alive.

15 DAVIS took Mutchler's words as a license to push ahead on C5, not full bore but at least fast enough to do engineering sketches and some basic computer analysis on the car. He passed the word to Design Staff and suddenly artists in three separate studios were at work again drawing future Corvettes.

John Cafaro looked at Randy Wittine's sketches, done in a back corner while others sketched shapes for the subcompact Cavalier, and put modelers to work turning three sketches into tabletop sculptures. In Tom Peters's studio downstairs, four sketches went to clay. And in another advanced studio down the hall, Jerry Palmer and Chuck Jordan gave the okay for a single sketch to be brought out to three dimensions.

A few days later, Jordan checked everyone's calendars and scheduled a show for February 28. It was far from time for a decision. But Jordan hadn't risen to the top of the GM Design hierarchy without understanding the company's executives. Chevy general manager Jim Perkins made no bones about wanting a new Corvette. Now if Mutchler was beginning to get the bug, Jordan wanted to dazzle him with futuristic models before he lost interest. Pairing him with Perkins could only help.

Jordan also did the politic thing by inviting Cardy Davis and his key engineers, along with many of Perkins's staff at Chevy. When Mike Mutchler arrived at the Design dome on that brisk late winter day, the show's audience was rigged in favor of a new Corvette.

The first thing Mutchler saw under the dome was a complete circle of artfully lit displays. To his left were eight scale-model Corvette clown suits, one-sided clay cars about sixty-six inches long, pressed against a mirror to give the illusion of a complete vehicle. Next was a full-scale photo of the California Corvette nearing completion at the Advanced Concepts Center. It looked aggressive and feline, and it was the first time Jordan had shown the car to anyone outside of Design Staff.

Then came eight large engineering boards with Corvettes of various dimensions and structures or full-size drawings of sports cars. One of the Corvettes was a mid-engine car. Cardy Davis had been alerted to its inclusion and had already taken steps to spike it. He wasn't sure that it would work. He was discovering that getting Jerry Palmer away from the mid-engine concept was tougher than getting a bulldog away from a bone.

The remaining space was given over to four interior bucks. Mutchler and Perkins would be able to sit in the no-roof models, get the feel of entry and egress, grip the steering wheel and gear shift, and look over suggestions for instrument panels.

Inside the circle of displays sat three cars. There was the old red Corvette Indy, done as a show car in 1986, with the slick mutant body of both Corvette and an Indianapolis race car. There was a yellow 1990 Corvette, strategically placed directly in front of a full-scale rendering of a red and black Acura NS-X, and flanked by a sleek new Honda motorcycle. The C4 looked old and dated. The third car was hidden under a cover.

"We just want you to look, smile, and kick the tires," Palmer told Mutchler. Chuck Jordan would be along in a while, after Palmer softened him up. "We're not looking for any decisions, just for you to see what we've got."

Jim Perkins came through the door and heard the last comment. "Hallelujah!" he laughed, thrusting both arms in a double victory salute. "No decisions! That's great!"

Palmer had the show planned for maximum psychological impact. He started them in the middle, at the engineering boards, with a drawing of the C4 package. "We can freshen it up, make it more dramatic," he said, "but when you start looking at things like all-wheel drive, traction control, and some of the other things, you start compromising. Then you lose some of the newness in how it will look."

Mutchler folded his arms across his chest and nodded, while Perkins jammed both hands deep into his pockets and scuffed his shoe on the floor.

"One way to get all that into the car and have it look new is to go to mid-engine," Palmer said. He pointed to the third big board, which showed how a mid-engine Corvette might look.

Cardy Davis glanced at it in disgust. "Didn't like it," he said later. "It wasn't a Corvette."

A phone call that morning from Mutchler to Palmer, at Davis's instigation, left no doubt that Mutchler thought a mid-engine Corvette was a nonstarter. So Palmer knew Mutchler's position and he played it smoothly. Before anyone could say fatal words in public, he diverted attention to the engineering board he had skipped and kept the mid-engine idea from being killed.

"But there's a compromise that gives you *almost* everything," he said, "and that's going to a transaxle package." He turned them toward a full-scale drawing that showed how moving the transmission to the rear and incorporating it in the rear axle would give more cockpit room for driver and passenger, while opening up space for all-wheel drive or other goodies.

That was about all Dave McLellan could take. He dismissed the Design Staff transaxle package with a wave of his hand. The only architecture worthy of consideration was the backbone structure being developed by the Advanced Vehicle Engineering people. "It's the proposal that has the most potential because it treats the engine like a race car does, as a drivable chassis," McLellan said.

If Palmer was miffed, he didn't show it. He simply regained control by moving the group to the clown suit models. All were either front-engine/transaxle schemes or mid-engine. Perkins wasn't impressed. Reminding Palmer that Corvettes have a long life cycle, he said, "We need to be radical. People are expecting the next Corvette to be radical."

Palmer was ready for that one. As Tom Peters pulled the cover off the third car in the circle, Palmer pitched: "It's a transaxle car, an all-wheel-drive package that's close to a Ferrari 348." His eyes twinkled and his grin was pure delight. "But it's definitely a Corvette. It has all the Corvette heritage. It's not a Honda. It's not a Ferrari. It's unmistakably a Corvette."

Mutchler and Perkins were intrigued. It wasn't quite the car they wanted, but it sparked ideas and discussion. One of the ideas came from Perkins, for a standard two-wheel-drive Corvette, a "boy racer," he called it, that would be a low-price entry car to attract younger buyers. His casual comment would have a lasting impact.

An hour into the show, Chuck Jordan strolled into the dome. He was a magnet, drawing them together for a wrap-up discussion. Jordan pointed to a photo of the California Stingray III. "They designed the California car as a convertible," he said. "Then they put the top on later. It's an interesting concept." He didn't tell them the quartering front view obscured the fact that it had a trunk, something missing from Corvettes for three decades. That was a surprise for another day.

Perkins was enjoying himself. Later he'd call that afternoon in the Dome one of the most memorable events of his career. "All the different architectures were there," he said. "That was the day that we could see where Corvette had been and where it was going. It turned into one of the liveliest discussions of product I ever had. People felt ownership for Corvette."

Mike Mutchler beckoned Cardy Davis to the side for a quiet word.

"You've now got to figure out a time line, figure out how to do a '95 car," he said. Davis let a half smile play on his lips. Mutchler was being infected with Perkins's enthusiasm. "How much time do we have to play around like this and when do we have to get serious?"

Serious? Davis thought. *We've been trying to get serious for the last year.*

Stop taking away our budget and I'll show you serious. Aloud he said, "We can do a backbone design a lot faster than a mid-engine."

Mutchler thought for a moment, then decided. "Get the plan together and get back to me."

An elated Davis caught Dave McLellan and Earl Werner at the door. Between Perkins and Mutchler, they were close to an official green light, to *another* green light. Then he had a sudden qualm.

"I wonder if some of this isn't backwards," he said. "We need to deliver a chassis to Design Staff and then have them do this swoopy, rounded styling."

McLellan instantly disagreed. "No, we needed an iteration with Design Staff to get their thinking. Now we can go away and do a package. We can incorporate what they're thinking, but we have the *real* engineering and maybe we can't do it all. But we can get back to them with something that's real."

Off to the side, Werner nodded. This was one where McLellan had it exactly right and he was letting Davis know.

"Okay." The program manager caught the signal and didn't miss a beat. "That's our job then. Let's get on it."

16 T H E Y didn't get on it. One more time—how many was a number nobody could remember—Corvette's people surged forward, then skidded to a stop. They needed only $2 million in additional engineering budget to start work officially on the 1995 C5 in August 1990. That was the Four-Phase date for a forty-eight-month program ending with production of a '95 car.

But in April, Mike Mutchler said no. For want of 2 percent of Corvette's own annual profit, the program was again being written on the shifting sands of corporate priorities. It was a few days after the corporation announced that on August 1, Bob Stempel would be the new chairman of the board and Lloyd Reuss would become president. Hundreds of people had gathered in the Design dome to hear the announcement. They cheered when Stempel's name came over the speakers. For the first time in decades, the top man at General Motors would be someone who worked his way up through the car side of the company instead of through the financial department. But when Reuss's name was announced, there was little applause and scattered boos. In the rank and file of middle management, there was not much confidence that he could do the job.

The announcement didn't make much difference to Mutchler, whose daily problem was money. Chevrolet-Pontiac-Canada lost money every year since its creation during one of Roger Smith's reorganizations. It lost money under Lloyd Reuss and it kept losing money under Mike Mutchler. The Chevy Lumina and Pontiac Grand Prix programs were destined to lose more than $1.3 billion in 1990 alone. Mutchler seemed to think that diverting money and engineering resources from Corvette to the other programs would help.

Cardy Davis tried to be a good corporate soldier. He didn't say that diverting $2 million to reduce a loss on other programs endangered hundreds of millions in future Corvette profits. He didn't have to.

Davis couldn't turn anywhere for help. "One of the problems across GM," he said, "is that Design Staff works independently. Engineering works independently. The marketing divisions work independently. I'm hoping Reuss will fix that." It was a vain hope. General Motors' multiple pieces would continue to work in the old way, sometimes against each other's interest, for another few years.

With no 1995 money, Davis struggled through the bitter months of 1990 by casting about for other solutions to getting a new Corvette on the road. There were none and he was ordered to plan an $80 million reskin for '95, changing body panels on the current car to give it a new look, but leaving everything else pretty much the same. The all-new car, Mike Mutchler told him, would be delayed until 1998.

A deep gloom settled over everyone involved with Corvette. Nobody thought that the reskin idea had merit. "I don't believe that Perkins was much in the loop [on the decision] and neither was I," Davis said. "I was just told."

Perkins instead was fighting a battle for Corvette's survival at the highest levels of General Motors. At least two management factions had their sights on the car. One group contended that Corvette was a frill that GM could do without. Another group argued that Corvette was not only too important to kill, but too important to be a Chevrolet. Corvette, they argued, should be taken away from Chevy and recast as simply "the General Motors Corvette."

"There are days when you go to work and battle for life and limb," Perkins said. "It got real exciting there for a while."

Perkins argued that Corvette had been a technological showcase for General Motors and that it put a shine on the company's entire product line. Killing off Corvette would be foolhardy. The news would be on the front page of every paper in the world. Magazines would do cover stories about a General Motors that couldn't hold up a forty-year tradition.

Removing the Chevrolet badge would also cost the company in terms of respect and legend. "If you make the ownership too broad and corporate," Perkins insisted, "you diffuse the Corvette name.

"There has to be somebody somewhere who owns the name and it has always been Chevrolet. People come and go, hell, cars come and go. But Corvette is forever. It's a symbol."

Jim Perkins won that battle.

At Design Staff, John Cafaro's Chevy 3 was again the Corvette studio, though he had a few people working on a full-size clay model of the new Cavalier. Cafaro was frustrated with the corporate waffling. He wandered listlessly through his studio, going through the motions. He thought the current state of affairs was just make-work. "So it's an eighty-million-dollar reskin," he said. "But it won't stay that way. They've got to change it unless they're ready to see Corvette sink out of sight."

Cardy Davis agreed. But he and chief engineer Dave McLellan discovered that getting marching orders for the reskin and being able to do the job were two different things in the GM of 1990. Most other car programs were in turmoil, too, and there were not enough parts engineers and drafters left in the company after the early retirements and buyouts of previous years to do all the engineering drawings needed.

The engineers assigned full-time to McLellan could do initial designs and set the specifications for Corvette components, but the detailed work and the all-important drawings that went out to suppliers came from other parts of the organization. In the vernacular of the business, GM was not just short of money, it was short of resources, a more correct word for "people." Wave after wave of downsizing had left GM as healthy as a bulimic teenager.

The usually upbeat McLellan came close to depression and his mood seeped into the entire team. A few days before Roger Smith turned over the company to Bob Stempel, a parody of a Civil War song appeared briefly taped to a wall.

> When Roger Corvette comes marchin' home,
>   Hoorah, hoorah.
> When Roger Corvette comes marchin' home,
>   Hoorah, hoorah.
> You hiven't a plan and you hiven't a hope,
> You've given your troops the hangin' rope,
> And now we're swingin' like some pitiful dope,
> Oh Roger, we hardly knew ya.

Nor would they miss him. Other comments about the state of the company were more blunt. Frustration was being replaced by anger. McLellan's deputy and Davis's engineering eyes, Earl Werner, boiled over in a meeting where C5's unknown future was discussed. "You get to a level in General Motors where success is the only acceptable report to bring to a meeting," he grumbled.

Davis again turned his ire on the W-car program that was losing so much money. "By the end of every development program, most of the key people who were there at the beginning have been transferred," he said, pointing out one of the most obvious flaws of the GM way of doing things. "The top people have almost certainly been promoted. So if there's anything wrong, and there always is, both the old guys and the new guys have a common interest in not making waves.

"They try to cure the symptoms, but they never examine the causes. In government circles, this is called a cover-up. Inside GM, it's called quality improvement."

All the raging aside, Davis laid down a simple law for the Corvette program: "We are not going to tolerate a situation that makes us fail!"

Near the end of summer, Chevrolet was increasingly opposed to the '95 reskin. Jim Perkins wanted a new Corvette, not a warmed-over C4 with new body panels. Davis and McLellan agreed, but the '95 program was a bird in the hand. "If you guys don't want to do that," Davis told Harry Turner, head of Chevy's Sporty Car Segment Planning and Engineering Department, "then you have to put together the case for doing a two-hundred-fifty-million-dollar program. But if you do that, I predict it will then become a '97 or '98 program anyway, so all that will have been done is that we've lost the '95 program."

Turner demurred for the moment. "But I do think there's an opportunity here for doing some concept alternatives, like a convertible with a trunk."

On that, there was agreement.

Then more hammer blows fell on Corvette. Dave McLellan's 1991 engineering budget request, to cover changes already scheduled in the '92, '93, and '94 Corvettes, plus getting started on definitive engineering for the '95 reskin, was chopped from $37.75 million to just $16 million. It was McLellan's turn to hurl angry words at the family sedan debacle.

"Arv [Mueller, chief of all CPC engineering] is held hostage by the [sedan program]," McLellan raged. "Its engineering budget is ten times what Corvette gets."

"Dave hit it right," Davis chimed in. "[It] is absolutely the worst thing that has happened to General Motors in its eighty-year history. It's a disaster."

"Isn't it great that this is a company where nobody can be accountable?" an engineer in the back of the conference room asked sarcastically.

"Right," said Davis, focusing his wrath on the sedan program and the manager who ran it during much of its development phase. "You know who I mean. Gary Dickinson."

On that day Dickinson was in overall charge of the General Motors Technical Center. He would enjoy more promotions in later years. Sometimes it happened that way.

Whether or not Cardy Davis's animosity toward Dickinson was justified, it made both the man and the sedans convenient targets. They were Cardy Davis's safety valve for letting off steam inside his program.

Then it all changed again. The emotional roller coaster carried Corvette from utter despair to yet another upswing of hope. It came in the form of an LRS, one of those "Lloyd Reuss Says" commands that could make things happen. Now Lloyd Reuss was president of General Motors. He asked for and got a presentation on Corvette in October. It was still one of his favorite cars. He heard Chevy's complaints about reskinning the C4 and he agreed.

Cardy Davis bounded late into a business meeting of his direct reports with the news. "Reuss's reaction was to support the two-hundred-fifty-million-dollar program and the backbone structure for 1996," he announced, giving Corvette its fourth target year—'93, '94, '95, and now '96

—in less than twenty-four months. "But he also said several times that unless GM is a moneymaker in the meantime, it might have to be pushed back."

So there was good news and bad news. But the good dominated. Jim Perkins brought up his idea of an entry-level Corvette again, calling it a "Billy Bob," in the $25,000–$30,000 price range.

That would be another challenge for the C5 program. "Reuss said to go full bore on engineering the backbone design for '96," Davis said. "But he also wants a meeting in the near future on how Corvette will survive between now and then."

They set about the business of making a new Corvette happen for 1996 while General Motors continued to crumble around them. By Christmas, the roller coaster was on another emotional downslope. Pete Liccardello, an ebullient engineer with a flair for organizing, had been given the job of 1995 model year manager back in the months when the reskin was the top priority. Now he was trying to map out the route to a C5 in '96.

After gathering together all of the schedules involved in a Four-Phase effort—everything from how long does Design Staff have to style a body to how long will it take the assembly plant to convert from the old car to the new car—he came up with a discouraging number.

"Right now," he told the first meeting of the new C5 steering team, "we have a forty-four week overrun."

"That's a six-year program!" Cardy Davis sputtered. "We're sitting here saying this is already a 1997 vehicle."

There was worse news. Harry Turner, head of Chevy's Sporty Car team, cleared his throat and delivered it. "Reuss doesn't remember asking for the interim stuff on how to keep Corvette alive and right now, February twenty-fifth is the first time we can get Perkins, Mutchler, and Reuss in the same room to hear us."

A groan went around the room. Suddenly that gilt-edged "Lloyd Reuss Says" was fluttering toward the wastebasket.

For the second consecutive year, Corvette's Christmas looked more somber than joyful.

17

CARDY Davis had predicted that 1990 would be the most traumatic year in the business that any of them had ever lived through. He was right—with the single exception of a small group of California designers living on the edge of Corvette.

For the lucky few at the General Motors Advanced Concepts Center, 1990 was a very good year. Nineteen eighty-nine wasn't too bad, either.

The Advanced Concepts Center was housed in a tiny industrial park off U.S. Highway 101 in Newbury Park, northwest of Los Angeles. Its function as a distant arm of Design Staff back in Michigan was to bring a fresh, youthful look to automotive design. A California look. Artists and engineers from Design Staff spent a year or three in the California sunshine, then were expected to bring back a new perspective to the production and advanced studios at the GM Tech Center in suburban Detroit.

Now and then ACC got an assignment filled with real excitement. One of them came when Chuck Jordan stalked out of John Cafaro's studio in early 1989 and ordered ACC to begin work on designs for the new Corvette. John Schinella, ACC's director, was delighted. Schinella was a slender, silver-haired and silver-tongued designer. His gift of gab, combined with his proven artistic talents, made him a popular chief when he ran one of the Pontiac studios back home and equally popular when he came out to California on a three-year assignment. He knew how to motivate.

Schinella had been John Cafaro's first boss more than a decade earlier. The chance to pit his talents against those of the young upstart, and of the even younger Tom Peters in a Design Staff advanced studio, was an irresistible challenge.

John Schinella preached a theory of automobile design that opened his artists' eyes. "Monitor the guys who park cars at restaurants," he told them. "They know because they see 'em all and they decide the pecking order. Watch where they park a car, out front where it can be seen, around in back where it can't, under cover where it'll be protected. These are things that count in car design."

And where better than southern California to test the theory?

Soon after Chuck Jordan's call, Schinella had a huge open bay dedicated to Corvette and filled with inspirational displays. Some showed Corvette's competitors, others were tacked with research reports on Corvette buyers, still another was a blank-paper comment board for Schinella's young artists to fill with their musings.

Schinella expected from the first that the California Corvette would be a show car. His California Camaro was a hit at the 1989 Detroit International Auto Show and he wanted to repeat with a Corvette in 1990. An ambitious schedule was plastered in large letters along one wall. Chuck Jordan wanted the ACC car shipped to Detroit on July 19 for a head-to-head showdown with cars from the studios of John Cafaro and Tom Peters.

The final item on the schedule was "Monday, 24 Jul. ACC Beats Design Staff."

The youngsters at ACC, most of them in their twenties, responded with passion. Back home, they were constrained by the Detroit environment. They came to work in shirts and ties, they designed to the party line, and they often went home at night feeling discouraged. At Schinella's ACC, they worked in cutoffs and Ts, wore running shoes without socks, and sometimes skipped shaving. They designed to the whim of the muse and they went home dreaming of swoops and shadows.

It was a kick. They even dug the part where Schinella had them competing against each other in a winner-take-all design fight over whose car would go back to Detroit.

Chuck Jordan came to town on St. Patrick's Day, 1989, to see for himself. He got an eyeful. Schinella and his boys got an earful.

He strolled from model to model, all of them clown suits, and each designer tried to curry his favor. "It's brutish . . . round, but aggressive," one said of his muscled car.

"This is the bad-boy design," offered another, hoping that the insectlike mandibles he created in place of a front bumper would catch Jordan's eye.

"We'd Di-Noked this one in yellow last night, then somebody said you hate yellow," another youngster said. "When I saw you walk up today wearing a yellow tie, I said, 'Whew.' " The car was dubbed an exoskeleton design, with bumps and protrusions on the hood that reflected the engine and other components underneath.

"Yellow's got nothing to do with it," Jordan said, not unpleasantly. "I don't care what color you put on it. I care about the design statement it's making."

He walked away from the models to examine a sketch of a more traditional, slightly rounded future Corvette. "It's nice to see something that's not so cartoony," he said, and most of the artists by their models winced.

"It's a breath of fresh air." Then he emphasized the point by leaning into the sketch and inhaling deeply. His smile when he turned back to the clown suits said, *Get my point?*

Now he got down to the business of critiquing two months of hard work. "There's some relief on this one," he said, examining another model with mandible jaws up front, but one that had been softened and made less mean and nasty in the last twenty-four hours. "It gets me away from some of the spastic things happening on the others."

There were more winces. "Spastic" is not a word an artist wants to hear from his supreme leader.

Finally Jordan backed off from a global judgment. "It's too much to absorb in one look. There's too much cartoon here and not enough design."

That wasn't what John Schinella was waiting to hear.

Early the next morning, a Saturday, Jordan had Schinella and his top people back. None of the artists were invited to hear Jordan relax and philosophize.

"We can always face-lift a car," he said, sitting uncharacteristically on a drafting table and letting his loafered feet dangle. "But the basic design has to last ten years. On this car, I want to make a statement that's as profound as the '63 Corvette. And that takes basic design.

"This car's important. It's special. If you just put a pretty face out there, you're not going to win. Now what are you going to do about these Corvette designs?"

"We've got three to take forward," Schinella responded, and listed the models that had elicited some positive comment from Jordan the previous afternoon.

Jordan glanced at one and dismissed it. He pointed to another done by Jim Bieck, Schinella's assistant chief. Its roof was small and rounded, almost like a beanie or a yarmulke. It was the brutish Corvette, described by Bieck as "round, but aggressive," and the roof didn't detract from the impression. Jordan accepted its possibilities. "It has good lines. It's just overdone."

Bieck moved in like a protective father. "It's a design that can be dialed up or dialed back. Whatever you need."

"Restraint," Jordan said flatly. "That's what's needed. I thought that's what California is. Smooth. Free-flowing. I don't see smooth in these cars."

Jordan sat down again on the table and looked at Schinella and his chief engineer, Don McFarland. "This is a significant car," he said. "Tell me how you're going to do it. Tell me dates."

"We're aiming at July twenty-fourth in Detroit for a car," McFarland said, "then November for a final design." McFarland was thinking about a production design, not a show car. Jordan ignored the implication.

"Let's work it the other way," Jordan said. "Say you've got a design on April twenty-fourth. When can you send me a running car? I want a running car from you."

Schinella's face lit up. But he couldn't find an answer better than "Get back to you on that, Chuck."

Then Jordan described the path he wanted ACC to follow. "The interior is going to be as important as the exterior. I think the interior will dictate the exterior.

"I'm going to give you fair warning. You've got to think about this as a total car, not a cute little scale model. You've got to think about the car inside and out."

Jordan paused and thought about what he wanted to say. His face said that he wanted the next words to be right.

"I'm not asking you to get conservative. But what you've got here isn't right. Here's what I'm asking. I'm asking for good design, not just style."

And on that note, he grinned. Nobody else did. The interpretation of what differentiated design from style was as murky as when he started talking.

The schedule, though, was clear. The Advanced Concepts Center was now making a running car. July was a deadline no more.

The summer of 1989 settled in with typical California speed. One day the sky drizzled with the last of the rainy season's moisture, the next day Schinella's boys began six or seven months of arid days and cool nights that would parch the surrounding hills from emerald green to brittle brown. In the cavernous main bay of ACC's converted warehouse, a beat-up '85 Corvette shipped in from GM's Desert Proving Ground in Mesa, Arizona, sat stripped down to its chassis, waiting to be fitted with the new pieces that would turn it into a running show car. Cleaning it up was grueling; every crevice was filled with sand and desert grit from years of abuse in the name of development testing.

Chuck Jordan was in and out, checking progress, picking at this design, dropping a kind word or two about that one. One design called for a V-6 Corvette, a radical departure from the traditional V-8 that was part of the legend. Jordan liked it. It made the car shorter. But the body work had flaws.

"You've got all the pieces, but it's sagging a little in the middle," he said. "I think you can take some out of the rear end. It's too beefy. And take some off the front.

"I like the idea of pursuing a shorter car. It's a good thing for us to do."

None of the ACC designs took firm hold until August. Then Schinella merged three of them into a single slinky Corvette V-6. They rolled it out for Chuck Jordan, a full-size clay model covered with foil in a deep eggplant purple. Schinella did it Hollywood style. The room darkened to full black, with indirect red floodlights coming up to throw a glow around the California Corvette. It was a topless car, a coupe, and it would have a trunk. *Also sprach Zarathustra* welled from hidden speakers. Dry ice packed around a rear wheel poured out a chilly fog that flowed around and under the shiny model.

Jordan was enthralled. *All this just for him.* He was dressed for the moment, cashmere herringbone gray sport coat, a blue dress shirt open at the neck and with monogrammed cuffs, navy slacks, black loafers, and a yellow kerchief in his breast pocket. There were no short pants or cutoffs among Schinella's artists, either. They were neat and tidy and grown-up. Jordan liked that.

Lights up, fog gone, music faded to silence. Jordan walked around the car smiling and nodding. "It looks a lot smaller. Did you tighten it up?"

"Yeah, it is smaller," Schinella answered from inches away.

"Did you solve the rear end problem? Yes, I see it. Boy, you really tuned up the front, got rid of all the curves and wiggles. It's more flat."

Exposed cat's-eye headlamps peered forward and the mandible-jawed front bumper was muted by an air scoop insert that filled in the gap. Jordan knelt down at the rear, nodding at the four ovoid taillights, the quad exhaust pipes centered between wide tires, and the slight dip in the trunk.

"Now that's interesting," he said softly, pointing to a spoilerlike wing just behind the seats.

"It's a pop-up roll bar," Schinella grinned. The innovation was intriguing and good-looking. But engineering it into anything other than a race car could be difficult. Still, the Stingray III was supposed to be a collection of ideas, not necessarily a design ready for production.

Jordan stood up. The dozen people gathered around the car waited in stomach-sucked silence while he studied the showy Corvette. When he finally spoke, his words were decisive.

"Cast it up," he said. "Don't fool with it. It has a certain spontaneity to it. You're making a statement."

Two dozen lungs exhausted simultaneously and Schinella's boys high-fived in a gabble of relief. Jordan turned to Jon Albert, who was taking charge of interior design. "Would you see doing it with a full interior?" he asked.

"We don't see doing it any other way," Albert said.

It took another nine months to get the car to Detroit. Fiberglass panels were cast on the clay model, formed at a specialty shop in Santa Barbara, and hand-fitted and smoothed. The V-6 engine was mounted to a modified structure in the old Corvette at ACC. Seats and an instrument panel were designed and built.

They had some fun and felt secure enough to take a poke at Chuck Jordan and the Ferrari F40 he had on order. One of the gauges rolled up and out from the instrument panel at the press of a button. It was a gunsight with the words "Lock On Target" and the crosshairs centered squarely on the rear end of an F40.

When Jordan saw it, he laughed and turned to Jon Albert. "You're a bad guy. A bad guy."

Schinella rented a nearby ranch for another Hollywood-style rollout in mid-April 1990. They came in droves from Detroit to see this car that was the only thing good happening in the Corvette program. John Cafaro was there, muted by the stalemate back home, but eager to see what California had wrought. So was Jerry Palmer, grinning like an elf.

Schinella's show started with a parade. He knew how to grab an audience. Corvettes rolled by in stately review, an original polo white 1953, then a '62, a '67, a '69, and an '88; the crowd yelled in appreciation. Then filling a moment of silence came a throaty roar and the deep purple Stingray III blew past so quickly that the oohs and aahs barely formed before it was gone.

The California Corvette was a hit and a miss. John Cafaro thought it missed the mark. He got a small measure of revenge for the intrigue and excitement surrounding the car by bending its suspension when he drove it too fast into a driveway turn with Jon Albert riding shotgun. But he got a surprise, too. As he and Albert passed slowly in front of the crowd, Jordan announced loudly: "These are the two guys responsible for doing the new Corvette. They've got it from now on."

John Schinella led the applause. Albert would return to Michigan to take over an interior studio and Schinella, too, would go home to supervise all of the Chevy and Pontiac studios. Cafaro's confirmation as the primary Corvette designer didn't mean that he wouldn't have competition, however. Chuck Jordan would see to it that someone was always nipping at his heels.

A few weeks later, Stingray III got mixed reviews in a show under the Design dome. "It's not a Corvette," Cardy Davis said. "The V-6 engine is ridiculous."

"There's not enough family resemblance," Tom Peters griped with a designer's eye. "And the headlights, Corvette shouldn't have exposed headlights."

Gary Dickinson, now Chuck Jordan's titular boss, at least for administrative support at the Tech Center, took the opposite view. "Really remarkable. A Corvette convertible with a trunk."

Dickinson's view carried the day when Stingray III was unveiled to the public and the automotive press. Long before anyone knew what C5 would look like, Stingray III, after being shown selectively to automotive journalists and a few others for a full year, was the hit of the 1992 Detroit International Auto Show. The press loved it and badgered a basking Jordan about whether it would be built. It wouldn't, but Jordan enjoyed dangling possibilities before automotive writers just to whet their appetites. When Chevrolet licensed the design to Revell, the model kit company, and to Matchbox Cars, the flashy coupe from ACC became a favorite on bookshelves and in toy boxes, too. It wasn't C5, but it had major impact on the creative thinking at Design Staff.

18 "CHUCK has a problem with me," John Cafaro said. "He liked my car, but he hates me. He liked it so much, he changed it."

Cafaro's resigned observation came in the spring of 1991, a day after another major patio show of competing Corvette designs. He and his studio were back full-time on Corvette after the Cavalier program was slipped a year, to 1995, to temporarily save the company capital investment. But at best, designing Corvettes was just something to fill the days. The year was already in danger of spinning out of control for General Motors, with losses mounting, sales battered by a recession, and top management increasingly in turmoil.

It all ran downhill onto Corvette, where the program was being turned on and off like a blinking light. At Design Staff, Chuck Jordan launched new and divisive competitions to design a C5 Corvette that no one was sure would be built. On the business side, at the platform or program level that included engineering, mixed messages heightened frustration and shortened tempers.

Mike Mutchler was now using $150 million as the budget for the new Corvette, down $100 million in only a few months, and even that was ephemeral. "He says that the corporation wants to do a new Corvette, but nobody knows where the money's coming from," Cardy Davis told his business team. "If there's money, it'll be done." Then within days, Davis discovered the possibility of shutting down the Bowling Green, Kentucky, assembly plant was being discussed. Corvette might move into some other plant, somewhere, where it would share facilities. It didn't happen, but the discussions were a measure of how desperate GM's situation had become.

The long-overdue meeting with GM president Lloyd Reuss to discuss ways to keep the C4 Corvette alive until a C5 could be delivered finally came in late March. Reuss vehemently vetoed a proposal to "decontent" Corvette to produce a C4 that could be sold for under $30,000. "To take content out, you're hurting our owners," he said. "I don't support going in with a stripper model on the Corvette. We shouldn't be talking about taking anything away."

So the Corvette team proposed a three-model scenario for C5, a hardtop targa, a convertible, and a fixed-roof coupe. The coupe would fit Jim Perkins's concept of a "Billy Bob," an entry-level Corvette priced around $30,000. It would be a distinct model, not a Corvette with many features taken away. And the convertible and coupe would have trunks, something missing from Corvette for more than three decades. Reuss accepted the idea. It was okay to plan a lower priced model for C5, but not to reduce the perceived value on C4.

None of that changed life for John Cafaro. Chuck Jordan was making him miserable with constant carping about his Corvette designs and renewed threats to pull the program and give it to another studio. Jordan may have been acting out his own frustrations. With his retirement only eighteen months away, there was no way that he'd be going out on a tide of acclaim for the new Corvette. He was more likely to be remembered for the tub-like Chevy Caprice and for the slope-nosed series of compact vans that had been panned by writers.

Then there was the Ferrari. The Tech Center's Quality Council, made up of union members, GM hourly employees, and management, complained to Gary Dickinson about Jordan's new F40 Ferrari. He drove it to work and parked it in a heated garage, where it was washed and shined by GM employees. It sent the wrong message, the council said, when the company was losing money and one of its vice presidents not only didn't drive a GM car, but kept his $400,000 Italian sports car in the company garage.

Dickinson ordered Jordan to cease and desist. It was an embarrassment that Jordan didn't take lightly and only obeyed in part. The Ferrari continued to show up now and then. It was just Chuck Jordan asserting that he couldn't be tampered with in his own domain.

Cafaro approached the late-April Corvette competition with both worry and confidence. One of the thirteen designs that would be judged in the glare of Patio daylight was his and his alone. He'd done the first sketches in February and worked with one of his sculptors to create a full three-eighths-scale clay car, not a half-car clown suit. It was sleek and tomorrow, definitely a Corvette. The windshield had more slope than a C4, and there was an elegantly subtle air scoop indented behind the front wheels and extending into the doors. The hood raked suddenly to the bumper. The rear was race-car wide with four oval taillights in the Corvette tradition and deck glass that implied unusually abundant baggage space.

Only one design would survive the day, according to Jordan's rule. That one might be refined, then be cast up to create a fiberglass car with real glass and lights all around, and maybe a real interior.

"It's gonna be wild," Cafaro said while he and studio engineer Steve Allen put the finishing touches on his scale car. "This is like a combination of Caligula and *Bowling for Dollars*."

The models, mostly clown suits Di-Noked in silver, were lined up on the Patio for Jordan's inspection. They came this time from half-a-dozen studios, including Tom Peters's. The buzz from the forty-odd sculptors, artists, and studio chiefs watching was that Peters was the only competition Cafaro had.

"Peters's car looks too cartoonish, but it's the one Jordan likes and that's what he's going to choose," predicted sculptor Gary Clark from Cafaro's studio. "The rest of them are out here to prove his point.

"Then he'll go back to John's car and decide he likes that one, too. In the end, he'll pick Tom Peters, but he'll tell him to take big pieces of John's car and incorporate them."

If Clark had been a Vegas handicapper, he'd be a rich man.

The Peters car had muscular fender bulges front and rear, but its most distinctive feature was a huge indented air scoop that dominated the side view. Jordan passed his hands over the model, chatting with Jerry Palmer, then did the same at John Cafaro's car. He spent only seconds at many of the models, dismissing them with a hard glance, longer at others, where he walked back and forth to see them from various angles.

Finally he waved everyone into a circle. "This is tough," Jordan said. "You guys have come a long way."

Then he picked Tom Peters's model. "But I want you to take the scoop out of the side," he told Peters. "We call it the rhinoceros dent. It looks like a rhinoceros rammed you broadside.

"Then take the rear off that car," he said, pointing to Cafaro's model, "and the side and doors." Before he made a decision on a full-size fiberglass model, he wanted to see more work in scale.

Tom Peters stayed poker-faced when Jordan delivered his ruling. It was hard to say whether he'd won or lost. John Cafaro was not so reticent. "In the end, it's gonna end up looking more like our car," he said, "because we understand the architecture."

"And that's where we knew we'd wind up."

19 REORGANIZING is a favorite General Motors game, one it seemed determined to keep playing until it got it right. The reorganization in mid-1991 subdivided Mike Mutchler's Chevrolet-Pontiac-Canada group into two pieces, one to handle front-wheel drive cars, the other to do rear-wheel drives. Assembly plants that had been managed by a separate organization were brought into the fold, too, giving program managers more control over the plants that assembled their cars.

Cardy Davis accepted the change with equanimity. He now had a new layer of management between Corvette and Mike Mutchler, but it probably wouldn't matter. "For most people in CPC, the reorg is a nonevent," Davis said. "The platforms have been operating that way anyway, so it was bringing the organization into line with reality."

But what seemed like a nonevent in the summer of 1991 was the camel's nose under the tent. It would lead to two more reorganizations in 1992, one of them killing off CPC entirely. Before that, other concerns were generating stomach acid. They involved people.

John Cafaro's emotional war with Chuck Jordan wouldn't end until Jordan retired. And Cardy Davis was focusing more and more on his problems with Corvette chief engineer Dave McLellan.

"He's got to go," Davis said abruptly in late May, "but I don't know if I can make that happen. He's just not a team player. He doesn't like to go to meetings because he doesn't want to be bound by what happens there. If he doesn't want to do something, doesn't want to carry out decisions made in a meeting, he just goes his own way. Hell, he goes his own way most of the time anyway.

"Sometimes he doesn't even show up for his own staff meetings. Jeff Yachnin [the C4 model year manager] runs them. Or Earl Werner. He wasn't in our business team meeting yesterday. He was just sitting in his office. That's got to stop."

But the Reuss connection continued to make McLellan untouchable. Davis couldn't dump him, couldn't change him, couldn't really control him.

Across the tracks, Chuck Jordan continued to churn emotions and artistic impulses at Design Staff by pitting studio against studio and demanding a seemingly endless series of futuristic body styles for the car. John Cafaro and the others felt that they'd done the groundwork over and over.

Meanwhile, the C5 program almost went through another Concept Initiation review. The Advanced Vehicle Engineering people used their own budget to work closely with Corvette on the backbone structure and with each passing month it looked better. And under Cardy Davis's direction, the marketing and financial people assigned to Corvette continued to refine C5 plans. A life-cycle plan was in place that called for a new removable roof model, a convertible, then the "Billy Bob" entry-level fixed-roof coupe that Jim Perkins wanted.

With that foundation—C5 was in many ways now a three-year-old program—Mike Mutchler thought he could get it past the Concept Initiation gate once more and lock in a firm budget. Presentations were readied, filed, then readied again as the proposed date for making their pitch to a board headed by Mutchler and Lloyd Reuss slipped through August and September, then into October. By then, General Motors' financials had gotten worse and worse. After losing $2 billion in 1990, including a restructuring charge (the huge CPC loss, which had ultimately reached $3.3 billion, was partly covered by profits from other parts of the company), projections for 1991 grew ever more dismal.

Mutchler finally decided that getting any serious development and capital money for C5 in late 1991 was impossible. But with the Corvette team primed and practiced, he wanted to hear their pitch just in case. They called it a "CI Scrimmage." Lloyd Reuss wouldn't be there, but the new guy who'd just taken over the rear-wheel-drive operation would. His name was Joe Spielman and before long Cardy Davis was calling him the best boss he'd ever had.

A few days before Davis and key people faced the Mutchler board, GM reported an incredible $1.1 billion loss for the preceding quarter. The CI Scrimmage went ahead anyway. Most of the money needed for C5 development, Davis said, was budgeted in the out years. It would be spent in the last two years of the four-year program on tools and dies, on building a fleet of test cars, and on converting the assembly plant to build the car. He outlined how far they'd come in three years and pushed hard on the Four-Phase rules that required detailed engineering and selection processes after CI that would lead up to settling finally on the car's looks and its components. They could do that, he said, on a minimal budget.

But under the rules, they needed something to take around inside GM that said they'd passed CI. It was the only way to get internal support and respect. Mutchler and the others agreed, and granted Corvette $1 million transferred from Advanced Vehicle Engineering's budget—AVE was all but done with their engineering design of the backbone structure anyway.

Everyone knew that a CI Scrimmage was nowhere to be found in GM's lexicon and letting Corvette go was based partly on sham, partly on prayer. They were off and running one more time, on shakier ground than ever.

"A good beginning," Mutchler said at the end of the meeting.

It would have been except that Dave McLellan was suddenly tilting his influence toward a mid-engine car. At Design Staff, sketches and models of mid-engine Corvettes continued to appear despite the objections of Cardy Davis and Mike Mutchler. McLellan was beginning to like some of what he saw. The backbone structure was all but locked in, yet he agitated for Corvette to take another look at the mid-engine.

Cardy Davis was furious and so was rear-wheel VP and general manager Joe Spielman. The last thing they needed after the CI Scrimmage was for word to get around that Dave McLellan wasn't fully on board with the foundation of the car.

It didn't help that Davis and Chuck Jordan had an angry confrontation over who was in charge of Corvette's future. With Earl Werner all but functioning as chief engineer, the platform worked with John Cafaro to provide his artists with a basic set of engineering goals, restrictions, and content for C5. They called it "the box." It allowed Cafaro's studio to get real on their sketches and clay models. They would be in synch with the engineers and not be wasting time on designs that were out of the box. The mid-engine car was not in the box. The backbone was.

Davis was on Jordan's turf in early November when the two met in a hallway. Jordan immediately went on the offensive.

"All this crap about 'the box,' " he snapped, "we can't live with that. You can't put restrictions on us. We're going to design a Corvette on our terms, not yours."

"Nobody's cutting off your artistic turf," Davis replied. "But we have to put some limits on what we can do and what we can't do. 'The box' is how we're defining the limits."

"I'm the one who sets limits around here," Jordan said.

"We all have limits, Chuck. We've finally got a good team going here and we need you with us."

"Don't count on it," Jordan sputtered. He turned and walked away.

Davis let him get a few yards down the hall before he said softly: "With you or without you, Chuck. With you or without you."

If Jordan heard, he didn't respond. But "the box" stayed.

That made Dave McLellan's new interest in a mid-engine car all the more intolerable. But he wouldn't back down. Joe Spielman was still new in his job and unsure of McLellan's strength. Davis had tried and failed to get McLellan to toe the line on a growing list of issues.

That left a con job. They did it by turning a McLellan suggestion back on him. A new fad was sweeping through General Motors, a new way to reach difficult decisions. It was called decision risk analysis, or DRA.

It was a six-to-eight-week series of meetings to explore issues in depth, study and rate alternatives, then end with total agreement on how to plunge ahead with a major program. It worked like the modern corporate equivalent of a tent revival, with a lot of observers, a few hallelujahs from the audience, and a charismatic facilitator leading the flock.

General Motors wanted it put into practice in those months of multiple crises. Dave McLellan suggested that Corvette give it a try. Cardy Davis and Joe Spielman jumped on the idea. It would cost $50,000 for professional help, including facilitators, from a company called DRA, Inc.

"Once McLellan committed himself, I had him," Davis said when the plan was set in motion. "He's agreed to abide by the DRA results because he thinks he can manage the process. But he can't because I'm going to. We'll do DRA, get McLellan and everybody committed to the plan, and then we can get on with doing a new Corvette."

Decision risk analysis involved two groups of people. The Decision Team, of analysts and worker bees, would do all the work in outlining plans and proposals, list the pros and cons, analyze budgets and schedules. The Decision Makers would give guidance, set parameters, and ultimately make the final decisions. Spielman and Davis agreed that the Decision Makers would be a seven-man board.

Davis quickly appointed Dave McLellan to the Decision Makers, a slot McLellan coveted. Pete Liccardello, the C5 model year manager, headed the Decision Team. "Dave can help set the framework for Liccardello's people," Davis said, "but when they come back with recommendations, he's only one vote out of seven in approving them or disapproving them."

The preliminary meeting to approve DRA for Corvette set the tone. McLellan followed his pattern of arriving late for the meeting. That gave the others a chance to talk about him.

"McLellan hit me again Friday with the idea of a mid-engine car," Cardy Davis said. "Anybody else hear that?"

Liccardello and Dale Jordan (no relation to Chuck), the lead Corvette systems engineer, buried their faces in their hands and shook their heads.

"If he mentioned it to me, he's mentioned it to others," Davis said.

"Just when you thought it was safe . . ." Dale Jordan muttered.

"Dave is a great idea man, very innovative," Davis said. "But he isn't worth a shit at implementing ideas."

Heads nodded around the table and Rob Kleinbaum from DRA, Inc., put the question on the table. "Do you want to take forward this process on the Y-car [the Corvette designator]?"

"You're the program manager," Dale Jordan said to Cardy Davis. "You have to make the decision on whether we use this or not. Is this system the answer to the McLellan problem, or just something that delays the work [on the '96 Corvette]?"

Cardy pondered a moment before answering. "The positive side is that when McLellan comes in with a new scenario later, we just have to say 'No, we can't do that.' The negative side is that to do this smoothy and quickly will take tremendous dedication and time." It could take a lot of twelve-hour days, seven days a week, for six to eight weeks.

Moments later McLellan walked in. "We've been weighing the pluses and minuses of DRA," Kleinbaum told him.

"You don't have to convince me," McLellan said.

That response sealed the decision.

The con carried into 1992 when the decision risk analysis working group settled on nine strategies to be considered for the 1996 Corvette. Each would be analyzed in detail as to cost, timing, market impact, profit, and other factors, over the coming weeks. Then the best would be taken to a vote by the Decision Makers and Corvette '96 would have a single architecture. No more deviations would be allowed.

McLellan hoped to tilt the process toward a mid-engine design, exciting in looks at some small cost in performance, but setting Corvette on a new course outside its forty-year tradition. But Cardy Davis and Joe Spielman picked the members of the working group and they made it bluntly clear: Their purpose was to thwart McLellan, bury the mid-engine concept, and move ahead with a front-engine, rear-transmission Corvette.

The day before the final showdown, Corvette got news of another kind. Cardy Davis was leaving, assigned to the W-cars he so much despised. Spielman had looked at his record of success in building cars profitably and in turning around programs in trouble. He needed a fireman and Cardy Davis was it. Corvette's new boss would be an unknown fellow named Russ McLean, just brought up by Spielman from Mexico, where he had been in charge of all GM manufacturing in the country.

No one had time to give McLean's arrival or Davis's pending departure much thought. All eyes were focused on the DRA and the day of decision.

Three options for C5 were more or less viable; that is, they would produce a car the Corvette enthusiasts would buy. There were significant differences between them, including development cost. The three were listed on a large display:

A *momentum* architecture that left the Corvette with a front engine, a rear transmission, and an evolutionary body style that followed Corvette tradition. They called it "momentum" because it was the backbone structure that had been on the front burner for more than two years. Everything in the engineering plan was based on it and to change now would put them back close to square one.

A *mid-engine* architecture that put the engine and transmission behind the driver and offered Corvette stylists dramatic new avenues for designing the car's exterior.

A *stiffer and lighter* Corvette that would combine aspects of both.

All three would be profitable for General Motors. All three involved risk in development, though the mid-engine was the riskiest and almost certainly could not be developed in time to be a 1996 car. The stiffer and lighter car had the best chance of meeting the $150 million engineering budget and other cost constraints but involved the most trade-offs in styling, comfort, performance, and overall quality. The momentum Corvette would make the most money and would have the highest initial quality of the three.

Through the three-hour presentation, Dave McLellan circled the cost and risk figures on his packet of charts and made a few notes and exclamation points next to the mid-engine styling predictions. But worker bees were recommending the momentum car. It was clearly the right decision and nobody had to fudge the engineering data or financial numbers. As McLellan asked questions and made comments, it was increasingly obvious that he was being swayed, either by the facts of the case or the realization that no one else in the room was interested in the mid-engine risks. If he voted for the mid-engine, he'd be all alone.

Joe Spielman made his position clear. "If we all pull together, decide what we want to do, then we can pull off a '96 program," he said, tugging open his tie and walking around the room. "We don't want another three months of study. . . .

"We *have* to have a '96 program. I'm willing to sit down with Chevrolet and everybody else to make that happen. . . .

"We are on the brink of bankruptcy," he said as he paced, "on the brink of having our bonds downrated to junk bonds. And that's the start of the end. There's not one-half of one percent of people at the Tech Center who understand that we are on the verge of going out of business.

"Guys, we are in deep shit.

"The best thing for me, for all of us, is to be ready to go through another kind of decision gate on August 1 and to say to CPC management, 'By the way, we need another seven million dollars or whatever to get on with it because we've got the best damn thing ever here and we have our business case nailed and Chevrolet is salivating for this car. They're even ready to give up pink mud flaps on the Monte Carlo to get it.' "

"Wait a minute," said Bob Bierley, Chevrolet's chief planner, laughing. "You've gone over the line now."

"I take it back, Bob. No pink mud flaps."

Everyone had a say, Decision Team members and Decision Makers alike. Finally Spielman stood up, his six-five frame dominating the room. He flipped a red pencil from hand to hand and took full charge of the meeting.

"We're here today to decide on what kind of car we're going to build," he said. "Does anybody here have any question about that?"

"Not me," McLellan said.

"The turbine car," John Cafaro, one of the Decision Makers, said to tension-releasing laughter.

"You're learning," Spielman joked.

"You know how design guys are," Cafaro rejoined. "We've been working on the momentum car for a year, maybe two. And if we go to stiffer and lighter, we're back in the basement reinventing the car."

"Okay," Spielman said, "I'm calling the board. I want us to go out those doors and all be in the same direction. Let's go around the table."

Cardy Davis: "Momentum!"

Dave McLellan didn't pause, not even a little: "Momentum!"

John Cafaro: "Momentum!"

And so it went, around the table with the seven Decision Makers casting their votes. It got back to Joe Spielman.

"Momentum for me, too." A round of applause went up from the other twenty or so people in the room. Spielman continued: "We got everybody on the same side. No backtracking. We're committed, right? If anybody asks what kind of car we're going to build, what do you say?"

A voice from the back responded: "Mom! Mom!"

The McLellan problem was solved, at least for a while.

Spielman fixed the room with a stern glare. "If we walk out of here and anybody says, 'Yeah, we sort of decided, but I've got another idea that I want us to look at,' then I say we get the firing squad, give 'em a last cigarette, and shoot 'em."

And then Joe Spielman did something strange, almost certainly never done before inside the conservative environment of General Motors. It was a defining and emotional moment that bound the people in the room in ways none of them understood at the time. But as the months and years went by, it was the single moment that indelibly settled the future of C5.

Spielman rolled up his right shirtsleeve and exposed his wrist. "I left the knife at home," he said, "so this is symbolic. We're in this together, bonded in blood."

He made an imaginary cut on his wrist and held it out to Cardy Davis. Cardy bonded his own wrist to Spielman's in a slapping movement. Spielman moved on to Russ McLean, who had observed the day's events, and McLean put his wrist against Spielman's. The big man went around the table and around the room. Bare wrist to bare wrist, the Corvette people took that blood oath to bond together—one team, one architecture, one goal.

Somebody asked if Spielman had taken an AIDS test. "If anybody violates this agreement, he's got more to worry about than AIDS," Spielman growled. "AIDS is too slow."

20 THE fates of General Motors and Corvette were settled in 1992. Key players disappeared and new ones arrived. Budget was given and budget was taken away. Corvette was turned, twisted, stood on its head, applauded, buried, and resurrected all in the space of twelve tumultuous months.

After the company reported a 1991 loss of $4.5 billion, rumors floated freely that president Lloyd Reuss was on the way out. They subsided briefly when chairman Bob Stempel announced yet another "restructuring and rationalization," a major reorganization of GM in North America.

The two big car groups, Chevrolet-Pontiac-Canada and Buick-Oldsmobile-Cadillac, along with the thriving Truck and Bus group, would disappear over the next year. New organizations would replace them, a car group that would itself go through an interminable series of mini-reorganizations while trying to find a management formula that worked, a truck group, and other groups for powertrain, components, and sales and marketing. The organizational structure built by Roger Smith in the 1980s was gone. His single-car plants were being closed or converted to multivehicle use. Except for the hole he had dug for General Motors, and his purchases of Electronic Data Systems (EDS) from Ross Perot and of Hughes Electronics, little of Roger Smith's era remained.

Stempel also created the North American Operations Strategy Board to make the major decisions affecting car and truck production, individual programs, marketing, and much more. Its members were the most senior executives in the company, including Lloyd Reuss, Mike Mutchler, and Gary Dickinson.

Reuss wouldn't be around to share in the decision making. General Motors' board of directors, in the first phase of a revolt, dumped him forty-one days later and named Jack Smith, no relation to Roger, president. Reuss was demoted to executive vice president, given a make-work job, and left the company before the end of the year. Stempel was replaced as chairman of the board's executive committee by outside director John Smale.

Years down the road, Stempel's company reorganization and creation of the Strategy Board could be seen as a major factor in improving GM's fortunes. More years of huge losses came first, but at least some kind of control was being exercised. It just wasn't easily seen in the glare of bad publicity. The car group would have to muddle its way through defining itself, almost a trial-and-error process over the next four years. That muddling, combined with overcoming the fainthearted and sometimes inexplicable product decisions of earlier years, would have grave impact on the company in 1992 and 1993. A company so huge can only be turned around slowly.

Corvette, hammered by years of reorganizations and seemingly capricious delays, received the changes numbly. There was an unspoken decision not to worry, but to move ahead under the optimistic leadership of Joe Spielman and the yet unknown Russ McLean. Cardy Davis, already deeply immersed in fixing quality and image problems on the family sedans—the Chevy Lumina and near twins marketed by Pontiac and Oldsmobile—came back in the weeks before Reuss was demoted to get a plaque and a cheer-up from his old team. "We'll still loan you Corvettes," jibed C4 model year manager Jeff Yachnin, "but only if you promise not to return the favor."

Davis promised not to make them drive Chevy Luminas, but said he'd still be coming around to offer advice. When a groan went up, he laughed. "Oh, you want advice already? Okay, here's a pearl. Never complain about another organization. You might have to go over there and fix it."

He turned serious and stuck a hand in his pocket. "I complained a lot about the W-car and now I'm paying for it. The W-platform is losing more than any car in history, in any company, and I'm supposed to turn it around."

He glanced at his watch. "GM's lost forty-five thousand dollars on the W-car while I've been here," he said with frustrated sadness. "I'd better get back to work."

Russ McLean's first big decision was a groundbreaker. He and John Cafaro agreed to move eight of Dave McLellan's engineers into the design studio to work minute to minute on Corvette packaging and styling instead of week to week. It was an unheard-of invasion into Chuck Jordan's turf, so Cafaro didn't tell Jordan until it was a fait accompli.

"If I'd asked permission, he'd have said no," Cafaro said, "and then yelled at me for even considering the idea. Once I brought them in, he couldn't throw them out. He still yelled at me, but what the hell, I was going to get yelled at either way. This way I have what I want, engineers in the studio from the beginning so we can avoid all those delays later on when we've spent months designing something that engineering can't build."

The engineers stayed for months, smoothing the process of styling a Corvette exterior over a hidden structure that was radically new. Early in the process, they got a look at how Design Staff worked, when Jordan put on a Corvette show on the patio for Chevy general manager Jim Perkins.

Blustery late-March weather threatened, but the show was going on, indoors or out. The high-walled Patio first filled with real Corvettes, driven gingerly out onto the hexagonal tiles by their keepers. There was a classic '53 with wire-screen headlamps, a Mako Shark from the mid-sixties, a Sting-ray, and an early-seventies show car. On the far right sat a 1992 ZR-1.

Four more Corvettes were pushed, dragged, nudged, and wheedled into position in front of the old cars, sitting broadside to the huge curved windows of the Design Dome. If the cold wind whipped too severely, Perkins could view the cars from inside. It did and he did.

On the left was the eggplant-colored California Corvette, already more than two years old and no longer a secret. Jordan used it as a prod. "Whatever we do has to be better than this," he told Cafaro repeatedly. Jordan also ordered an Acura NS-X and a new Porsche set off to one side for comparison. "Nice cars," he conceded, "but we can do better."

Next to the California Corvette sat a maroon Corvette of futuristic origin. It was a fiberglass beauty with a custom interior, an engine, and almost two thousand miles already on its odometer. It was the car designed by Tom Peters and selected by Jordan as his favorite (modified) in the building-wide competition eleven months earlier. Peters's Corvette had morphed into a low-slung speedster, with a sudden drop-off in front that gave the impression of a wide-nosed armadillo snouting for grubs. Tom Peters loved high-performance jets and his Corvette showed the influence in a mostly transparent bubble roof shaped like a fighter's canopy.

The third and fourth Corvettes waiting for Perkins were from John Cafaro's studio. Cafaro called them mainline designs to show the direction that Corvette would take when the 1996 model finally debuted. One was bright and lively, a full-size clay model covered with foil, red for the body, black for the roof, silver for the windows. By Cafaro's words, it was an evolutionary Corvette, still too broad in the rear, but with side lines and a greenhouse that showed its heritage.

At the end of the line sat a hot black Corvette, the design that most people favored. It was another fiberglass model, similar to the red clay car, with a difference. It was another car you could sit in and drive, a car that looked to be in motion even when it sat still, a car with the steepest front-end plunge of any car out there. It also was a product of Chuck Jordan's conscience. After giving the nod to Tom Peters's car long ago, he faced up to the fact that Cafaro's car was better. So he authorized both of them to cast fiberglass bodies and build drivable cars. Now Cafaro's fiber-glass car, sporting tires too wide for the 1996 Corvette and built over a "birdcage" chassis that had been mostly abandoned in the new design, drew eyes wherever it sat. Because the body was on a "birdcage," the black car would need serious modification to fit over the backbone structure. But Cafaro and McLellan's engineers had already examined the design and decided that it could be done.

The design team wanted some direction from Perkins in this show. After nearly an hour of presentations and musings, he rendered a semiverdict. "I like the black one," he said, knowing that it could fit over a backbone structure. "The red one still has a ways to go. It needs more reach. This car has to survive in the market for maybe twelve years, out to 2008. I'd say you've reached maybe five years, to 2001. It's a good start, guys. Just give it more reach."

"We're already doing it," Cafaro grinned after Perkins left. "But we really needed him to say it in front of Chuck." He cackled and slapped his fist into his palm. "Reach! My favorite word!"

The car by Tom Peters was finally out of the running. Challenges to John Cafaro's Corvette supremacy would continue as part of the emotionally charged styling game, but each time he rebuffed one, he emerged more firmly as the dominant Corvette designer.

Nobody expected Perkins to point to one of the cars and say, "Build it!" And nobody was disappointed when he asked for something better.

Cafaro went back to his studio happy—but only briefly. Joe Spielman brought the bad news.

"I love Corvette," Spielman told the Corvette business team, "but I'm afraid that for '96, the money won't be there to do the car I want."

It wasn't, but Spielman brought the latest version of good news back from a Strategy Board meeting. "Corvette is solid for '97," he announced, putting a happy face on the umpteenth delay since someone decided back in 1988 that there should be a new Corvette for 1993. When he saw the green faces in the room, he tried to mitigate the depressing news. "Hey, we could still do the program in '96, but the money just isn't there. It's strictly a money problem, not design or engineering or a bad business plan."

Then just as faces were relaxing, he dropped the rest of the bad news. "But we will have to do another CI in January."

One more walk around the garden, some of them thought. *Will we ever get a program that lasts?*

Aside from the slip from '96 to '97, the organizational upheavals were having little impact on John Cafaro and the rest of Design Staff. Cafaro's two big concerns were refining his Corvette design and worrying about who would succeed to the throne when Chuck Jordan retired in October. Cafaro and most of the other studio directors wanted Jerry Palmer to get the job. He'd been in training for it long enough and insiders at Design Staff knew, if the corporate chiefs didn't, that it was Palmer who most often kept Jordan from excesses.

But there was a dark horse on the scene and Cafaro was worried. His name was Wayne Cherry, brought back from GM's European design center by Jack Smith with the obvious intent of challenging Palmer for the top styling job in the company. When Cafaro took his latest Corvette model into the Patio in late June, it was Jordan and Cherry who examined it. The full-size clay was now Di-Noked shiny black and it incorporated the changes Jim Perkins had requested a few months earlier.

Jordan knelt at the front of the Corvette, looked into the curved and uplifted air scoops that gave the car a distinctive head-on appearance, and uttered the words that some said later he had rehearsed. "It looks like an insipid, grinning hyena," he said with sugary venom. "I don't like that look."

He walked around the car. "The back end is too fat."

He squatted. "I don't like the way this rear quarter panel flares into the door."

He stood off to the side. "The upper looks funny. You know, those people over at the platform want more headroom. I suppose we'll have to give it to them."

Then he gathered the design studio people around and changed directions completely.

"All in all," the Chrome Cobra said, "I like it. You people have done a helluva job. A couple little things I mentioned and I think we've got a Corvette."

He turned and walked away. John Cafaro and his people stared after him slack-jawed. *What the hell* . . .

Three weeks later, the model was significantly changed. The *insipid, grinning hyena* look was gone, replaced by air scoops more rounded. The rear end was trimmer. The roof was a full inch higher. The fender flares were more subtle.

Like every other Corvette model created in Cafaro's studio since 1988, it was a car that would have Corvette lovers salivating.

Cafaro waved his hand at the revised car and did a Steve McGarrett impersonation, "Build it, Danno!"

Then his brief grin faded. "What's really going to happen is that the new guy, whoever replaces Chuck in November, is going to take one look at this car and then have it crushed down into Play-Doh. We'll be starting all over."

On that one, John Cafaro got it wrong.

The GM executive committee met in early August and within hours the rumor mill was calling Wayne Cherry the new vice president for design. Cafaro and half-a-dozen other studio chiefs put their heads together to scope out the future. "We all agreed on two things," he said. "One was that we weren't happy with Wayne Cherry as our boss.

"The other was that Chuck Jordan's support of Jerry Palmer was counter-productive. We were afraid that the suits downtown were thinking that Jerry was just a younger version of Jordan. But Palmer's no Chuck Jordan. He's got vision that Jordan didn't have on his best day. And he loves Corvette."

Cafaro then proved that he still hadn't learned the corporate art of keeping his mouth shut. "What the hell," Cafaro said, propping his feet on his desk. "Once more into the breach."

The breach this time was an appointment with forty-five-year-old Mike Losh, one of the four or five most powerful men in the company.

Losh was a contemporary of Jerry Palmer, only a few years older than John Cafaro, and was known for keeping lines of communication open downward as well as upward. Cafaro figured he was risking his career, but that didn't stop him from asking for a half hour with Losh. He got it.

"We were right," he reported back to his cohorts. "The top dogs were thinking that Palmer was going to be too much like Chuck Jordan. Why else would Jordan be pushing him so hard? Losh was wide open to discussion and was glad to hear the viewpoint of the studio chiefs. He seemed kinda surprised that we like Palmer because he knows we all hate Jordan.

"Will it make any difference? I don't know and he obviously didn't make any commitment. But he did say that he'd do a lot of asking around and that this whole thing would be a renewed topic of conversation.

"Oh, yeah . . . I didn't get fired, either. I'm still here."

While that issue fomented, Corvette's chief engineer Dave McLellan bowed to the obvious and turned in his retirement papers at the stroke of eight on the morning of August 24, 1992. He would stay on as Corvette chief engineer under a consulting contract until his replacement was named. Joe Spielman had suggested the move to McLellan and after weeks of an-guished contemplation, McLellan did it.

Why now? he was asked.

"Now because the money was right," he said frankly. "The window for early retirement closes September 1 and I had to make a decision. And now because we just added another year in doing the new car. I've been chief engineer for what, sixteen, seventeen years? I don't know that I could keep fighting these wars for another three or four years."

His eyes reflected the sadness he was feeling, and the frustration and the exhaustion. "It takes a lot out of you going through this cycle of starting, stopping, starting again." He looked at his staff, some of them frantic at the idea that McLellan was leaving, others sitting in enigmatic silence. "I'm not telling you anything you don't know from your own experience."

It took twenty minutes to shake hands all around and to listen to the pleas, the condolences, the words of genuine regret. Whatever he was or was not as a get-your-hands-dirty chief engineer, Dave McLellan was almost as much a legend as the Corvette itself. Finally he raised his hand for the room's attention. Even his detractors were moved by his next words.

"I'll be around," he said quietly. "Anytime any of you want to talk, you have my number.

"I'll always be Corvette."

The next question on everyone's mind, most particularly Earl Werner's, was, Who's going to be the new chief engineer? Whoever it was would have huge shoes to fill and a new Corvette to take through the engineering process.

It would take three months of corporate turmoil, another boardroom revolution, and a near obituary for Corvette before the question was answered. Another issue was settled first.

Wayne Cherry got Chuck Jordan's job.

The board of directors met by phone in mid-September and did it. Jerry Palmer got the news on a Friday afternoon. What he heard was that he had lost his chance at the golden ring but got a promotion anyway. At the recommendation of Bob Stempel and Jack Smith, the board made a Solomon-like move. It gave Cherry the vice presidency. But it made Palmer director of design for North American Operations. In theory, Cherry would handle the vice presidential things—budget, administration, personnel, the overall operation of Design at GM. Palmer would run all studios and be the dominant force and influence over the actual design of new cars.

"If it works, we'll be a lot better off than we have been," Cafaro said. "Jordan has messed with the studios from day one . . . [but] we can work with Jerry. When he doesn't like something, he knows how to tell you what's wrong."

Amazingly, it did work. Cherry knew that he wasn't the first choice of the studio chiefs and he knew who to talk to about it. He sat down with John Cafaro and in a long, quiet conversation they came to terms. One of Cafaro's options was to give up the new Corvette and take a three-year tour at the Advanced Concepts Center in California. It wasn't an option he wanted. Above all, Cafaro was a realist. He shook hands with Cherry and climbed on board. "I've lipped off around him," Cafaro said later when he and the other chiefs got back down to business. "But now he's got the job and I'll support him. It's time to get back down to business and get behind Cherry one hundred percent."

Within a month, the question once again was whether there would be a Corvette to support at all.

At Design Staff, one more studio competition was under way and Chevrolet was planning to take the winning models to a November marketing clinic in Los Angeles. Then as General Motors continued its spiral down into financial disaster, the Strategy Board held its fateful weekend meeting in late October.

"I want everybody to take a deep breath," Corvette platform manager Russ McLean told his key people on that Monday morning. "The Strategy Board met all weekend. There'll be an announcement about another reorganization in the next day or two.

"But the impact for us . . . well, all programs after '96 have been put on hold or canceled. Since we were a 1997, all I can say is for you to clear your calendars, stop everything, and go into a holding pattern. Right now, things are pretty confused. . . ."

Chaos had arrived.

21

T H E weekend reorganization was the third major shuffling of GM's structure in 1992 and left questions everywhere. The Corvette people, once again facing an unknown future, were distraught.

One uncertainty was quickly resolved. Bob Stempel figured things out and resigned. The news leaks were right, and so were advisers on Stempel's personal staff who had warned him that the board was in revolt. The unmistakable message came on October 22 after Stempel asked the board for a public statement of confidence. He got something else:

"The GM Board of Directors has taken no action regarding any management changes at GM. However, the question of executive leadership is a primary concern to the Board of Directors of any company and GM is no exception. The GM Board of Directors continues to carefully reflect upon the wisest course for assuring the most effective leadership for the Corporation."

Stempel took the next day, Friday, and the weekend to think things through. First thing Monday morning he issued his own statement. "I sincerely hope that my decision to resign will end the chaos of the past several weeks. . . ."

He was replaced as chairman by John Smale, who once ran Procter and Gamble and engineered a turnaround. As an outside director, Smale was a key player in GM's boardroom revolt. Corvette people placed hope on the fact that Smale drove one of their cars and loved it. But for the immediate future, what Smale drove didn't seem to matter.

"I feel like a dog on a chain," one young Corvette engineer said. "Every time I start running, somebody yanks me back."

The latest changes left real casualties. One corpse was the underlying philosophy of the previous reorganization that had separated GM's car products into small, manageable groups and made programs like Corvette into mini—car companies, responsible for their own engineering, their own purchasing, and their own assembly plants. Platform or program managers had real power. For the first time in years, their authority matched their responsibility. Most important, each platform was a profit center. At the core, profit was how performance would be judged.

Program managers loved the idea. "Everybody wants to be chairman of the board," Russ McLean said one day soon after taking over Corvette. "Now we can run our own show."

Almost none of the strong-manager philosophy survived in the new organization. The plan put together and approved by GM president Jack Smith and his North American Operations Strategy Board that October weekend was just the opposite. Car programs would henceforth share key elements of engineering and manufacturing, without having managerial responsibility for either. Sharing saved money by avoiding duplication. But it also divided resources and loyalties. Even worse, it created mini-kingdoms. At the Midsize Car Division, where Corvette struggled, it would cause major trauma.

Platforms would still be expected to make a profit, but they'd have to do it with less autonomy and more subservience to the larger organization. Corvette would no longer be a mini-company on its own. It was once again a piece of something bigger.

There was a big winner in the reorganization. Joe Spielman picked up several platforms and he suddenly had the biggest piece of North American Operations. The Rear-Drive Automotive Division disappeared as quickly as it had arrived. His empire grew to take in all midsize cars and mini-vans, not just the rear-drive models like Corvette that had been his previous responsibility, and his assembly plants would produce more than 40 percent of all General Motors cars built in North America. Spielman now ran the new Midsize Car Division and his power grew exponentially.

Design studio chief John Cafaro paid attention to the shake-up at the top, but he had more immediate problems. His position still wasn't secure. Months earlier, Chuck Jordan had ordered yet another internal competition, pitting other studios against Cafaro. The carrot Jordan dangled was that someone might yet take Corvette away from Chevy 3.

The day after Bob Stempel resigned, artisans wheeled nine scale-model Corvettes out to the Design Staff's high-walled patio, where they could be viewed and judged in natural light. The man running the show was not Chuck Jordan. His long-pending retirement at age sixty-five was at hand and his successor, handpicked and already announced, was taking over. Wayne Cherry had spent all but a few years of his GM career in Europe. He was the opposite in almost every way from Chuck Jordan, who dressed with verve, had shiny silver hair, and still drove his Ferrari to work now and then. Cherry was tall, dark-haired, and somber-looking. He favored black suits, white shirts, and conservative ties, and he drove a

General Motors sedan. Now he was a key player in deciding the future of Corvette.

In a masterly subterfuge, Chuck Jordan wouldn't be at the show. With five days to go before he officially turned control over to Cherry, he was being taken to lunch—"A long lunch," Cafaro grinned—by a half-dozen secretaries and other women in the building. They planned to keep him away until the show was over. Any decision about Corvette now belonged to Wayne Cherry and Jerry Palmer.

Cherry insisted that more eyes than his and Palmer's study the models. At least a dozen people would have votes in the contest. Cafaro and his competing studio chiefs would mark secret ballots to rank the models. So would a few members of the Design Staff administrative staff. Then Cherry asked several executives from Chevrolet and the Corvette platform to take part in the process. Among them was Corvette's lame-duck chief engineer, Dave McLellan.

The winning Corvette models were to be photographed against realistic backgrounds. A few weeks later they would be displayed to about three hundred carefully selected sports car owners at a marketing research clinic in southern California. The lucky few would see full-size projections, artistically lighted and almost three-dimensional, of Corvette contenders. They'd see the cars from the front, side, and rear. They'd sit in a full-size seating model called a "buck" that was complete with instruments, electric seats, and (mostly) working controls. Their reactions would be carried back to Detroit for analysis and deliberation.

Four of the candidate models came out of John Cafaro's studio. Three more were shipped to Detroit from the Advanced Concepts Center outside of Los Angeles, where freethinking stylists had created the Stingray III a few years earlier and now entered new and wild models in the competition. The last two models were done in one of Chuck Jordan's advanced studios where stylists worked on futuristic designs, but with less slap and dash than their California counterparts.

The afternoon show brought a brilliant autumn sky dotted with puffy white clouds. It would be a beauty contest, with Cherry and Palmer setting the tone for the judges.

Cherry's openness surprised them all. "It's a real departure," Cafaro said. "Chuck Jordan would have looked at the models and made the decision by himself. At least Cherry's asking for input, whether he actually uses it or not. Party on, Wayne! Party on, Jerry!"

While his people moved their models to the patio, Cafaro bounced over to his glass-walled office, returning with a special ballot he'd prepared. "Our Design Analysis Department has the real ballot, but I think this is the one we ought to use," he grinned. He taped the ballot to the model Corvette he had designed over the last two months.

Please Check One

❏   Love it

❏   Like it a lot

❏   Like it somewhat

❏   It's okay

❏   Dislike it a little

❏   It sucks

❏   Hate it

❏   Hate you

❏   You're fired

Additional comments:

Signed:

The ballot stayed in place through the show. Wayne Cherry chuckled when he read it and turned to Cafaro. "I'll let you know when I'm ready to use your ballot," he said with a genuine smile.

The lead yes or no item on the official ballot approved by Wayne Cherry was "Looks like a futuristic Corvette." The three models from California failed miserably. One looked like a short, stubby Volkswagen Karmann Ghia. It was anything but a Corvette. The other two just left the judges bewildered.

"Why did they do that?" Cherry said in deep puzzlement. "None of the California cars are even close." He looked closely at one model. "I find this car impossible to evaluate. The overhang is all wrong. There's no Corvette heritage."

"I think the designer has been on drugs," Palmer joked. "He must have done this in rehab."

The other California model had a front air scoop with uplifted corners merging into the hood. "It looks like it's smiling at me," Cherry said. "When I look in my rearview mirror and see a Corvette coming up, I want to be overpowered. I don't want a friendly Corvette smiling at me!"

The judges walked up and down the line, marking their ballots and offering comments. At one point, the difference between Wayne Cherry and Chuck Jordan was striking. Cherry wandered in front of one judge, blocking his view. After a moment, he realized that the man, trained in the days when no one said anything to Chuck Jordan like "Excuse me, you're in my way," was standing there patiently. With a touch of chagrin, Cherry moved out of the way. "Sorry," he said.

After forty minutes, the ballots were collected. Cherry asked that the top four models be selected by consensus, not by his singular decision. John Cafaro's car was a winner. So was a model done in the advanced studio. Randy Wittine's car also would be shown at the California clinic, a tribute to a guy they called "Mr. Corvette" because of his twenty-eight years in the Chevy 3 studio. The fourth car was a toss-up between a sleek model done by Dan Magda, Cafaro's deputy studio chief, and another model from the advanced studio.

"Maybe we'll send five to the clinic," Cherry said at the end. "Let's see what the Chevy people have to say." He looked directly at Cafaro and at the rest. "And I want you guys to go back and tell your people how great these models are. Everybody did a really good job."

Compliments from the boss! Cafaro's face registered shock. Then his eyes softened and he nodded. There were some things happening here that he'd have to get used to.

Moments later, Chuck Jordan walked out onto the patio. Everybody froze. He glanced at the models, then turned to Cherry. "You all done?" he asked.

"We're waiting on the Chevy people," Cherry said. "You want to take a look?"

Jordan didn't hesitate. "No, not today," he said. "It's your decision now."

There was a stunned silence, but the Chrome Cobra didn't notice. "You've got good people out here," he said. "They'll do the job." He clapped Wayne Cherry on the shoulder and walked back into the building.

Nobody knew what to say. So they didn't say anything.

Half an hour later, the Chevy people completed their review. They agreed with Design Staff's choices, picking the same five models in slightly different order. The afterglow conversation turned to Corvette's future. One of Chevy's men at the show was Bob Bierley, the division's director of planning.

"We need this car," he said. "We have to have it and everybody at Chevrolet knows it. This car has to be in production by '96, as a 1997 model. We have four programs for '97 that have to go ahead, and Corvette is one of 'em.

"That word to shut down everything after 1996 was taking things too literally. It was an overreaction. Corvette is a mainstream program for the corporation and it's going to stay that way."

There were whoops and hollers on the patio. Corvette was no longer on life support. C5 was definitely alive.

Joe Spielman confirmed it in a phone call originated by Jerry Palmer.

"The clinic in Los Angeles," Palmer asked. "Do we stop or go?"

"Go," Spielman said. "Whatever you heard about canceling the new Corvette, forget it. We need that car and I'm not going to see it delayed."

'43 Corvette

EARLY SKETCHES IN THE BUBBLE-UP PHASE OF 1989 AND THE STOP-AND-GO DESIGN PERIOD OF
1990 AND 1991 HAD TOO MUCH IMAGINATION. THESE CARS, CHEVY DECIDED, WOULD NOT MAKE
FUTURE CORVETTE BUYERS HAPPY.

AN EARLY CLOWN SUIT MODEL SHOWED C5 IN A SLEEK TOPLESS RACING VER-
SION. THIS DESIGN HELPED SET THE PATTERNS THAT LED TO THE 1997
CORVETTE.

KIRK BENNION'S CLOWN SUIT WAS DONE IN THE CORVETTE SKUNK WORKS IN
1989. IT WAS ONE OF THE FAVORITES OF THE TIME.

IN A COMPUTER
RENDITION, THIS CORVETTE'S REAR
END WAS TOO RADICAL. IT WAS ONE
OF HUNDREDS OF DESIGNS
REJECTED OVER THE YEARS.

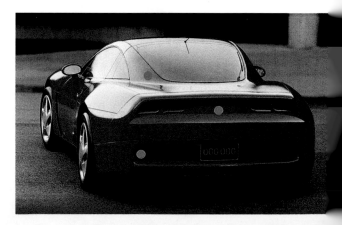

JOHN CAFARO'S BLACK CAR SURVIVED ONE OF CHUCK JORDAN'S INFAMOUS INTER-
STUDIO COMPETITIONS. IT SET THE THEME THAT ULTIMATELY EVOLVED INTO THE
C5 CORVETTE.

AS C5 MATURED, SCULPTORS AND ENGINEERS IN THE CHEVY 3 DESIGN STUDIO
WORKED TO SHAPE THE CAR'S FINAL LINES. THE PROCESS WAS PAINSTAKING AND
PRECISE.

THE BASIC SHAPE OF C5 WAS
APPROVED IN 1993. IT TOOK
ANOTHER YEAR TO SETTLE SIDE
AND REAR-END TREATMENTS.

THE SIDE SCOOP ON THIS C5 MODEL WAS
CONSIDERED TOO RADICAL. SO WERE THE
SLASH-TYPE MARKER LIGHTS NEAR THE
REAR.

FREQUENT STUDIO REVIEWS LET CORVETTE
AND CHEVROLET MANAGEMENT TRACK
CHANGES MADE IN THE CLAY MODELS.
From left: DAVE HILL, JIM PERKINS, HARRY
TURNER, AND FRED GALLASCH.

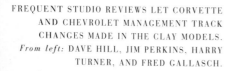

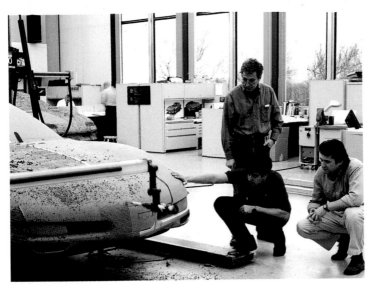

HIS HANDS-ON APPROACH TO DESIGNING THE NEW CORVETTE MADE JOHN CAFARO *(kneeling at left)* ONE OF GM'S PREMIER STUDIO CHIEFS. DEPUTY STUDIO CHIEF DAN MAGDA *(kneeling at right)* AND CHIEF MODELER CLAUDIO BERTOLIN MONITORED THE PROGRESS OF A CLAY LATHE TO ENSURE ABSOLUTE ACCURACY IN THE FINAL MODEL.

HOOD HEIGHT WAS A QUESTION DECIDED WHEN JOHN CAFARO PUT A CLAY C5 NEXT TO A CURRENT C4 CORVETTE. THE LOWER HOOD LINE, ON THE DRIVER'S SIDE OF THE CLAY MODEL, WAS AN OBVIOUS WINNER.

THE DISTINCT SCALLOPS OVER C5'S TAIL LIGHTS CLEARLY DIFFERENTIATED THE CAR FROM ITS AGING ANCESTOR. BUT THEY WERE SACRIFICED TO GIVE THE CAR BETTER AERODYNAMICS AND EASE OF MANUFACTURE.

THIS JIM DUNNE SPY PHOTO CAPTURED A HEAVILY CAMOUFLAGED C5 ON A ROAD TEST LATE
IN THE DEVELOPMENT AND TEST-DRIVING PROCESS. *(Jim Dunne)*

TEST DRIVERS PUT C5 ON ROADS
WHERE THEY COULD LITERALLY
SHAKE IT OUT IN THE REAL
WORLD. THIS CANDID PHOTO BY
THE AUTHOR CAUGHT A C5 CROSS-
ING A DRY CREEK BED IN THE
ARIZONA MOUNTAINS.
(James Schefter)

UNDER THREATENING SKIES, DRI-
VERS STOPPED FOR A PHOTO
OPPORTUNITY AT ROOSEVELT
LAKE IN THE MOUNTAINS EAST OF
PHOENIX. THIS ROAD TRIP IN
DECEMBER 1995 WAS CRUCIAL TO
FINDING PROBLEMS IN C5'S
DEVELOPMENT PHASE.
(James Schefter)

MORE THAN SEVEN YEARS AFTER HE FIRST BEGAN SKETCHING C5
CORVETTES, JOHN CAFARO *(seated on hood)* AND HIS STUDIO TEAM HAD
ONE TO SHOW OFF IN THE DESIGN DOME. EVEN THIS ONE
WASN'T FINAL; SOME CHANGES IN THE PARKING AND FOG LIGHTS CAME
AFTER THIS FIBERGLASS CAR WAS BUILT.

NO ONE WOULD DOUBT THAT IT WAS A CORVETTE. BUT THE FOIL-COVERED C5 CLAY
MODEL IN THE FOREGROUND WAS A DISTINCT EVOLUTIONARY CHANGE FROM THE
CORVETTE THAT HAD BEEN ON THE ROAD SINCE LATE 1983.

THE INTERIOR OF THE C5 CORVETTE, AFTER MONTHS OF ARGUMENTS
OVER EVEN THE SMALLEST DETAILS.

MORE THAN ANY OTHERS, THEY FOUGHT FOR THE C5 CORVETTE, SAVED IT, AND PRODUCED IT.
From left: DAVE HILL, JOHN CAFARO, JOE SPIELMAN, AND RUSS MCLEAN.

22

I N just over three years on the Corvette program, Earl Werner had earned his keep. He backed up Dave McLellan seamlessly, letting the fabled chief engineer travel the country and the world as an apostle for Corvette, and letting his vision for the car be a constant motivator for people battered by a corporation thrashing in a financial wilderness.

Behind the scenes, Werner kept the engineering team focused on the dual jobs of making improvements in C4 and laying the necessary groundwork for C5. When McLellan announced his retirement, Werner saw a clear path to finally winning the title of Corvette chief engineer. It didn't work out.

In the corporate upheavals, Werner had lost his two supporters. Arv Mueller, formerly engineering director of Chevrolet-Pontiac-Canada, moved on to become director of the Technical Center. Mueller's replacement in the organization now known as the Midsize Car Division had no inkling of Werner's special role in providing the engineering management that seemed to come from McLellan. And Cardy Davis was busy saving the last few years of the W-car platform from utter disaster. He put in a good word with Joe Spielman and Russ McLean, but it was too late. Werner wouldn't get the job.

One of the dark-horse applicants was a slight and soft-spoken engineer from Cadillac named Dave Hill. He was a full ten inches shorter than Spielman's six-five, but only an inch or so under Russ McLean. He had a thick mustache, thinning hair, and pale eyes that could mask his emotions with a thousand-yard stare. His memory bordered on total recall and he had the kind of work ethic and success record that matched McLean's.

"My chief engineer has to have killer instincts," McLean said. "He has to see the problem, attack the problem, solve the problem, then go on to the next problem." During their first interview, he wondered if Dave Hill had the fire. McLean would ask a question. Hill would sit silently thinking, sometimes for so long that McLean would begin to fidget. Then he'd answer. The answers were good, but McLean wasn't sure until they talked more. McLean went back to Joe Spielman and reported.

"I have the impression that he will not carry on the legend of McLellan or Zora," he said. "On the other hand, he burrows into things. Like me."

Dave Hill had the kind of desire that Spielman liked. He wanted the job badly. After twenty-seven years at Cadillac, he was ready for the kind of challenges Corvette offered. Finally he convinced Spielman, a Corvette fanatic of the first order, that his only interest was in building the best sports car in the world.

They offered him the job in late November. But Dave Hill had a surprise for them. Before he accepted, he asked for a meeting with McLean. The Corvette manager had a reputation for getting too involved in details down the chain of command. McLean himself knew that it was a problem.

"How do you operate?" Hill asked bluntly. "I've heard stories."

"They're true," Russ McLean said. "But times are changing, getting more disciplined. If I have confidence in a person, I'll do my best not to get in the way. You understand that when I give you this full responsibility, that's, to me, unorthodox."

"But you'll do it?"

"I'm going to trust you to the nth degree. I want people who think the way I do, the way *you* do."

"What about the outside stuff?"

"You'll have to do some of it, but for a while, we need it less right now. You know, the platform manager's public image is confusing and a question mark, and that's all right. But the chief engineer for Corvette, that's mystical. That mystique, it has to be there. You'll have to go out, but only once in a while."

Hill was quiet, thinking about McLean's words. He'd survived interviews with the press over at Cadillac, staying off the soapbox, but giving precise, simple answers to questions. A little bit of the spotlight didn't worry him. Whether he could work under a boss who got involved in every detail was another question. McLean caught the hesitation.

"I'd like to be out there, making those decisions side by side with you," McLean said. "But I have to discipline myself, and not do that."

Hill recognized that McLean was baring his soul. It was a rare moment at General Motors, where personal feelings often fell under the plow of an impersonal corporate culture. More than that, Hill knew opportunity when he saw it. It was one thing to be in the right place at the right time. It was something else to be smart enough to recognize it. He stuck out his hand.

"Okay," he said. "Let's do it."

Dave Hill's reputation at Cadillac was strong. But Corvette was not Cadillac. The two were very different, and so were the people who worked on them. There were two camps in Corvette engineering. A handful of diehard McLellan supporters resented Dave Hill, partly because he was an outsider and partly because Earl Werner didn't get the promotion. The others knew that Corvette desperately needed a chief engineer like Werner, who got his hands dirty and could actually *manage* the work that had to be done. Werner was good at managing the troops, but without the cachet of a chief engineer, he lacked the muscle to have a big impact with senior executives.

After Dave Hill got the job, Werner confronted Joe Spielman and demanded an explanation. "You're a good manager," Spielman said, and offered Werner the chief engineer's job on one of the sedan platforms. Werner's reaction was blunt.

"Hell, no," he said. Six weeks later, he doubled his Corvette salary and authority by becoming engineering vice president for Harley-Davidson. It was a bittersweet victory for the man who loved the two American icons, Corvette and Harley, and had climbed into high engineering positions at both. Years later he was asked which icon he considered greater. "It's hard," he reflected, "but I have to say Harley-Davidson is the greater icon. But only for one reason. I never heard of a Corvette fanatic with the logo tattooed on his dick!"

Dave Hill knew nothing of the Earl Werner history, except that Werner was gone and Hill could start with a clean sheet. Spielman and McLean thought Hill might even acquire a public persona one day, putting him up there with McLellan, though perhaps not as flamboyant. They were willing to wait and see.

At times Hill's smile was quick. At other times he'd sit poker-faced in a four-hour meeting, betraying nothing to the people who were laying their plans and their problems before him. He usually remembered to thank his engineers when they did well. He kept his public criticisms to a minimum, taking engineers behind closed doors when there was a foul-up or a failure to deliver.

He was not brought in to be an outside man. Just the opposite. The bosses who gave him the job made a conscious decision that they didn't want another gregarious showman. "We need a guy with fire in his heart for Corvette," Joe Spielman said, "somebody who will fondle it, help it, and get in the trenches and lead the team." But they weren't afraid to let Hill handle the press when the opportunities came up and they were willing to let him earn the respect of the Corvette people who bought the car and attended Corvette club meetings and rallies. But not right away. The first thing was to let him engineer a world-class sports car. They were tired of hearing about squeaks and rattles and water leaks. Every survey of what Corvette owners wanted—something GM calls the Voice of the Customer—rated the term *well-built* right up there with *performance* and *safety*.

Corvette was seldom challenged on performance or safety. But there were cars in Corvette's price range that delivered high quality far beyond the Y-car, and had speed and handling that came close. All of those cars were Japanese.

They were the competition and because Porsche had priced itself out of the market, none of them were European. Corvette bosses called them rice burners. The next Corvette, they said, needed a chief engineer who could deliver a car that would leave the C4 Corvette, and the rice burners, somewhere back in the dust.

They found Dave Hill.

He arrived in the maelstrom.

23

CORVETTE lived. It had a new chief engineer on the way. But it didn't have any engineering money.

Joe Spielman went to his boss, Mike Mutchler, who now ran an upgraded successor to the old Chevrolet-Pontiac-Canada group called North American Passenger Car Platforms. It was the bureaucracy that sat between Spielman's Midsize Car Division and North American Operations. Passenger Car was one of the interim stops in GM's frenetic attempts to find itself during the time of chaos. It was a superstructure that absorbed the old Chevrolet-Pontiac-Canada and Buick-Oldsmobile-Cadillac organizations created by Roger Smith. Mutchler had been the man at CPC's helm and he still held Spielman's purse strings.

The November 11 meeting between Mutchler and Spielman was tense. Corvette's original engineering budget for 1993 was $28 million. That was *BC,* the new phrase for anything that happened before October 19. *Before Chaos.* Russ McLean pared his budget to a bare bones $18 million, reasoning that "if we ask for $20 million, we'll get all beat up, so give us $18 million and we'll figure out how to spend it properly."

Spielman took the $18 million request to Mike Mutchler. Mutchler cut it to $9 million.

Spielman brought the news back to a meeting of the Corvette core team, the people wrestling with how to get all this work done. He tried to be upbeat and when he did, the six-five Spielman dominated a room.

"Our mission is to do this car program and do it well, so don't let all this increase your stress levels," he cautioned. "Think of us as scuba divers in calm, clear water thirty feet below the Caribbean. Everything is wonderful and peaceful for us, until we look up and see that there's a force five gale at the surface."

"Yeah," said Dave McLellan, who was still around part-time. "What we have to avoid is rapture of the deep."

"Don't be too concerned about the nine-million-dollar number," said another senior man in the room. "That's Mutchler." And in a time of extreme budget pressures, it was.

Some good things were happening for Corvette, even without money.

One of the smartest things to come out of GM's October revolution was an experimental organization called the Vehicle Launch Center. The VLC was to be both a process and a place. All new-car programs would pass through it on the way to getting the big money tap turned on.

"It's a new piece of Four-Phase," Spielman said. "And you guys get to be among the first."

Eyes rolled at the mention of the General Motors Four-Phase process. The mutant was rearing its ugly head again with yet another change, they thought. In effect, the Vehicle Launch Center became both bubble-up and Phase Zero in the Four-Phase process. But no longer would bubble-up be a freewheeling time to explore and dream about what this new car might be. It would become a formal thing, fourteen months or so long, in which *corporate* processes and procedures would be built into a program. Much effort would be spent shopping through other programs for parts that could be used by *your* program. A specific purpose for the VLC would be "to disallow proliferation of processes and components." That was a decidedly good idea in a company where a 1990 study found that among all of GM's vehicles, only fourteen parts were shared by all. Three of those were little fasteners; the others were fluids and labels.

So Corvette, having previously done an idea-generating bubble-up and having twice in earlier years been passed through the Concept Initiation gate, where the real work begins, once for real and once for practice, would go back to the beginning and become a resident in the Vehicle Launch Center. Because of its earlier work, it got special dispensation to bypass some VLC processes. But still, for a team of people with stars in their eyes, it was like going back to kindergarten. Except that there was no teacher. Corvette people found themselves helping to write the VLC textbook, innovating their way around the many murky parts of this new addition to Four-Phase.

Along the tortuous road from C4 to C5, Corvette's people found that Four-Phase was both road map and roadblock.

It was a hard way to get to where they were going.

GETTING the money at the end of 1992, at least part of it, wasn't that hard. A little creative accounting by the Corvette team helped. So did an angel willing to skirt the rules by diverting certain invoices away from Corvette and paying them from another account.

A heavy December snow was falling when a core team of Corvette people gathered at 8 A.M. Many of them staggered in late, stomping snow from their shoes and tossing heavy coats into a growing pile on a drafting table outside the door. Driving conditions were abominable, but no one wanted to miss this day.

The pivotal meeting for Corvette's future was in a cramped engineering conference room at the General Motors Technical Center in Warren, Michigan. Two hundred yards away, barely visible through the storm, was Cadillac's headquarters building, which company president Jack Smith had commandeered to get himself and most of his senior staff away from the stultifying influence of GM's corporate headquarters.

"A couple more minutes," said Pete Liccardello, the short and feisty engineer whose position as model year manager for C5 made him something of a senior coordinator. Not many people in the room knew that the way he coordinated Corvette was reflected in the coordination it took to juggle home and work. Liccardello's wife suffered from an incurable, degenerative nerve disease and was rapidly becoming an invalid. He'd hired a full-time day nurse for her, but there were times when the phone rang and he had to rush home to handle a crisis. There were other times when the phone rang and the latest nurse in a long series said she was quitting. One thing never changed. The full-time night nurse was Pete Liccardello.

Liccardello's lot was not easy, though never once did he let on that there were worse problems in his life than the ups and downs of the C5 Corvette. His ebullient nature and his willingness to talk tough when the moment demanded it usually carried the day.

He stood there stroking his thick mustache until the last of the snow-delayed stragglers arrived. When he did start talking, he went straight to the budget: "We'll get to a couple of other issues in a few minutes and they'll affect all of you, but first let's talk about money."

It was a sobering moment for the thirty-plus people packed into the overheated room. In the on-and-off year of 1992, they'd managed to get by on a C5 engineering budget of barely $6 million. Much of that had gone for ongoing engineering design and analysis of the all-new Corvette backbone structure. To go much further would get into real money.

Joe Spielman understood. He was a Corvette fanatic and he wanted C5 as his showcase program. In early December, he wielded his power as vice president in charge of the newly minted Midsize Car Division and boosted C5's 1993 budget to $12 million. But even the $12 million Spielman promised wouldn't get the job done.

"At twelve million dollars," Liccardello told the team, "we have to develop a detailed budget that Russ McLean can take to Spielman and defend. We're only two working weeks from the end of the year and whatever we do has to be in place in early January."

Questions erupted from the people sitting in chairs around the walls and from the early dozen who got seats at the conference table. One of the lucky ones was Dave Hill, in one of his first appearances as chief engineer. He listened and he watched, but he didn't say a word. The others were trying to talk over each other.

"Wait 'til I'm finished," Liccardello snapped, holding up his hands. "I've got some suggestions."

First, he said, the future Corvette would take advantage of the current car, C4. The 1993 'Vette was rolling off the assembly line in Bowling Green, Kentucky. Engineers and administrative people were still working on the '94, and the '95 and '96 models were yet to come. All administrative staff would henceforth be carried on the C4 budget, including those devoted to C5. The identical move had worked in 1989 and 1990, keeping a modicum of work going on C5. It would work again by shifting at least part of the C5 load onto C4.

"That's 17.5 heads," Liccardello said, "that won't be charged against C5, about $1.4 million for 1993 alone. And we'll probably move a few more heads to the other budget, too. Regardless of where the budget sits, these people work on C5. Anybody object?"

It wasn't exactly by the book, but there wasn't a dissenting voice. When Liccardello added that all travel would henceforth be charged to C4, the grins widened. A few million diverted to getting C5 off and running—again— wouldn't be missed.

"There's one more big chunk here," Liccardello said, pointing to the spreadsheet projected on the front wall. "We've got more than one million dollars in this line item for a demonstration vehicle. We've got to find someplace else to charge it."

The demonstration vehicle, also called a mule, was a vital piece of the

C5 strategy. The backbone structure for the new Corvette still existed only on paper and in computers. The Advanced Vehicle Engineering people had decided that the structure would do everything Corvette needed and had turned their studies over to Dave McLellan. The structure was a massive framework onto which all the rest of the car would be attached and, at least on paper, might bring a host of desirable attributes to C5, affecting everything from safety to handling to passenger comfort.

But manufacturing the frame required techniques never before tried, except for little two- or three-foot pieces. The C5 side rails would be single tubular pieces, fourteen feet long and hollow, bending and bowing to spectacularly rigid specifications. Even if such pieces could be manufactured—and GM's tool and die experts thought it could be done, though no one anywhere in the world ever had—the final test was to build a car and drive it. Tool and Die was working on its end, designing a huge machine that could manufacture large numbers of side rails, and working with specialists at GM's Advanced Manufacturing Division to have a few test rails made. Once a handful of acceptable rails were available, the Corvette teams wanted to build a car around them and test it on GM's tracks at the Milford Proving Ground about forty miles to the west.

The money to build that car was the issue. Corvette's own budget couldn't do it. That didn't mean that it couldn't be done. A little fear helped. At the Chevrolet marketing division, engineers conveyed their doubts to Chevy general manager Jim Perkins. They just weren't sure that the backbone concept, with its difficult-to-build tubular side rails, would live up to expectations. But they weren't sure it wouldn't, either. What they were sure of was that Corvette needed to put a backbone car to the test and settle the doubts one way or the other. A new Corvette was just too important to Chevy's future to gamble on a theory that hadn't been proven on the track.

"We have an offer from Chevrolet to pay for the car," Liccardello announced. Surprised murmurs filled the stifling air. Only a few in the room were privy to the offer beforehand and there were difficult kinks to be worked out.

In the General Motors organization, Chevrolet and the other badges—Pontiac, Oldsmobile, Buick, and Cadillac—had long ago become marketing divisions, not designers or builders of cars. Chevrolet people attended meetings, influenced car specifications and designs, and even at certain points in the Four-Phase process, had limited go/no-go decision powers. But in the end, Chevy was a middleman, buying its cars from an organization like the Midsize Car Division and sending them out to dealers. Except at that point, there was no transfer of money.

Now Chevrolet and Corvette proposed to bypass the system.

"There will be another meeting immediately following this one to discuss exactly that," Pete Liccardello said. "I've already asked the required people to stay. The rest of you, keep this under your hats. It's not something that outsiders need to know."

To Liccardello, outsiders meant all other car programs and most of GM's top management. Midsize Car Division vice president Joe Spielman was the highest executive in the know, and that was unofficial. Officially Spielman didn't know.

Two more items were on the agenda. C5 would be one of the first programs sent through the new Vehicle Launch Center. The VLC would take up most of a building on the west side of the Tech Center. The building was connected by a tunnel to GM's Design building and there would be a steady flow of people between John Cafaro's studio and the engineers.

But the hooker was that the building, formerly part of the Advanced Vehicle Engineering organization, required extensive remodeling. Offices and hallways would be converted to giant open bays where people could work with each other more freely. Conference rooms had to be built for those endless meetings that are GM's lifeblood. So did mock-up rooms, almost mini-garages, where full-size models of cars could be pieced together from cardboard, metal, wood, and plastic.

C5's move date would be in late March or April 1993, Liccardello said. "Optimist," came a prescient voice from the back of the room.

There was more. By any standard, the C5 program was already an antique. These senior people and the engineering cadre who worked for them had been through years of stop-and-start hell. An enormous amount of work on C5 was behind them. But the Vehicle Launch Center was supposed to be a starting point for new programs. Somewhere in the GM hierarchy, the disparity was recognized; Corvette was more than four years past its real starting point. It didn't have to go back to square one and take a year to get to the first big decision point.

"We're going to do a thin Four-Phase," Liccardello said. "We'll do another Concept Initiation in June. . . ."

As one of the first programs into the Vehicle Launch Center, Corvette could also help write the rules for how it would work. That was a prospect that appealed both to program manager Russ McLean and to chief engineer Dave Hill. The men had definite ideas about how General Motors should develop cars. Their ideas didn't always mesh with corporate policy.

Part of the problem they would face was that GM had shed itself of vast numbers of senior engineers through the mid-eighties and early nineties. The downsizing was all part of Roger Smith's plan to streamline the company. In the process, GM streamlined itself out of much hard-earned experience. Its institutional history, resident in the memories of its people, was thinned from a multivolume set to a thin tract. Many lessons would have to be relearned.

"The mean experience of release engineers in the company today is five-point-four years," said Bill Todd, who would have charge of recording Corvette's VLC experience. Release engineers design parts and "release" them to the purchasing department. "But the average on any given program is only two-point-four years. Is it any wonder that there is no corporate memory, no library of engineering notebooks, no one who remembers where the alligators are waiting?"

So the C5 Corvette was on the point. Everyone in the room understood that battling the alligators was about to be an even bigger part of their job.

At last Dave Hill started to talk. It wasn't something he did often at meetings in his early months as chief engineer. Hill was still a cipher, not yet a presence, and quite unlike the dashing white-haired McLellan. He spoke quietly, with a measure of self-effacement. He was on trial in front of these people and he knew it.

"Starting on Wednesday, the weekly packaging meeting is reinstated," he said, and the expressions on faces in the room told him that everyone knew the real work was starting again.

One of the most difficult aspects of doing a new car is packaging—figuring out where every piece goes and making each fit without conflicting with its neighboring pieces. But it's not enough to fit ducts and fans and a radio and instruments and door handles and window mechanisms and miles of wire and electronic devices and mufflers and a gas tank and an engine and transmission and all the rest under Corvette's gleaming skin. The engineers also have to consider future maintenance and repairs, safety, human function and comfort, and a great deal more.

Packaging a car is not just difficult. It's a terror.

"I want to start with the most perplexing packaging issues and work our way down the list," Dave Hill told the people who were not yet his. "I want you to put me to work as your chief engineer. I'm accustomed to working in these activities, to coming up with alternatives, and to coming to a decision."

At the word *decision,* some eyes popped open. *Decision* was not a favorite in Dave McLellan's vocabulary. Maybe this new guy was actually going to be different.

"If we can't make a decision at the time," Hill continued, "we go off with a plan of action and we come back for a decision in one week."

Now the murmurs flowed again. "A *week?*"

Hill spoke softly, in a low voice, but his emphasis was strong. "This is one of the most important ways I earn my paycheck. This is what we're going to do."

He went quiet, waiting for questions. There were none. So Pete Liccardello adjourned the meeting. "Those of you I asked, stick around," he said. The rest went out into the snow, where drifts were building up against the cars and visibility was, if anything, even worse than it had been at dawn.

Now there were only fourteen left, the most important engineers and managers in all of Corvette, and they clustered around the conference table. Dave Hill was ready for them.

"It's in our best interest to get some physical manifestation of what we've been talking about," he said. "We've got to demonstrate that we are talking about a real car, not a theory. We've got to get some momentum outside of our immediate Corvette group, get our bosses and *their* bosses excited. And we've got to get some confirmation that our designs are sound."

He'd thrown down the gauntlet. Chevrolet was ready to pick it up.

"We have a generous offer from Chevrolet to donate some money to the cause," Hill said.

The offer had come through the back door a week earlier when Russ McLean took Dave Hill on a tour of the Corvette assembly plant in Bowling Green, Kentucky. That evening, the pair had dinner with Chevy's Harry Turner, who let them know that Chevrolet general manager Jim Perkins was willing to bend the rules by supplying money to build a test car.

"But if we spend it on a show vehicle, we will not have spent it wisely," Hill told his new team. "If we spend it on an engineering property, we will be doing the right thing."

He showed a transparency with his ideas for what the mule should be. But he wasn't just telling. He was asking for feedback. "This is a straw man meant to generate some discussion," Hill said.

Discussion? Feedback? The pent-up frustrations after years of chaos at General Motors, after working for a chief engineer who had little interest in discussion or feedback, caused a long moment of silence. Then a dozen voices began talking at once. Hill listened. It quickly became obvious that everyone agreed that the mule should be a convertible. If their innovative structure worked for an open car, it would work for any car. Hill began checking off additional points.

"I want to see us confirm structural integrity with a full-size vehicle," he said. "I want to know about ride and handling. I want to demonstrate traction and braking. I want feedback on the car/driver interface.

"I want a three-thousand-pound curb weight with body work cobbled from the current car and I want adequate safety equipment to let us operate the car on the GM proving ground in daylight, in open configuration, at speeds up to one hundred miles an hour."

There was more and the meeting moved on for more than an hour. Hill was clearly in charge, beginning to exercise authority as chief engineer. But he deferred to his people, too, repeatedly saying, "You're the experts. I need to be educated on these things. I need to learn from you."

They responded with growing excitement. It had been a long time coming. Now they were going to build a car.

Chevy's Bob Applegate took that chance to toss out words of caution.

"You know," he said, "we can't just write you a check. We don't want your management to find out about this. They'll just say, 'Well, we gave you a twelve-million-dollar engineering budget and now Chevy is giving you a million, so now we're only giving you eleven million.'

"We can't have that happen."

Applegate's voice got more strident as he talked. Chevrolet desperately wanted a new Corvette, he said. It was the premier car in Chevy's fleet and brought people into dealerships even if they didn't buy one. Jim Perkins liked to say that there was a little bit of Corvette in every Chevrolet. But the GM system was more likely to obstruct Corvette than help it in these critical times. Chevrolet wanted the obstacles removed. Perkins was willing to end-run the system to jump-start C5.

"Our thinking is to do the vehicle off-site," Hill said. He'd discussed this possibility with only a few of his staff. The smiles in the room broadened and there were a few nods around the table as Hill continued, "Basically, we're going to be keeping it from management's view."

The Detroit metropolitan area is full of companies, some of them in buildings not much bigger than oversize garages, that do specialty work for GM, Ford, Chrysler, and even the Japanese automakers. They build one-of-a-kind parts or even one-of-a-kind cars. Chevrolet had one of them in mind, and Hill agreed: TDM, Inc., which was tucked away on the far side of Detroit. It could build this car and keep it a secret. Even better, the small company's executives were eager to have a little piece of the new Corvette. There was magic here and they wanted in.

But first the money.

"Remember that the offer of money runs out at the end of the year," Dave Hill cautioned. "I don't want to give answers here, today, that you will consider direction. I can't direct you yet because I don't have your knowledge or even know where you are in this whole process. But still, we have decisions to make."

The most immediate decisions involved locking in the money and setting up sub-rosa channels that would allow Corvette engineers to build a mule car off-site and off-budget. Christmas Eve was just two weeks away. General Motors would be closed tight as a drum from December 23 to January 3. Some of the people in the room had vacations scheduled to start within a week.

There wasn't much time. The Corvette senior staff—not yet Dave Hill's staff, but beginning to develop a new allegiance—went out into the storm to make it happen.

25

FROM Chaos to Christmas, Corvette changed.

Corvette and Chevrolet worked it out to build the engineering car, the mule, outside of the system. Corvette engineers would design the car, and order the parts from suppliers, both inside and outside of General Motors. The parts would be delivered to TDM, Inc., where the cars would be built under direct Corvette supervision. The invoices would go directly to Chevrolet.

It was all a big secret. Keeping the car physically far from the General Motors Technical Center stifled the rumor mill. The small group with a need-to-know specifically excluded senior General Motors executives.

Two vice presidents knew this was happening. Joe Spielman, who ran the Midsize Car Division, knew, and so did Chevy general manager Jim Perkins. He and Spielman agreed, through their designated representatives, to let Corvette move ahead with building the test car while sending all invoices for parts and for TDM's services directly to Chevrolet. If nothing showed up in the Corvette accounts at Midsize, there would be nothing in the budget for senior management to question, or take away. When the money finally surfaced during a future audit, hell came home to roost at Chevrolet. But by then, the crucial test car had been built.

Officially the mule would be a Corvette Engineering Research Vehicle, called CERV-4. Research Vehicles were rare in General Motors history. Only three such cars had been built going back to 1958 and all were Corvette-ish in looks and engineering. Each of them served its purpose as a test car, then was displayed proudly at major auto shows.

But this one was different. It would never be a show car. It was deliberately designed to look like a current Corvette. It could roll down any street in the country and only the most sharp-eyed Corvette lover would notice anything amiss. It had a trunk. Corvettes hadn't had trunks since 1962. CERV-4 did. In almost every other way, it was indistinguishable from a 1993 Corvette. But under the skin, it was not like any Corvette ever built.

"You could be passed on the road and never notice that you've been time-warped by a research vehicle," Dave Hill would say later.

Hill eased into his new job, listening and watching through Corvette's interminable schedule of meetings by day, devouring armloads of documents at home by night. Even during the Christmas shutdown, he found himself waking at 3 A.M., thinking about Corvette, then going down to the kitchen to read and make notes. Except for the one meeting, he still hadn't said much at work and people began to talk. He'd made a good impression at that meeting, but now they were wondering again, not *when* he'd take over, but *if* he'd take over.

Dave Hill had no such concern. On the first Sunday in 1993, he sat at his kitchen table and glanced around at the 1940 Grosse Pointe house that he and his wife, Karen, had almost finished restoring. It was their second restoration, after a 1928 Tudor in northwest Detroit, and they would soon sell it in favor of another 1928 Tudor in Grosse Pointe that needed a lot of work. He liked old houses, liked working on them and getting his hands dirty when he came home from General Motors. So it was in that setting, in a restored 1940 kitchen that was built three years before Dave Hill was born, that he sat and organized his thoughts. Then he dialed up the General Motors voice mail system, punched in the codes for his five key assistants, and left a twenty-minute message.

Succinctly he outlined his impressions of the Corvette program. He listed problems as he saw them—the new car was growing too much in weight; the engineering organization was too fragmented; budget problems had to be faced and if they needed more money than the $150 million currently anticipated for the total multiyear program, he and Russ McLean would go to Joe Spielman to fight for the cause. Those were the key points, but there was more and Hill talked in knowledgeable detail.

"If I'm wrong on any of this, let me know," he said into the telephone. "If I've missed something you think is important, let me know that, too.

"I'm probably going to ask a lot of stupid questions in the next few months. I need you to bear with me and help me understand. The bottom line is that we're going to do the best damn Corvette anybody ever did, and we're going to do it together."

The impact of Hill's message was dramatic. It was played and replayed throughout the Corvette engineering organization on the first day of work after the holidays. It was bootlegged from engineer to engineer, some of them hearing it three or four times before 9 A.M. And it broke the logjam of pent-up work. Corvette had a chief engineer and Dave Hill had new respect from his team.

A few days later, Dave Hill spent most of a morning listening to Dale Jordan, Corvette's systems engineer, lay out his plan for putting C5 together. Jordan wanted to divide the car into six zones, assign a manager and an assistant to cover each, then give them the responsibility for packaging all the right parts into their zone. When the meeting ended, Jordan went away happy.

One by one Hill's other direct reports stopped by to talk. When he told them about the zone plan, they nodded and agreed. It was a good plan. Each discussed his role and made suggestions, and each went away feeling good. The fifth-generation Corvette was beginning to take shape.

A week later, thirteen days into 1993, a revitalized Corvette team started in earnest.

26

D AV E Hill was still trying to get a chief engineer's firm grip on the Corvette program when the gas tank question overflowed into his consciousness.

Where do you put a gas tank? What does it look like? There was a time when the answers were easy. In a car with the engine in the front, the gas tank went somewhere in back. It was made of galvanized sheet steel. It looked like a big metal pillow or a fat seat cushion. If you looked under your car, there it was, tucked up below the floor of the trunk.

Steel gave way to high-grade plastic in the eighties and nineties as engineers struggled to save weight in the cars they designed. Even so, gas tanks generally retained the pillow shape and were packaged under or just behind the trunk.

Those days were gone for Corvette.

The Corvette designs taken to the Los Angeles clinic in November had a common flaw caused by the gas tank. The engineering package, approved months earlier by Dave McLellan, located a flattened pillow of a tank behind the front seats and just under the rear cargo floor. The tank lay across the top of the central tunnel, where it would be easy to engineer for safety concerns and simple to install by assembly workers when C5 was being built. It was, in every sense, a cop-out.

Potential buyers—Corvette lovers and owners of competing cars alike— hated what it did to the car. It raised the rear cargo platform so high that a grocery bag couldn't stand up there when the hatch was closed. Golf bags would fit just fine, but two suitcases couldn't be loaded one atop the other. Anything more than maybe eight inches tall either didn't fit or blocked part of the driver's rearward vision.

For more than half of the clinic participants, it all combined to make the car a "no-sale." Even Corvette lovers wouldn't buy it.

The engineers came up with a quick fix. They flattened the tank design to free up more cargo space. But now the gas tank barely held ten gallons. C5 would have no driving range at all. It was another cop-out, and as he came on board, Dave Hill would have none of it.

There were weeks of five o'clock mornings when he crawled out of bed and his first thought in the winter dark wasn't *Coffee*, it was *Gas tank*.

By 7 A.M. he would be in a conference room at the General Motors Technical Center listening to engineers debate the great gas tank problem facing the C5 Corvette. The problem was both simple and terrible.

Packaging engineers ran into a solid wall of trouble in Dave Hill's first month as chief engineer when they wrestled with the tank design. The engineer trying to make the tank fit was Bob Stein. In the first days of 1993, he broke the bad news.

"No matter how we try to fit the tank in," Stein told Dave Hill, "it intrudes up through the floor and into the rear compartment. A twenty-gallon tank would come up so high that it would block part of the driver's vision in the rearview mirror. The only way we can keep a standard tank under the floor is to cut it down to about nine gallons."

That would give a Corvette about the same range in city driving as an electric car. Hill's reaction was predictable. One of the rules in designing C5 was "no take-aways." If something was on the current Corvette, C4, it had to be at least as good and preferably better on C5. The C4's range was almost 350 miles in city driving. Even at 70 mph on the highway, it would go more than 470 miles between fill-ups. Anyone poky enough to drive a 'Vette at the current speed limit could stretch the highway range to almost 600 miles.

"Not good," Hill mandated after listening to Bob Stein's woes. "Starting tomorrow, we meet at seven A.M. *every day* until this thing is solved."

The predawn meetings lasted until late January. There was grumbling at first. It stopped when it soaked in that Dave Hill always showed up, sometimes coming from a meeting with program manager Russ McLean even earlier. By the end of the month, Stein and his little strike team of design engineers had come up with several solutions. None of them would be easy.

They found ways to fit in three varieties of oddly shaped dual tanks, hanging them over the transaxle. Each side could hold about nine gallons of gas, with another two gallons fitting into the connecting piece between the twin tanks. It was their favorite solution, but it depended on finding a supplier who could blow-mold the tanks to precise specifications.

Another idea called for two independent gas tanks located in odd spaces under the cargo compartment. Each tank would have its own fuel pump, but there would be thin pipes so that gas from tank B pumped over to tank A, then on to the engine. It was an expensive solution with an extra pump that could eventually fail, and it required extra wiring.

Finally they showed Dave Hill drawings of a "spaceship" tank that looked like a winged vehicle out of the *Star Wars* Trilogy. It had multiple bends, angles, and protuberances to take advantage of every open space under the cargo floor. But its most striking feature was an open central hemisphere that would provide pass-through space for the transaxle. It would be a nightmare to manufacture.

Each solution brought new problems, ranging from where the filler neck would be located, to how to get gasoline into all the bends and corners, to how to stop the sloshing and slurping noises that would drive Corvette owners crazy. There also were questions of cost. Any solution was going to add more than $1 million to C5's development costs. Then there was the "piece cost." Would the tanks be so expensive to manufacture that they'd add noticeably to C5's sticker price? And other questions were even more important. Were the tanks safe? Would they survive rear-end or side-impact crashes without breaking open? Could they be assembled and installed in the car without great difficulty?

Still, Dave Hill was pleased with the ingenuity he saw. He liked the twin-tank design and thought it might be the answer. So he called off the 7 A.M. meetings and sent Bob Stein's group out to do the next level of evaluations.

While that was happening, there was plenty else for Hill to do.

27 T H E freezing rain started just before midnight. It was a sharp contrast to the blizzard a month earlier. By 7 A.M. cars left out overnight were coated with an eighth of an inch of ice, glowing like Jurassic insects under the predawn streetlights. Detroit radio station WWJ reported the temperature at 34 degrees and announcers read long lists of school closings. A mix of rain and ice continued to fall, keeping streets and freeways perilous. In every part of metro Detroit, worried people looked out windows and wrestled with the question of whether or not to try their luck.

John Cafaro looked out, too, through high second-story windows facing north to catch the best daytime light. Beyond his reflection in the glass, all he saw in the dark hour before dawn was pelting rain and the rim of lights framing a ten-acre reflecting pool. At the far end of the pool, just before the low-rise building housing the research laboratories, he knew that a few dozen geese, ignoring winter's icy message to fly south, floated near a warm-water outfall. The birds had almost lost the will to be wild. Cafaro didn't have that problem. He was pushing thirty-eight, approaching middle age, and still had a job that encouraged flirtation with the wild side.

He turned back into his studio and instantly forgot the treacherous forty-minute creep-and-crawl drive from his northwestern suburb to the General Motors Technical Center in Warren. Whatever January brought to the wintry outdoors didn't matter. Here in his Chevy 3 design studio, John Cafaro's fantasy was finally taking shape.

He looked left and right, walked to the center of the huge room, and turned full circle to soak in the sleek and secret models that surrounded him. Modeler's clay, a light pinkish tan, remained the medium of art for auto stylists. A half-dozen clay cars, crafted to three-eighths scale, sat on wheeled platforms around the studio. Each was a clown suit, half a car split front to rear, about sixty-six inches long and snugged up against a mirror to give the illusion of a complete automobile. Each was a recognizable Corvette, but each was different. Cafaro and his artists continued to experiment in their search for the perfect design.

Two more cars in the studio were full size. One was gleaming black, cast and crafted in fiberglass, the result of the long-ago interstudio competition that had briefly set designers at each other's throats as a way of achieving art. The designer of the black car was Cafaro himself. The second full-size car in Chevy 3 was sculpted from clay, brought up to size from a series of sketches by Cafaro's deputy, then modified and tweaked over the last few months.

Cafaro squatted to stare into the face of the futuristic car. Bringing a design up to full size showed it truly. The magic stood out. So did the flaws. Corvette owners and others invited to the recent marketing-research clinic harped on the flaws. C5's interior, done in another studio, flunked badly. Cafaro's exterior got fewer complaints, but enough. He was hurt, but he also knew the critics were right.

From his low angle, he looked into the double maw of a sloping front end. The wide air scoops, separated by a plate for the car's name, still carried a hint of a grin. Their corners tilted up, calling attention to the muscular curves of the fender bulges. But a smile was not what Cafaro wanted drivers to see in their rearview mirrors when this car stormed up from behind. He wanted them to see an aggressive oncoming Corvette that made them reflexively slide to the right to let it pass.

He leaned over to look down the car's low-slung side, noting the proportions of the front and rear wheels, and shook his head at an awkward curve in the rear quarter panel. Three quick steps brought him to the offending lines. He looked around for a sculptor's spatula or a sharp-pointed scribing tool, but the guys had cleaned up and put things away the night before, so he used a fingernail to scratch new lines in the clay over the left rear wheel. Cafaro knew that the studio's four journeyman modelers and their Italian-born chief would be showing up any minute, winter rain and ice be damned, and that they'd spend the morning carving and scraping away slivers of clay to give the car just a little more tightness in that curve.

"We're getting closer," he muttered.

But not close enough. The car was still too big, too bulky. One regular studio visitor had the temerity to stand behind it and compare the wide and rounded rear end to the hips and buttocks of an old farm woman who'd eaten too much butter. Cafaro had gritted his teeth, then grudgingly nodded. That kind of criticism could provoke angry words, and sometimes did. If Cafaro disagreed, or thought the critic didn't have the standing to back up his observation, he might lash out with seething sarcasm. He was more restrained, though sometimes not much, when criticism came from senior company executives, or from his own Design Staff management. But just as often, Cafaro knew that such comments contained an element of truth, and that other eyes brought fresh vision to the creative process. He'd done enough cars to understand that a new Corvette slaloming through mountain curves or gobbling up freeway would be the product of conflict as much as cooperation.

The hippy rear end on this version of C5 was part of an ongoing conflict. Engineers were still struggling with their own pieces of the car that would be packaged under the skin. The cargo space—under the hatchback glass for the targa model, but a real trunk for the convertible and fixed-roof coupe that would round out a new line of three Corvette models—had to be big enough to hold those two sets of golf clubs. The gas tank shape and position, concealed under the cargo floor, was an engineer's nightmare, but Cafaro was confident that Dave Hill could keep the tank from intruding through the floor.

But some things were beyond any control by artists or engineers. There was a federal judge out there who thought he knew more about emissions than automakers did and was about to mandate the addition of a gasoline vapor catcher—the engineers called it an evaporative emissions canister—for all new cars. Nobody had ever engineered such a thing for cars and it would not only have to be tucked away out of sight, but be protected from exploding in an accident. The alternative solution, putting vapor catchers on gas pumps in the few areas of the country such as Los Angeles and Denver where the vapor problem was real, was opposed by the oil companies and it was a battle they would win. Instead of one-time modifications on pumps at a few thousand gas stations, the judge-made engineering would have to go into each of the 15 million or so cars manufactured annually in the United States and on all the imports. Every car buyer would pay the price, no matter where he lived.

Then there was the problem that the exhaust system still wouldn't quite fit under the new Corvette's plastic skin. No matter how that one was resolved, Cafaro and his design studio would be involved. The number of tailpipes, as well as their size, shape, and placement, was both a styling issue and an engineering issue. The clay car Cafaro eyeballed had four tailpipes, two on the mid-left, two on the mid-right. The placement had nice eye appeal. It was balanced. But Cafaro could foresee the possibility that all four pipes might eventually be clustered in the middle. Even worse, the four-pipe arrangement could be cut to two if things got so crowded that four pipes couldn't be packaged. Cafaro squatted to look straight into the exhaust pipes. "Four's nicer," he said. Eventually the engineering team made it work and Cafaro got his tailpipes two by two.

Another controversy was less easily settled. Cafaro fought against the adamant insistence by Chevy's Jim Perkins that this car have a spare tire.

"We don't need a spare tire," Cafaro grumbled as he stood up and walked around the clay car one more time.

Technology had bypassed spare tires. For buyers who wanted them, there were optional tires on the current Corvette called run-flats, or, in General Motors techno-speak, EMTs, for extended mobility tires. Goodyear made them and even without air they could be safely driven at 55 mph for 100 miles or more. They were more expensive and required electronic sensors that alerted the driver to tire trouble.

A Corvette with run-flats didn't need a heavy spare, a jack, or a tire iron. That saved weight in an era when pounds equated to miles per gallon and it freed storage space in a car that had almost none. Many Corvette buyers opted for run-flats already. They didn't think about fuel economy or luggage. They thought about hefting one of the car's bulky flat tires into the rear and ruining a nice coat or shirt in the process.

So Cafaro argued for run-flats as standard equipment, not an option, on C5. So did the engineers under Dave McLellan and then Dave Hill. But Jim Perkins, prodded by his marketing staff, wasn't convinced that Corvette buyers would be comfortable without a spare tire. So the current C5 design included space for one, and for a jack and tire iron. It chewed up a lot of space and weight.

Cafaro's argument had nothing to do with any of that. It had to do with looks. What the car *really* needed, Cafaro thought, was bigger tires all around. He'd begun a quiet lobbying effort with the engineering side to add an inch to the front and rear wheels. With eighteen-inchers on the front and nineteen-inch wheels on the back, the proportions of this car would approach perfection. The current specifications supplied by the engineers called for seventeens in front and eighteens in back. And they were resisting anything bigger because of their own considerations on weight and fuel economy. Cafaro had hopes of winning them over. But if packaging a huge spare tire stayed mandatory, it would doom any hope Cafaro had for bigger tires. *There'll be battles on that issue before this car is done,* Cafaro thought.

He walked back to his large design board under the windows. His glance caught the no-top interior buck, a full-size Corvette interior formed of clay, wood, metal, and plastic that sat in a corner of the studio. Interiors were the responsibility of another studio, but after the negative returns from the research clinic two months earlier, the work had been moved into Cafaro's domain. The theory was that cooperation between the studios would be easier with exterior and interior designers working side by side. Cafaro didn't like the theory and was pushing to have the entire Corvette interior studio swap places with the Chevy 2 studio next door. Then each studio chief could have his realm, with only a door in a movable wall separating them. It didn't take long for Cafaro to get his way.

The icy rain still fell, but daylight had come while John Cafaro thought about his new car. Doing a Corvette from scratch was the dream of his career and the assignment was finally his alone. This one would make or break Cafaro's reputation. He'd be forty-two years old when C5 hit the streets. It was still four years off and he could hardly wait. Turning forty meant nothing to John Cafaro, not when it was just a waypoint to C5.

"We're getting there," he muttered, taking up a pencil and sketching new lines, modified lines, for C5's broad butt end. "It's really starting to take shape."

That phrase *take shape* meant different things to artists and to engineers.

While John Cafaro sketched on that rainy and bitter mid-January morning, Corvette engineers gathered on the other side of the Tech Center for the first big packaging meeting in the new, fully revived C5 Corvette program. Dave Hill was five minutes late, coming over from a meeting with the gas tank team. Dale Jordan waited for him before laying out his zone plan, virtually as he had shown it to Hill. As usual, the chief engineer listened without comment.

"This is a new concept for management of a car," the impish Jordan said. "The zone managers will be responsible for engineering solutions to packaging issues, for generating alternative solutions, for communications, and for reporting out biweekly at this meeting."

In two sentences, he had established the engineering framework that would carry C5 from paper to product.

"The zones are the front compartment—that's where the engine is, for those of you who never lift the hood—the occupant compartment, the rear compartment where you put your luggage, the body, the chassis, and the front of dash. That one is the transition zone between the engine and interior. Lots of stuff gets hung on there."

The Wednesday packaging meetings would become one of the most substantial Corvette events of each week. By March, the 8 A.M. to noon meeting wasn't long enough to handle the conflicts, the trade-off discussions, and the reports necessary to fit everything under Corvette's skin. Nobody complained when the starting time was moved back to 7 A.M., nor when meetings ran through lunch. On some Wednesdays, the packaging meeting ended only because some other meeting had the conference room scheduled at 1 P.M.

Toward the end of the organizational meeting, Dave Hill finally spoke up. Two days earlier, he'd given the chassis people a message. Now he repeated it for everybody. "Contrary to past events, the new Corvette is not going to stop this time," he said as people strained to hear his words. "So we need to recognize that having the right people on board and getting things in order is crucial."

Then he got into details. He'd just listened for more than two hours to the zone organization plan and to a long report from Design Staff market researchers. Speaking without once referring to notes, Hill made his presence as chief engineer felt. His first remarks took aim at the A-pillars, the left and right posts on a car that frame the windshield and help hold the roof. Design clinic participants didn't like them; they were too fat and obtrusive.

"The current Corvette has elegant, thin pillars," he said, looking at the Design Staff researchers and at Ron Nowicki, the lead engineer in Cafaro's studio. "The clinic car had clumsy pillars. The goal here *has to be to improve on the current car,* so if we have to go to rolled steel instead of aluminum to get thin pillars, even if it adds mass, that's okay." He shifted his gaze to Dave Dolby, the body manager who reported to Hill himself. "This is both an engineering problem and a styling problem, so we have to work together. Until this A-pillar problem is solved, it's number one on the agenda for this meeting."

Hill's tone was matter-of-fact but determined. It was the first time he'd spoken so bluntly, at least in a group, about the engineering designs he'd inherited from Dave McLellan. Looks of surprise flashed around the room, replaced quickly by small smiles and nods of approval. For the first time in years, they had a boss talking about details. "Now that's a chief engineer!" whispered C5 model year manager Pete Liccardello. Hill didn't seem to notice the stir he was causing.

"The next thing," he said, "is I want to see some greater attention to detail on how C5 looks. I use the word 'elegant' again. Specifically, I want you body engineers to design rabbets at skin joints."

Dave Dolby grinned and nodded, but a few people looked puzzled until Hill took a marker and drew an L-shaped flange, a rabbet, on an overhead transparency. The bend in the shape filled in the gap where two body parts came together. "I want rabbets at skin joints and cut lines," he repeated, "so you look down at a body-colored gap instead of a black hole. This is the kind of thing that gives a car an elegant finish. It shows attention to detail. I want it at hood gaps, at door-to-fender gaps, at any gap you can look into.

"If we think about this now, chances are we will see it in the car. If we don't do it now, we probably will never go back and do it. This is the kind of detail that separates good cars from really excellent cars. I want our Corvette to be an excellent car." He stressed *our.*

"Hear, hear!" The approving words came from several corners at once.

Hill quickly sketched a Corvette door on the overhead transparency, adding the rabbet flange. "We need to chase these rabbets all over the car," he joked, getting his first laugh as chief engineer. "I'm now on record on this issue."

A few engineers clapped tentatively. As the meeting broke up, the room buzzed with side conversations. Dave Hill packed up his file folders, tucked them under his arm, and walked out. He left the first solid evidence of a new Corvette team behind him.

2 8

DAVE Hill knew how to make decisions. One of the toughest he made as a boy was whether to follow the mean road toward a music career or to see what college had to offer. He was the oldest of three brothers, but not a serious student like middle brother Robert, and though he knew he was adequate on the trumpet, trombone, and baritone, he didn't have youngest brother John's true musical talents. What he did have was an interest in cars, picked up working in gas stations and garages around Niagara, New York. So he enrolled in a technical school in Buffalo, got a lab technician job at Union Carbide, and found a life.

The Arts Associate degree and the job together convinced Hill that he could compete. He looked around for what he called "a real college" and settled on Michigan Tech in Houghton. He didn't know where Houghton was, but the school looked good. When he discovered that the town was nestled in a Lake Superior bay on the far northwest corner of Michigan's Upper Peninsula, where winter days were short and frigid winds howled in off the frozen lake, he went anyway. "I thought there would at least be girls," he remembered. There weren't; Michigan Tech's student body was predominantly male.

That left studying and playing gigs in the U.P. to help pay for school. Early classes started before winter dawn. January dark settled on the town before 5 P.M. Hill concentrated on school, got a summer internship at GM's Harrison Division in Lockport, New York, as a production engineer, and when he graduated in 1965 took an offer to join Cadillac. He was there more than twenty-seven years, finishing up as chief engineer on the two-seater Cadillac Allante, then doing the DeVille luxury sedan introduced in 1993. When Corvette beckoned, the DeVille was all but done. It was time for something new.

At Cadillac, Hill was known as a working engineer who demanded results. Corvette engineers learned that early.

Homework made the difference. A young engineer assigned to Corvette walked out of a meeting shaking his head. "Dave Hill's knowledge of Corvette is encyclopedic," he said.

It got that way quickly. After taking the job as the car's new chief engineer, Hill spent a week in a windowless room at Chevrolet headquarters soaking up Corvette lore, statistics, marketing schemes, and future plans. Chevy's Fred Gallasch and Bob Applegate loaded him with documents and reports, and spent hours regaling him with Corvette stories.

When he was finished reading piles of marketing research reports, minutes of meetings that helped define the C5 Corvette, and wish lists submitted by dealers, GM middle management, and working engineers, he asked for more. He invited key Corvette engineers over to air their wants and complaints, and to give their analyses of what was right and what was wrong with the program.

"Chief engineers have to be focused on getting the job done," Joe Spielman said. "That's Dave Hill. He's not a cover boy. He's not effervescent. He's just going to drive the team and get the job done."

Hill put reciprocal faith in the key executives championing the new Corvette. He left a strong career at Cadillac behind and didn't want his new career to brand him as a loser. As events would unfold, it didn't.

"I have to trust the momentum that Jim Perkins of Chevrolet and Joe Spielman of Midsize have going," Hill told intimates. "The company can't delay Corvette anymore. They've killed off every other interesting car in GM. It was easy to kill the Fiero, then the Reatta, and finally the Allante because there was always something left. But now we're down to one. If GM killed Corvette, that would be it. So we can't do that."

But he brought a dose of realism from Cadillac that left him with genuine fear that Corvette might yet be a target for extinction. "There has always been resentment in the company for Corvette," he confided. "Corvette has been special and aloof. It's a public figure." Those were feelings he had felt himself when Corvette hogged the limelight and his cherished Cadillacs didn't get the attention he thought was their due.

Now the shoe was on the other foot and Hill supported the overt emotionalism that Joe Spielman had for the car. "The next Corvette is my car," Spielman said in meeting after meeting. And he backed it up with stories about the eighteen or nineteen Corvettes he'd already owned.

"You gotta get the fever," he said in one pep talk to Hill and his key engineers. "You can't get it in business terms. You can't get it on a balance sheet. You have to feel it in your gut. Last weekend I backed my '73 out of the garage, washed and waxed it, put the top down, and then drove it around for a few minutes. It just made me feel good."

Corvette fever was part of being there and it didn't take Dave Hill long to catch it. He'd been chief engineer for less than three months when he experienced an epiphany on the dark drive from Warren to Grosse Pointe. "I went home with a feeling that, by golly, I do belong here and I'll do okay," he said. "I can make a contribution."

Spielman and program manager Russ McLean conferred often in the early months when Corvette was getting back on track. On the day that McLean said he was giving Hill full control of C5, Spielman agreed readily. That left McLean free to concentrate on improving C4 and preparing the looming presentation to the North American Operations Strategy Board.

"Just remember," Spielman said, "you're not doing that presentation for a bunch of engineers. I want you to give them a factual presentation, no bullshit, no smoke and mirrors. Don't tell them anything we can't deliver. I want them to know that what Corvette says, they can take to the bank."

Dave Hill left those worries to Spielman and McLean. "I hope I'm not misplaced here," he said. "A better politician would worry about looking good for the board, but I'm more concerned that the car looks good, engineering and styling."

Spielman heard of those comments and relaxed, but only a little. By 1997, the current Corvette would be an old, old car.

"If any of my cars fail," Spielman said, "it's my people who fail, my people who get laid off, my people who can't support their families and send their kids to school.

"The new Corvette's gotta be the right car," Spielman said. "We can't wait thirteen years for a new one and then do it wrong."

29 THE day after Dave Hill laid down the law about the A-pillars, the engineering team got into its cars and drove to the other side of the General Motors Technical Center. They had to pass through the car tunnel and coming out the other side was still like changing worlds. It was still the ducks coming to visit the swans.

But it wasn't as different as it used to be. The changes had started in the Corvette studio, with John Cafaro and Cardy Davis talking to each other as equals instead of adversaries. The changes would reach fruition in the Corvette studio, with Cafaro and Dave Hill and Russ McLean completing a real car. The changes might have happened sooner, except that the previous Corvette chief engineer, Dave McLellan, had been all but banned from entering the building called Design. When Chuck Jordan ran Design, he and McLellan were not friends. Jordan couldn't forbid McLellan from visiting, but he wanted to. For his part, McLellan had stayed away from the studio except when absolutely necessary.

Now in early 1993, there were new attitudes at Design. With Wayne Cherry in command, Cafaro didn't have to subvert the system to be reasonable and cooperative with the Corvette engineers. He could do it openly and with Cherry's blessing.

The issue that day was redesigning the A-pillars for the new Corvette. In the Chevy 3 studio on the second floor, they gathered around the full-size clay model of C5. "We're going to do another clinic," Cafaro announced, "to get ready for Concept Initiation." The clinic was tentatively scheduled for late April in Los Angeles and the results would be critical if C5 was to pass the Concept Initiation gate the third time.

Concept Initiation was scheduled for mid-June. It was still the all-important meeting when a program looked for a green light from GM's most senior executives. Under the new rules of the day, those executives would now be GM president Jack Smith and his North American Operations Strategy Board. If the clinic results weren't good, it was a dead certainty that those harried men would turn thumbs down on the next Corvette.

"We want a car that is more customer-acceptable," Cafaro said, "particularly in the cargo area. We'll have the clinic results evaluated by mid-May, then we'll have a general management review of the car here at Design Staff."

The cars they'd taken to the November clinic flunked badly. Almost three hundred people had looked at high-quality photos of four possible Corvettes and only Cafaro's car got partial approval. "Most preferred . . . but not distinctive enough or exciting," the clinic report said.

John Cafaro was there and he had listened. Two features were especially liked on his design. The roof was a compound curve with a longitudinal dip running fore to aft. It gave the roof a subtle double-bubble look, something like side-by-side jet fighter cockpits. People smiled when they saw it. Then the dip carried through into the rear hatch glass, called the back light. The glass itself would be subtly indented so it, too, was a double bubble. That brought more smiles.

Another feature got mixed reviews. Cafaro and his artists had put the double-bubble feature into the top of the rear fascia, the vertical panel at the car's backside, so that Corvette's traditional four taillights were accented below strong bulges in the plastic surface. The studio people and most of the engineers liked the feature a lot. Cafaro's mentor and second-in-command of Design Staff, Jerry Palmer, did not. For the time being, the feature stayed.

The interior design bombed and many of the criticized features were already being fixed. More than half of those at the clinic preferred digital instruments, at least for the speedometer. They wouldn't get them, but the designers and engineers were trying to address everything else, including complaints about the gear shifter, the steering column position, and uncomfortable seats.

Market research is a General Motors strong point. The company had researched feelings about a new Corvette to extraordinary lengths, both through surveys and clinics. The surveys, mostly done in the late eighties, with a tune-up in late 1992, turned into that document called the Voice of the Customer, the VOC, or just the Voice. Now Dave Hill threw a dash of reality into the stand-up meeting in the studio.

"It's important to make the next clinic property meet the Voice," he said. "But it's just as important to make the car real."

A clay model that everybody loved wasn't much good if the engineers and manufacturing people couldn't figure out how to build it. That had happened before in General Motors, and at every other car company in the world. The collision between fantasy and reality was called a "no-build." Those were words no one wanted to hear.

"That pillar is a major item," Hill continued. "We want it committed by the clinic. It has to be redesigned for both beauty and strength."

"But we're not going to the clinic with something we can't deliver," Russ

McLean said. "You and I both want a great-looking car, John. But we have to be real."

Cafaro nodded. He knew that tough days were ahead. Changing the A-pillars meant that additional changes would ripple into the roof and the windshield, into the doors and door glass, into the fenders, into the hood. The A-pillars touched everything around them. The changes would not be just a matter of carving clay to sculpt new shapes. The engineers and stylists would have to work side by side to find shapes that were beautiful, strong, safe, and ultimately, able to be manufactured.

They had only a little more than three months to make it happen. In mid-January, it seemed like just enough time. It wasn't.

Cafaro ran his hand along the clay A-pillar on the driver's side. Earlier in the month, he'd spent many hours at Cobo Hall in the Detroit International Auto Show, one of the largest in the world. "We have to do it and we can't wait," he said. "When you go down to the auto show, you see that the company is falling further and further behind. But this is a new car and we don't share it with anybody inside GM. So we have to do it right. No excuses."

Then he looked around. His studio people were lined up at the rear of the clay model. Russ McLean, Dave Hill, and the engineers were by the steeply sloped hood. Cafaro stood between them.

"Looks like the OK Corral here," he said quietly. "We almost have a fence between us. What do you say, let's stop it."

Russ McLean stuck out his hand. There, by a clay Corvette, they shook on it.

30

J O E Spielman, the vice president in charge of the Midsize Car Division, made sure everyone knew that the 1997 Corvette program was on track. He dropped in unannounced to meetings, usually tieless after he declared "business casual" as the dress mode for his division, sometimes in the red golf shirt given to him by Corvette program manager Russ McLean. The shirt had a Corvette logo embroidered on the right breast, surrounded by the words "Bury Me in a Corvette."

"I'm serious," he said often, "I want to be buried in one of my Corvettes." He was only forty-eight, so the prospect didn't loom large. He currently owned two Corvettes and was looking for a '60 convertible identical to his first 'Vette "so I can return to my Walter Mitty past." Even so, he was greatly disappointed a year later in 1994 when a fellow in Pennsylvania beat him to the Corvette burial idea. After a long fight with the Brush Creek Cemetery in Hempfield Township, George Swanson's widow Caroline buried George in his 1984 white Corvette. George loved that car. "I wish I'd known him," Spielman said wistfully. "He sounds like my kind of guy."

Chevrolet wanted a new Corvette badly, too. It was quietly funneling money into the program while doing everything it could to keep C5 alive. In earlier and happier times, 1993 was to have been the year C5 hit the road. Instead the 1993 Corvette looked to the civilian eye pretty much like the 1984 Corvette, except for the ruby red paint job and flashy insignia on special "40th Anniversary" cars. The major differences were under the skin, including engine improvements, better suspension, and the beginnings of solutions to the nagging problems of squeaks, rattles, and water leaks.

Immediately the issue of dividing up the meager Corvette team arose. They still had to produce a '94, '95, and '96, and McLean demanded that each year be better than the last. Simultaneously they had to develop an all-new 1997. It was a challenge more awesome than anyone foresaw.

The C5 would be the most complex new car ever attempted by General Motors. It had a new structure and new chassis. A new engine was being developed, a small-block aluminum V-8 called the Gen III that would deliver more than 340 horsepower. It had a new body and a new interior. It had new computers and new software to make it all work. It would have new tires. Once all the new parts were done, many of C5's manufacturing and assembly techniques would be new, too. Some were radical. It had to be that way because C5's goals included sharply cutting the number of parts from C4 and making it easier to assemble, in fewer man-hours, and at less cost.

There wasn't much in C5 that wasn't new. Fasteners like screws and rivets might be common. Maybe too the guts of some electrical switches, and a few things borrowed from the vast General Motors supply bin, like door handles or mirrors. But the truth facing chief engineer Dave Hill and program manager Russ McLean was that General Motors had never attempted to revamp a car with so much "new" all at one time.

McLean and Hill began dividing up Corvette engineers. Some would work only on C4 in its last years, meeting demands for improved quality and performance. John Heinricy, a Corvette veteran both as a program engineer and as a famed Corvette race driver, got the job of running C4. Dave Hill would look over Heinricy's shoulder now and then but concentrate on C5. A handful of other senior engineers would monitor C4 while focusing on C5. And at the next level down, engineers would be assigned to one car or the other, but not both.

Other changes would come in the next months. Dale Jordan left the program to take a job in management of the Vehicle Launch Center. And an engineering management system that would leave everyone bewildered was soon to be inaugurated at the Midsize Car Division. Corvette endured it all.

All around, General Motors continued to battle red ink. But there were signs that the corporation still had life. Jack Smith as president was an invisible man, but his policies and his commands were being felt. Unlike Roger Smith, who was seen everywhere, or Bob Stempel, who was seen in the halls frequently until he withdrew at the end of his GM career, Jack Smith led by being decisive and firm while seldom being seen at all. He could have walked down almost any corridor at the General Motors Technical Center without being recognized. Years later he was still so anonymous that he was denied entrance to the Detroit International Auto Show when he forgot his badge, because the security guards didn't recognize him and wouldn't take the word of his badge-carrying subordinates. (He finally got in by borrowing an auto show badge from one of them.) John Smale, the chairman of the board, was an even more ghostly presence. No one in Corvette could remember laying eyes on him, but no one doubted his influence. Smith and Smale were having their impact on GM. In two of the last three months of 1992, North American Operations actually made money. The full year would be a disaster, partly because GM was about to write off more than *$20 billion* in future health care and retirement obligations. That was a bookkeeping loss. Overall, GM would report a 1992 loss of $24.2 billion, and $4 billion of that was real money.

Joe Spielman took advantage of the little bit of good news about North American Operations to firm up Corvette's future. Despite low-level rumors inside the company about Corvette's demise and an occasional press story that stirred the pot by predicting that GM would abandon the car as a cost-saving measure, there was going to be a new Corvette. It was never in doubt. The company couldn't kill a crown jewel, a true cult car, like Corvette. But it did back itself into a corner on the subject.

When it slipped the new Corvette from 1993 all the way to 1997, GM ran headlong into new federal side-impact standards. There is little in automobiles that isn't regulated, from dimensions for this part to the curve radius of that part. The amount of light that passes through glass is regulated. So are the specifications for air-conditioning, brake, and transmission fluids, and for thousands of other components and operations in a car. Those rules fill volumes and many of them are logical. Design engineers follow the government's myriad of rules scrupulously. The biggest complaint they have is that the rules inhibit creativity and innovation. Too often, innovations get into cars only when the lawyers or lobbyists are able to get the rules changed, sometimes having to go state to state as well as lobbying at the federal level. Convincing a few holdout states to drop the requirement that all cars carry spare tires finally opened the way for Corvette to offer high-technology run-flat tires as an option.

Some rules are at odds with each other. Rules that added items to cars made them heavier. Heavier cars burn more gas, on average losing one-third mile per gallon for every 125 pounds of added weight. But other rules mandate that cars get better and better gas mileage. The first way to improve mileage is to reduce weight. The government's position on these opposing rules is simple: Don't argue, just do it.

Most rules go through a process that has an inevitable conclusion. They are proposed, almost always by the National Highway Traffic Safety Administration, or NHTSA (pronounced "nitsa"). Comments are sought from the general public, if the general public reads the *Federal Register* or sees a news story, and from the industry and consumer groups. After the comments are digested, the rule is adopted, most often with relatively minor changes. But sometimes new rules being proposed are so inane or idiotic that they actually die. One of those was proposed in 1992.

It involved the amount of light that could lawfully pass through car windows. The National Highway Traffic Safety Administration proposed a rule requiring *more* light to pass through than was currently allowed. The rule was requested by industry groups that tint car windows and that may have thought that people would buy more tinting to reduce the light back to tolerable levels, and by Florida cops who thought they ought to be able to see into cars more clearly to determine if the driver or passenger were packing heat.

Heat was indeed the question. After Corvette engineers spent months analyzing the proposed rule in terms of what it would do to their car, they were horrified. More light passing into the car translated into more heat building up in the Corvette's interior. The word "oven" was used in some meetings. There was so much heat that under worst-case conditions, say a parked Corvette on a Phoenix street at high noon in July, the heat would begin to melt the covering on the instrument panel. That could be corrected by changing material. Materials resistant to the excess heat would cost more and weigh more, but it could be done.

Then they discovered that the extra heat meant that Corvette would need a larger compressor for its air conditioner. With a larger compressor, it would need a larger radiator. And a larger, more powerful alternator. All of that added weight to the car, so its fuel economy would deteriorate. Some of the standard glass used in cars, not just Corvette, wouldn't meet the proposed light transmission standard, so glass manufacturers would have to abandon products they'd made for decades and go through the costly process of converting to new glass that let more light pass. Between the new glass, the new material for the dash, and the new and bigger components under the hood, the price of a Corvette might go up by $1,000 or more. And even then, the driver and passenger would never be as cool and comfortable as they were on the day the rule was proposed.

A fellow at NHTSA who didn't have much else to do, and who realized that the existing rule had been around unchanged since 1955 and therefore ought to be changed "just because," was pushing the flaky idea. The change had no impact on safety, he admitted to an inquiring reporter, but what the heck. More than a year after he floated the rule proposal, and after Corvette, other GM car and truck platforms, and presumably engineers at every other auto company had spent thousands of hours and certainly millions of combined dollars analyzing it, a Corvette insider mentioned the rule to a writer for *AutoWeek* magazine. Soon a story appeared exposing the bureaucratic nonsense. And soon after that, the rule proposal was withdrawn. It was a small victory for common sense, and a small handful of Corvette engineers who had wasted much time and spent thousands of dollars on analysis went back to working on more important things.

All of NHTSA's rules are arbitrary, but not many are so ill-conceived.

Of them all, no regulations are more rigidly followed by automotive engineers than the regulations affecting safety. In the early nineties, NHTSA announced a new, more stringent rule governing broadside crash protection, to take effect in 1997. The rule was arbitrary and had downsides. But because it was safety related, it became bureaucrat-mandated law. No one in the auto industry dares to argue too much against a safety rule.

There were no simple solutions to the side-impact rule. New barrier rails inside doors would add weight, or new structure around the doors would add weight, or new crush zones to protect drivers and passengers would add weight and reduce fuel economy. Doors would become thicker, taking away shoulder and arm room from drivers and passengers. Door storage compartments would shrink or disappear, just as glove boxes did when the passenger-side air bag was mandated. People with disabilities would have a harder time opening and closing the heavier doors. The cost of designing and engineering the changes, along with the cost of the additional materials needed, plus a margin for profit, would be passed along to car buyers. By 1996, the average cost of a new car in the United States topped $20,000, a good deal of the sticker price being for government-mandated this-or-thats, and that was before the side-impact standards took effect. A 1996 University of Michigan study forecast another 25 percent increase in sticker prices by 2004, *just for the government rules still known to be coming.* (Other inflationary factors would drive the price even higher.) The study didn't say where the average family would find a small fortune to buy an average car.

Almost no car on the road in 1992 could meet the 1997 side-impact standards. The C4 Corvette certainly couldn't. Neither could the Ford Taurus, the Honda Accord, nor any of them. Every car builder faced one of two certainties: They had to find a way of modifying their current cars to meet the new standards, or they had to design all-new cars.

For Corvette, the cost of reengineering and testing a C4 to meet the 1997 rule would exceed $80 million.

"That leaves us with three choices," Joe Spielman said when he dropped in on a Corvette meeting and gave a pep talk. "We can spend the money on the current car, we can just close the plant and have no Corvettes to sell anymore, or we push ahead with the new car. The first two choices are big losers. The new Corvette makes a profit.

"We're doing the car as a '97. Period." Nobody in the room doubted him. Nor did they doubt that it would meet every rule in NHTSA's massive library.

To make his point, Spielman promised to move the program's budget back up to $250 million, about where it was when the C5 program was young and fresh in 1989, and $80 million more than the upper limit ordered by top management during the days of Chaos. And he wasn't done.

"If we need more money than we have now, I know where to get it," he said. "And I will. We've learned a helluva lot in the last four years. We can do a car, a better car, for a lot less money. I won't let this car out the door if it isn't world-class. And *my* boss won't let it out the door if it goes over budget. But I can raise the budget if it comes to that. So that's the envelope, and we sure as shit can do it!"

The engineers in the room burst into applause.

It was vintage Spielman, profane, charismatic, to the point. He knew how to inspire people. Inspiration was something he learned at home, where his father owned and edited the Trimont (Minnesota) *Progress.* Young Joe listened to his dad rail on about politics and watched him get out the vote for Minnesota's Democrat Farmer/Labor (DFL) party. The old man was good at it. He served on the DFL state committee and was an early supporter of a young politician named Walter Mondale. When Joe graduated from high school, Hubert Humphrey dropped by the house with a card, a crisp bill, and a pep talk.

Inspirational people surrounded Joe Spielman during his formative years. He soaked it up. But he had the full measure of a kid's rebellious nature and he loved a challenge. He became a Republican. "It's too easy to be a liberal in Minnesota," he explained. Spielman didn't like things that were too easy.

He also went off to the college that is GM's crucible, General Motors Institute in Flint, Michigan. One kid from Trimont had gone there ten years earlier and GMI continued to send catalogs to Trimont High. Then Joe's older brother went to GMI, along with another boy from town. Finally Joe Spielman applied and was accepted. Trimont, Minnesota, population 1,500, soon had the highest per capita population of GMI graduates in the country.

At GMI, he picked a rough road, majoring in mechanical engineering with a minor in electrical engineering. GMI students called it ME/Suicide. Spielman survived. Part of it was the way he buckled down to his studies. Part of it was his personality. Joe Spielman knew people.

Because he did, he came to know snakes. There was a large rattlesnake encased in plastic on his desk after he became a General Motors vice president. It got there the hard way.

Joe Spielman rolled up to General Motors' Arlington, Texas, assembly plant one day in the early nineties for a 7 A.M. meeting. He'd spent a few years in the plant earlier as an up-and-coming manager and now it was time for him to put up or shut up.

The entrance to the plant's administration building was blocked by a crowd of workers, mostly union guys off the line. One of them was J. R. Martin, a gangly union man stripped bare to the waist. Spielman himself stands a strapping six-five. He took one look and knew what was coming.

"Hey, Joe," J.R. said. "You promised for years. Now you're a hotshot VP and you don't go into the plant until you learn a couple of lessons."

Spielman grinned good-naturedly, stripped off his jacket and tie, and rolled up his sleeves. "Okay," he said. "Let's go!"

The pair walked over to a pickup truck topped with a camper shell. The bed was filled with cages of snakes. Some of them were loose. They represented J. R. Martin's other job—snake hunter. He'd ragged Spielman for years to join on a hunt for Texas rattlesnakes. Spielman's constant answer: "Sure, but not this time. Ask me again."

On that hot spring day, *again* became *now*.

For the next forty minutes, while people waited inside for the vice president from Detroit to join their meeting, Spielman learned about snakes. He pinned down four-foot rattlers with a prong and picked them up. He milked venom. He dodged striking snakes. He snagged them bare-handed from cages.

The mostly union crowd loved it. When the lessons ended, one of the assembly-line guys handed him that snake-in-plastic. Spielman displayed it with unabashed pride.

"They say there's a difference between a manager and a leader," one Corvette subordinate said off-handedly in a later coffee machine conversation. "Well, Joe's the guy they were talking about. If he's leading, I'll follow him up the hill.

"Even the wrong hill."

A lot of executives have open-door policies, knowing that few on their staffs will come in without an appointment. Joe Spielman's office door never closed and people actually did drop in to chat, discuss problems, complain about things that mattered to them.

"I might not be able to solve every problem," Spielman told them. "But I'll always listen. And if you think I'm wrong, you'd better tell me now. Any sonuvabitch who comes back later and says he knew I was wrong, but kept his mouth shut, is in deep trouble."

Spielman could be a charismatic leader. But he'd already made the worst mistake of his career. He charged up the wrong hill when he selected a new engineering director and nobody told him, at least not loud enough to make it stick. When the choice came back to haunt him, and to haunt every car program in the Midsize Car Division, it came back in spades.

31

ANGRY words spilled into the hall. Corvette program manager Russ McLean and chief engineer Dave Hill accosted Jerry Palmer, design director and second-in-command of the General Motors Design Staff, at the door to his office.

McLean and Hill were livid. They'd made the trek one more time from the east side of the Technical Center to the west, for a regular Thursday morning meeting, the time and day changed from Wednesdays after considerable juggling to accommodate everyone's calendar.

Most important, the place—one of Design Staff's own conference rooms—was chosen to make it easy for Jerry Palmer and his boss, Design vice president Wayne Cherry, to attend. The room was a thirty-second walk for Palmer. Cherry needed ten seconds more.

John Cafaro usually showed up. But since the weekly meetings restarted four months earlier, Cherry showed up just once. Palmer didn't show up at all.

On this day, neither did Cafaro. In the fun of designing a *real* C5, he'd forgotten. Russ McLean was steamed as he looked around the conference room. It was Design's room, in Design's building, on Design's side of the railroad tracks. But the only Design Staff representative in the room was a junior administrative aide with no decision-making power.

McLean and Hill were there to get decisions. It was the end of January 1993. In the General Motors Four-Phase process of developing cars, even the mini-Four-Phase that would apply to Corvette, two major gates were looming. One was another Concept Initiation, the third for C5, when the team would present its plans, *and its preliminary styling designs,* to the Strategy Board. McLean didn't want to take any risks. There was always the chance, however slim, that the Strategy Board would turn thumbs down when Corvette came knocking again on June 14.

The second gate was scheduled for August 10. It was called Concept Alternatives Selection, or CAS, and was a grueling event that would run for several days. A board of experts from the Midsize Car Division, Chevrolet, Design Staff, and Corvette itself would review options for every major part of the new Corvette—from the instrument panel to the battery to the entertainment center to shock absorbers, tires, and everything else of any importance—and pick one for further development and inclusion in the car. They'd also look at two or three or four exteriors, each closely following the theme presented at CI, but each different in some way. Those exteriors were John Cafaro's responsibility. The CAS review board would pick one and it would be carried through to become the new Corvette.

Concept Alternatives Selection was a big deal. In the normal course of events, programs would have four or five months after CI to get ready for CAS. Corvette would have fifty-seven days and of those, the entire company would be shut down in July for seventeen.

For both Concept Initiation and Concept Alternatives Selection, good designs from the Corvette studio were mandatory. McLean and Hill wanted assurances from the top people at Design Staff that somebody in the building other than John Cafaro actually cared.

Hill had three discussion points and while they waited for somebody in power to show up, he tossed them on the table.

"The car in the studio looks like a pumpkin seed," he said. "It grew four inches wider and two and a half inches longer in January alone."

The Design Staff aide checked his notes. "That was to meet the engineering criteria," he said. "Cafaro's working on trimming it back."

Hill accepted the small reprimand. His own engineering staff furnished the criteria. Cafaro was just trying to find a skin that contained it all.

"The aerodynamics are a big concern," Hill went on. The C5 Corvette needed a miraculously low coefficient of drag—the measure of how much it was affected by air flow. The goal in the vehicle technical specifications was a c/D of 0.29. The lower the number, the less the air resistance. That was better for the car in terms of fuel economy, and it improved its top speed. "They've already tested six models in the wind tunnel and only one had a low enough c/D to be within striking distance."

That model came out of the tunnel at 0.319. Not good enough. The others all exceeded 0.34. More tunnel runs were scheduled in the following week. They'd each cost $25,000, charged internally against Hill's engineering budget.

"They're going in with a model that isn't within striking distance," Hill complained. "If I'm paying, I have to be involved in making those decisions."

The only Design Staff representative in the room nodded and took a few notes. This was a question he had no power to resolve.

Finally Hill brought up the second of three Corvette models that would be part of the C5 package. The targa coupe with its removable roof panel and hatchback body style would come out in 1997. A convertible and a lightweight, entry-level fixed-roof coupe based on the convertible—the car Jim Perkins had long dreamed of and still thought of as the "Billy Bob"— would follow.

"Nothing's happening on the convertible," he said. "We should be seeing some themes in the studio." But there were none yet, no sketches, no scale models in clay. The studio was working to its limit on the targa model. McLean and Hill hoped that they could persuade Cafaro's bosses to give him another sculptor/modeler or two. The studio desperately needed more bodies. But with neither Wayne Cherry nor Jerry Palmer in the room, the question was moot.

That was when tempers burst. One of Hill's engineers looked around and said, "Why are we wasting our time here when they don't show up?"

"Let's go find out," McLean said. He and Dave Hill marched down the hall. They caught Jerry Palmer just leaving his office.

"We want to know whether you guys are committed to Corvette," McLean said brusquely. "It doesn't look like you are."

It was a direct challenge that Palmer couldn't ignore. He'd been the Chevy 3 studio chief for the C4 Corvette and he loved the car. When it was named *Motor Trend*'s Car of the Year in 1984, and the convertible got the same award for 1986, it was as much an affirmation of Jerry Palmer as it was of Corvette. And though the new car belonged to John Cafaro, Palmer cared about C5.

Russ McLean's challenge brought him up short. He took the barrage of complaints and couldn't do much beyond agreeing. Finally he did the only thing he could do. He scheduled a meeting.

They got together a few days later. Wayne Cherry, Jerry Palmer, and John Cafaro were there. But it was Dave Hill, a man not given to cusswords, who got in the first blow.

"You people aren't showing up when we need you," he said harshly.

Palmer looked chagrined. "Yeah," he said, "we're fucking the whole thing up."

"Then maybe we oughta stop fucking up," Hill retorted. He spoke slowly and stressed each word.

Wayne Cherry sat quietly through the confrontation. It was his way. He was a rarity at General Motors, a man who went overseas to GM's German operations and almost didn't come back. He was there for twenty-seven years, eventually taking over the European design studios. Nobody in the room knew that a corner of his heart belonged to Corvette. The first new car Wayne Cherry ever owned was a silver '63 Corvette open-top roadster. He paid on the spot and still had the canceled check he wrote to the dealer. But those weren't the kind of personal admissions that Cherry made in public. He kept close counsel, unlike the man he succeeded. Chuck Jordan's emotions flew like battle flags planted in his soul. Wayne Cherry's were masked by his Teutonic training.

When he finally spoke to the Corvette people, Cherry offered both apologies and promises.

"You'll have people senior enough to make decisions at every meeting," he told Russ McLean and Dave Hill. "And I'll be there myself at least every other week."

He didn't quite live up to the last part of the deal. But the rest of it stood.

32

"WHAT we have here is a mock-up with teeth in it."

The voice came out of the back of the crowd. It was 7:30 A.M. on a late-February day and the room in Livonia, Michigan, was filled with Corvette people. They'd driven under blue skies that hinted of spring to a tightly guarded facility owned by TDM, Inc., more than forty miles west of the General Motors Technical Center. A cardinal event in the development of the 1997 Corvette was under way.

The CERV-4, the secret Corvette Engineering Research Vehicle that was crucial to all their plans, lay before them in skeleton form. The first structural parts were being fitted together. When the car was built and tested, it would prove whether or not the unique backbone structure envisioned for C5 lived up to its promise for improving handling, increasing both crashworthiness and occupant comfort, and reducing squeaks, rattles, and water leaks.

Boxes of doughnuts provided by TDM were being quickly depleted. It was only two days after Fat Tuesday, known in Detroit as "pcznski day," and the crowd was taking advantage of the hospitality to pump up on pastry for the second time that week. Pcznskis, pronounced "punch-kee," are jelly-filled Polish pastries. The Detroit area's large Polish community and everybody else celebrates Fat Tuesday by gorging on pcznskis.

The Corvette offices were no exception. "I'm having pcznski withdrawal," said one engineer, going for his third doughnut.

When the doughnuts had disappeared and coffee cups were refilled, development engineer Jeff Yanssens herded people around two sets of rails set on stands that held them just above the floor. Yanssens was assigned to the Corvette program at GM's Milford Proving Ground northwest of Detroit. He'd be one of the drivers putting CERV-4, and all future Corvette test cars, through hell. He'd been picked by Dave Hill to ramrod CERV through its high-speed development and assembly process. Now he had something to show.

"What you see here stays inside Corvette," he said. "Nobody talks outside about this car. Not at home. Not to your neighbors. Not to people back at the office who aren't part of Corvette. Understand?"

TDM's Livonia facility had the contract for assembling suspension and design-check mock-ups and would put together the structure for the real CERV-4. Another TDM facility, in Madison Heights and much closer to the GM Technical Center, was fabricating the fiberglass exterior and would assemble the final car.

"It doesn't look it yet, but this car's going to be a bastardized version of the current car," Yanssens said. "The width is coming out almost exactly like the ZR-1, so we'll be using a ZR-1 rear panel."

The ZR-1 was Corvette's "king of the hill" car, wider in the rear than the regular car to accommodate bigger tires and packing an engine that let it set a world record on a track in San Angelo, Texas, in 1991 by averaging 176.2 miles per hour over a twenty-four-hour period. The drivers stopped only to refuel.

"We'll have a quick and dirty removable top with zip-in side windows," Yanssens continued, "mostly for storing the car. We can't leave it in the garage at the proving grounds full-time; too many people would see it."

Few places in all of General Motors are more secure than the proving grounds at Milford and at Mesa, Arizona. Yet even inside the grounds, CERV would be largely protected from curious eyes.

"With the top, we'll also be able to do some driving in cold weather."

Engineers crowded around a long table to sort through engineering drawings. For many of them, it was their first look at the face CERV-4 would show on the test track. It did resemble a current car. The general lines were there. The same hood and fenders boxed in the engine. The ZR-1 rear end was familiar. Look casually and it was just another C4.

Except for one thing: It had a trunk. No C4, neither hardtop nor convertible, had such a thing. But there it was in the drawings, a flat deck extending from the tonneau. It was definitely a trunk. An idea that had floated around Corvette for several years, and that was incorporated into the loved-and-not-loved Stingray III, was right there in the drawings. The future C5 convertible and fixed-roof coupe would have regular trunks. The CERV-4 would have one in 1993.

The group turned to the mock-up rails and they were massive. ". . . a mock-up with teeth in it," one engineer said. "God, it's big," said another. "Jeez," whistled a third.

It wasn't close to being a car yet. It was just the beginning of a car. The mock-up stand, showing how the pieces fit together, had two long tubular side rails and looked like a giant tuning fork. Cross members were welded in place to hold them together. The TDM engineers had dropped a mock-up engine into the front compartment to check size and location. The center tunnel, welded sheet steel that ran lengthwise through the structure, ended with a transmission housing at the rear. The housing, Yanssens said, would soon be sent back to GM's Powertrain Division to be filled with the real thing.

Next to the mock-up, the real CERV-4 structure was mounted on a stand. Only the side rails and cross members were there, with welders at work. This one would become the structure of the test car.

It was the rails that caught everyone's attention. Nothing on the new Corvette was more important. Or more radical.

The rails were the major elements in the new Corvette's structure. They were part of the car's comfort package, allowing the car to absorb shocks and vibrations more effectively than any sports car in the world could do. They were part of the ride-and-handling package, in theory contributing to C5 maneuverability beyond even a Corvette dreamer's dreams. They added safety to the car by making it stronger and stiffer. They were part of the mass reduction package to make the new Corvette more than a hundred pounds lighter than the current car.

They were much of the reason for CERV-4. If the theory of the side rails, and the big central tunnel that ran through the car's midline, didn't prove out on the road, the 1997 Corvette would be in deep trouble.

The rails at TDM that day were made under trial-and-error conditions at GM's Advanced Manufacturing facility inside the Tech Center. The trick would be making them for full-scale production. Corvette engineers had committed the program more than a year earlier to making the rails with a risky process called hydro-forming. It was one of Dave McLellan's legacies and would be a lasting contribution to automotive design.

All cars have side rails. They bend in and out, up and down, and are hung with all sorts of gear. Like the suspension system and wheels. Or the gas tank, the engine cradle, the passenger compartment structure, and the outside body of the car. Rails are welded together in sections to form the ins and outs. C4's side rails were put together from twenty-four different pieces. They were heavy. They ate up man-hours of production time to put them together. And there was no way to guarantee that each rail was identical to all the others. The process of welding them together introduced variation; their lengths might vary by a few thousandths of an inch. That, in turn, led to squeaks and rattles and other irritating problems when a complete C4 was finally assembled and rolled off the line.

Hydro-forming eliminated most of that. The problem was that hydro-forming had never been attempted anywhere on a production basis for pieces more than four or five feet long, and maybe three or four inches in diameter.

C5's side rails were fourteen feet long before being bent, thirteen feet after. They were nine inches in rectangular height. They had to be one continuous piece, not several tubular sections welded together. Making that happen would be part art, part science. The Tool and Die experts and the specialists at Advanced Manufacturing figured they could do it. They already were well along in the process of designing the machine that would do the job. It was a two-hundred-ton machine, eighteen feet high, twelve feet wide, and twenty-four feet long, to make rail sets for C5 production at the rate of fifteen sets an hour.

The process would start with rolled steel sheets two millimeters, about a thirteenth of an inch, thick. A sheet would be rolled into a six-inch tube and be laser-welded along its fourteen-foot length. Laser-welding leaves a surface scar so smooth that it can barely be seen or felt. The bond is stronger than any regular weld.

Next the tube would go through a pipe bender to establish the basic curves of the C5 side rail. Finally left and right tubes would be laid into shaped grooves in the hyrdo-forming machine. The immense top of the machine would lower and lock.

Then came the tricky part. Water at hydraulic pressures of seven thousand pounds per square inch would fill each tube. Under that extreme pressure, the steel tube would blow up like a metal balloon. It would fill the die groove and become rectangular instead of circular. It would blow into corners and form bends of precision and strength. It would become a one-piece side rail with consistent thickness from front to back. And every rail set would be exactly like every other rail set—no bad welds, no variations in length or cross section, no difference in mass because one welder laid down more bonding metal than another.

The rails, in short, would be perfect. That was the theory. Making it happen took a while.

Meanwhile, CERV rails came from special tools that were little more than first attempts at making the process work on such huge components. The rails weren't perfect. But they were close. And once CERV-4 was built up around them, development drivers and test engineers could find out just how much stiffness they added to the car, just how much vibration they eliminated, just how much they added to Corvette's already extraordinary handling.

33

THE great tire debate started with lousy numbers from the wind tunnel. Until then, John Cafaro had his way. He wanted bigger rear tires on the new Corvette and he was getting them.

From generation to generation, Corvette tires had grown. Tires on the current car were so wide that they approached the dimensions of racing tires. They were big, too. The standard Corvette came with seventeen-inch wheels.

Cafaro was a big-tire advocate. He had pushed Dave McLellan's engineering team for bigger tires when the hot Corvette ZR-1 was being designed. Bigger tires in back would give the car a racy nose-down tilt that Cafaro loved, and extra width in the tires would add a muscular, don't-mess-with-me look from the rear. All of John Cafaro's talents as one of GM's top stylists, combined with his weekend racing experience when he charged around tracks in Michigan and Ohio with his old Datsun on a semipro race circuit, told him that big tires were better.

Now he was pushing Dave Hill to take the next step. The clay car in the studio had seventeen-inch wheels in front and nineteens in back. Cafaro was using the model to make his case. It presented a striking look.

Tires are a major contributor to any car's ride and handling. On a high-performance sports car like Corvette, tires are so important that they are specially designed just for the car. Today's battle would be over both engineering and styling issues. Those decisions belonged to the two chiefs, Dave Hill and John Cafaro. It was the regular Thursday gathering and the engineering people dribbled into the design studio from their early-morning meeting at TDM in Livonia.

Dave Hill was stoked. "This is an historic day," he announced to Cafaro and his studio staff. "We have the start of a new Corvette."

"All right!" Cafaro grinned. "Gimme details." Hill told them that CERV-4 was on the way. They'd have it at the test track before June, giving them real engineering numbers and real driving experience that they could take to Jack Smith and his Strategy Board.

Cafaro's designers and modelers shared his mood. Some of them had been on the program for four years and were still waiting for the first running car. A real Corvette, not a glittery Stingray III, was now only months away.

"Okay," Cafaro said. "The issue today is aero. Let's get started."

The model from Cafaro's studio had been to the wind tunnel without Dave Hill's input. Scheduling tunnel time was an art in itself and there had been no way to get a Hill-approved model ready for the time slot allocated to Corvette. That wouldn't happen again.

Aerodynamics engineer Kurt Romberg, a young self-effacing expert assigned to Design Staff, took over the presentation.

Romberg cited the coefficient of drag (c/D), the measure of how slippery the car was through the air, as 0.32. That was a better number than Hill expected but still a long way from the goal of 0.29. Romberg had increased Corvette's slickness by adding three belly pans—flat covers that made the underside of the car almost perfectly smooth—to improve air flow under the car. He'd also scraped clay to reshape the rear end slightly. He had a few more tricks up his sleeve to get the c/D down ten more counts to 0.31, but those last ten counts to 0.30 were going to be tough.

And the counts to get to 0.29? Hill wondered.

A second engineer spoke up. "If you can't live with the belly pans, the next thing is to lower the front end." Belly pans were simple but expensive. Worse, each would add several kilograms of mass. Hill was already pounding on his design engineers to reduce the car's weight. Even grams were being sought. Adding thousands of those grams for the sake of aerodynamics was not an attractive thought.

John Cafaro saw the look of consternation on Hill's face. "We're working on shortening the car a couple of inches," he said. "As we shorten it, we can drop the front down."

"Looks cheated now," model year manager Pete Liccardello said, using design slang for "not quite real." "How much aero will you lose if it's brought up to criteria?" He could see that the clay car didn't match up with the engineering specifications, the criteria.

Modelers and styling designers cheat the clay in the early stages to exaggerate curves, push it lower to the ground, or highlight visible cues that make the car different. Cheating adds eye appeal in the studio and makes the heart beat faster. But a cheated design won't look quite the same when the car is built to real-world conditions.

Cafaro was ready for the question. He assured Liccardello that with a few modifications they could meet the criteria and keep the c/D at 0.32. "There are a lot of aero advantages to shortening the car," he said. "It improves the looks, too. We've got it down to one hundred seventy-nine inches overall. The new Toyota Supra is one hundred seventy-eight, so we're in the hunt. It's pretty exciting stuff."

Liccardello had been caught up in Cafaro's infectious enthusiasm before. He felt it happening again, so he tempered it by asking what other modifications Cafaro had in mind.

"Well, the front air dam is a factor," Cafaro said. "Curb heights and haul-away requirements have to be considered. And belly pans in the middle of the car don't yield much compared to the effort and expense. We can get as much aero by doing a flat undersurface on the front fascia."

"What about the B-pillar?" Dave Hill asked. The B-pillar is the upright piece behind the driver or passenger that holds up the roof and frames the rear glass. "You could hold it where it is, but maybe bring the side glass in a half inch or so. That would keep air attached to the car by softening the break from the windshield to the side of the car."

Keeping air flowing smoothly around a car contributes to its aerodynamic numbers. If the air flow breaks away, it creates turbulence and friction.

Cafaro looked at the driver's window carved into the massive clay car. "Yeah, we can do that," he said.

Hill walked around the front of the car and pondered its design. "Shortening the car is good," he said. "The crash group was concerned about that, but the new car has a big cross beam in front, plus another hefty crossbar that the current car doesn't have. That should make crashworthiness as good as C4 and, in fact, it may already be better.

"So I think you should look at ways to take advantage of that beefiness and shorten the front overhang even more."

Now Cafaro was getting into the give and take. This was a chief engineer he could work with. They thought alike and Hill was giving Cafaro permission to do things that allowed for both good engineering and good styling.

Kurt Romberg brought up the tires.

"That rear wheel width is an aero problem," he said. "Sucking in the sides would help."

Cafaro gave him a sideways look, but Romberg pressed on. "Look down from the top and this car is wider in the rear than it is in the front," he said. "I know John doesn't like to hear this."

"Remember, you still have to work in this building," Cafaro warned. He was half smiling.

"I know."

"Please, keep talking," Dave Hill said.

"What are you doing for lunch today, Kurt?" Cafaro teased. "How about ten table dancers?"

Kurt Romberg blushed and grinned. "I don't have anything to say."

"Naw, let's hear it," Hill pressed.

Romberg shrugged and went on. "Skinnier tires will have a real impact if you want better aero. It's pretty simple."

Hill's engineers were enjoying the moment. "Yeah . . . definitely . . . skinny up them tires. . . ."

"Okay, Kurt, you've done enough damage," Cafaro grinned. And he turned to hear Dave Hill say the dreaded words.

"Maybe we can get all the aero we want with seventeen-inch tires," he said. "So maybe we go seventeen-seventeen instead of nineteen rear and seventeen front. But we have to look at ride and handling, too. What do smaller tires do to us?"

He knew the answer. Handling would deteriorate. The question was, how much?

Cafaro was legitimately concerned about the direction of the conversation. "The looks would be wrong," he argued. "You don't gain anything by making a skinnier rear end on a Corvette, not with the long length and wheelbase."

This was a styling issue to him and it was paramount. "We need to keep the ratios pretty much where they are. Plus the greenhouse is so big that narrowing the rear end would give the car a skinny look."

The greenhouse was the passenger compartment. Hill conceded the point. So Cafaro conceded one, too.

"I'd be willing to look at a car with seventeens all around," he said. "The Supra has seventeens. But remember, Corvette has always been a leader in tires. We've got bragging rights here and I'd hate to give them up if we don't have to." He paused to let that soak in. "But I agree with you, Dave, that ride and handling have to be big considerations, too. If we can have it all, that's what we want."

In a way, it was a ploy. Ride and handling would be degraded, all right. The differences between fat nineteen-inchers and skinnier seventeen-inchers would be obvious to any Corvette driver. But it didn't hurt to let Hill and his development drivers come to that conclusion on their own.

Glances passed back and forth between engineers and studio people. Whatever happened, they were seeing real negotiations between factions that more often in the past had butted heads. One or two wondered if John Cafaro was really giving up on big tires. Or would the great tire debate come back another day?

"It ain't over 'til the fat lady sings," whispered modeler Gary Clark.

Cafaro's studio engineer, Ron Nowicki, responded: "You mean fat tires. He'll settle for eighteens on the rear and get the width back." Months later, it turned out just that way.

The aerodynamics discussions weren't done yet. Romberg brought up turbulence discovered over the top of the windshield, around the outside rearview mirrors, and around the license plate well. Hill wasn't unhappy with the windshield news. Glass was expensive and he saw a way to save a little money.

The meeting had gone on more than two hours and it was well into the lunch hour. Dave Hill ignored the clock; his lunch was in a brown bag back at his office and he always ate between meetings, or even during them. But it was time to wrap it up.

"Okay, let's recap," Hill said. "For the next set of tunnel runs, you're going to remove the front and mid belly pans, which are a lot of expense for very little aero. Leave the rear belly pan.

"Get a license plate fairing that's aesthetically good and helps the aero.

"Get the height right.

"Also, to get more affordable glass, bring the base of the windshield in and wrap the lines back to the B-pillar. That trades a little panoramic view for better affordability and saves one hundred thousand dollars in investment.

"Then shorten the front overhang by two inches. Design Staff likes that, and it cuts the mass and the length of the car. You'll have to work with the crashworthiness people to determine any safety factors here.

"Also try a ten-millimeter-narrower cross section on the tires. Put seven-teens on the back, but leave the outside surface of the tires where Cafaro wants and bring the inside of the wheel well in. That will reduce the hole and cut the induced drag under the car.

"Then try different outside mirrors, do some vision studies. Existing GM mirrors might work for Corvette."

A few jaws dropped. Dave Hill had gone through the list without referring to notes. His near-photographic memory was more than just a rumor.

When John Cafaro started to say something about the tires, Hill held up a hand. "Just for the test, John. Just for the test."

Cafaro nodded. The debate wasn't over.

3 4 / THE power of the press is a cruel tool. When a respected automotive writer reported comments by Corvette chief engineer Dave Hill, his story made headlines around the world and sent the Corvette team into a deep, dark funk.

Jack Keebler was engineering editor for *Automotive News,* a weekly news magazine that is one of the industry's bibles. Dave Hill drew Keebler as a table companion at an automotive lunch in Detroit when he made his first Corvette outing into the world of journalism.

The conversation turned naturally to the next Corvette and Hill made a few offhand comments. One of them was the need for Corvette to make a profit. He dodged rumors that Corvette would be built as a variety of the Camaro and that if it came out at all, it would appear in 1996. Hill knew that his Corvette would be a 1997. But that tidbit hadn't been announced to the world and Hill wasn't going to leak the news. Keebler focused on the profit comment.

His story in the next *Automotive News* reported that Corvette was in dire danger. Detroit radio stations took Keebler's report a step further down the road to demise, and the story was picked up by the Associated Press and other wire services for dispatch to the world.

Corvette Must Tally a Profit or It Dies

—Automotive News

Corvette's Days Feared Dwindling

—Portland Oregonian

Corvette Endangered

—Associated Press

Corvette engineers and designers were shell-shocked. Some remembered the news stories about Bob Stempel a few months earlier. Rumors of his impending departure turned to fact and the reporters were right. Others had been through Corvette's fits and starts going back to 1988, leaving work one evening with a viable program and coming to work the next morning to discover that the C5 Corvette was delayed again. Many were convinced that history was about to repeat itself and began dusting off their résumés.

Chevrolet public relations and the Corvette team were flooded with calls from Corvette owners, Corvette clubs, Corvette enthusiasts, and especially Chevrolet dealers. The cries of anguish drove Chevrolet to do something it almost never does. It sent a letter to *Automotive News* refuting Keebler's story and stressing GM's commitment to both the current Corvette and the new car being developed.

Russ McLean and Dave Hill smoothed the internal distress. "No way is the program going away," they told everybody. But outside Corvette's walls, the rumors went on. Editors had been burned before by "ongoing commitment" statements. It took nearly two months before the automotive press turned around and believed that C5 wasn't dead.

Dave Hill eventually took it in good humor. As he walked through the dirty rooms that were being converted to Corvette's quarters in the new Vehicle Launch Center, he told his people not to despair about the mess. "Mighty oaks from little acorns grow," he joshed.

"Yeah," came a voice from the back of the group. "And from which limb of that oak are you going to hang Jack Keebler?"

Hill laughed. "After I draw and quarter him," he said, pointing first to one end of the ninety-foot-long room, then to the other, "we'll hang him from *that* limb, and from *that* limb, and from *that* limb. . . ."

Other stories impacted the new Corvette's design and content. The C4 Corvette had a digital instrument cluster. The speedometer showed a real number—63 or 55 or 79. Survey after survey showed that a slim majority of Corvette owners liked it that way. The new generation of buyers, raised on computers, arcade games, and push-button telephones, would agree even more strongly.

But automotive writers, aided and abetted by a hard core of Corvette traditionalists, almost all disparaged the new world of digital. They wanted the old analog instruments, a needle on a dial that pointed somewhere in the general direction of accuracy.

"Analog instruments are tradition in sports cars," they wrote. "Digital instruments are distracting and garish."

Year after year, press reviews of the C4 Corvette assaulted the digital panel with caustic, derisive comments. At formal press shows, automotive writers for *Road and Track, Motor Trend,* or *AutoWeek* would ask Corvette engineers and stylists the same question: "When are you going to get rid of digital instruments and give us back our analog?"

Mike Andalora was the lead engineer developing the C5 electrical system.

He held out long and strong for a digital panel. "It's more accurate," he'd say. "It's modern. It's where the future is going."

But at every review of future plans, someone would bring up the latest critique by an automotive magazine. The influence of the "buff books" was a frightening thing to people already sticking their necks out for the new Corvette. Auto writers who probably wouldn't buy a Corvette themselves wielded more influence in engineering meetings than loyal Corvette owners who were already saving up for a '97.

Andalora finally threw in the towel. "I don't care if it's the wrong thing to do," he said. "I'm tired of getting beat up by the auto writers. We're not doing a digital instrument panel on C5. We're going back to the old analog stuff."

MIKE Juras had a vision.

"We don't make cars," he preached. "We make parts. If the parts are right, the cars will be right."

Mike Juras took over as engineering director of the General Motors Midsize Car Division on January 1, 1993, reporting to Joe Spielman. He came with a history of engineering on cars and trucks, and his appointment raised a few eyebrows.

For all his experience, Juras was not a car guy. His office may have been the only one at General Motors that was barren of automotive artifacts. Unique among GM executives, he did not have a single model car on his credenza or bookcase, not a single Design Staff sketch or other car art on the walls. He had some plants, a street scene photo, and a photo of a brook and bridge. In every way, Mike Juras worked in a generic office. The man behind the desk could have been an accountant or a stockbroker. Yet Mike Juras was part of Joe Spielman's answer to a terrible dilemma.

The problem was that the Midsize Car Division didn't have the wherewithal to do its job. The money crunch at General Motors left the division with too few working-level engineers, no permission to hire more, and constant pressure from North American Operations to perform, perform, perform. Downsizing had a downside.

The Midsize Car Division produced more than 40 percent of all GM vehicles in North America. It was the heart of the company, building family sedans for Chevrolet, Pontiac, Oldsmobile, and Buick. It built slope-nosed vans for all of those but Buick. It built the hot F-cars, the Chevy Camaro and Pontiac Firebird.

And it built Corvette.

Virtually all of its product line was in flux, with new models of everything but the F-cars due out in 1996, 1997, and 1998. The all-new Camaro, designed by John Cafaro's studio, and a matching Firebird from Pontiac would be out before the rest, reaching dealers in late 1993. Cardy Davis had been shifted from Corvette to salvage what could be salvaged in the W-car sedan program while other engineers worked on replacement sedans for 1997. So the scarce engineering resources available were going to old cars that were losers and yet-to-be cars that everyone hoped would be winners.

GM compounded the problem by continuing to thin the ranks of its white-collar population by offering early retirements and buyouts. Experienced and talented engineers took the bait by the thousands. Many of them walked out with six-figure payoffs and went to work for the competition the next day. A standing joke around General Motors was that Ford didn't need a recruiting department. It had GM as its farm club.

The pressures put Joe Spielman in an impossible position. His engineering staff had been downsized through muscle and into bone. The demands on his people had increased. And he had too little budget to make it all work. Then he listened to Mike Juras lay out a vision for a matrix management system that theoretically got maximum use from a minimum number of people. It would save money, Juras said. It would move engineers hither and yon where they were needed, not leaving them assigned to a single-car program like Corvette. It was one of those ideas that seemed too good to be true. But it was the only idea around. Spielman thought it over and grasped at the straw.

It took Juras three months to roll out yet another reorganization of the engineering department at Midsize. Old ways were swept aside in the Juras vision of how to get the job done.

Juras was in GM's truck division in the 1980s, where he was one of the few engineers to follow programs from beginning sketches to ultimate production. Those were the years when the truck side of GM began a long series of successes, and some of the sheen belonged to Juras. When he became engineering director at Midsize, he brought the truck division's organizational philosophy along. He didn't question whether what worked for a relatively cohesive universe like trucks would also work in a chaotic cosmos like Midsize.

Juras unveiled his vision to an assembly hall filled with engineers in early April. He was a trim, gray-haired six-footer and he paced the stage in one of his trademark multicolored sweaters. Juras wore sweaters almost every month of the year. He talked fast and it was sometimes hard for the crowd to keep up. At first, he tried inspiration.

"We are the heart of the North American organization process and if we can't be profitable, there's no hope for General Motors," he said. Then he moved on to philosophy.

"[General Motors] is an org chart company," he said. "People talk about the organization chart, not about the organization philosophy."

His philosophy was to concentrate on the quality of parts from the first sketches to final production. He used a multipage org chart to show how it should happen.

• • •

In the Juras Vision, almost nobody on the engineering side worked for a car program. Programs like Corvette were no longer independent. Russ McLean and Dave Hill would have to requisition help. Generally the same senior engineers who'd been with the Corvette program would keep their positions but would have a second master in the form of a "homeroom" boss. The rank-and-file engineers were matrixed from one of eight home-rooms, like "chassis and power train" or "body/exterior." The homeroom boss assigned people out as they were needed to work on parts for a car. An engineer might work on Corvette one day and a family sedan or a van the next. It was the old union hall concept infiltrated into middle management.

There were homerooms for production and manufacturing, and for dimensional management—the technology of making all the parts fit together with specified tolerances. Both would be involved across the board with other homerooms as car parts came together to become cars. "Quality equates to dimensional management," Juras told the gathered engineers, and on that, he was right.

Someone stood up and asked Juras if Midsize would be bringing in engineers to fill existing gaps. He had to bob and weave with his answer. "Our proposed head count is two thousand three hundred sixty-four," he said. "But right now we're around twenty-two hundred and that may be where NAO forces us to stay."

Translation: No. Even worse, as General Motors lost more and more money, the engineering head count continued to fall.

Another engineer stood up and challenged the Juras organization chart: "Why isn't management thinning down along with the rest of us?"

"Our current level is four hundred managers to about twenty-four hundred engineers," Juras said. "So that's a six-to-one ratio, which seems low already. And it will thin more when some platforms are combined."

A veteran in the audience whispered loud enough to be heard four rows away: "Six to one? I remember when it was thirty to one and we thought there were too many bosses then!"

Juras heard the chuckles, but he missed the remark.

He also missed some important points. One of them was human nature. In tearing car programs apart by sharing engineers among them, the Juras Vision destroyed the esprit that engineers felt when they identified with their product. It wasn't long before people stopped saying, "I work on the new Chevy van," or "I'm on Corvette," and started saying, "I work on doors." Then they stopped saying even that and just admitted to being a GM engineer. Working on doors had no glamour. The cachet of a brand-new vehicle that they could point out to their friends and neighbors was gone.

In later explanations of his vision, Mike Juras liked to use doors as an example:

"A door fills an opening. A door keeps you dry. A door opens to let you in and out. Every door is supposed to do that, whether you have freestanding glass or framed glass or glass in the header.

"But the functions it performs are the same whether you are doing a Corvette or a van.

"So a door is a door is a door.

"It takes different experiences and skills to do a freestanding glass door or a header-in-the-roof door. So that's the only difference, because the functions are the same."

So door engineers worked on the sports car doors for Corvette and on van doors and family sedan doors. But it left them empty in the gut. The fire was being put out.

There were other problems with the Juras Vision, too, and they couldn't all be laid at Juras's feet. There were never enough engineers to go around. When an engineer got pulled off a Corvette door to work on a door for the new 1997 van, Corvette suffered. So did the van, because the engineer had to get up to speed on that door before he could solve its problems. Thus when work got done, it often was done late. The bigger programs eventually fell behind schedule. And it wasn't just because of doors. It was everything.

At first, not many people understood how the new Juras engineering organization was supposed to work. There were days of classes to teach the fundamentals to the people who had to implement the vision. There were meetings that conflicted with other meetings and people didn't know which to attend. There was frustration over who worked for whom because too many key people found themselves with two masters.

An engineer supposedly worked for Dave Hill and was charged with developing and testing key parts of the 1997 Corvette. But he didn't work *for* Dave Hill because he had some other master who controlled his paycheck and had assigned him to Corvette. Key people on the Corvette program stayed on the program. The homeroom managers weren't stupid and assigned large numbers of engineers right back to the program from whence they came. They just didn't work for the program anymore.

Sometimes an engineer would toss a grenade into a discussion of Corvette plans or designs: "My homeroom thinks we should be doing. . . ." The engineer would be conflicted because Dave Hill wanted one thing, but the homeroom wanted something else. Most of them felt real loyalty to Corvette and to Dave Hill. But their paychecks came from the homeroom.

Second-guessing consumed hours of negotiation. Sometimes Hill won. Sometimes he didn't. And sometimes he saw that the homeroom did have a better way and he switched sides immediately.

A small sign generated on someone's computer appeared one day in the Corvette offices: "Welcome to matrix management. If you understand what's happening, please let the rest of us know."

Corvette was the smallest program at Midsize and the most emotional. People loved working on Corvette. Dave Hill and Russ McLean used that lever, and a bag full of management tricks, to keep up the Corvette esprit, to get engineering assignments completed, and to stick to the program's calendar.

Eventually Corvette was the only program in the Midsize Car Division that was on schedule. A confused and confounded engineering organization failed to deliver.

The road to hell was paved with a flawed vision.

36 PETE Liccardello, C5 model year manager, slapped a transparency onto the overhead projector screen and grinned at the twenty-two people in the cramped and dirty room. It was just after dawn on a misty April 1993 morning. Halfway down the table, chief engineer Dave Hill smiled quietly. He knew what was coming.

"Here's the schedule for the preproduction prototype build," Liccardello said. "We're not only doing 'em at long last, but we're doing 'em sooner than we thought, and we're probably going to do more of them than this schedule shows. Right, Dave?"

"We've got ten cars on that build schedule," Hill said. "But after my meeting with Joe Spielman last night, I think we can count on doing a few more. More than ten for sure, probably less than twenty. Figure somewhere in the mid-teens."

The grins flashed around the littered conference room. It was still suffering the indignities of remodeling disarray and there was dust everywhere. But that hardly mattered. For the first time in an official meeting, Corvette people were in their own domain on the west side of the General Motors Technical Center in Warren, Michigan, in the unfinished Vehicle Launch Center. Except for the strangeness of being west of the tracks and stuck down in a windowless basement, they felt good. Just being there was a sure sign of progress.

Talking about real cars instead of engineering drawings or clay models was even better. These cars would come after the CERV-4 and they would have C5 bodies, not the revamped C4 styling used for CERV. The first cars to be built would be called "alphas," mostly hand built and crude. They'd use early parts from suppliers and a lot of them would have to be trimmed or shimmed to make them fit. Later they'd go to "beta" cars, built either with parts redesigned to correct flaws or with parts from suppliers that were close to final specifications. Then would come prototype cars, and finally prepilot and pilot cars. Prototypes had to be perfect, or nearly so, using increasingly improved parts and assembly techniques that approached the final processes to be used at the assembly plant. The prepilot cars would be the first cars off the assembly in August 1996 to validate the assembly process. Pilot cars would come in September 1996, and by the rules of production, they would be salable vehicles.

What Dave Hill knew, but didn't say, and the rest suspected, but didn't ask, was that even twenty cars of the alpha and beta variety wouldn't be nearly enough. Toyota, they said privately, built at least three hundred test cars and sometimes more. The idea of building only ten cars, even for the first and most basic phases of testing, was not realistic. Neither was twenty. It was just a start. Hill and Russ McLean would have to ask for more money later.

The alpha cars were major items in the Corvette development program. Their frames and chassis would be close to the final thing. Their interiors would have many of the components—also custom-made—of the ultimate car. Their exteriors would start out looking more or less real, though fit and finish would leave much to be desired. Most of them would be fitted with camouflage, weird pieces like long padded bras and passenger door covers and flat sheets taped over the hood. They would be deceptively gimmicked to mislead spy-photo auto journalists and competitors who might happen to see one on a back road somewhere.

Alphas would have geometrically correct versions of the new Gen III aluminum V-8 engine, but some early models would get cast-iron motors while GM's Powertrain Division perfected the aluminum block.

While Dave Hill and the key members of his engineering team were discussing prototype Corvettes that wouldn't make it to the test track for another fifteen months, Jeff Yanssens was ramrodding the secret round-the-clock operation to build a test car that would roll out in another month.

Crews at TDM, Inc., worked three shifts, seven days a week, to produce CERV-4, the Corvette Engineering Research Vehicle that only a handful of people knew was coming. Yanssens was a burly fellow who coached Pee-Wee Hockey in the winter and loved the Detroit Red Wings. The spring of 1993 was the only time in his life when he was relieved that the Wings weren't bound for the Stanley Cup. He was spending too many long evenings and late nights at TDM to have the time and energy to cheer a run on the cup.

And he was loving it. He'd drag in bleary-eyed with the dawn and say that it was the highlight of his career: "Doing a secret car for the next-generation Corvette . . . I feel great!"

Yanssens became the legendary madman with a mission. "Lead, follow, or get out of the way," he said to TDM's managers and crews, and they listened. When GM's Powertrain Division told him that they couldn't deliver a 5.7-liter Gen III engine for his car, he rumbled and ranted, and then accepted a 5.0-liter with identical outside dimensions.

"You just get me the right engine in time for testing," he said, "and we'll swap engines ourselves out at Milford." So CERV-4 went together with an underpowered engine up front, but all the connections were there to make it right when the car went out on the track.

Day after day through March and April, TDM fabricators hand made exterior panels patterned after the C4 Corvette, laying up fiberglass over carved wood forms, while structures and mechanics experts fitted the frame with suspensions, hydraulics lines, an electrical system, and all the rest.

Dave Hill gave Yanssens all the leeway he needed. One morning Yanssens showed up at the GM Tech Center to brief the Corvette team.

"We're either on schedule or ahead," he said, "except for Powertrain, and we've got a recovery plan in place on that. The car is going to be a dual-breather with panel inserts so we can get air flow to the radiator either up from the bottom or through the front."

The C4 Corvette was a bottom-breather, sucking air into the engine from underneath instead of through a traditional front-facing grill. Bottom-breathers are smoother and generate less turbulence because air flows smoothly around the car instead of ramming through it. But they tend to lift up a little at high speeds, which can degrade maneuverability and handling. A front-breather forces a car's nose down, improving the way the tires grip the road. But the drag penalty cuts fuel economy and top speed.

"We'll be able to run the car both ways," Yanssens said. "And if we don't get enough cooling, it can even be a dual-breather."

He laid out a test schedule that gave everybody a crack at the car on the Milford Proving Ground track before GM closed down for two weeks in mid-July. He didn't tell them about the two turndowns from Dave Hill before he convinced the chief engineer that a second CERV-4 might be a good idea to give them even more driving experience.

"Hill was a guy you could get a decision from," Yanssens said later. "The first two times I tried to make a case for a second car, he decided no. I figured I'd get fired, but I went back a third time."

That time Hill told him to poll the team.

"I want to know who thinks we could use a second CERV," he said that morning. "Now is the time to buy additional parts because the tooling [fiberglass molds and other special rigs to make parts] is up and done and additional parts would be cheap right now. But don't come back in forty-five days with your request, because the tooling will be dismantled by then."

Then he put some frosting on the idea. The first CERV was costing Chevrolet around $1.2 million. Yanssens pointed out that TDM could build an entire second car for $600,000 right now. He knew the result, but he had to ask. Everybody wanted a second car. In a few days it was a done deal. CERV-4b was written into the plan.

He had one last piece of news: TDM offered to add Corvette-style pop-up headlights to CERV. No charge. "They've been concerned about the looks of the car," Yanssens said. "They don't want to deliver something that looks like a piece of crap. It's their pride and reputation, so they want it to look right as well as drive right."

The first Sunday in May came too soon. Yanssens, a team of other Corvette engineers, and TDM crews worked through the day, then into the night. At 5 A.M. they loaded CERV-4a onto a truck and drove into the rising sun toward the GM Technical Center in Warren. They'd met a deadline set by Russ McLean. It had taken just ninety-one days from the first drawings to the finished car.

"I want to pull the cover off at the all-people meeting on May 3," he told Yanssens. "I want everybody to see that the program is for real."

When he did, the hall filled with surprised applause and cheers. Maybe forty of the hundreds of people there walked in knowing about CERV. Now they all did. Before the day was over, GM executives from Mike Mutchler up to the most senior ranks would know about it, too. But it was too late for them to do anything but smile, cross their fingers, and hope that Jim Perkins, Russ McLean, and Dave Hill hadn't overplayed their hands. The tale would be told on the track.

Hill and McLean weren't worried and if Perkins had qualms, he kept them to himself. Jeff Yanssens took CERV-4 to the Milford Proving Ground and turned it over to the development drivers. They all knew that in just six weeks, McLean and Hill had to show it to Jack Smith. His reaction would be the one that would shape the future for them all.

37

JUNE heat soaked the rented pavilion at the Los Angeles County Fairgrounds in Pomona. The November research clinic that came just two weeks after Corvette got the word that it was a viable program again had found flaws in C5's design. The June clinic came barely a week before Corvette was to take its case to General Motors president Jack Smith and his North American Operations Strategy Board.

If results echoed November's, they could kiss Corvette good-bye.

The auto industry loves its clinics. Every company does them, usually hiring a professional research firm to do most of the work. Many are held in Los Angeles on the theory that southern California auto buyers closely represent the world. Even if they don't, Californians buy a lot of cars and their opinions are valued. But clinics are also run in other cities. Corvette included Chicago, Cincinnati, and Dallas at various times, but its primary focus remained the L.A. area.

Lists of registered car owners were scanned by the research firm to produce an appropriate sample of people. For Corvette's clinics, the samples would include owners of Corvettes plus the major competition—the Nissan 300ZX, Mazda RX-7, Toyota Supra, and perhaps the Mitsubishi 3000GT/Dodge Stealth. The invitation list was three hundred strong in November and grew to five hundred in June. Arrival times were tightly scheduled to give each person from ninety minutes to two hours in the building, usually in groups of a dozen or so. Each was paid for helping out, typically $75 to $100.

Dave Hill was there, at his first Corvette clinic, and with two of his engineers and several people from Chevrolet. John Cafaro was on hand to watch faces and listen to voices. He wanted to feel the reactions on the spot. Two Chevy dealers, members of an advisory council, also watched. They had a vital stake in the car and wanted to know that it would be right.

They brought four cars again, in mural-size photo projections, for eight separate focus groups to study and discuss. Cafaro teamed with his assistant Dan Magda for one, and Randy Wittine had the second entry from Cafaro's studio. A third was by Joe Ponce from the Advanced 2 studio and the last came from GM's California studio. On day one of the clinic, only

Corvette exteriors would be tested. Separate groups would rate interiors on day two.

The Cafaro/Magda car got mixed reactions. In the focus groups, only first names of the people being questioned were used. "The front end is like a dustbuster," Rebecca said, "like it's going to suck up something off the road."

"I'd rate it a three as a dream car," Leroy said. "No, on rethinking it, I don't like it that much."

Jim called it a Batmobile. "I expect to see a guy jump out wearing a cape. But I like the side view."

They all liked the side view of the Cafaro/Magda design. Rebecca found it growing on her: "It looks cutting edge. A person buying this car wants something new and exciting."

"The taillights look like a 'Vette," Jason said. "And it's more streamlined. It would be a nice car to have."

Randy Wittine's car caught their attention. "It looks fast and expensive," Ellen said, rating it a 9.5 on her dream car scale.

The California car took criticism. "It looks too much like a Saturn," David said, "or maybe like a base Corvette with pieces stuck on that don't belong."

"Like a pregnant RX7," Grace added.

John Cafaro sat in a side room watching each of the groups on closed-circuit television. He sketched cars on his pad as he listened and took a few notes. When they talked about his car, he perked up and paid attention.

"It's more aggressive than the others," Daryll said. "I give it an eight."

It reminded Herb of the muscle cars of the mid-sixties, though he called the rear end weak. "A young guy will drive the hell out of that car and really enjoy it," he said.

A few yards away, John Cafaro grinned.

Walter called it traditionally Corvette. "I like that," he said. "The front is traditional and I like that."

"What do you expect in a Corvette?" they were asked.

"Something new," Ellen said. "Something old. I want to know what to expect, but to have new things, too."

The answer was straight out of the mainline of Corvette fanatics. "Give me something new. But not *too* new."

In the end, participants wanted to mix and match. They liked some of Joe Ponce's car ("nice front end, weak in the rear"), pieces of the Cafaro/Magda car ("mean and aggressive"), and pieces of Randy Wittine's ("not gee whiz, but enduring"). They didn't like much at all of the California studio's entry. That one, they said, sent the least focused message. It was "derivative and boring."

John Cafaro slept happy that night. He'd take his insights home and put the whole studio to work making a series of little fixes to the car he'd designed with Dan Magda. The dustbuster front end had to go. That fix wasn't so little, but it was easy. They'd borrow some of Joe Ponce's ideas, blend in a little Randy Wittine, and have a Corvette that could live into the next century.

The interiors did almost as well on day two. There were two, which could be lifted in and out of the seating buck. No focus group saw both. The benchmark car was a Nissan 300ZX and the procedure was simple. People got into the car, adjusted the steering wheel, got out, then back in. They checked out the Nissan, then one of the Corvette interiors, labeled only A or B.

"The ZX has more of a cockpit feel, but I like the overall layout of B better," Wes said.

"This is a lot easier to get in and out of than my Corvette" was a frequent comment.

"The gauges, the needles, are too ordinary," Pat complained. That comment would register strongly. The needles stayed, but the ultimate design would be far from ordinary.

"The center console isn't deep enough to be useful," Linda said. And that comment was admittedly accurate, but there was nothing the designers could do. The central tunnel running through Corvette, its "backbone," left little room for decent storage between driver and passenger.

"Entry and egress is great," Greg said with obvious feeling. The steering column no longer got in the way of knees settling into position.

"Visibility is definitely superior to the Nissan 300ZX," Jennie said, and almost everyone agreed. In the back room, Dave Hill was smiling. "This front pillar is a bit thick, but it's okay." Hill's smile slipped a bit. The A-pillars still didn't meet the "elegance" of the C4 Corvette.

Some items were beyond the designer's control. People complained about reduced size in the glove compartment without realizing that their storage space was more or less preempted by the requirement for a passenger air bag. The doors came inboard a bit too much, crimping shoulder room, but that was because of the government's side-impact standards forcing doors to be stronger and beefier. Passenger and driver were being packaged by law tightly inside a cocoon of steel and balloons. They were losing comfort and convenience but gaining a small fraction of safety. All it cost was out-of-pocket money and a bit of the pleasure they got from their cars.

The cargo area came in for some criticism. The reach-over to load a suitcase or a golf bag was still too much. "It's because we have that spare tire right there," Cafaro said in the viewing room. There was only one place for the tire, tucked vertically in a deep well against the rear wall of the car.

One way or another, the spare tire had to go. Then the reach-over would be nothing at all.

There were criticisms to be dealt with, but nothing like the bad reviews the Corvette designs got in November. None of the cars at Pomona was perfect, but three out of four cars had major features that the focus groups liked. Two might have been good enough to carry forward without change. But John Cafaro knew better. The job ahead for his design studio was to blend the best features of the three cars into one Corvette with a new look and a lot of class.

By Sunday night it was over. Dave Hill called it.

"Well," he said, "I think we've got a good story to tell Jack Smith."

38

JACK Smith was sick. The Corvette team was ready for him to be a grand inquisitor when they brought him their plans, but with chills and a fever, he slept poorly the night before and he was mostly quiet when his North American Operations Strategy Board convened on June 14, 1993. The rest of the board was only a little more feisty. But then, many of its members had been primed in advance.

Russ McLean started the preparations for the big day back in March, setting people to work collecting all the information they'd need and then some. He wanted dry runs in April and May. He scheduled a presentation to Joe Spielman and his Midsize Car Division staff, but Spielman added additional sessions that he'd attend without his staff.

"This has to be right," Spielman said. "If GM ever tried to drop Corvette, we'd all be looking for jobs because this company would be down the tubes. The world would see General Motors as a major loser."

A practice session highlight was Fred Gallasch of the Chevrolet Sporty Car section telling about another piece of the Corvette legend. The biggest Corvette show of them all, he said, was called Bloomington Gold. The 1993 gathering in Springfield, Illinois, only a few months hence, would attract more than forty thousand people with at least five thousand of them bringing their Corvettes.

In 1992, Gallasch said, he rode in the number six car during the Saturday evening road tour—1,609 Corvettes led by the local cops with lights flashing and winding through miles of countryside and small Illinois towns.

As the tour stretched across mid-Illinois, it passed crowds gathered everywhere. Where the seamless line of Corvettes crossed over Interstate 55, cars, pickups, and eighteen-wheelers stopped on the shoulders for a half mile in each direction; people gawked and cheered at the unending procession. Truck drivers stood waving their caps from the tops of their cabs, their cross-country schedules be damned.

"Along some of the back roads," Gallasch said, "farmers had pulled their pickup trucks into fields, put out ice chests and picnic snacks, and sat with the wife and kids, watching from lawn chairs." Many of them waved American flags at the passing parade.

"You see those good-old-boy farmers waving the flag at your Corvette and it's hard to remember that there's anything wrong with the world," Gallasch said, looking directly at Joe Spielman.

"Look at Jack Smith when you say that," Spielman interrupted.

Gallasch nodded. All the vintage 'Vettes were at Bloomington Gold, he said. The Indy pace cars from the fifties, sixties, seventies, and eighties. The high-octane Fuelies from 1957 to 1965. The original '53s with wire screen covers on the headlamps. He told about those Corvettes, some of them going back to day one in 1953, still being driven by their original owners. For contrast, there were Corvettes thirty years old with less than ten thousand miles on their odometers and newer 'Vettes with more than two hundred thousand hard miles behind them.

There were the Corvette Collector's Editions, the styling cars of the sixties and seventies, the experimentals of long-ago decades, and a factory pilot car of the 40th-Anniversary Edition of 1993. "We made sure that one was there," he said.

The warrior Corvettes were there, too, the racers and the dragsters, and the muscle beasts from years of Corvette Challenge races.

In the middle of the road-tour pack, Gallasch said, seven cars in a row flew the Canadian flag. They'd driven down from up north just for the weekend. Other Corvettes flew flags from Europe and Asia. Their drivers made the annual trek to Illinois and rented Corvettes for the road tour. Not even the craziest Corvette owner would ship a car overseas for a few days of fun at Bloomington Gold. He'd rent somebody else's instead.

"The small towns were amazing," Gallasch said. "The streets were lined with people, kids being imprinted with their own desire to own a Corvette, babies in carriages pushed by young mothers and fathers, and old men leaning on canes and wishing they'd been smart enough in the fifties to plunk down the bucks it took to buy one." When he told them about girls running out of the crowds to kiss drivers, Gallasch blushed. And when he told them about another town where the mayor shook hands with every driver, he couldn't help grinning.

"We finished the tour and went to dinner," Fred Gallasch said in a tone that approached awe. "When we came out two hours later, Corvettes were still streaming past the restaurant. The end of the parade was nowhere in sight.

"We're going back there in June," he said. "Any of you guys who doubts the strength of Corvette ought to come along."

Another preview was scheduled with Corvette's group executive and old friendly nemesis, Mike Mutchler, now running North American Passenger Car Platforms. But after listening to Spielman's enthusiasm, Mutchler settled for simply viewing a set of the slides that the Corvette presenters would use. He blessed them without a change. Both Mutchler and Spielman were members of the Strategy Board. They'd be ready to take on other members if the going got rough.

Joe Spielman came close on his promise to get the total program back to its original $250 million. He got it up to $241 million and said that Mike Mutchler looked happy when he said yes. It was a sign that General Motors, still desperately ill, was no longer dying. Russ McLean made a promise of his own. "You keep it there and I'll bring it in for less," he said.

"If you do," Spielman said, "we won't tell anybody until the very end."

"I'll keep a reserve in my hip pocket," McLean agreed conspiratorially. "You know how programs go. Something always costs more."

McLean's obsessive nature reemerged during the ninety days leading up to the Concept Initiation grilling on June 14. The administrative side of Corvette—people charged with overseeing finances, purchasing, warranty records, quality reports, program timing, assembly plant liaison, car testing, and more—were grilled relentlessly by McLean. He didn't just want to know about the data that would be fed to the Strategy Board. He wanted data two and three levels deeper, along with analyses, so he or Dave Hill would be ready to field any question that came up. He also wanted lists of questions that board members might ask. They were indexed with the locations of backup slides that he could call up on the screen. His answers would not only by verbal, but visual.

The more nitpicky he got, the longer hours his team worked. At the same time, they had to cope with making the move to the new Vehicle Launch Center and with the restructuring of the Midsize Car Division. Engineering director Mike Juras chose that time to begin implementing his vision and it hit Corvette quickly.

The new organization chart called for three senior systems engineers to support a program, in addition to a model year manager. Pete Liccardello's experience in GM plants in California and at the Bowling Green, Kentucky, plant that built Corvettes was too valuable to lose on administrative duties. He took over the manufacturing systems slot and an eager young Canadian named Gordon Duda became C5 model year manager. Fresh faces came in to fill the slots for dimensional systems and engineering development systems. They'd all get their turns at bat later in the program.

But for Gordon Duda, it was like being tossed into a cauldron. Before he found out where the bathrooms were, McLean loaded him with assignments for the Strategy Board presentation. Duda learned by immersion. Within six weeks, he knew more about Corvette than most diehard fanatics. He was at work before 7 A.M. and by evening each day he'd taken on the blank stare of a zombie.

While Russ McLean was cracking the whip at the General Motors Technical Center, Jeff Yanssens was having the time of his life at the Milford Proving Ground forty-two miles to the northwest. After showing CERV-4 to the Corvette team at an all-people meeting, he took it out on the secluded Milford track and fell in love.

"Incredible," he reported to Dave Hill after his first run. "It felt better than any car I've driven in my life."

Hill's gut told him that would be the case. But hearing it from Yanssens lifted his spirits all the same. The car was strong. It was stiff. It was what they wanted.

A soft car is bad on the bumps. It deflects and bends. It develops squeaks and rattles. Its steering is mushy and every vibration works up through the legs and backsides of driver and passenger. Stiff is better. One jolt might get through, but the suspension absorbs most of the road impacts.

They measured CERV-4 on special machines to get hard data. It was five times stiffer than the current Corvette convertible. It was four times more resistant to bending.

On every test, it exceeded predictions. And the predictions were high.

It was also too heavy. "Some of the good numbers were from mass," Yanssens reported. "A heavy car doesn't bounce as much as a lighter one. But we know how to diet when it comes to the real C5."

The important thing to Dave Hill was that Corvette's new structure was going to do everything they'd dreamed. The fundamentals were there. The rest was detailed engineering and fine tuning. Over at Chevrolet, Jim Perkins was a happy fellow. His gamble on authorizing under-the-table money to build CERV-4 paid off with a car that didn't just prove the backbone theory, but validated his own executive wisdom. After the troubles of the previous years, it was time for Jim Perkins to win one.

He'd already gone to the mat over the hidden money to build the CERV. The auditors discovered something amiss in Chevy's books and launched an investigation. General Motors' security people were called in, too. When the sleuths narrowed it down to a couple of people, and the word "embezzlement" was being considered, Perkins walked into a conference room and fessed up. "I authorized it," he said, and explained where the money went. "We needed those cars. It was that important. And if I have to resign my job and find a way to pay you back out of my own pocket, I'll do it."

The auditors thought it over, packed their briefcases, and went away. If Jim Perkins said that Corvette needed an engineering test car, that was good enough for them.

A few days before the all-important Concept Initiation meeting, McLean and Hill put their heads together and came up with one final scheme to get Strategy Board members on their side. Jeff Yanssens loaded CERV-4 into an eighteen-wheeler and delivered it to the General Motors Technical Center late Thursday night, four days before they'd show it to the full board. Three board members accepted invitations to drive it Friday on the Tech Center's small track.

Harry Pearce was GM's corporate lawyer and a man rising rapidly in the hierarchy. He would soon make his public mark by exposing how an NBC television program rigged its reporting of fire hazards in some GM pickup trucks and by getting an on-air apology. When Pearce got into the driver's seat of CERV-4, he was eager but skeptical. And when he took the car around the track with Dave Hill in the shotgun seat, he wondered about Hill's claim that the next Corvette would handle the road so much better.

"This track's too smooth," Hill said. On the spot, he proved that he was a man who knew when to break his own rule about keeping the car in hiding. He waved to Jeff Yanssens to open the gate and Harry Pearce gunned CERV-4 out of the Tech Center's grounds and onto Van Dyke Avenue, where winter potholes still hadn't been repaired and ripples in the blacktop gave the car a legitimate test.

They were back in five minutes, hair rumpled and grinning like truant schoolboys. CERV-4 was solid, stable, and shake-free. Harry Pearce's vote to approve the new Corvette was in the bag.

Hill followed with board members Arv Mueller, the vice president who ran the Technical Center, and executive vice president Bill Hoglund, GM's chief financial officer, who formerly ran both Pontiac and Oldsmobile. Hill let them feel the car through their fingertips and their backsides on the smooth track, then told them to run the car out to the real world of bumps and potholes. He already knew how they'd react. Two more voices for the new Corvette would be ready to argue for Corvette approval on Monday afternoon.

Monday dawned bleak and stormy. Hill was working at dawn, honoring a request from another Strategy Board member, Mike Losh, for the chance to drive CERV-4. When the lanky Losh pulled off bumpy Van Dyke and squealed back into the Tech Center, he was shaking his head in awe. Hill mentally tallied another vote for C5.

Russ McLean was still fretting the last-minute details. He had the Design dome set up for the meeting and it was to be a full day for the Strategy Board. In the morning they'd pore over corporate issues. In the afternoon they'd consider Concept Initiations for Corvette and a new family sedan. When the board broke from its morning session, the ailing Jack Smith managed a 7UP and some soup for lunch, then tried to catch a short nap in Wayne Cherry's plush office on the second floor of the Design building.

He didn't get much rest. A violent thunderstorm broke overhead, filling the sky with jagged lightning bolts and immediate booms. Across Mound Road from the Design Dome, lightning struck an open field and threw up gouts of sizzling dirt and steam. Torrents of rain marched on wind gusts across the reflecting pond and the geese and swans tucked their heads in submission.

Inside the Dome, the Corvette team was oblivious to nature's hammer. They were setting up displays for the show-and-tell, ready to let Strategy Board members touch and feel the past, the present, and the future. They brought in one of the original 1953 Corvettes, its polo white paint still gleaming and its red interior looking hardly the worse for its thirty-nine years.

Four more bright red cars were driven onto the Dome's floor: a new 1994 Corvette just off the assembly line in Bowling Green, Kentucky; a Dodge Stealth; a Mazda RX-7; and a Nissan 300ZX convertible. The Mazda and Nissan were major competitors and the Nissan was the benchmark car that Corvette intended to beat. The Stealth was there to let them see a low-end sporty car that didn't take away from Corvette sales. The Strategy Board could take a close look at the real competition and at a wanna-be. Russ McLean wanted them to see the other cars first, then to hear that Corvette would be better.

The seating buck used in the early June clinic was there, too. If Jack Smith or any of them wanted to sit in it to see for themselves, they were welcome. Then there were three scale models, three-eighths-size Corvettes that had been seen as photos at the clinic. The California model wasn't there. And the primary model by John Cafaro and Dan Magda was in new garb, with its dustbuster front end replaced by aerodynamic air scoops separated by a license plate well, and with subtle changes to the sides and rear.

There was a fourth full-size car sitting mysteriously covered to the side where Jack Smith couldn't miss it. Midway through the presentation, Dave Hill would lift the cover and Smith would get his first look at the shiny black CERV-4.

Jack Smith walked in just after 1 P.M., looking worn but managing a smile. His dark hair showed a few more strands of gray than a year earlier when he moved up to the presidency, and he'd added a few pounds to his medium five-nine frame. He filled a glass with ice water and took his seat at the center of a horseshoe-shaped table, and the show began.

It was Joe Spielman's place to make opening remarks. They were short: "Corvette has been in bubble-up for five years, Jack. I'm here to tell you that we've got it right!" He pointed to Russ McLean. "Russ will open up and tell our story." That was it. Spielman sat down.

McLean grinned like a new daddy. He was nervous when the lights dimmed, but when he started to talk the little shake in his voice went away quickly. He'd rehearsed so often that he seldom referred to the slide on the big screen in front or to brief film clips. He knew his material. He bowed briefly to Corvette's history. He talked about the competition and how Corvette had increased its market share for three years running. As good as they were, Nissan and Mazda were falling farther behind and Corvette was increasing its dominant position. He pointed to the '53 and '94 Corvettes.

"No other car has this heritage," he said. "Corvette as a cult buries Harley-Davidson. Kids get imprinted with the Corvette desire in their teens. A fireman at our clinic in L.A. saved for five years to buy his new Corvette. Another guy was a collector. He had seventeen Corvettes in his collection and said he buys them like some guys change ties. Except he never sells. He still owns every Corvette he ever bought."

When McLean showed the models that represented Corvette's chosen direction, Jack Smith perked up. "Why are you evolving rather than changing dramatically," he asked. "If Corvette doesn't change dramatically, why not?"

McLean was ready for the question. "Corvette buyers want the heritage, the continuum, not something dramatic," he said. "New and dramatic cars come around all the time. They grab a big bite for a year or two, then they fade away just as fast. Corvette just keeps going, and going, and going. If we get dramatic, we risk being hung out to dry like a dinosaur."

Smith nodded and sipped his water.

Around the table, GM's top executives sat in silence. The Strategy Board already had earned a reputation for interrupting, for asking harsh and pointed questions, for finding the flaws in presentations and ripping them open. Russ McLean talked for thirty-nine minutes, gliding from point to point as he built the case for the '97 Corvette. There were no interruptions. There were no more questions. Two minutes before McLean finished, Jack Smith got up to fetch himself a fresh glass of ice water. McLean took the cue and wrapped up his piece of the show.

Chevrolet's Fred Gallasch took over to outline the marketing plans for the new Corvette. "Corvette is the only General Motors car to increase market share in a decreasing market," he said. That got their attention. Then he told his story about Bloomington Gold, and the board members listened and nodded and glanced at each other with smiles.

Finally there was a question. Executive vice president Bill Hoglund asked why they were waiting until 1997 for the new Corvette. "Why this timing?" he asked. "Is it money? Design? Engineering?"

"It's primarily getting the engineering done," Russ McLean answered. The biggest problem, he said, was that corporate downsizing left Corvette with too few engineers and drafting experts. Every platform in the company had the same problem.

"Then maybe we ought to get you some," Hoglund said.

Jack Smith rubbed his eyes and leaned forward on his arms. "You're talking about starting production in February 1997," he said. "Why not try to make it earlier, at least a little?"

"We're looking at a plan to start shipping to dealers in December 1996," McLean said. Under that plan, he didn't say for fear of looking too optimistic, production on the first pilot cars would start on September 3, 1996. Not so coincidentally, that was Russ McLean's birthday.

"If it's possible, we'll do it," Joe Spielman interrupted. He stood up from his seat on the left arm of the horseshoe table and let his six-five bulk emphasize his words. "And it looks possible. More than possible. With your help."

The Corvette people in the dome held their breath. The Strategy Board didn't offer to give platforms *more;* it was more likely to take budget away and tell them to make do with *less*. Spielman and McLean didn't push their luck. They both sat and let the thought soak in.

Dave Hill had yet to talk, but the board's mood was clear. "In this segment of the business," said GM executive Dick Pompa, "there are only two choices: Corvette and all the others. I think that's pretty neat!"

When Hill started, he skimmed over the nuts and bolts, and how it would all be coming together. He talked about the new Gen III engine being developed. It was aluminum to save weight and it used push-rod technology that had been around since the beginning of Corvette. From the dark at the edge of the table came a single word: "Why?"

"Corvette owners want performance, not gadgets," Hill said. "They want to squirt through traffic and they don't want the lag from turbocharging. And we can give it to them without gimmicks like thirty-two-valve engines."

Hill had, however, come to the Gen III engine reluctantly. He preferred a version of the super high-tech thirty-two-valve Northstar engine that he'd used on Cadillac programs. He'd been swayed by the Corvette veterans to go with Gen III, but he still wasn't convinced. When another questioner asked about the possibility of Gen III delays, Hill quickly answered that the C5 Corvette would "package-protect"—or ensure that space was available —to put the bigger Northstar engine under the hood if necessary. Package protection proved impossible in later months, but by then it was a moot point.

When Hill got to the CERV-4, the board was primed. He stressed the results of early CERV-4 testing and was immediately interrupted. "I'll second that," said GM vice president Mike Losh. "I drove that thing at six o'clock this morning and it's like nothing I've ever seen."

Hill immediately called a fifteen-minute break, pulled the cover off CERV-4, and watched the grins under the Dome. They didn't need translation.

All that was left was the business case. For the $241 million investment, the new Corvette should sell an annual average of more than twenty-five thousand cars over a seven-year lifetime. It would be profitable. It would dominate the sports car market. And it would bring more than money into General Motors. It would remake an American legend and show that General Motors could still build a world-class car.

Joe Spielman stood again. Outside the rain had stopped. Sunlight reflected off the Patio's puddles and wet tiles and beamed through tall windows into the Dome. Spielman held up a piece of paper and waited for a copy of his script to appear on the screen. Tom Hoxie of Chevy's public relations department had authored an emotional and fictitious article from the distant future. It could be from the December 1996 *Road and Track* magazine, Spielman said. He started to read. Some members of the ferocious Strategy Board followed along on the screen. One or two leaned back with closed eyes and listened. Jack Smith rested his head in his hands.

The piece unblushingly extolled the '97 Corvette, maybe too unblushingly. *Road and Track* writers would have screamed indignantly at the fictional liberty, at the lush prose and lusher praise. But when Spielman finished, the board applauded. Including Jack Smith.

"Well done!" shouted Dick Pompa. "Bravo!"

"I wish all the programs we see in here were this good," said Mike Losh.

"Don't underestimate your volumes," Bill Hoglund said. "You're going to sell more cars than you think."

Mike Mutchler had been quiet most of the afternoon. He'd been the instrument of most Corvette delays since 1989, or at least the bearer of bad news, and was now the instrument of its bigger and better $241 million budget. He was not given to strong reactions, but his smile was big and wide.

"This is the best CI presentation I've ever seen," he said, standing at his seat. "You all deserve our congratulations for the work you've done and for having such a strong program under way.

"I'm confident you can deliver. I'm confident you *will* deliver!"

Finally it was over. The afternoon had been a lovefest. Russ McLean was exhausted, but he stood his ground and asked for more questions. There was only one. "What else do you need from us?" Bill Hoglund asked.

McLean was struck dumb. It was a question nobody anticipated. McLean was ready to defend his program. He wasn't ready to ask for more. But he recovered. "I'll send you a list."

Jack Smith coughed lightly. Then he said the words that would be quoted throughout the Corvette team in the coming weeks.

"It's pretty clear we have a program," he said. "Anybody object?"

The Dome went dead quiet. On the huge screen, a sign-off slide appeared. There were three blank boxes:

❑ APPROVED

❑ DISAPPROVED

❑ DEFERRED

Jack Smith nodded and the screen flickered.

☑ APPROVED

39

T H E Y got their green light from the Strategy Board and with it a mild dose of confidence that this one might be for real. Now they had to perform. They had to take five years of paper, plans, and preliminary designs and turn them into a 1997 Corvette.

Jack Smith and the senior executives at General Motors came close to doing what enlightened bosses are supposed to do: Set the goal, set some guidelines, get out of the way. In the all-pervasive General Motors culture, getting out of the way was the hard part. But they tried.

It was just that GM is neither static nor predictable. From the outside, corporations appear to be logical, uniform, and structured. Perhaps some are. But not GM. It is an amorphous, sometimes erratic, always changing beast with rules, procedures, and reporting lines that shimmer in the glass of today and may look quite different seen through the glass of tomorrow.

Bobbing and weaving across GM's unstable bureaucratic landscape is a required skill for getting anything done inside the company. Corvette would still waste valuable time dodging bullets and complying with the rule of the day. Executive tunnel vision would hide the waste from the senior bureaucrats who caused most of it. At the top, Jack Smith and the people around him fought a daily battle to get their hands on things, attempting to bring order to a disorderly corporation. Every change they made, the good and the questionable, filtered down through the ranks. Every change brought grief to someone, at least until the ripples of change smoothed into something either manageable or understandable, or ideally both. So while the upper ranks may have thought they had gotten out of Corvette's way, they still did their share of burdening the program with too frequent changes in how things were to be done. Just complying with those changes added untold months to bringing a typical GM car to market.

Tom Krejcar offered a pick-me-up example for the beleaguered Corvette team. The financial manager, a cheery finagler who loved the car and had been a key conspirator in keeping money flowing to C5 either on budget or off, grew a mustache. He promised to keep it until the first C5 rolled off the assembly line at Bowling Green, Kentucky, in late 1996. He kept the promise, but not the way he wanted. Nine months later he was dead from metastasized tongue cancer. Most of the Corvette team showed up at his wake. The mustache was intact and in his lapel was the Corvette pin Russ McLean had given him a few weeks earlier.

In the months before he died, Krejcar knew that C5 was in a fight, but maybe at last, a fair fight. Russ McLean kept him on distribution for every memo and called him every few days with updates. Even when Krejcar could only listen, McLean would talk at length about how it was going. "You watch," he said in one of the last calls. "You'll like the way it turns out." McLean knew exactly what he was saying. So did Tom Krejcar.

The first fight for the people working for McLean and chief engineer Dave Hill was to sort out the mixed messages and get their own psyches straight. The inflow of new people, assigned to help design and package all the parts that went into the car, helped allay concerns that another stop order was imminent. The move into the Vehicle Launch Center helped even more.

The VLC was on the west side of the tracks at the GM Tech Center, the side where the artists and the elite among GM's scientists and engineers worked. For a year or so, the Corvette team would work there, too. The tunnel down the hall was another psychological boost. It was protected by a security door that opened when Corvette people ran their ID badges through a card reader. Once past the door, they entered a gloomy and humid corridor that led underground to Design Staff's basement, where a quick elevator ride brought Dave Hill and his engineers to within a few yards of John Cafaro's studio. For the duration, gloomy and humid were just fine. At least they didn't have to make the drive across the Tech Center to meet with the people styling the new Corvette, or to see the latest changes in the studio clay. Now it was just a seven-minute walk.

Corvette's VLC quarters were in an engineering building basement with no windows. A sedan program got the second floor with a view of the reflecting pool and its geese and swans. The basement area was still under construction as workmen finished conference rooms, installed cubicles, and ran telephone and computer lines through floors and ceilings. It was to become Dave Hill's subterranean empire for the next fourteen months. Russ McLean stayed behind with his financial and administrative staff at Midsize Car Division headquarters to manage C4 and maintain overall coordination. The Vehicle Launch Center was for engineering, a place where a car team could bring itself together and where it could call upon experts from other parts of GM to pitch in and lend a hand. It was what bubble-up and Phase Zero had been in the original Four-Phase development plan. But now it was formalized and confined to a single location. If you needed the C5 Corvette, here it was. And if C5 needed you, Dave Hill had the power to get your services.

One area away from Hill's office was being filled with computer tubes and designers who would trace out parts and components to be fitted in the C5 chassis. In the crucial year when most parts took on their shapes and specifications, the drafters or designers drawing the lines on the screen had the C5 engineers close enough to be called on for clarification. Or close enough to be looking over shoulders in the crunch times.

Another pair of adjoining rooms was outfitted for full-size mock-ups of the car-to-be. The mock-ups were vital to packaging. It was how they made sure that all the pieces fit. The rails and backbone structure were carefully formed of wood and metal. The rest of the parts—from body panels to gas tanks to instrument dials to the windshield washer reservoir—were fake, too. Many were cardboard and paper. Others were lightweight plastic, or foam, carved and bent to shape. Doing the mock-up became an exercise in putting together a full-size three-dimensional puzzle. As parts were designed and given their first approvals, expert model makers turned out replicas for the engineers to try. When they didn't fit exactly, the parts were redesigned and a new piece showed up for another go.

"Cardboard is cheap and easy to change," the mock-up chief, Dave Salada, preached to the Corvette engineers. "Seeing your parts in 3-D helps drive your designs, so don't be afraid to make changes." After a while, they weren't.

The final piece that straightened out the unspoken concerns of the Corvette team fell into place a month after Jack Smith and the Strategy Board turned on the green light. It was a simple thing but telling. Overnight, decisions were being made and they stuck. Joe Spielman looked at a clay car in John Cafaro's studio and made a decision right then and there. On one side of the clay, Cafaro had seventeen-inch wheels front and back. It looked like its rear quarter had been slammed by a truck in traffic. On the other side, Cafaro had an eighteen on the back. Spielman walked around the car, listened to Dave Hill talk about the weight they'd save with the smaller wheel, and overruled him on the spot. "Save the mass somewhere else," Spielman said. "Cafaro's right. The car needs big tires in back."

A few days later, Cafaro showed Hill a new look for the C5's hood, a five-degree slope toward the front wheels that gave the future Corvette a racier look. Hill and his engineers had pushed for the slope to improve forward vision. The problem was that the extra slope meant interference between the hood and the engine under it. "You do the five degrees and I'll get the engine packaged under it," Hill told Cafaro. It was the right thing for both the driver and for the car's looks, but it was a decision that would cause Powertrain fits a few years later.

At the same time, Pete Liccardello, now in charge of manufacturing liaison for C5, decided that the basic structures for the first twenty-three preprototype, or alpha, test cars should be built at the Bowling Green assembly plant. Hill reversed the decision, citing the need to keep it close at hand. The frames would be built in the mini-assembly plant called Bumper-to-Bumper located in the huge back end of Midsize headquarters.

Hill also backed the first of several changes in Corvette resulting from the "Juras Vision." The Midsize Car Division's engineering homeroom for doors decided that it didn't like the way Corvette planned to assemble doors. Without warning or discussion, it announced that Corvette's way was out and that it would design all-new doors to its own liking. It was a challenge that the independent-minded Corvette engineers wanted Hill to answer. Instead he looked at the schemes and decided that it wasn't a fight they could win. "They're the real experts on doors," he said quietly and with less than hearty conviction. "We have to give them a chance."

Like it or not, he told several of his people privately, they had to learn to live with the Juras engineering system. It was all they had. "And maybe it'll work," he added.

The mass of the car—its weight—was a subject for endless decision making. Whenever Corvette engineers fought over the mass of this or the mass of that, the term "test weight class," TWC, came up. Federal tests on engine emissions and gas mileage frequently vary according to how much a car weighs. Test weight classes come in 125-pound increments. When the C4 Corvette was first planned, it was supposed to be in the 3,000-pound TWC, weighing more than 3,000 pounds but less than 3,125. It came in far above that, in the 3,625 class. Test weight includes two adult passengers at about 150 pounds each, a full tank of gas, full loads of oil, transmission fluid, and coolant, plus an allowance for baggage. So a Corvette with a curb, or empty weight, of 3,100 pounds could easily be in the 3,625-pound TWC.

The goal for C5 was to deliver a car in the 3,375 test weight class. At that weight, the Gen III engine could easily deliver superior gas mileage, maybe twenty-four miles per gallon, in government tests while exceeding all emissions requirements and giving Corvette enthusiasts a high-performance sports car. At heavier weights, the engine would work harder and the numbers would degrade. There were other factors, too. A heavier car needs heavier brakes, heavier shock absorbers and springs, a heavier structure to carry the loads. So a pound here and a pound there frequently meant even more pounds somewhere else.

Dave Hill decided to put a dollar value on mass. His systems engineer, a relatively new addition named Tadge Juechter, put together a committee and worked it out. The numbers were instructive.

"The elasticities are measurable," Juechter reported. "A one percent increase in the acceleration time from zero-to-sixty mph equals a one-point-twenty-five percent increase in Corvette sales. A one percent increase in miles per gallon equals a one percent increase in sales."

Acceleration and fuel economy both go up when weight goes down. If improvements made sales go up, profits too would go up.

"Then what we have is this," Juechter said. "One test weight class equals a six-point-three percent change in performance. That translates to a seven-point-eight-seven-five percent increase in sales."

At the numbers being estimated for C5 sales from 1997 through 2003, it all added up to significant additional profit per pound saved on the performance side of the equation. Then Juechter threw in the fuel savings, the benefit of keeping C5 from paying a gas-guzzler penalty to the government, plus savings in fuel costs for the car owner on each tank of gas.

"The bottom line is that mass equals money," he said. Instead of keeping the profit, they could spend it on mass reduction.

Hill took it in and made a decision that rippled through the team for the next three years. "Okay," he said, "starting now we will use ten dollars per kilogram to rationalize mass reductions."

The decision meant that Hill's engineers were free to spend ten dollars in the cost of a part for every kilogram of weight cut. They could switch from cheap steel to expensive magnesium, for instance, or they could tell suppliers to use a more costly process to make a part, as long as that ten dollars per kilogram measure was met. They could even, as they would do more than a year later, make the floor under the driver's and passenger's feet out of balsa wood grown on a farm in Peru.

The ten-dollar rule was a major turning point in shrinking C5's weight to an absolute minimum. It gave them a new tool to catalyze their thinking in the few weeks remaining before they had to face Russ McLean, Dave Hill, and a board of C5's senior engineers and administrators in early August with their own decisions at the impending gate called Concept Alternatives Selection.

That wasn't much time.

40

CORVETTE was a maverick. Its people complied when they could but continued to maneuver around the system when they had to. In the end, Russ McLean and Dave Hill proved their point. In mid-1993 General Motors had nearly a dozen new cars and vans scheduled for introduction in 1996 and 1997. Only the C5 Corvette stayed on budget and on time.

It wasn't easy. To help make it happen, McLean used something he called a "deep dive," an intense piece-by-piece review of the program and the car itself. It forced his people, particularly the engineers, to stay focused.

Platforms at General Motors were divided into engineering subgroups called product development teams, or PDTs. For the last half of Corvette development, there were nine of them. A development team was responsible for its own part of the car. Each had its own senior engineer who reported both to Dave Hill and to an engineering homeroom, plus a cadre of engineers assigned to the program, and another cadre of engineers from the homeroom who helped design parts, kibitzed and critiqued plans, and sometimes took over this piece or that to do it their own way.

The Corvette product development teams were: PDT-1, powertrain—the engine and transmission; PDT-2, chassis; PDT-3, heating, ventilation, and air-conditioning (HVAC), plus engine and transmission cooling. Then came interior, body, exterior, occupant information and controls, and electrical power and signals. The ninth product development team was called "vehicle and assembly." It was the oversight team, headed by systems engineer Tadge Juechter. The members of PDT-9 were the chiefs of the other eight teams plus Dave Hill and several administrative support people. It was where the major decisions were made, particularly when conflict arose among the teams.

McLean combined C5's first deep dive with the internal gate called Concept Alternatives Selection. Each engineering PDT now had years of experience in getting ready for CAS. They'd met internally and with other PDTs to settle basic questions such as C5's size and basic dimensions, its weight and performance goals, and its general layout. The engine would be in the front, the transmission in the back, and it would be a rear-wheel-drive car.

It should accelerate from 0 to 60 mph in 5.1 seconds. It should get at least 23.5 miles per gallon overall, and have a range of at least 450 miles between gas stops.

There would be no take-aways. If the current Corvette had it, so would C5. If the current Corvette did it, C5 would do it as well or better. It would do all this with fewer parts than it took to build a C4 and it would be assembled at Bowling Green in fewer man-hours.

It would include as much advanced technology as could be reasonably incorporated into an automobile. That included multiplexing, the black magic of sending scores of electrical and data signals along the same wires, leaving C5's computers to sort out what was what and make the right things happen. Corvette would be a multiplexing test bed at General Motors. It reduced the number of wires in the car and saved mass.

The C5's engine would be the push-rod Gen III being developed at the Powertrain Division. No postmodern thirty-two-valve, double-overhead cam engine would be inflicted on Corvette purists. The engine itself would be a marvelous mixture of old and new. The mechanics were old and had been around for at least five decades. But in Gen III, the engine would be run by computers. A computer would decide when to feed gas into a cylinder, and how much. A computer would mix in the right amount of air, bring back the right amount of exhaust for emission control, and decide when to fire the spark plug.

The accelerator pedal in C5 would be an anachronism. The Gen III would use ETC, electronic throttle control. The driver might think that his right foot was going pedal-to-the-metal, but ETC would be in the way. Under that pedal an electronic sensor would be measuring his foot's force and sending a flood of bits and bytes to an engine computer. The computer would decide whether to obey, and sometimes it wouldn't. For instance, when the driver wanted full throttle but the computer had warnings from the traction control system or antilock brakes (controlled by other computers) that a skid was impending, or when sensors reported that emissions limits would be exceeded or even that the engine wasn't sufficiently warm, the computer would override the driver's wishes.

The engine experts who would test and perfect Gen III would not be mechanics. They would be electrical engineers and computer science majors who wrote software and used laptop computers to reprogram cars on the spot.

The requirements for C5, the vehicle technical specifications (VTS), ran to hundreds of pages. They included comfort factors for passenger and driver, luggage or stowage space (two sets of golf clubs minimum), visibility through the windows, kinds and quality of paint (C4 had been notorious for paint jobs that didn't meet the standards of Corvette aficionados), and much more. If the members of the Corvette engineering teams could imagine it, and if it was even marginally important, there was a specification for it that had to be met.

In creating the VTS they had been aided, it seemed, by every owner of the nearly 1 million Corvettes still on the road; by every GM employee from the janitor to Jack Smith, all of whom had an opinion on what Corvette should be or not be and were mostly unafraid to express it; by the automotive press, whose writers were articulate and opinionated and had no idea of the influence they wielded; and by their friends, neighbors, spouses, and kids who all knew that a Corvette would be coming home and it darned well better have this or that. Or else.

Now it was time to make it happen. At Concept Alternatives Selection, each product development team brought in its proposals. Part of the bubble-up process, and the early months of Phase Zero in the convoluted Four-Phase process of developing a new car, called for PDT engineers to examine different ways of doing things. They were directed *not* to automatically take the old tried-and-true part and bring it forward into the next car. Instead they were to examine alternatives, look for something better, find a new and more efficient (and thus cheaper) way to do whatever it was that needed doing. A sign on the wall in both Corvette's old quarters at the Midsize Car Division headquarters and in the underground Vehicle Launch Center put it succinctly:

> If You Always Do
> What You've Always Done,
> You'll Always Get
> What You've Always Got

Grammar aside, it was a sentiment that profoundly affected C5 from its earliest days to the very end.

Now it was time for everyone to look at the alternatives and to pick one. They'd been working for years, and balls to the wall since the previous November when Joe Spielman promised that this time they wouldn't stop. Their best guesses had been part of the presentation to Jack Smith and the Strategy Board. They'd been melded into the financial numbers that made up the business case and the performance numbers that predicted what C5 would do in the hands of a Corvette driver.

But guessing was over. Deciding was now. This size battery or the next size bigger? This kind of lighting in the interior or that? Aluminum wheels or magnesium? Which carpeting at what cost and what weight? How thick should the body panels be? What kind of material for the floor pan, the rear tub, the wheel-well liner? Not every decision would be made at CAS and they all knew it. There were too many. And some issues had been boiled down to only two or three choices. Outside help was needed to go further, particularly from competing suppliers. Where two choices looked equally good, or equally confusing, a supplier's bid on the investment it would take to do choice A over choice B, or vice versa, and the "piece cost" the supplier would charge often tilted the decision.

Piece cost was a big part of CAS. The exact price that Corvette would pay for each part, or at least the best available estimate, had to be factored in wherever possible. Could the part be bought cheaper from a different supplier? Was it available in the so-called world parts bin? That mythical place was the sum total of all the parts from all the cars in the world. There were more than fifty thousand parts in GM alone. There had to be more than a half-million individual and discrete parts for cars worldwide. Did Toyota have a unique electrical switch that could be incorporated into C5? Did Ford use a catalytic converter that would fit C5's exhaust system? The possibilities were practically endless and nobody could examine them all.

But it was important to try. Some of the answers waited across the road from the Technical Center, in a nondescript warehouselike building. Here was GM's Competitive Assessment Center, nicknamed Mona Lisa because cars ended up in pieces, hanging on the walls like paintings. At Mona Lisa, skilled workers took brand-new cars purchased from competing dealers and tore them down. Piece by piece, wire by wire, nut-bolt-screw-and-fastener, they took apart Fords and Infinitis and Mazdas and selected models of almost every car on the market. Corvette had asked for a teardown of a Nissan 300ZX and a Mazda RX-7, to see what made those cars as good as they were.

To walk through Mona Lisa was to walk through an automotive wonder world, a supermarket of car parts and car technology. All the parts of a car were carefully attached to tall display boards. Engineers could examine shock absorbers, for example, and see how Lexus fit them into the chassis. Each piece was carefully labeled, complete with all the fasteners and other pieces that surrounded it. Structures were set on the floor in front of the displays, which took many boards to complete. The electrical system was there, fully diagrammed in both schematic and physical layout. Parts were weighed and measured and tested. Their specs were available in full reports and volumes of loose-leaf books that documented how the competition did this, or built that, or assembled these parts to make whatever.

Every car company has its Mona Lisa. It's one of the ways they keep track of what the competition is doing right and doing wrong. Corvette engineers spent hours and days wandering through Mona Lisa and thumbing through volumes of reports on cars no longer on display. Sometimes they found a part they could use, if only the supplier could be convinced to sell it to

General Motors as well as to Ford. Sometimes they found a different way of doing something and incorporated it into their own thinking. Usually they found nothing. But the exercise was useful.

There was help at the corporate level here, too. Under the short-lived reign of Jose Ignacio "Inaki" Lopez as GM's chief of purchasing, a subgroup called World Wide Purchasing was put in place to scour the globe for parts. Lopez soon disappeared after betraying his friend and mentor, Jack Smith, by jumping ship for an offer at Volkswagen in Germany. But many of his philosophies, and World Wide Purchasing, remained.

A unique part, a Corvette-only part, had to be designed from scratch. Costly tools and dies had to be built and tested so the part could be manufactured. Then engineers had to remember that Corvette was a low-volume car. After the initial investment in tools and dies, and maybe even complete new manufacturing machines and production lines, a supplier would charge more per part—the piece cost—for sixty-six thousand pieces than it charged for a million pieces. So if a part could be found that did the job, and if Toyota or Ford or some other car company was already buying 2 million of them a year from a supplier, then Corvette not only could avoid the initial investment costs, but could buy its sixty-six thousand or whatever small number of parts at a greatly reduced piece cost.

Reduced piece cost equaled reduced total cost of C5. Many parts would be unique to the all-new Corvette. But every penny saved by finding a part in the world parts bin, or on some other GM car, could be passed on to the customer. That was because the first new Corvette in thirteen years had a most unusual pricing target.

After everything was figured in—investment costs, piece cost, profit for GM—the sticker price for a C5 on a dealer's showroom floor *had to be equal to or less than the price of a comparably equipped C4.*

It was not just a tall order. It was gargantuan. It violated every precept in the automotive world and every cynical conviction held by the buying public. New cars cost more. A new Corvette that goes faster, handles better, gets more gas mileage, meets or exceeds every environmental and safety standard existing or contemplated, and costs less than today's car? Hogwash! That naturally made it a point of pride for everyone working on the new Corvette. *Hogwash? We'll show you hogwash!*

First they had to show Russ McLean. The decisions surrounding Concept Alternatives Selection ran to the thousands and McLean decreed that CAS would not be a simple presentation of what each PDT had decided. It would be a deep dive.

McLean, Dave Hill, and others from Corvette would hear the pros and cons, and the full range of ifs, ands, and buts. McLean wanted his engineers to dive so deeply into their systems and its parts that when they stood before the CAS board, they could not only report decisions, but defend them. He wanted to hear about the alternatives. He wanted detail. He wanted controversy. He wanted to walk away at the end and feel confident each PDT, each individual engineer, truly understood his piece of the Corvette. And he wanted them to demonstrate that they also understood how their piece fit with the other pieces, or in some cases, did not.

That was just for starters. Dave Hill added to the CAS burden by mandating that every part be reexamined using the ten-dollar-per-kilo rule, and that mass calculations be a part of every decision. The PDT leaders rolled their eyes, rolled up their sleeves, and passed the word.

Concept Alternatives Selection would begin on August 10, less than two months after the new Corvette got its green light. And for the first time, GM would be closed for the last two weeks of July, a cost-saving vacation ordered by Jack Smith that would become an annual tradition. Engineers packed up their documents and their laptop computers and took them home to do what had to be done. *Vacation? What vacation?*

When CAS, and Russ McLean's first deep dive, ended, they'd look back at working through the downtime and think again. Maybe that had been a vacation after all.

T H E deep dive wasn't exactly a bloodletting, but it left them exhausted and exhilarated in equal measure. Three product development teams, chassis, structure, and powertrain, went away in a sorrowful state. Russ McLean ordered them to come back in two weeks with a better story. He and Dave Hill would both come in from vacation for a day to decide whether the team used the time to get it right.

Diving deep turned into a grueling four-day process in the largest of Corvette's Vehicle Launch Center conference rooms. Even then, observers and presenters overflowed into the engineering bay and the air conditioner had a difficult time keeping up. McLean and Hill demanded detailed rationales for everything the PDT engineers wanted to do. One of the first up was Steve Mackin, chief of the interior team.

"We've selected smaller air vents and components behind the dash to give Design Staff the look and space it wants without moving the shifter," he said. "We're looking at a mid-mount for the passenger air bag to make room for a small glove box, but we need more design on that."

One decision involved planning ahead. A heads-up display, or HUD— which used special projection optics to give the driver the illusion that some instruments, like a digital speedometer, were floating out over the hood—might be added in some future year. But its hidden parts could be incorporated now.

"We need some brackets under the instrument panel," Mackin said.

The tooling investment would be minimal if the brackets were in the original design, but would be costly in the future when the change might involve tearing up existing parts. Mackin favored the preparedness route and got the nod.

The cup holder was a problem because the only space available for it was close to the shifter and even closer to the instrument panel. People with huge hands, less than 1 percent of the population, would scrape knuckles on a pop can in the holder. When a can was there, the ashtray wouldn't open.

"You can drive and drink," commented one of the engineers. "But you can't smoke and drink. So somebody's eventually going to have a problem."

Mackin shrugged. "There are always compromises." He got his cup holder.

Finally he described the options for the underside framework, or carrier, to which the instrument panel would be attached. "We picked the nonrigid carrier," he said, "so all the touchable surfaces are soft. There are no hard plastics there."

Dave Hill nodded. "I like it, but I want to make sure that Design Staff also is on board with us."

The Design Staff people in the room, representatives from John Cafaro's exterior studio, Jon Albert's interior studio, and the admin staff, gave a thumbs up.

"Okay," Hill said, "that's the decision."

Russ McLean rapped his knuckles on the table and Fred Gallasch from Chevrolet jumped up. They'd set up the interruption as a team builder. Even Dave Hill didn't know what was coming.

"Hey, we got some decisions," Gallasch said, "and Chevrolet wants to say *thanks*. This has been a long time coming and everybody here deserves some warm fuzzies."

He walked around the room handing out the newest Corvette lapel pin, along with specially printed "thank-you" certificates signed by Chevy general manager Jim Perkins. Corvette pins are collector items, produced in limited quantities and rarely presented. That particular pin was small and elegant, a gunmetal miniature of the Corvette logo. Some said then, and held the opinion years later, that it was the finest Corvette pin ever produced.

Team building was a Russ McLean canon. Most platforms at GM were not much more than places to work and esprit was just a word. But McLean wanted more. He accepted the notion that Corvette was special and was determined to use it to every advantage. One of model year manager Gordon Duda's added duties for the duration—his regular assignment was handling the paperwork and keeping the team on track through the crucial Four-Phase gates—was making McLean's plan happen. He found himself helping to set up Corvette family picnics in the summer, Corvette team golf tournaments, and Christmas parties, and arranging for an ongoing series of Corvette handouts—mugs, posters, and other goodies that could be presented to people who'd done something special. In later days, when there were problems with union workers putting together C5 prototype cars, McLean had Duda order in decorated cakes and soft drinks and assemble them for a pep talk. He used the cake trick often, too, just to give folks a half-hour break and to walk around saying "well done."

The Corvette pins were the opening move in McLean's campaign. The surprised looks on faces at the CAS review were followed by engineers and administrative types alike pinning the emblem to collars and shirts. McLean said later that he thought that there was a touch more pride in the presentations after that.

There also was controversy, and plenty of it to come. Arbitrary changes in the way the C5 door would be assembled brought sharp criticism from Mike Andalora and his electrical team. The question was whether the door would carry structural loads on the inside or the outside. C4's door was an inside-load design. For C5, the body people wanted an outside-load door. It was more difficult to design and assemble, but it had significant advantages. But they were overruled by the body homeroom. Terry Jinks was the homeroom engineer assigned to do it and he wanted no part of an outside-load door, no matter what the product development engineers assigned full-time to C5 wanted.

The electrical team complained loudly when their time came to present decisions. The outside-load door weighed less, they said. It had fewer parts, fewer squeaks and rattles, and better protection from water leaks. With an inside-load door, they'd be forced to redesign wiring that ran through the doors. Even worse, they'd have to provide additional waterproofing for switches, stereo speakers, and black boxes inside the door structure. "It's going to be C4 all over again," moaned one of Andalora's engineers.

Another argument surfaced from the corporate people responsible for service and maintenance. Their jobs would be easier with the outside-load doors. Everything from water leak tests to adjusting the window mechanism was improved.

Dave Hill told them to get their facts together; the question could be reopened.

Next came the controversy over whether C5's instrument panel would be all analog, with needles pointing approximately to numbers on dials, or be a combination of analog and digital, with at least a digital speedometer that gave speed in an exact number like 67. To Andalora's ongoing consternation, analog gauges weighed less, cost less, and required a smaller up-front investment in tools and manufacturing machinery.

"We'd already made the decision for analog based on all those damn magazine articles," Andalora lamented. "I'm the guy who was getting beat up. Our customers are split fifty-fifty, but the magazine guys love analog and hate digital.

"We'll do a HUD [heads-up display with instruments projected onto the windshield] for the people who want digital and we'll mainstream the analog gauges," Andalora said. "That's the decision we made a long time ago and that's what we want to do now. So what'll it be?"

Mass and piece cost overrode any other consideration. "Going once," Russ McLean said. "Going twice. Sold!" C5 would have analog instruments. That didn't mean they couldn't be as good-looking as possible.

"I want you to do something to make the lighting on those gauges elegant and special," Dave Hill said. "Look at the great lighting in an Infiniti, a Lexus, or a BMW. Then come up with something better."

That was a challenge that the electrical guys savored. Mike Andalora grinned and some of his team members jammed their fists in the air. "Yes! Yes!"

Another electrical decision went by without argument but brought some chuckles to a corner of the conference room. The driver information center, DIC, on C4 was a black screen about three inches high and five inches wide. Messages appeared on the screen when something happened, like "ABS Off" or "Tire Low/Flat." For C5, Andalora's group proposed a one-line scrolling display under the speedometer. Through programming tricks, it would give the driver much more information than its C4 predecessor, including such added goodies as multiple trip odometers. Its control switches would even offer drivers the option of turning off those odious daytime running lights (DRLs) that the company had ordered be incorporated into all GM cars as a special, and controversial, big-brother safety feature.

(Daytime running lights reduce battery life and cut a car's mileage by upward of a quarter mile per gallon. The glitter and flare of badly adjusted DRLs also affect people in other cars, who find themselves changing rearview mirrors to the nonglare setting even at high noon to avoid the discomfort of a GM DRL car behind, thus losing sight of all cars except those with their lights on. And the only studies showing that DRLs reduced accidents were done in Canada and Sweden, high-latitude regions with chronic low sun angles. Even those studies only covered the first year of DRL use, when drivers had not grown accustomed to them. General Motors went ahead with DRLs anyway. Image was more important than fact.)

The ability to turn off the DRLs in the C5 Corvette by manipulating the driver information center switches brought quiet cheers. But it was the miniaturized DIC itself that got the laugh. "Sure is small," an administrative guy whispered to one of Andalora's engineers.

"Hey," the engineer whispered back. "When you've got a Corvette, you don't need a big DIC."

Hill and McLean missed the comments and could only look with puzzled eyes at the giggling group in the back of the room.

One big decision didn't get made. When Terry Jinks presented the case for the inside-load doors, he cited numerous problems with the competing design: It weighed more and cost more, he claimed; there were difficulties in attaching the outside door handles and locks; and the solutions pushed the outer corner of the door so low that it violated corporate curb-clearance standards.

His arguments contradicted everything that the Corvette door people believed. McLean ordered all parties to convene in one week, with the warning that they'd better have facts to back up their contentions. "This decision will be made next week with no finger pointing, no recriminations, just doing what's best for the car," he said.

(With backup experts from the body homeroom, Jinks subsequently convinced Hill and McLean that the technical risks on the outside-load design were too great. Whether one or the other cost more or weighed more was not a consideration if the job couldn't be done at all.)

Bad news had been dribbling in on the first two days of the CAS presentations. Despite the ten-dollars-per-kilo allotment, C5 was still running heavy. On the last two days, it got worse before it got better. The structures team under engineer Doug Ego was wrestling with weight. They went into the last weeks before CAS fat by 60 kilos (132 pounds). They cut some by recommending that the driver/passenger cockpit be aluminum instead of steel. The piece cost was up, but the investment went down and so did the mass.

They cut a little more by devising a rear compartment tub that integrated the outer body panels into the structure. In C4, the tub was one piece and the panels were attached later. The new scheme saved money and mass. "Anybody who doesn't want to do this one?" Dave Hill asked facetiously.

The side rails gave them another big cost saving. The best outside estimate for the high-technology hydroforming process came in at $1.5 million for tools and dies, with a $380 piece cost. That was an economic killer. But structures engineer Ego pulled a rabbit from his hat. General Motors' own internal tool and die operation, usually the high-price bidder on almost any part, thought they had a better way. Staying inside the company cut the investment to less than $1 million and the piece cost to under $150.

There was stunned silence when structural engineer Rich MacCleery read off those numbers.

"How can GM offer us a cost so much less than outside?" Hill asked. "Can we be confident that GM can really do this?"

It was a tough question to ask about his own company. But it came from long experience with GM's high labor rate, often double or triple the rate of nonunion outside suppliers.

MacCleery held out the engineering estimates. He'd spent weeks with the internal tool and die people, and he liked the way they were approaching the hydroforming puzzle. Inflating a steel tube like a water balloon was their kind of challenge. Besides, he told Hill, this was exactly the kind of advanced technology that GM excelled at, and the internal group wanted to push ahead of the world on this one. "It's a risk," MacCleery concluded, "but a reasonable one."

General Motors got the job.

But all of it put together wasn't enough to keep the structures team off the hot seat. In the end, they found only twenty-eight kilos (about sixty-two pounds) of mass reduction. Hill expected at least forty kilos. "Twenty-eight is marvelous and you've done really well on the financials," he said. "But you're still thirty-two kilos over your target weight."

"We picked up a lot on piece cost," Doug Ego replied. "We'll look more at using some premium materials to get the weight down."

Hill pressed on. He wanted pressure on the structures team and he knew how to apply it. "We've done a lot of things on mass and we'll just have to add it up. But this may not allow us to pass CAS. We'll know Friday afternoon."

Hill used similar threats on the chassis and powertrain teams. Both were overweight, particularly the Gen III engine. Hill wasn't happy with the mileage projections, either. At its current weight and power ratios, the engine would give Corvette only an extra one-third of a mile per gallon. "If that's the best you can do," he said sharply, "Corvette might be limited to a five-point-two-liter engine instead of the five-point-seven."

And that, everyone understood, would cut the car's performance to unacceptable levels. That kind of Corvette would not be a Corvette.

Russ McLean stepped into that issue. "Jim Perkins just went to the Strategy Board and said he wants all the effort directed at Corvette. So that's the direction from the very top. Do the five-point-seven for Corvette and do it right.

"Powertrain is the heart of Corvette."

The engine people went away with a list of options to run through their computers before reporting back in two weeks. When they did, they'd found enough mass-reduction potentials, everything from a lighter differential to a new design for the manifolds, to put some optimism back into their team.

Chassis had similar troubles. Most of its decisions were ratified, but the chassis remained overweight and the team was ordered to spend two weeks finding kilos that could be trimmed. The gas tank question was back, too, because at least one supplier was refusing to bid on it. Hill and his engineers had settled on a dual-tank design. The tanks would straddle the central tunnel, with connecting lines to pull gasoline from one tank into the other, then on to the engine. A tough polyethylene material was chosen both for its high strength and its relatively low mass. But the tanks had to fit into spaces under and behind the passenger compartment that already contained other components. Because of the odd tank shapes that resulted, the supplier thought that its "rotational molding" process might not do the job.

Hill ordered more design work to find ways to trim the mass without compromising safety issues. They would modify the shapes again, and the changes worked.

It came down to the last afternoon, an exercise in summing it up. A diagram of C5 was on the overhead projector screen. The last calculations by systems engineer Tadge Juechter showed that it was still almost 119 kilos too fat. Its front overhang beyond the tires was 92 mm (3.6 inches) less than C4 and its rear overhang was 146 mm (5.7 inches) less. Its overall length was down by 40 mm (1.6 inches), but its wheelbase was up 25 mm (1.0 inch). C5 was taller than C4, and wider by 78 mm (3.1 inches). Driver and passenger got more headroom but a little less shoulder room because of the doors reinforced for the new side-impact regulations.

"What lies between the overhangs is drastically larger," said packaging manager Bill Johnson. "It's not surprising that we went up in mass."

Dave Hill took the floor. "I'm going to get up on my bandbox and say that to get the fuel economy and to get the performance and to get a car that's well built like a five-thousand-pound Mercedes, and to get all that in an open car [the convertible would be built of the same structure as the 1997 targa], we had to do things like a radically new structure, like the big central tunnel.

"We wanted a car that was unique and superior and weighed only three thousand pounds. Well, we got unique and we got superior. But it weighs thirty-five hundred pounds.

"And the only other car in the world that good weighs five thousand pounds. So we wanted the impossible and what we got was the improbable. But, you know we still want the impossible. And maybe that's not right anymore."

The mass issue was paramount. But to get the kind of a ride and the kind of maneuverability they wanted—measured by the natural vibration frequency of the car—required mass. Vibration frequency is something drivers and passengers in every car already measure without knowing it. It's that seat-of-the-pants feel that makes a ride comfortable or jarring when a car hits a pothole or shimmies down a rippled road. Engineers measure it more precisely, using the hertz rating, or vibration cycles per second. The higher the number, the better the ride, because the car absorbs the bumps. C4's natural frequency was around 16 hertz and it wasn't that bad. But C5's targa-top model was coming in between 23 and 27 hertz, a level reached by few cars except the heaviest Mercedes and GM's own Oldsmobile Aurora, both at 25 hertz. No convertible in the world, not even a Mercedes,

came in above 18 hertz. C5's convertible was also coming out of the computers at an astounding 23 hertz.

"We've been looking at this like the vehicle technical specs came down
from Moses," Hill said. "But it didn't. It came from us. And we have the
final obligation to balance the car."

The fixed-roof coupe design showed that mass could still be reduced, he
said. It was already nudging the thirty-five-hundred-pound test weight class
and had enough mass-reduction potentials on the various engineering lists
to push it much lower.

The question driving the discussion was simple. Does the C5 pass the
Concept Alternatives Selection gate or not? Tadge Juechter listed the salient
points.

"It looks like thirty-five hundred could be the natural test weight class for
this new car," he said. "We have some confidence that the long and growing
list of mass-reduction potentials will get us there. Right now the list shows
one hundred thirteen kilos that we think can be taken out and there are a
lot of items on the list with no estimate yet. So the real potential is significantly higher.

"We're still seven hundred twenty-two dollars over budget on piece cost,
but we improved by one thousand dollars just since June. When the purchasing people start negotiating real contracts, they say that they'll get us
what we need. So that's where we are."

"The biggest negative is that we don't have a car in the three-thousand-
three-hundred-seventy-five test weight class," Hill said. "But we can go
forward if the team understands that we never had a chance at making
three thousand three hundred seventy-five. *Nobody* can make a car this
good at three thousand three hundred seventy-five."

"And nobody can do it at thirty-five hundred," Juechter added quietly.
"Except us."

There was silence in the room, broken by Pete Liccardello, the former
model year manager who had been given the task of bringing C5's manufacturing plans into line. "We've come further at this point than any program
I know," he said. "[Concept Alternatives Selection] says we are now select-
ing the concepts to *begin* final design on. And we are truthfully way past
that.

"Other programs go through CAS with a confidence level of under fifty
percent. Ours is much higher."

"True," said model year manager Gordon Duda. "But maybe that's one
reason those other programs got into so much trouble."

"Yes for them," Liccardello answered. "But here's where the bad news is
supposed to come to the surface. We're seeing it, so do we think we can
handle it?"

A new voice intruded. Bob DeKruyff was one of the senior executives assigned to the Vehicle Launch Center organization. He was given the job of watching programs at work, of looking for the pluses and minuses that would feed into how the VLC handled things now and in the future. He'd been listening quietly for the full four days. Now he spoke up.

"It's never black and white on these Four-Phase gates," he said, and his words had people leaning through the conference room door to hear what this outsider had to say. "You have tremendous understanding of your car and its potential."

He paused and delivered a verdict. "I'm more confident than anyone in the room, I think. We've all got to fix the system more than fixing the car. We've got to get you more help from GM's technology centers. My gut feel is that you can meet your targets.

"You have a level of understanding of your product that goes beyond anything I've seen. That means ever. You've got the most focused product, the longest heritage, and the best understanding of your customers. I think you can do it."

A few hands tapped on chairs. It wasn't time to applaud.

"There should be anxiety at this stage," DeKruyff continued. "If this job was easy, we'd have NHTSA do it." The reference to the industry's primary federal regulatory agency—the National Highway Traffic Safety Administration—brought guffaws and the tension level dropped by half.

"Well, the investment levels sure look good," Hill said, "one hundred ninety-five million dollars to do three new cars! That's unprecedented."

Engineering and plant conversion would bring the total package up close to $250 million. And that was unprecedented, too. When Chrysler numbers were reported for its 1996 mini-van, they showed that the company spent $675.8 million just for tools, dies, and something called material handling. Chrysler's research and development costs alone on the mini-van were $247 million, just about what Corvette spent for its entire program, without yielding a fraction of Corvette's advances and innovations.

The pressures of detail work were beginning to tell on the Corvette team. "Maybe we didn't have the right to tell you what mass to make the new car," said Chevy's Bob Applegate. "The customer cares about performance and doesn't give a darn about mass. And we're willing to talk to you about that gold-plated VTS, too. Maybe there's some things where we set our sights a little too high. What we really want is the best sports car in the world, and one that's better than C4. It looks like we're going to be there anyway."

Russ McLean polled the table. What he heard was something between "pass" and hesitation. Nobody said the word "fail."

"My own verdict is that I'm reluctant to say we passed the gate," he said.

"We passed the gate with our shadow. Now we have to get our bodies through.

"But you don't get through a gate by voting. You get through by consensus. Around this table, I see consensus. And let's not change the VTS yet. It's what we're shooting for and some we're going to beat, some we're going to meet, some we're going to miss. As long as we give it our best shot, which is a pretty damn good shot from you Corvette people, the future's as bright as ever.

"I want a review in two weeks on those areas we've taken exception to. For the rest of you: Go! Keep refining your product."

"So what do we reflect to the outside world?" The voice from the side wall was asking for all of them. If the rest of GM didn't get the right message, all the help and support that Corvette was looking for would dry up overnight.

"The message is we provisionally passed pending a two-week review of powertrain, chassis, and structure. The message is that we are within striking distance on investment and piece cost. That alone is remarkable.

"And the message is that Corvette is a single-focus team, dealing with the emotion of the car, but with cold calculations about what's best.

"You tell 'em we're green. Maybe with just a tinge of yellow." And not a red light on the board, McLean was saying. The reviews two weeks later would turn the light unmistakably green.

The tension level dropped by half again, with enough smiles and handshakes to give them reason to take the weekend off. After that, McLean told Gordon Duda as they left the conference room, C5 would be on a twenty-four-hour schedule.

"What does that mean?" Duda asked.

"It means we schedule meetings between seven A.M. and seven P.M.," McLean said. "And if those times are filled, you schedule us at six A.M. or nine P.M. or whatever it takes to get the job done. We don't delay anything because of conflicts during the day. If we have to, we start before dawn or we go on into the night."

Duda made a note on his big yellow pad. "Gotcha," he said. "From now on, the clock doesn't matter."

42

GENERAL Motors had been getting knocked in the press for years over its look-alike cars. When it did come out with something that looked different, it got knocked even worse. Its slope-nosed vans were derided as dustbusters and the massive Chevrolet Caprice was called GM's version of the *Titanic*. In Saudi Arabia, where the Caprice had been the top-selling sedan for years because of its good maintenance record and big interior, they got even more personal. Caprice was nicknamed Lifebuoy because it looked like an oversized bar of soap.

Joe Spielman, as vice president of the Midsize Car Division, played activist, and with a much-quoted decree of "no more ugly cars," he became a familiar figure prowling the halls and wandering into studios at Design Staff.

"If I think a car's ugly, I'm going to say no on the spot and send 'em back to the drawing board," Spielman said. Two or three times a week, sometimes for a full afternoon, Spielman looked in on the studios designing a series of new midsize cars and an all-new family van for the 1996–1998 years. The cheerleader enthusiasm he displayed for the Corvette was only a bit less robust for his sedans and van. "I used to feel like Attila the Hun going into a studio," he mused one day. "Now it's different. Wayne Cherry is part of it. He's made us feel welcome."

Cherry continued to let Jerry Palmer exercise most of the artistic authority over the studios, while Cherry focused on administrative and organizational issues. But like Spielman, Cherry couldn't stay away from the Corvette studio. The two vice presidents agreed that C5 was GM's chance to display real innovation.

Ford's original Taurus had beaten the competition with its aerodynamic and shapely skin. Chrysler made a breakthrough in its "cab-forward" design that moved the wheels out closer to the corners. "So what's the next step?" Spielman asked. And the answer, he decided, was Corvette's new backbone structure that could be skinned with a beautiful body by John Cafaro's studio and engineered by Dave Hill's team to be one of the smoothest and sweetest sports cars in the world.

Palmer kept Cafaro's feet to the fire. The pair were friends and even when they were in Palmer's basement tinkering with his huge electric train collection, they talked about design. One day Palmer reminded Cafaro that Ford's new Mustang would soon be on the streets and would make an impact on buyers who opted for hot cars. Cafaro wasn't concerned. "This thing [C5] looks nothing like a Mustang," he said. Then he got an impish gleam in his eyes. "But Wayne came in and said he really likes the Mustang. I was thinking, Hell, what's he saying? when he sort of smiled and said, 'Yeah, it's going to help us sell a lot of Camaros.' "

As Cafaro refined the C5 clay model and worked out problems discovered by the engineers—the fog lamps weren't positioned quite right, the dipping curve in the back glass was too difficult for easy manufacturing, the spare tire was in, the spare tire was out, designers were experimenting with curves and gaps to drive aerodynamic drag down, and scores more—styling got closer and closer to the final shape that would earn C5 raves or jeers.

The general shape, the "theme," in styling vernacular, had been given direction at the Concept Alternatives Selection review. C5 was a double-bubble car, not the rounded marshmallow of Taurus, but the sleek bubble curves of jet fighter canopies and fuselages. The roof dipped in the center, creating longitudinal bubbles that enhanced the image of driver and passenger in separate side-by-side cockpits. A similar cue ran down the center of the hood.

Inside, the dashboard swooped over the driver's instrument cluster to add yet another double-bubble element to C5. But the most dramatic styling effect was the double dip over each set of two taillights. From behind, the C5 Corvette was race-car wide and sports-car low. But instead of a flat surface flowing into the hatchback glass, the ledge over the taillights undulated dramatically and would be instantly recognized by anyone driving behind.

Joe Spielman looked at the changes in his car between June and October, and his enthusiasm bubbled over. "If you can't get excited about a car like this," he said, "you'd better check your GM benefits. You're probably already dead. They're gonna hear about this car from Bangor to Botswana."

The changes were increasingly subtle and involved the engineers as much as Cafaro and his stylists. It was excruciating work. Days would be spent getting the curve of a fender just so. Each change was measured by the engineers and run through their computers to plot its impact on other parts and to get an estimate of how the change impacted mass. By early October, the targa model of C5 was only eight kilos fat and some of the grams saved came from Cafaro's deep understanding that C5, which was *his* car, too, wasn't just a pretty face. It also had to perform.

Every Thursday morning the Corvette planning team, the overall coordinating group that kept things flowing between the engineers, the design studio, the assembly plant, and the massive GM bureaucracy met in a Design Staff conference room. Its job was to make key decisions—ratifying the long-argued design for Corvette's outside mirrors was typical—and to settle disputes between the various factions. When the key design players, mostly Jerry Palmer and Cafaro himself, began missing meetings again, Russ McLean and Dave Hill took the issue straight into the studio. They understood that much of the planning team's agenda was boring to Cafaro and too mundane for Palmer. But on the pure design issues, they needed a dialogue.

They demanded and got a new mandatory meeting in the studio at 5 P.M. each Wednesday. Hill and McLean would be there, along with any engineer they needed for the issues du jour. Cafaro and Palmer would be present— the stand-up meeting would be in Cafaro's studio, making it impossible for him to be anywhere else—along with the studio's artists and modelers. Whenever necessary, which turned out to be almost always for the next year, Jon Albert's interior studio next door would join in. On a slow week, the review of the clay exterior and of the various proposals for interiors was over in an hour. More often, it ran long into the evening.

Finally they felt ready to get more opinions from the outside world and took the designs to another marketing clinic, this time in Chicago. A big question was whether or not Corvette buyers could be comfortable driving a car with no spare tire. The answer brought a big smile to Dave Hill's face.

"It was decisive," reported John Wagner, now Design Staff's administrative manager for Corvette. "They're eager for run-flat tires, but not because of the extra storage space they get or for any styling reason. They want run-flats because they don't want to change a tire. Never, never, never!"

The run-flats being developed at its own expense by Goodyear Tire and Rubber Company would allow drivers to go a hundred miles or more at 55 mph, even if all the air was gone. The "more" was something of a secret because nobody wanted to let drivers think they could go forever without getting an airless tire fixed. But at least one Corvette engineer eventually put more than 200 miles on a flat tire of the current C4-option variety before he had the leak plugged. Then he drove it another 20,000 miles.

Goodyear's concern was that it didn't have a C5 contract yet. It had supplied Corvette tires since 1978 and promoted the connection in its advertising and marketing literature, and on the racetrack. Goodyear and Corvette were like apples and pie. They just went together. But in the new world order of Inaki Lopez and the drive to trim every possible penny from piece cost, GM's purchasing organization was entertaining bids from all comers. To the horror of Corvette purists, and to Goodyear, the Japanese company of Bridgestone Tires was making a strong run at C5. Bridgestone appeared ready to undercut any bid by Goodyear, even to the point of losing money, if only it could say that its tires were on the new Corvette.

It was a challenge that wouldn't be settled for several more months.

The Chicago clinic sent some bad news home to Detroit, too. Participants didn't like the big air scoop flowing from the fenders into the doors. *Grossly overstated,* they said. They didn't go for the roof. *Too rounded.* The rear deck needed work, notably on the double bubbles over the taillights. *Bold, but overpowering. And the deck's still too high to make the lift-over for luggage or golf clubs quite comfortable.*

They did like the way the front fenders rose and fell over the front wheels. That macho bulge was a Corvette characteristic and they were glad it was still there. John Cafaro took the criticism in stride. In the years since he'd started on C5, he'd matured in subtle but telling ways. He knew that he could fix it all without artistic compromise. At the clinic, Cafaro was on the phone to his artists and modelers back home, directing them to make changes that would be apparent, but no *too* apparent. And somehow a real car always looked a bit different from the clay model. There was something about being able to look through windows and about seeing real gaps between body parts, not just lines etched in clay, that deadened a clay but gave life to a car. Cafaro knew in his mind what the *car* would look like. He also knew that fresh eyes from real Corvette customers brought insight that was dulled in people who saw the clay every day. Even himself. The changes, he decided, were the right thing for the car.

By midautumn, another Four-Phase gate was looming. This one was called Concept Direction. Russ McLean ruled that it would be their second deep dive. Concept Direction was too important to do anything else, he said. If they passed the gate, that would be the day the diddling stopped. The new Corvette would be all but locked in. Susan Stanczak, C5's timing manager, put up a chart to let everyone know exactly what they were facing. There were thirteen points to be satisfied by a mid-October 1993 deadline for the Concept Direction gate.

They were all important, items like updating engineering plans and beginning to select suppliers for C5 parts. But it was the final item, covering the months following CD, that sent chills up Corvette's collective spine. In those months they had to prepare for yet another major gate. Concept Direction was internal; they could do the review themselves and give themselves a passing or failing grade. But after CD came CA.

Concept Approval (CA) would only be granted after they made their case once again to Jack Smith and the North American Operations Strategy Board. Concept Approval was the external gate they all wanted. It marked the end of Phase Zero. Go through the gate into Phase One and they would be moving heavily into testing real-world cars. The alpha cars, the first preprototypes, would be under construction when they reached the gate. Paper and clay would give way to steel and aluminum. Real cars with traditional plastic bodies and the new Gen III engines could be running on the tracks within months after CA. Concept Approval was on the schedule for April 20, 1994. So CD-13, demanding that Corvette have the resources lined up to get itself in front of the Strategy Board six months later, brought a dose of realism to the proceedings.

The deep dive took five long days, spread over two weeks. Each started at 7 A.M. and ended ten to twelve hours later. Hill's product development teams were on the spot, some of them for half a day of intense questioning, explaining where they'd reduced mass and what they'd done to get parts firmed up and in some cases under contract with suppliers. Diving deep, some of them found things that had slipped through the cracks. Engine aesthetics was one of them. The powertrain people had been so focused on solving engineering problems with the Gen III engine and reducing its mass that they'd skipped over how it would look under the hood. A good-looking engine was something every platform wanted for its car. But nowhere was it more important than for Corvette. Owners by the thousands showed their cars at Corvette clubs and rallies, and how that engine looked with the hood up was more important to many of them than the look of a passing blonde in tight shorts.

"We'll try to get an illustrator assigned to the Powertrain Division so we can do some roughs," said engine expert (and race driver) Jim Minneker. "Then we'll send 'em over to Cafaro."

Dave Hill agreed. Cafaro had the final say on the issue, but Hill wanted him to keep working on C5's body. "He also has to get started on the convertible and the coupe," Hill said, "so thanks for the help."

Some open questions were resolved as the dive continued. Interior engineering manager Steve Mackin had been struggling with positioning for the switches controlling the one-line driver information center. From an engineering perspective, the easiest place to line them up was along the bottom of the instrument cluster. That made wiring easier and left room on the vertical face of the instrument panel for other items. "What do you say?" Mackin asked Henry Iovino, assigned as C5's human factors expert.

"If I had three choices," Iovino said, "that would be number four."

The switches went on the vertical panel to the right of the instruments.

When the deep dive moved to the design studio, Jerry Palmer and John Cafaro showed off the latest clay. "This car is just about perfect," Palmer said. "We've been working on it for five years and to see this one alongside today's car makes you really feel good."

"Maybe it's a bit conservative, not radical," Cafaro said, "but it's still a helluva next step for the Corvette tradition. We've done it all, from way-out and overaggressive to understated and too conservative. We've gotten here by being there and I'll tell you, I love this car.

"It's exactly where we want to be."

At least, as a theme. Even then, it hadn't been blessed by Chevy's top management and that couldn't happen until late October, when everyone's hectic schedules could mesh for the required hour or two.

Other things were in far worse shape. By the last day of the deep dive, Russ McLean was listening to bad news. Piece cost had soared in the previous months as engineers got real about their parts and some suppliers licked their chops with inflated preliminary estimates. And with new estimates on charges for everything from warranty costs to freight charges, the car was price heavy by $1,500 to $1,750. Tom Krejcar wasn't there to pull another rabbit from the financial hat. His cancer was flaring and it fell to a temporary fill-in, a young financial analyst named Kevin Brim, to spread the gloom. But on the plus side, Brim reported, they'd found almost $1,500 in cost-saving potentials that needed to be pursued. The purchasing department alone promised that it would wring at least $367 from piece cost. Warranty costs might fall by $300 when the final parts list was complete and the engineering finished. "We think we can reach the target," he said, "but we're not there yet."

Mass of the car was even more gloomy. Dave Hill knew that every car got heavier when it went through actual testing, and that today's reserve would get eaten up tomorrow. Problems would be found that could only be fixed with heavier parts. Hill set a target of 1,616 kilos (about 3,555 pounds) for the test-loaded car. That would be within the 3,500-pound test weight class. Systems engineer Tadge Juechter flashed a picture of an old General Motors locomotive on the screen. "This is the new shape that meets our mass targets," he said. The conference room erupted in tension-easing guffaws.

"... the new aero version, too," jibed Chevy's Fred Gallasch.

"And it corners like it's on rails," added structures boss Doug Ego.

"The real truth is that we're now fifteen and seven-tenths kilos over the target," Juechter said. He'd just run the latest numbers after four days of the deep dive and C5 had gained seven kilos as team after team brought in their news.

"So with all the improvements in two months, we have a negative reserve?" Hill asked dispiritedly.

"Right."

"The question is, how do we get it back?" asked Russ McLean.

Juechter was ready for that one. "Things are happening on the plus side, but we've got negative potentials, too. The fuel tanks are getting heavier and we still have to account for any changes after crash testing.

"But we have one hundred ten kilos of positive potentials. Well, we had that much, but there have been some decisions here that eliminated a few. Putting the parking brake handle on the center console instead of on the rocker by the driver's left knee cost us three kilos right there."

That was a decision based on the driver's comfort and convenience, and on the need to route brake cables through the central tunnel anyway. The brackets and braces needed on the console location ate up valuable mass.

Dave Hill delivered an awful verdict. "We can't make this gate with a negative reserve," he said. "I was hoping that the improvements would make us positive."

Bob DeKruyff was sitting in again as the designated observer from the Vehicle Launch Center organization. "My impression is that the team hasn't had a fair chance," he said. "With all the disruptions and personnel changes, it hasn't been possible."

He was referring to the impact of the multimaster matrixed engineering system devised by Mike Juras. Now more than eight months old, it was no more settled than it had been after eight weeks. So many people had been shuttled in and out of Corvette, and every other car platform in the Midsize Car Division, that the new guys spent more time finding out what had already been done than rolling up their sleeves for the work yet to do.

"The problem with a matrix organization," DeKruyff said sardonically, "is that when you call for help, your own phone rings."

Russ McLean seized the opening for a tight-lipped blast at the "Juras Vision." "Dealing with a matrix always takes longer because you're constantly negotiating to get things done instead of actually doing them. Then you run into those gray areas," he said, and pointed his fingers in different directions, "where somebody says 'It's *his* responsibility, not mine.'

"The MCD reorg has created a lot of turmoil. In a group that wasn't as tough as we are, people would have gone insane with the difficulties that have been thrown at us."

A sour mood settled on Corvette. Almost without exception, the engineering development teams had cited multiple instances of homerooms promising and failing to deliver final designs for parts or systems, of drafting resources not available because the dearth of experts in running the computer design tubes left gaping holes in the system, and even of new engineers arriving at Corvette, then tearing up long-completed designs and starting over from their own points of view.

Plans for manufacturing and assembling C5 were late for many of the same reasons. Schemes laid out and approved both by Pete Liccardello at the platform level and by representatives of the UAW and management at the Bowling Green, Kentucky, assembly plant were being challenged inside the Juras engineering organization. The latest argument was whether to bond and seal the exterior rear quarter panel to the rear tub, making it a single piece as planned, or to change to a separate and heavier bolt-on panel. Bolt-on parts were easier to replace and could affect insurance rates. But the bonded parts wouldn't squeak or rattle, and they would help cut the car's mass. By the last day of the deep dive, it still hadn't been settled.

The business side was troubled, too. General Motors' purchasing organization was in turmoil and even the process of getting early costs estimates from outside suppliers was running months behind. Some critical parts were under contract, but many were not. Outside the company, suppliers were moaning over Inaki Lopez's demand for price concessions and his threats to tear up existing contracts by exercising obscure quality-control clauses.

The C5 team had just seventeen days before taking its case to Joe Spielman and his senior staff for a formal go/no-go on the Concept Direction gate. The key Corvette people looked at each other, and their expressions slowly changed. None of them wanted to be part of a losing effort. Bob Hard, C5's purchasing manager, broke the silence. "We needed some kind of a shock on this, and we got it," he said. "But I think we can lay out a plan and pass in a few weeks."

He promised to get the logjams in the purchasing area broken, or at least eased, and to get some real numbers on piece cost and investment.

"But we have to come up with a mass plan," Dave Hill said, and Russ McLean echoed the concern. The argument over exterior body panels was the third major worry, but now the tide was turning. They agreed to resolve it one way or the other in twenty-four hours. (The homeroom would win that one when it promised the next day to offset the 1.2-kilo mass increase in bolted panels with savings somewhere else in the C5 body.)

"It's not an insurmountable problem," Bob DeKruyff said. "The initiatives for mass reduction are there."

McLean tossed it to his chief engineer. "You're the guy on the spot, Dave. What do you want to do?"

Hill didn't respond for almost a minute. Thirty-plus people in the crowded conference room watched him in absolute silence. The only sound was air hissing from a dust-coated ceiling vent. Then Hill decided.

"We have to pass the word that we didn't make CD," he said, and shades of despair closed over the faces around him. He paused to frame his next words exactly as he wanted them, ". . . and that we're going to work damn hard on them to get this turned around by November fifth. We're going to do the job before the Spielman review."

The faces perked up as quickly as they had closed down. When Russ McLean added, "You have three hundred sixty hours to cover the red items, and that's it," they nodded and many of the engineers began right there to make notes on their pads.

Bob DeKruyff stood up. "I gotta get my two cents in one more time," he said. "I've been sitting in on all the teams [doing new cars] and I haven't seen anybody take the deep dive into the details that you have. You understand more about where you are and what you're doing than anybody. But the result is that you get yourself depressed.

"So I see it just the opposite from Dave. I think you're doing damn fine. You just have to pay attention to the *intent* of the Four-Phase requirements, not to the exact words."

It was exactly the pep talk they needed, especially coming from an outsider.

Outside an autumn chill gripped Detroit. In Corvette's basement quarters, they were drooping at the end of the grueling deep dive. Hill and McLean still faced the regular Wednesday night meeting in the design studio before they could head home. Hill admitted to exhaustion but promised to provide details by the next morning on what he expected to be done in McLean's 360 hours. "DeKruyff made us feel good and that makes me proud," he said. "So if you want to go home and have a drink, that's great.

"And if you want to do something else, take home your mass potentials list and put it under your pillow—after you've spent a few of those hours working on it."

D AV E Hill put his elbows on the work table in his office and stared off into space. He'd been chief engineer of Corvette for almost a year. The car dominated his thoughts by day and his dreams by night. He'd taken a watercolor class on a few Tuesday evenings to divert his mind. He and his family had slipped away once or twice to their cabin up north, where he could windsurf or hop on his Honda trail bike for a speed run through heavy forest.

Those moments were rare. Corvette was more stressful than a greedy mistress. Tomorrow Joe Spielman would look at C5 on the Design Staff Patio and two days later Hill and the rest would face a moment of truth with their Concept Approval pitch to Spielman and his staff. Hill thought they were close, maybe even there.

Fred Gallasch from Chevrolet made Hill's day in one meeting when he reported on tires. The Chevy general manager was willing to stick his neck out for Corvette again. "Jim Perkins wants American tires on Corvette," he said. "No Japanese rubber. I've drafted a letter for his signature that says Chevrolet will only accept Goodyear tires on C5. We may have to let the purchasing people put Japanese tires on some other Chevy, but they will never go on a Corvette."

Hill's systems engineer, Tadge Juechter, brought more good news. He'd ridden the product development teams hard for two weeks, forcing them to reexamine every part and every possibility for mass reduction. Gram by gram, the reports came back. Engineers looked hard at the way General Motors built things. If the federal spec on a part was "1," the GM spec was "1.4," and most engineers made it a "1.5" just to be on the safe side. General Motors doors were the heaviest in the industry, so heavy even before the new side-impact regulations that many disabled people couldn't open or close them. General Motors fenders were thick to ward off the little dents and dings. General Motors brackets, bolts, and binders like glues and sealants were thick and overengineered. On fenders alone, Jeuchter reported, they'd just saved 3.4 kilos (7.5 pounds) by using a different plastic for the wheelhouse liner.

In one meeting, Hill jibed electrical team boss Mike Andalora about the weight of the C5's battery. "When are we going to see the zinc-air battery? I read about it in *Popular Science* twenty years ago."

"I don't know about that," Andalora retorted. "Maybe we should put a windmill on the roof. *Popular Science* did those stories, too." Then he promised to keep searching for the perfect battery that would have minimum weight without disrupting his power system.

Overall, Juechter reported, the teams had trimmed mass by 37.8 kilos (83 pounds) in the past two weeks. That gave them a 22-kilo reserve against the 3,500-pound test weight class. Hill smiled and let out a small sigh. It was the right kind of news, but he was still worried.

"We really have the gun to our heads because we can't built C4 for 1997," he said. It wouldn't meet the federal side-impact standards. "But then, GM is so good at postponing cars that it doesn't matter how good we are." He remembered his last Cadillac, the 1993 DeVille, internally dubbed the "K Special." In the financial panic of the early nineties, the K Special was postponed until 1994 for no reason that Hill ever understood. When it did come out, it was a hit with customers. "That was the Reuss era," he said. "Maybe that couldn't happen anymore."

But now completing C5's engineering was dragging Hill down. His eyes showed it and so did the slump of his shoulders. "Mike Juras has the opinion that his system will work because it combines the focus of my immediate staff with the effectiveness of a resource pool that grows the talent. Well, it's theoretically possible. But will we have allegiance to the car or to the parts? That remains to be seen.

"The whole Juras theory is that the vehicle people like us make the plan and then the big organization executes that plan. They don't mess with the plan once they've agreed to it."

It was the last part that was going very, very wrong. The big organization did mess with the plans and it was putting the entire Midsize Car Division in the tank.

"It's a sizable chore to do all this in a stable organization," Hill said. "In a violently changing organization, it's even more uncertain how it will come out."

Joe Spielman dispelled some of the uncertainty, at least for C5, at the next day's Patio show. It was chilly and windy, under threatening skies. Spielman and Wayne Cherry made some sort of fashion statement, Spielman in a leather jacket and dark aviator's glasses, Cherry in a white anorak that was a daring contrast to his usually somber suits. The two vice presidents, one from the product side of the business, the other in charge of style and beauty, walked around John Cafaro's latest iteration. Spielman was ebullient.

"It's a Corvette," he announced. "The last version said, 'Hi, I'm a Corvette and I'm nice.' This one says, 'I'm a Corvette and I'm a beast.' " He clapped Cafaro on the shoulder. "The front end's right. It looks like its gonna bite you in the ass. Whatever you do, don't change it again."

Claudio Bertolin, Cafaro's chief modeler, jumped up with a car cover. "Cover it up! Cover it up! We're done!"

"Not yet," Cherry said. "You got the front perfect, but you lost a little on the back end. You're almost there, but not quite." The rear was still too wide, he said. It needed to be brought in. Just a little. The double bubbles over the taillights were gone, too. The clinic hadn't liked them that much and the engineers knew that a flattened surface offered less wind resistance.

Spielman accepted Cherry's verdict. He was happy. "We got a helluva car," he said. The Chevy guys there, and Dave Hill and Russ McLean, started to applaud.

It was Cafaro's turn to put a hand on Spielman's shoulder. He had to reach up to do it. "How could anybody so big, so good-looking, and so lucky have a car this nice, too?" he teased.

Spielman's grin was wide and proud. "It's your design, buddy," he said. "Your design."

That night a scale model of the car was in the General Motors wind tunnel across the street from Design Staff. Thirty-six hours later John Cafaro was part of the group briefing Spielman and his staff at the final Concept Direction review.

Cafaro flashed a slide of the car on the screen and the room broke into applause. "I just got the aero numbers," he announced. "We got the c/D (coefficient of drag) down to zero-point-two-eighty-six." When the second round of applause settled down, he chuckled: "The guy that did it is out in Las Vegas with a couple of blondes. I gave him some R and R."

If the numbers could hold up all the way to final assembly in late 1996, the new Corvette would be the sleekest, most aerodynamic production car in the world. Spielman patted the Corvette logo embroidered on the right breast of his black golf shirt. "One damn rocket ship," he grunted.

The rest of them made their reports.

Russ McLean: "This is the overview. The car looks good and so do the financials."

Tadge Juechter: "We've got a small positive reserve on mass. We met the twenty-three hertz requirement [on structural integrity]." Spielman jammed both fists forward and let out a breathless "Damn!"

Pete Liccardello: "We got the cockpit build settled." (The dash assembly would be assembled as a separate unit and dropped into the chassis.) "Dave reminds us daily that we will have no wind leaks, no water leaks, and no noise. We're there." Spielman interrupted again: "Plus structural integrity. Look what you've done for the front end of the car."

Kevin Brim: "The business case has turned around completely in the last two weeks." He showed a profit margin on the car that guaranteed Corvette's future. Spielman just grinned some more. Almost every other car in his division was losing money. He could smell turnaround in the years ahead.

Dave Hill: "Summing it up, we think we've passed the gate. Now we have to move forward on the preprototype cars. No matter how good the prepro is, if it's late, it's a failure. We're going to do everything we can to make it come out on time."

At the end, Spielman looked around the conference table at his staff. One by one, they nodded.

"What can I say?" Joe Spielman hooted. "First of all, it's approved." He was interrupted by cheers and applause. Whatever was happening in the rest of General Motors, Corvette people had learned to wear their emotions on the outside. They weren't afraid to gripe when things were bad and they weren't afraid to cheer and holler when things were good. When the room quieted again, Spielman took a jab at Chrysler's super-expensive Viper model:

"I can't wait to see the magazine articles comparing this car to that Chrysler garter snake. There was a time not long ago when nobody believed this company could do a car like the new Corvette. Well, we can. So keep moving, keep kicking, keep shoving. Because this is *my* car.

"Execute, execute, execute," Spielman concluded. "And if anybody gets in your way, execute 'em."

EXECUTION at dawn was once a tradition. Russ McLean used dawn to exert another kind of pressure. When engineers continued to report static from their homerooms—often prefacing remarks apologetically with the words "my boss says . . ."—McLean developed a standard reply: "Tell your boss to be in my office at five-thirty tomorrow morning. I want to hear it from him."

The homeroom chiefs complained to the Midsize Car Division's engineering director Mike Juras and Juras complained to vice president Joe Spielman. Spielman had no sympathy. They owed McLean an explanation and if 5:30 A.M. was the only time McLean had free, then they'd just have to be there.

McLean used the sessions to get the support that had been promised but not delivered. The usual excuse was that resources, meaning people, were needed on the bigger programs like the sedans and the new van. Their profit potential dwarfed Corvette's, and they were all in deep trouble, behind schedule, and over budget. McLean didn't care. He knew that Corvette's needs were a pittance compared to the big programs and that giving Corvette what it needed would, in the long run, have little or no negative impact on the rest of the division. On the contrary, he saw the impact as wholly positive.

He usually got what he needed. Not always, not in the quantity he demanded, nor as quick as he wanted, but close enough. Nobody liked getting up at 4 A.M. to beard Russ McLean at 5:30 in the man's own den. As for McLean, he was usually in the office by then anyway—frequently the only executive in all of MCD to arrive so early. ("I get a good parking spot," he liked to say.) A cup of vending machine coffee and a quiet confrontation when he thought he had the angels (and Joe Spielman) on his side was just a good way to tune up for the rest of the day.

Nearly fifteen months had passed since the boardroom revolution that ousted Bob Stempel as chairman of General Motors and since the day Corvette almost died. Russ McLean, Dave Hill, and all the rest had slogged their way through those months to get the C5 program over hurdle after hurdle and to keep it on schedule. But it was still two and a half years before the assembly line would be cranked up in Bowling Green. What they'd done was ephemeral, the mist and the magic and the paper. Now they needed to get real.

They needed to start building cars. They needed to put those cars on the tracks at GM's two proving grounds, at Milford, Michigan, and Mesa, Arizona. They needed to take cars out on frigid days at Kapuskasing, Ontario, and in Michigan's Upper Peninsula, and again in August heat at the bottom of Death Valley. They needed to drive early versions of C5 to their limits and beyond, and when something broke, they had to find out why and then fix it.

Before they could do any of that, they needed to have parts. They couldn't build alpha cars, the earliest of all test vehicles, without side rails and central tunnels that could be fitted with chassis parts like steering knuckles and springs, shock absorbers, fuel tanks and lines, brakes, wheels and tires, and all the rest. Above the chassis they needed engines and transmissions. Around the chassis they needed fenders and hoods, doors, windows, roofs, and the front and rear pieces called fascias. They needed all the electrical parts, wire harnesses, switches, dials, gauges, radios, fans, air conditioners and heaters, and even lightbulbs. They needed complete cockpits with seats and pedals and steering wheels. They needed screws, bolts, clip fasteners, glue, and rivets.

For each C5 alpha car, they needed 2,823 parts. That was more than 1,400 fewer than it took to build a C4, an amazing reduction in both parts and cost. It was one reason that they could still hope to see C5 with a sticker price lower than C4's. But the alpha cars would be a challenge. C4 was built on a modern assembly line partly by robots and mostly by experienced workers with special tools and machines who knew C4 backward, forward, and inside out. The C5 alphas would be built by skilled workers, too. But none of them had ever seen one because theirs would be the first. They had no robots and not much more than their hands and their toolboxes. The whole thing would happen in the Bumper-to-Bumper Shop that occupied the southern end of Midsize Car Division's ground floor.

(As General Motors continued to morph itself from the old GM into the new GM, Bumper-to-Bumper became part of a new group called the NAO Prototype Shops and there was a bureaucratic move to find a more sophisticated name. Nobody paid any attention. Bumper-to-Bumper it had always been and Bumper-to-Bumper it remained.)

At Russ McLean's direction, most of the alpha car assembly process would take place in a narrow, crowded corner on the west wall. The corner was eventually walled off to create a room and security guards sat at the door twenty-four hours a day. It took special permission to get in and more than half of Corvette's own engineers were not on the access list. Those who were had to wear special photo ID badges that got them past the guard.

Inside the room, away from the curious eyes of GM employees and the few visitors allowed into Bumper-to-Bumper, alphas would be hand-built, one by one, on hydraulic lifts that resembled those in the old corner gas station. Security was a big deal to Russ McLean. The outside world knew that a new Corvette was coming for 1997. The car magazines and GM's competitors were eager to know what it would look like. McLean took every step to make sure they didn't have a clue.

Not all of the alpha cars would be driven, or even be drivable. Some were destined for a long series of crash tests to ensure that C5 met the federal government's safety standards. There would be complete cars sent to the crash unit at Milford, and partial cars, or bucks. A whole car wasn't needed, for instance, when a test involved smashing a ram into this part or that. Early sets of hydroformed side rails were dropped in silo tests or rammed at high speed into fixed barriers. Complete structural frames were dropped or crashed. Some had cross straps for reinforcement, some didn't. They all passed and Corvette's lead safety engineer, Dorian Tyree, was more than satisfied. "When you get these kinds of results in preliminary tests," he told Dave Hill, "you can feel pretty good about the car passing future crash tests."

Making it all come together in Bumper-to-Bumper was the next major challenge. That was the good news. The bad news was that the Midsize Car Division's engineering organization was going to make it difficult. Corvette wasn't told about a whole new series of meetings, reviews, and interventions until it was almost too late. They were only a month from another deep dive that would end with a double gate called Agreement to Build Alpha (ABA) and Divisional Design Approval (DDA).

Divisional Design Approval was the moment when Chevrolet looked at the whole package—styling and content—and its general manager, Jim Perkins, gave the high sign. It meant that C5 was locked in, except for necessary engineering fixes and the most minor of styling changes.

Agreement to Build Alpha was exactly what it sounded like. Everybody got together and looked at the parts list to make sure that enough of everything was on order and could be delivered. Bumper-to-Bumper would be ready to supply people to do the work. Dave Hill would have his key engineers on virtual seven-day standby to be called in when parts didn't fit. (Early parts from suppliers are usually rough. Final tools and dies haven't been completed, dimensions haven't been verified, and preliminary materials are not always the same as the final specification. Alpha parts have the same level of sophistication as the alpha cars themselves: not much.)

Then a representative from Mike Juras rolled out the new Engineering Functional Activity to Corvette; the most common reaction was purchasing manager Bob Hard's. "Damn, damn, damn," he muttered, holding his head in his hands.

The homerooms now would be called "commodity areas" and there were eight new meetings—design readiness meetings, they were called—required to get their approval for parts. Meetings were now needed to load parts into the parts data base, to track the total number of parts, to order parts, to get parts shipped to a GM warehouse (usually in Pontiac, Michigan, about twenty miles away), to get parts out of the warehouse and delivered to Bumper-to-Bumper.

What was worse to Russ McLean was that Corvette's dedicated engineers would not be in the loop for any of the reviews. They were the guys who needed the parts and were responsible for fitting them together to create an alpha car. But they wouldn't know even the simple details of when parts were approved and would be available.

McLean objected strenuously. The C5 team was approaching ABA and wanted to start building cars. Now here was a whole new series of roadblocks. The man from engineering, a newcomer named Bruce James, tried to be sympathetic. "Nobody from C5 ever talked to me," he said.

"Nobody told us we had to," McLean retorted. And what he said was that Corvette would continue its present course to get parts and build cars. "We've got this Juras organization that is supposed to do stuff, but when we go to them nothing happens and we have to do it ourselves. Our choice is to wait around and lose, or do it ourselves and get people mad at us.

"So what we're going to do is get people mad. Until this sorts out and gets working right, we still have to get our job done."

Dave Hill was even stronger in his condemnation. "Every phase you gotta take out your do-it-yourself kit and figure out how to do it. It'll be a miracle if we can do the prepro, just a superhuman effort to plow through the crap that's in our way.

"Like the prototype work being moved to NAO. The only trouble is, NAO doesn't work yet. We're planning on coming through with a program and, holy shit! NAO is still getting organized."

North American Operations was, in fact, still in the throes of upheaval under Jack Smith. Responsibilities were being shuffled here and there in the attempt to create a new and more efficient General Motors. But the immediate result was that NAO only delivered more confusion and frustration.

"We can't get a damn thing done," Hill complained. "We can't get anybody to write orders. We can't get a parts list. People are saying 'I won't do this until you do that' and the people they're talking about don't exist in the new organization. Every time we go to use a service, it's not there anymore."

At the same time, Hill's own engineers were working with the home-rooms to refine parts for later builds. Most parts for the alpha cars were on order, or at least somewhere in the purchasing system. The beta cars would be significantly better than the alphas and their parts were being refined almost daily. One result was that C5 was like a fat man on a yo-yo diet. Its mass went up, back down, up again. Even tiny changes in exterior parts meant that aerodynamics were fluctuating. The coefficient of drag had gone back up over 0.316, then down to 0.294, then back up to 0.302.

"It is really a touchy car," aero expert Kurt Romberg told Hill. "You look at it and it goes goofy. You try something for the wind tunnel and it doesn't work, and then you can't get back to where you were." Somehow, he promised, whether it meant going to a movable front air dam, sealing over the underside with flush belly pans, and changing shapes on the wheel wells, he'd deliver a sleek c/D of 0.290. Changes like belly pans added mass and cost, but Hill accepted the compromise.

"At that c/D, we have a one-hundred-eighty-mile-per-hour car," Hill told his engineers, "and that's where we're going to test them." General Motors' proving ground gurus would not allow such speeds, even on their closed tracks. The alphas and betas might be speed-restricted, Hill said, but the prototype cars in late 1995 and 1996 would have to be driven at 180 "no matter where we have to go, just to see what happens." If they couldn't run fast on GM tracks, they'd find other tracks more amenable to speed.

One important test demanded a fast track. Hill's test drivers would run a prototype C5—a car as close to the final production model as possible—at full throttle for twenty-four hours. As long as the car didn't break, they'd stop only for gas and to switch drivers. It would be the final verification that the new Corvette met its top-end specs, in both performance and endurance. But that was still almost two and a half years in the future. The C5 team still hadn't built its first car.

They did another deep dive before the upcoming gates and came out smiling. Mass had fallen well below the 3,500-pound test weight class. They had Dave Hill's 25-kilo (55-pound) reserve in hand. A chunk of it came from Mike Andalora's electrical team. They'd worked with Bose to cut 2.5 kilos (5.5 pounds) from the speaker system while increasing sound quality. They'd also convinced the high-tech sound manufacturer, Bose, which wanted badly to be part of the new Corvette, to cut its price by $75 per car. Then Andalora revealed that they'd saved another $45 per car by combining the radio transmitter/receiver for the passive keyless entry system (no need to push a button on the key fob to lock or unlock the doors because the transceivers were automatic) and the low-tire-pressure warning system needed for the run-flat tires.

"You got my attention on that," Joe Spielman said at the gate review.

Russ McLean played his cards shamelessly to grease C5 through the gates. He started by showing a blowup of a Corvette ad, the one with a kid holding a model of a '67 Stingray at the top and a speeding C4 at the bottom. But this one had Joe Spielman's face in place of the kid.

"That's my high school graduation picture," Spielman sputtered. "Where the hell did you get it?"

"Your high school annual," McLean grinned. "Your wife helped."

The ad was made into a poster that stayed on Corvette walls for months.

McLean laid out the plan for putting the new Corvette through two years of intense testing. "Starting this summer, we'll have two full cycles of hot and cold testing," he said. That was the minimum. Problems that couldn't be completely solved in the first seasons of hot or cold weather could still be addressed a year later. And in the worst case, there were options to send cars to the southern hemisphere, where the seasons are reversed. It was not common, but GM and other companies had sent cars to the icy tip of South America in July or to Australia's outback desert in January to work out the last-minute fine points.

Mass was good for the moment, Tadge Juechter said, but Corvette still needed more help from the homerooms to keep it that way. "These are hard times," engineering director Mike Juras responded. "We don't really have excess people."

After more than five years of downsizing and cutting costs, GM was being outbid for engineers by Ford and Chrysler. "I'm having a hard time finding people on the streets with signs saying that they'll do engineering for food," Spielman quipped. Then more soberly, he added, "And I have three other programs cooking for '97. They're all saying the same thing."

It was what they'd expected to hear and McLean and Hill already had factored it into their plans. What they really wanted was the agreement to build alphas and they got it. They'd gotten Divisional Design Approval from Jim Perkins a few hours earlier. He'd heard some of the same pitches as he walked around the silver-Di-Noked clay in John Cafaro's studio. He loved the car and he loved the new Corvette insignia designed by Cafaro—a pair of wavy checkered flags crossed over a small Chevy bowtie logo.

He even liked the way the interior looked in Jon Albert's studio next door. The round analog instruments would glow a pure and pleasing white and the gauges themselves were three-dimensional circles that partly overlapped and protruded different distances from their background. It was a striking effect, still in clay but soon to be real.

Perkins brushed clay from his pants after sitting in the interior model.

"Last time I got in a clay," he said, laughing, "my wife accused me of running around with Tammy Faye Bakker. It looked like I had Maybelline all over my suit."

A few minutes later, Perkins and his staff, along with Hill and McLean, put their pens to the Divisional Design approval sheet. Fred Gallasch had it blown up to poster size for the signing. Wayne Cherry didn't sign that day and nobody knew why. But it wasn't long before he did.

C5 had a new set of green lights. It was time to build some cars.

45 T H E alpha cars gave them fits. Just getting ready to build the first one took nearly three months. At one point, the final designs for twenty-nine important parts had yet to be completed by the commodity areas, or homerooms. In those cases, the parts on order for the alphas came from preliminary designs and were close, but not perfect.

Some Corvette people likened the commodity concept to medieval trade guilds. There was a guild of body engineers, a guild of chassis engineers, a guild of purchasing agents. Some caustic engineers said there was even a guild of bean counters and a guild of meeting goers.

The biggest difference between the medieval guilds and the commodity areas of the Midsize Car Division was that the guilds worked. The commodity areas—with the notable exception of the electrical group, which consistently delivered on its promises—were dysfunctional. They would stay that way as long as the "Juras Vision" of engineering procedures remained in place.

Compounding the challenges Corvette faced, the commodity bosses got together and ruled that Mondays and Fridays must be reserved for the growing list of meetings. That left Tuesdays, Wednesdays, and Thursdays for Corvette-only engineering get-togethers. Forty percent of MCD's engineering work week, at least as far as work dedicated to a single-car platform like Corvette, disappeared in the blink of a memo. Even Dave Hill wouldn't be available for much of each Monday. He'd be in a meeting with other chief engineers, all telling their tales of woe to engineering director Mike Juras and his staff.

Hill needed some respite and got it by resuming his Tuesday evening watercolor class. It was a tiny release valve, but it gave him a few hours' relief from the tensions at work.

There were some moments of pure joy. The second pseudo-Corvette, the Corvette Engineering Research Vehicle 4b, was delivered in mid-January. It still looked like a C4 Corvette with a trunk. Underneath it had the hidden backbone structure and the chassis of a C5, with a Gen III engine up front. The engine was an early iron block model, not the aluminum block that was still giving the Powertrain Division trouble. But it developed much the same horsepower and did the job for tests of structure and ride and handling. Development drivers ran CERV-4b for a week at the Milford Proving Ground, gave it to Goodyear for a week to measure chassis dynamics for designing the all-new tires that C5 required, then shipped it to the Desert Proving Ground at Mesa, east of Phoenix.

The car was in the desert in time for GM's semiannual private showing of what's new to the board of directors and to senior company executives. Hill flew to Arizona in early February 1994 to spend two days in the car whipping it around the proving ground's high-speed oval track and weaving it through multilane courses where the road conditions changed every quarter mile or so. He wanted to feel the effect of the new backbone structure through his own backbone. And in the corner of his mind, he wanted one more reassurance that they were doing the right thing in putting so much engineering faith in the radical new structure.

On a Sunday afternoon, he took half-a-dozen outside directors and Strategy Board members onto the track at Mesa to see for themselves. They were enthralled. "It handles better than a C4," Hill told his key people two days later. "It's quicker and more direct. It responds at once to steering input and then holds the line. It has high-speed stability . . . well, it doesn't go really fast yet, but at one hundred twenty miles per hour it has a definite world-class feel and high-speed-lane-change capability."

Nobody challenged his definition of "fast." At 120 mph, even a C4 Corvette hadn't started to breathe hard. It was the high upper end of performance that made the mid-range of 60–80 mph so spectacular. A Corvette in even average hands responded with verve in tight situations.

From the exhilaration of his desert ride to the most mundane of a chief engineer's tasks was not much more than a heartbeat. Hill had no sooner finished telling his engineering team about CERV-4b than the next agenda item brought him crashing to earth. The subject was labels. Geri Mertens was the label engineer for both Camaro and Corvette. It was her job to start gathering the information for all the labels that would be required in the new Corvette. C4 had fifty-five labels.

"A lot of them are CYA," she said. People are supposed to read the labels, learn what to do and not to do, and then not file a law suit when they did it wrong and smashed a thumb or burned a finger. Labels could not be obscured by hoses, wires, or other parts. Some had to be printed in contrasting colors to make them more obvious. One label newly required as part of the air-bag-and-seat-belt safety system had to be attached to the front of sun visors. It said simply: "See Other Side," where another label offered lengthy verbiage on safety dos and don'ts.

"Can't we just have one label that covers everything?" Hill moaned. Labels, here, there, and everywhere would detract from the beauty they'd spent so much time and effort to perfect for C5.

"You'd need a bed sheet," needled Powertrain engineer Jim Minneker. " 'Don't put your fingers here, don't pet the fan, don't touch hot surfaces . . .' "

"Get me a list of every label on C4," Hill said. "We'll start with that on the C5 mock-up cars. The only way to make good things happen is to plan ahead."

"Good things" is a relative term. When the first C5 rolled off the assembly line, it was stickered with dozens of separate labels.

Hill skipped the next trip to the desert, leaving it to his chief development driver and engineer, Dave Wickman, to host Chevy general manager Jim Perkins for a drive in CERV-4b. With two CERVs on hand, and the promise of fourteen alpha cars to be delivered between the end of June and the following January, Wickman and the dozen engineers under him would begin emerging as some of the most important players on the C5 stage. It would be their job to drive the alphas, then the betas, and finally the prototypes and pilot cars that represented the first cars off the production line, to find and fix problems, and ultimately to get C5's performance fine-tuned to the extreme. Other test cars would be driven by engine people and by the heating-ventilation-air-conditioning/engine-cooling experts for the same reasons. Still others would go to the so-called "durability drivers," who would amass tens of thousands of miles on cars by putting them through bone-rattling, teeth-jarring, and often completely boring test drives just to see what held up and what degraded, what broke and what survived.

Now Wickman's chore was to shepherd Jim Perkins, at the wheel of CERV-4b, through the Desert Proving Ground's maze of roads. What Perkins found was what the rest of them already knew: The new Corvette structure gave a ride that was tight and smooth, with almost no road vibration. It leaned in the corners less than a C4 but held tighter to the steering line. On his third circuit of the test roads, Perkins snapped the test car back and forth between road surfaces just to feel how it reacted to ripples one second, bumps the next, and potholes the second after that. He got out of the car smiling.

"That is going to be one fine car," he said, and started chatting about Dave Hill. "He wants to do the best damn car ever. He's straight on that, like he's on rails. And he's a bear on mass."

Development engineer Jeff Yanssens, who had ramrodded the once-secret CERV project from the start, couldn't resist. "Does he give you that silent stare when you ask for something to be added to the car, or do you get professional courtesy?"

"Not hardly," Perkins said. He smiled widely, took off his sunglasses, and did a passable imitation of Dave Hill's voice, if not his vocabulary: "You must be the dumbest sonuvabitch I've ever met," Perkins intoned. "How many times do I have to explain this mass shit to you?"

Yanssens, Wickman, and the rest broke up. Perkins was living up to his reputation as an earthy and effective general manager. "He's one helluva chief engineer," Perkins went on. "He'll tell it to you straight every time. That other guy, McLellan, you ask for something and he gave you Waltzing Matilda.

"If anybody can give me a great Corvette, it's Dave Hill."

Two thousand miles away in Detroit, Hill had moments of doubt. He was getting new evidence that "great" was still just a word and that getting there was a long, painful process. He was about to discover that one of the commodity groups had dropped the ball in almost unforgivable fashion. When a design engineer went on pregnancy leave, the homeroom boss failed to reassign her work. Now C5 was coming up on its first alpha build and not only was an important part not on order, but it didn't even exist on paper.

But first Hill and McLean had to deal with other bad news. A giant die used to make early versions of the hydroform side rails had failed. The steel rail tube blew out when it was filled with high-pressure fluid. One worker needed stitches; another had a bruised shoulder.

The blown die was made of kirksite, a weaker metal than would be used in the final production hydroform machine. Kirksite is often used in early tooling because it is more malleable than heavy steel and the first test tools can be ready months sooner. But the material is also more fragile and wears out more quickly. Its failure threw a pall of indecision over rails to be produced by a private supplier to GM. The supplier was supposed to provide the one or two hundred hydroformed rails for the alpha and beta cars while GM experts completed work on the room-sized unit that would produce side rails in production quantities for years to come.

Now with only a month to go before workers in the Bumper-to-Bumper Shop were to begin building the structure for the first alpha cars, the source of their rails was in doubt. Nobody could be sure that the die would last long enough to do the job.

"Alphas were always going to be tough," Hill said. "But I knew we'd make it. Now? I don't have the foggiest."

THE leak hit the press when *Motor Trend* magazine ran a two-page spread in its April 1994 issue, complete with a color rendering of a 1997 Corvette.

"Great story," said John Cafaro, holding an advance copy of the unsigned piece and walking around the full-size C5 clay model in his studio. It was better than that. It was the perfect story in the eyes of Chevrolet public relations and both Russ McLean and Dave Hill. It was perfect because it drew the attention of the automobile world for the first time to the new Corvette taking shape inside General Motors—and because so much of the story wasn't quite right.

It was the latest skirmish in a gentleman's war over the Corvette. The C5 team did everything to keep the new car under wraps. On the other side, skilled and knowledgeable journalists probed their sources, picked up on clues, and tried to give their readers a look at what could be the new-car story of the decade. A new Corvette was important to GM. It was just as important to the journalists, partly because of Corvette's cult status and partly because a new one was a rare event. A writer or photographer who could blow GM's cover would have bankable stature in a tight-knit profession.

Motor Trend was up front about the story. In the second paragraph, it told readers that its information was "culled from sources within GM and its suppliers" and that parts of the story were "good, solid rumor . . . extrapolation, and . . . our very finest wild speculation."

The car shown with the article was off by enough to make Cafaro chuckle. "It's based on some early work," he said, "not what we have now. The roof is sort of right, but the rear-deck line came from an earlier model. And they missed the big scoop in the sides completely."

But the rear deck was right enough to let McLean know that somebody, probably an outside supplier, had talked out of school. He debated about launching a security investigation. But when he reread the text, he shrugged it off. The rumormongers hadn't known that the internal code for the car was C5. Instead they'd confused the car and its engine, telling *Motor Trend* that the new engine was a Gen 5, not Gen III. They got the front-engine/

rear-transmission configuration right but missed the unique hydroformed side rails. A drawing of the new Corvette's structure showed a large central tunnel (correct) with Y-shaped structures at each end (wrong). They speculated that the car would have a shorter wheelbase (it was longer) and a steel floor pan (it was then a composite plastic, which would give way to balsa wood).

Most important to Russ McLean, the story implied that C5 would still have just two models, with a fixed-roof coupe replacing the targa-top model with its removable roof. The rumor mill didn't know that C5 would be the first Corvette to have three models and that the 1997 targa would be followed by a convertible and a fixed-roof coupe. That wasn't a secret that could be kept forever, but McLean knew that it would only cause more confusion when the truth finally leaked out.

Such encounters in the journalist-C5 war became routine. There would be more in the next two years. Russ McLean's most realistic hope was that the war would end in a draw.

The more immediate concern was to get parts to build the alpha cars. Alphas were an innovation being tried for the first time with C5. For decades, GM had built both preprototype and prototype cars as more-or-less finished products. The cars were built later in the development program using mostly-complete designs and engineering drawings, and parts that were close to if not exactly like production parts.

Doing it that way stretched out programs because the builds started late. When the exhaustive test-drive schedule found problems—as it always did —they led to delays in getting the cars into production. The invention of alpha cars in the ever-changing Four-Phase process of developing cars made sense.

The alpha cars were to be quick-builds, using early designs for parts. The cars existed to validate the basic concepts that went into the designs, to do the initial thermal tests both under the hood and in the cockpit, and to get an early start on the many crash tests required to meet federal and GM safety rules.

What they learned in driving or crashing the alpha cars would begin to feed into the beta cars. From there it would flow into the prototype cars and very quickly after that into regular production. The alpha-beta-prototype scheme was supposed to shorten the time it took to get into production. It also was supposed to be cheaper. There would be fewer prototype cars needed because most of the problems would have been found in the alphas and betas. Toyota was rumored to build up to five hundred preprototype and prototype cars for a typical test schedule. General Motors typically built between two hundred and three hundred cars and bucks in the prototype process. Corvette intended to do the same job with fewer than a hundred.

But without side rails, Dave Hill wouldn't have any cars for the test program. The kirksite die, a type of mold, was worrisome. If the die wouldn't last through making a few hundred rails, it would take months to get a new one built. It was nearly two weeks before the supplier decided that their die and the hydroforming process probably was robust enough to make all the side rails needed for the alpha cars.

Probably, Russ McLean mused. *"Probably" won't cut it.* This was just another in a series of delays and the supplier already was three weeks behind in its deliveries. The first usable rails were now promised for delivery on Friday, March 25. Instead, the supplier sent word it wanted more time to make practice rails on its die. Maybe some usable rails could be delivered on April 1.

McLean came out of GM's manufacturing side. He knew about die shops. "The biggest and meanest guy who talks last is going to get his parts," McLean said. He cited a rule of thumb that die shops want to make four runs to tweak the dimensions and get the process right. After that, they should be in business. Then he hopped into his car and drove out to the supplier's shop. He wasn't that big, but he knew how to act mean. He returned with a promise that the supplier would work overtime to complete the trial runs and the first production rails.

"They'll deliver over the weekend," he told the workers in the Bumper-to-Bumper facility. "You can start building alpha structures Monday morning."

The first of anything is always a bear. It took nearly four weeks before they had the first structure far enough along to tell what it was. By then, rails for eighteen cars and bucks had been delivered and were stacked around the welding area, or were being brought together with cross members to form the basis of a car. S7Y001P was the first. The S meant it was a buck, not a drivable car. 7Y was for a 1997 Y-car, the Corvette platform designator. P was for prototype; it was not a car that could be sold. This one would be the structure for the mock-up master. It was to go upstairs on May 27 to Corvette's mock-up room and eventually be fitted with most of the parts to make a car. The days of cardboard, wood, and plastic mock-ups in the Vehicle Launch Center were all but over. This mock-up would be close to the real thing—a combination of handmade parts and early-run parts from suppliers. It would be used to work out the changes and conflicts that were certain to occur in the coming eighteen months.

The second structure was labeled 17Y002P. The 1 in the place of the S made it a drivable car. It was to be delivered on June 20 to Dennis Sheridan, lead engineer in the HVAC/engine-cooling product development team. It wouldn't be on time. When reality intruded on the schedule, reality always prevailed. There was just too much to do.

In four weeks, the welders and the manufacturing experts had perfected jigs and frames to hold the rails stable while cross members were welded to them. Already others were using the basic design to begin laying out the tools and jigs that would be needed at the assembly plant to turn thirty rails into fifteen C5 structures every hour at full plant speed. Developing the assembly process was a key part of building alpha and beta test cars.

The first frame was being fitted with its long central tunnel by the fourth week in April. The broad bow that formed the rear structure of the cockpit was in place and where welding was yet to be done, huge C-clamps held parts in place. Most of them were festooned with dangling pieces of paper: welding notes with engineering instructions on what was expected.

Russ McLean and Dave Hill had instituted an early-morning routine with their key engineers and with Bumper-to-Bumper managers, including Joe Lopez, assigned full-time to Corvette. They called it a "floor walk" and it started each morning at about the time the union workers began their day at 6:17 A.M. (The time was worked out in painstaking negotiations between GM and the United Auto Workers union. It was decided by plugging in so many minutes for each break, so many minutes for lunch, and so forth, then marching it backward from a quitting time of 2:42 P.M. to make a seven-and-a-half-hour working day. Nobody had a good explanation for that last number. It was just one of those things that happens when union leaders and management sit down together.)

The group of them, as many as twenty people on some mornings, walked through each Bumper-to-Bumper station that was building sections of C5. They looked at the progress, or the lack of it, and chatted briefly with the union people. They looked at the large pads on easels at each station where workers noted problems. Sometimes it was a missing part or an instruction that didn't make sense. Sometimes it was a part that didn't fit; its dimensions were wrong, either on the original spec sheet or in the way a supplier had manufactured it. In that case, the workers took out their files or cutters to make the necessary adjustments and noted the results on the easel pads. Joe Lopez and his people checked the comments daily and set to work informing release engineers that they had a problem and needed to make it right.

"Good work," McLean or Hill would say, or "What do you need?" or "How can we help?" The word got around Bumper-to-Bumper and it was the kind of word that had been said about no other program: *These guys are serious. They're here when we are, up with the birds and walking the floor.*

"This thing is strong," a welder said to Pete Liccardello on the morning that the rails had turned into something resembling a car. "It's going to crash real good. It's a tough one." Liccardello smiled and chatted for a few moments about the intricacies of getting a weld just right. It was one of his concerns as the platform's lead manufacturing engineer and he and the union guy saw eye to eye in the dawn of the day and the dawn of a new Corvette.

Managers on other Midsize Car Division programs showed up to check their cars later in the day, almost always after 8 A.M. By then McLean and Hill had walked the floor, had done a forty-five-minute sit-down meeting to sort through problems that had come up and assigned people to fix them, and were off doing other things for their car.

It was the kind of hands-on management technique that union workers understood and liked. When the really troublesome problems cropped up later, it helped to have that kind of relationship with the folks building the cars.

The other early-morning walks were "wall walks." McLean and Hill participated every Thursday at 7 A.M. Other engineers walked the walls daily. The walls were eight-foot-high cardboard partitions set up in a cramped room at the Vehicle Launch Center. Giant paper clips held standard sheets of paper. Eventually there would be no open spaces, and some spots held several sheets. Each described a step in the assembly process, maybe a station on the future assembly line that would be installed at Bowling Green, Kentucky, or a step-by-step description of one task to be done at that station. Anyone could walk the walls from beginning to end and see the steps by which the C5 Corvette would be assembled.

The "wall," they called it, after their first few months in the Vehicle Launch Center, and everyone knew that they meant "the assembly process wall." Like much of C5 at that stage, it was a living and changing thing. Engineers began with the machines and processes that already existed at Bowling Green. They took what they could use for C5 and began inventing the rest.

It gave them a visual method to track assembly and to determine what new machines they needed, or what new procedures they had to develop so that C5 could be assembled in an efficient and logical way. That naturally led to conflicts. Under the direction of Pete Liccardello and with the help of assembly experts from both the plant's management and the union side, they discovered the places where the logic was wrong or the machines didn't fit into the space available. Sometimes they found that they'd done the usual General Motors thing and overengineered something for the task at hand, making assembly-line machinery too strong or too complicated.

Russ McLean's eye was keen on 7 A.M. Thursdays. He was at heart a plant guy who'd worked from the most junior jobs up through foreman and plant manager to finally becoming manufacturing director for all GM plants in Mexico. Each Thursday he looked at a different part of the wall. Dave Hill would be along, but this was a part of the job where he deferred to McLean's expertise. He looked at it as part of his own education. "Why do you need a ninety-thousand-dollar fixture here?" McLean would ask. "All you need is something to slide the thing into and hold it steady. A thousand-dollar rig is all you need. You're not talking about tight dimensional stability at this point. That comes later."

The younger engineers would nod and accept the chastisement. Off in a corner, Pete Liccardello nodded, too, because he'd told them the same thing when they brought in the plan the night before and put it on the wall. Eventually they learned.

The wall would move back to Midsize Car Division with Corvette when they left the Vehicle Launch Center. It was a valuable tool that would be used to refine the assembly process all the way into 1996, when Bowling Green would stop building C4s and be converted to C5 production.

CORVETTE was in its fourth deep dive in eight months, another four-day examination of systems and parts beginning on April 14, 1994. This one included all the manufacturing and assembly details that had been developed since January.

As always, its purpose was to get ready for another in the long series of gates in the Four-Phase process of doing new cars at General Motors. This gate, Concept Approval, was more important than most. It would put the C5 Corvette back in front of GM president Jack Smith and his North American Operations Strategy Board. Passing through the gate meant the end of Phase Zero and the beginning of Phase One. The paperwork would be all but done and the focus would shift to hardware.

More important, the Strategy Board was being asked to write the check that would complete the development program and take C5 to the brink of full-scale production.

"The money comes, or it doesn't come," platform manager Russ McLean told them solemnly on the first morning. "And if it doesn't come, it probably *won't* come. Ever."

He let that soak in before he cracked a bit of a smile. "Talk is cheap; it takes money to buy whiskey," he said with a stand-up comic's lilt. "After this, the talk is done and it's time to buy the whiskey, to buy the car." He looked at the representatives from GM's Powertrain Division who were first up to talk about the Gen III engine. "Well, can we buy the car?"

McLean and chief engineer Dave Hill already knew that only two chunks of C5 were in trouble, the engine and the chassis. Both were still overweight. Greg Cockerill was Powertrain's representative to C5. For this day, his boss, Ed Koerner, was on hand and feisty. Cockerill decided to go with the good news first.

Corvette's share of the up-front investment in Gen III was $12 million under budget, he said. The engine would be Corvette's alone in 1997 but would be shared with other vehicles in future years. Their volumes far surpassed Corvette's and the other programs were picking up the lion's share of investment. The piece cost—how much Corvette would pay for each engine—also was down, about 4 percent under earlier estimates.

"That doesn't include investment for premium materials which are likely to be needed for mass," Cockerill said. And that brought him to the bad news. The manual transmission engine was still 13 kilos (about 28.6 pounds) too heavy and the automatic transmission engine was 10.8 kilos (about 23.8 pounds) on the fat side.

Hill and McLean were adamant about the mass problem. "I don't think we can pass the gate with thirteen and ten over," he said. That brought Ed Koerner, the Gen III's chief engineer, to his feet.

"Look," he said, "you have to take into consideration that this engine is delivering much more horsepower at comparable mass levels than Cadillac's Northstar, or even anything Lexus has. And part of the problem is Getrag [a German supplier]. They low-balled their bid on axles in both cost and mass. We're holding them to their cost, but they're not making their mass."

The look on McLean's face delivered his silent message: *That's your problem, Ed.*

"I want a summit a week from today to review these things," McLean said. "That mass has to come down and I want it looked at strongly in the next few days."

Of all C5 systems, none was more weight-critical than the engine. It all sat in one place and tilted the car's balance forward. Ride and handling for C5 was predicated on a mass distribution of almost fifty-fifty for the center of the car. A nose-heavy Corvette was not acceptable.

Koerner spread his hands in supplication. "I appreciate what you're saying. We do owe you some better numbers on the flywheel and I think we have some reductions within significant reach. But I don't know how I'm going to squeeze more blood out of that turnip in *the next few days.*" He stressed the last words to make sure that McLean got *his* message.

"I'd also like to know that the other teams are getting this same level of scrutiny," Koerner said. There was a dejected bite in his words.

"Everybody's in the same frying pan," McLean said. "But you should know that chassis is the only other significant problem area."

It was a small rebuke and Koerner understood that his Gen III engine was a millstone around Corvette's neck. "A week from today," he said. "We'll have something." They did better than Koerner could have predicted. In a week, partly spending some of their reserve on lighter weight materials, partly by holding Getrag's feet to the fire, they cut nearly 6 kilos (13.2 pounds) from the two engines. Along with Powertrain's promise to keep digging for every gram, it was good enough to send C5 forward.

Jim Lloyd took his place on the hot seat to face the music for the chassis team. "Mass is eleven kilos (about twenty-four-point-two pounds) over target, but we have sixteen-point-three kilos (about thirty-five-point-nine pounds) of potential reductions, plus another list with no numbers, just question marks."

Too many issues had to be settled during alpha car testing, Lloyd said. He couldn't give a hard number on mass today and maybe not for another year.

"What will you sign up for?" McLean demanded. The important thing was that an engineering team promise to meet its goals sometime before production, not necessarily at this early stage. That almost every team had met its goals or was close, and that all were still working on more mass reductions, was not typical of any GM car whose production was still twenty months away. McLean and Hill privately felt that C5 would meet its mass requirements with room to spare. But their public posture was to maintain the pressure on mass reduction now because they knew how cars grew during testing.

"I already signed up for my target," Lloyd said. "We'll get there."

The big blow-up came on the the deep dive's second day. There was no hinge for the hood. The homeroom in charge of hinges looked at a design used by Mercedes-Benz but couldn't get it packaged properly in the C5 nose. They'd evolved a design that would fit in the limited space available, but hinge stability deteriorated to the point where the hood wouldn't stay up. A more robust hinge was tried and it, too, wouldn't package.

Then the engineer in charge of the process went on pregnancy leave in September 1993. Nothing happened until she came back in January. Her commodity group boss had ignored the whole thing. Now the group's engineering analysis was raising fears about any hinge being good enough. The hinge she'd promised in January, and that did fit in the space available, was not good enough. Dave Hill was as close to furious as he let himself get in a meeting.

"The history of Corvette is forward hinging of the hood," he said forcefully. On the C4 Corvette, the hood and fenders had become one piece. The "clamshell" opened forward to expose the entire engine compartment and front chassis components. They'd gone away from the clamshell on C5. The fenders and hood were again separate pieces. That made the car easier to assemble and cut costs. It would reduce repair bills after accidents, too, because pieces could be replaced instead of a complete clamshell. Finally, it would make future changes in styling easier to execute. If they decided to reskin C5 in 2003 or 2004, dramatic changes could come at minimum cost.

But they refused to make C5's hood open from the front, as do most hoods. The forward hinge and rear latch would be retained as part of Corvette's tradition and mystique. Now there were no hinges.

Hill knew that the argument was coming. He'd received a formal letter from Phil Boulanger, chief of the body/exterior commodity group, notifying him that they could not support the way the hood opened. Hill demanded that Boulanger be present at the deep dive and fixed him with a stare as he recited more history.

"This is another example of the system in turmoil," Hill said. "Everything changed at the end of August and you got responsibility for hood hardware."

Boulanger nodded in agreement. "But we didn't get involved until January," he said. "We certainly had little or nothing to say about this." Boulanger's attempted excuse didn't explain who else should have been in charge between September and January. "We had a lack of data. We had designers who couldn't decipher what was supposed to be done."

It came across as a combination of *not our fault, not on our watch, we couldn't help it.*

Russ McLean put some bite in his voice. "Who's responsible for developing hinges?" he asked.

"We are," Boulanger said. "But the platform is supposed to come in and give us the data."

"We gave you the data."

"It still has to be packaged." Boulanger was being backed into a corner and was looking for a scapegoat. Packaging manager Bill Johnson flared at the implication.

"We packaged the last thing we got," he snapped.

"It doesn't work!"

"He's making it sound like the packaging team didn't do its work. That's bull!"

"Well, we still need to package a hinge that works."

Johnson sneered. "And we'll be glad to help you out. Again!"

"It's going to be front hinges, Phil," McLean said. His tone cut off argument.

"You're saying that we don't have a hood system because the platform didn't design it," Hill told Boulanger. "But in this commodity organization, we're not allowed to do that. There are a lot of things on this car I'd like to have more control over. But I don't have it."

Boulanger saw the truth of the situation. Another meeting went onto the schedule for the next week. This one would include Boulanger's most senior engineers. Corvette would have a design for its hinges. This time they would work.

Tom Krejcar, still carried by Russ McLean as Corvette's financial manager, died of cancer sometime during the day. When McLean announced it the next morning, there was a long moment of silence. Part of his legacy, McLean said later, was that C5 would be on or under budget. Another part was that C5 existed at all. Krejcar's willingness to finesse the books had helped keep it alive during the dismal days. It would always be his car, too.

The deep dive ended as McLean hoped it would. Bob DeKruyff was there again, still cheering them on. This time they all believed it. McLean let them in on a company secret.

A new marketing clinic had just been held in Los Angeles. Neither he nor Dave Hill was allowed to attend. Nor was anyone present from Design Staff. It was called the "volume clinic" and it was run by corporate-level people. They looked for independent verification that not only did people *like* the car, but it would *sell.* One of the most important numbers to come out of the survey was a projection of C5's volume, how many cars it could be expected to sell in the seven or so years of its nominal lifetime.

The C4 Corvette captured around 37 percent of the high sports market in 1994 and that number would grow steadily through the mid-nineties. But the numbers for C5 were astounding. Invitees to the clinic were selected to reflect current market shares. Thirty-one percent owned Corvettes; the rest owned competing models such as the Nissan 300ZX and the Toyota Supra. They looked at the latest exterior and interior for C5, then at Corvette's competition. Finally they were asked which car they would buy.

The corporate people went home shaking their heads. The new Corvette blew away the competition. The number to be entered into the business records for C5 was all but unbelievable.

Sixty percent said they would buy C5 over the competition. No GM car had ever come out of a volume clinic with that kind of number.

Dave Hill put his own spin on the report: "We're going to put a lot of rice burners back on the boat."

"When we go before the Strategy Board," McLean predicted, "we're going to rock their socks."

48 THE Strategy Board came to work wearing cast-iron socks. Jack Smith's were stainless steel. The *Wall Street Journal* that morning in early May carried a page-one story critical of General Motors for not turning its finances around fast enough, for being too slow in bringing new products to market, and most scathingly, for long delays in changing over plants from old models to new ones.

One of the plants cited as a particularly bad example belonged to Joe Spielman.

Smith was stung by the article. It put him in a testy mood that was picked up by other members of the board. Instead of rocking their socks, Russ McLean found himself facing a contentious group of senior executives who needed to let off some steam. The handiest target was Corvette.

The attacks came out of left field. Jack Smith got up abruptly and left the Design dome before Russ McLean could build up momentum in his opening remarks. He hadn't returned when Chevy's Fred Gallasch started talking into a dead microphone. By the time a technician found the loose connection at the amplifier, Gallasch was halfway through his marketing pitch and growing hoarse from trying to make himself heard in the big open arena.

That was when executive vice president Bill Hoglund challenged him on an apparent omission. "What about any overlap between the Camaro Z28 and Corvette? Is Camaro going to take sales away from Corvette?"

Not even one, Gallasch said. All the surveys showed that the price differences were enough to attract buyers who wanted to create different images.

"What about the engine?" Hoglund pressed. "Gen III is old technology. I'm worried about how it will be accepted."

"It's what Corvette people want. In fact, I think it's a positive for us." Then before Hoglund could frame a new question, Gallasch triggered a slide show. "And now," he announced, "your new Corvette."

The music swelled, a Prince song with a rapid beat, and images of the all-but-final C5 flashed on the screen: C5 alone, C5 surrounded by earlier Corvettes, C5 against the competition from Nissan, Toyota, and Mazda. Gallasch slipped away from center stage as exterior studio chief John Cafaro and interior chief Jon Albert took his place. "That'll give you a hard-on," a voice in the small audience whispered.

It was the car they'd been waiting for. The show faded to black and as the lights came up, John Cafaro spread his arms to reveal a display of cars off to the side. "This is a momentous day for us," he said with a wide grin. "We invite you to walk up and take a look."

Jack Smith still wasn't back, but the rest of the board applauded as they moved toward the display. McLean and Cafaro had set it up carefully. There were four old Corvettes, an original 1953, a '61, a '67, and a '78. On the far right sat a deep red 1994 C4.

Smack in the center was a bright red fiberglass C5, a perfect replica of the Corvette they were asking the Strategy Board for permission to build. It cost half a million dollars of Chevrolet money to build and this was its moment. Board members could crawl in and out, try the driver's and passenger's seats, open the rear deck lid, where two golf bags were laid with room to spare. After today, the model would be on occasional display at Design Staff before retiring to a warehouse filled with fantasy cars. But its immediate job, giving the guys who held Corvette's fate in their hands something that was touchy-feely, made the investment worthwhile to Chevrolet.

There were two other displays intended to boggle executive minds. The S7Y001P structure was there, complete with a full cockpit frame loaded, and painted glossy black. It was massive and intimidating. It looked strong. To the board members with engineering background, it was a look at the future of automobile design. To the rest, it was an impressive hunk of metal and they walked around it and nodded.

The last display was another fiberglass model. It was the rear end and trunk that would go on the convertible and the fixed-roof coupe. "A Corvette with a trunk," said Strategy Board member and top GM lawyer Harry Pearce. "I like it."

A few feet away, Design Staff's John Schinella reminded other execs that the Stingray III had a trunk. "When did we start that out in California?" he asked rhetorically. "Five years ago?" It was a concept then, a reality now.

Jack Smith returned just in time to see Bill Hoglund clap John Cafaro on the shoulder. "You really pulled it off," Hoglund said. Smith walked through the displays smiling and took his turn sliding in and out of the fiberglass model. It wasn't the last time he smiled that afternoon, but it was close.

Dave Hill ran down his list of C5 achievements. "As you just experienced, entry and egress are much better than the current car.

". . . Targa top latches and unlatches without a tool.

". . . Human factors have gone from bottom of class to top of class, a dramatic change that people will see and feel.

". . . In curb weight, only the Acura NS-X, a very expensive all-aluminum car, and the Mazda RX-7, which got low weight with extreme compromises that made it a small car, are lighter.

". . . Convertible sales penetration is going way up."

". . . Manufacturing shows a significant improvement in hours per car of assembly time."

He was about to go on, when executive vice president J. T. Battenberg, head of GM's Components Group, one of the largest parts manufacturing operations in the world, interrupted. He wasn't a happy fellow.

"How can you ask us to approve the program when you haven't completed your sourcing?" he demanded. He was right about that. Parts were on order for C5's alpha and beta cars, but final contracts remained unsigned for almost half of the major systems that would go into the production car. Hill tried to walk around Battenberg's question.

"We've only had a ten-and-a-half-month Phase Zero," he replied, "and the requirements keep changing. Sometimes major new requirements come in only two weeks before gates." One of those recent changes said that all contracts should be signed by now.

Battenberg waved him off. "Let's get back to the original question," he pressed.

But Hill was chief engineer, not program manager. His engineering answers didn't satisfy Battenberg and he was being beaten down by Battenberg's increasingly belligerent tone. Russ McLean gave the confrontation about sixty seconds before getting in the fray. He called for a backup slide. It showed that a final purchasing plan was in place, and that all contracts would be signed in the next two months. He repeated Hill's statement that the purchasing requirement was brand new.

Battenberg wasn't willing to drop it. "Then you're saying the policies adopted by this corporation are wrong? It's not you that's wrong, it's the corporation?"

That was dangerous ground. The corporation *was* wrong. McLean was debating how to answer when Jerry Collins, director of the Vehicle Launch Center, stood up in the small audience of executives allowed to witness the Concept Approval session. He took the heat.

"There are mismatches in the timing," he said, addressing the full board. "We've only had a few programs through the Launch Center and we are looking at this. I already have people on this problem, with the timing."

Battenberg was a bulldog who wouldn't let go. "If it's the policy that's wrong, then we should change Four-Phase, or we should be questioning this right now," he said, his voice heated. "I feel very strongly about this. Fifty percent of the major systems on this program are not sourced. I've built a lot of prototypes in my life and I see this as big trouble."

On the opposite leg of the horseshoe conference table, Joe Spielman reacted. He stood up to his full six-five and stared across at Battenberg. "This is the best program ever presented to this board and given the time they had, they've done the job," he said. "They have a plan in place to finish it up and we should let them."

That turned it into a confrontation among board members. Rick Wagoner, soon to be named president of North American Operations, weighed in. "The next program up will have this same problem," he observed. "It doesn't suggest that either the platforms or Four-Phase are right or wrong. It does say that there is some inconsistency here."

Which was exactly what Dave Hill and Russ McLean had been saying for nearly a year and Jerry Collins had just said, too.

Battenberg seemed to hear the message at last. "It could be that the policy is wrong. Maybe we ought to go back and change the policy. We have to have discipline in the system when we try to hold people accountable."

An almost audible sigh went through the board. Mike Mutchler, executive vice president for North American Passenger Car Platforms, looked out in the row of straight-backed chairs for Jerry Collins. "These are all good points," Mutchler the Negotiator said. "Jerry, I want to be sure that you take that on and look at the programs that are coming through the Launch Center."

Collins was about to say yes, when Battenberg went off in a new direction: "It seems that our competition doesn't have these kinds of problems."

"Toyota doesn't have this problem, that's right," Spielman retorted. "Before they start, they know that the same supplier is going to provide parts who provided them last and the time before that. Here we're playing four-dimensional chess."

The board went silent for a moment. On one level, Spielman had touched on a problem that they all recognized but couldn't bring themselves to address. General Motors rarely gave life-of-the-car contracts to any supplier, preferring to go out for rebids every few years as a wedge to drive down prices. That often worked but made supplier loyalty virtually nonexistent. It had another counterproductive side, too. Suppliers hesitated to make big investments that would improve efficiency in their own plants. With no guarantee that they wouldn't lose a contract in two or three years, there was simply no incentive. The result was never-ending turmoil, fear, and even ill will surrounding GM's purchasing operations.

On another level, Spielman's remark could be seen as a direct challenge to J. T. Battenberg. General Motors' parts-making operations were his. But in the new wave of cost cutting, he often couldn't compete against outside suppliers. His labor rate exceeded forty-five dollars an hour, against nonunion outsiders who sometimes booked rates a third as high. Battenberg's divisions and plants, once mandatory suppliers to GM platforms, were losing business to cheaper competitors. No program in the pipeline had ignored Battenberg as much as the C5 Corvette.

Dave Hill used the silence to try to get back on track. This time it was Bill Hoglund who interrupted. "You *are* challenging the policy," he said pointedly.

Hill could only agree and he did it quietly but firmly. "The policy is difficult to follow. The Four-Phase deliverables have been changing the whole time we've been in Phase Zero. They've been growing and growing just ahead of hitting the gates. It's been a perspiring experience.

"We know we are not where today's policy says we are supposed to be, but we are well ahead of any other program and we will have this in hand by our quarterly report in August."

Finally they let Hill go back to his presentation. He got to the part about converting the Bowling Green plant from C4 to C5. The process would start in April 1996 and run to August. The assembly line would crank up slowly and the first salable C5, called a pilot car, would begin to come together on September 3. He didn't get to mention anything else before Jack Smith's usually quiet voice broke in archly.

"That's taking way too long," he said. His tone said it was an order, not an observation. The morning's *Wall Street Journal* article was too fresh in his mind. It had cited the Oshawa, Ontario, plant that was still not producing midsize Chevrolet Monte Carlos seven months after its conversion had started. Part of the reason was that a key supplier was delivering inferior parts. Spielman's division was responsible and a new supplier was cranking up. But the bad parts should have been spotted by the Midsize engineering organization. They weren't and Spielman, as division head, was taking the rap.

Russ McLean stood up again. The Bowling Green plant conversion was his pride and joy. "The timing is for two reasons, Jack," he said. "First, we need time to get the plant ready for later work, and second, we already pulled up production by three and a half months." The reminder that C5 production had been on the books for start-up in early 1997 didn't placate Smith.

"This is a disaster," he said. "We can't be down that long. We gotta be able to move in a couple of weeks."

But the Corvette plan had a sound basis and Spielman defended it. "Jack, we're going from the old '84 body shop to a new and modern shop that will carry us out through C6. We have to have the time to do it right. Sure, we could do it faster. But the cost doesn't make sense."

"The *Wall Street Journal* ate our lunch on Oshawa," Smith argued back. "It went down in November and it's still not back up. We can't have that."

McLean brought up the money factor. His plan called for Bowling Green to reduce conversion costs by using equipment from other GM plants being closed. "But that means modification," he said. "It ends up being a lot cheaper, but it does take extra time."

Smith mulled that one over. "Could Chevy sell more of the current Corvette if you ran longer?"

Chevrolet general manager Jim Perkins took that one. "The danger is having old cars on the lot when the new Corvette comes out," he said. "We don't want to sell the old car alongside the new car. We end up cutting price and losing money."

Once again Smith analyzed the trade-offs. "Well, maybe this car doesn't matter," he conceded, "but we sure as hell don't want this kind of plant downtime happening on other programs."

Spielman heaved a sigh of relief. It was premature. "I know that, Jack," he said. "Even on Corvette, we could shorten the conversion by spending more money. But I can't move the start-up back any more. All I could do is run the old car longer to keep the plant open and that's not right, either."

On any other day, Smith might have let it drop there. But he didn't like being trashed in a national newspaper. "You're right in saying you can't do this on other cars," he said sternly. "Maybe you can't sell any more Corvettes, but you could have sold those cars from Oshawa. I don't want to see any more plants coming in with this long a conversion."

Joe Spielman got the message and sat down quickly. He'd just had his wrist slapped hard and in front of both his peers and his troops.

By now the session had run more than two hours and more questions were coming. The Strategy Board was living up to its feisty reputation. It focused on finances, particularly an $11 million increase in overall investment. "Does it really add value to the car?" Smith asked. "Do you get all of it back?"

"Absolutely." The answer came from Jim Perkins. He'd put his money on the line for C5 from the beginning. He knew that the car would be profitable. But Smith wanted more details.

"It's the new paint shop at Bowling Green, and the hydroforming process," McLean explained. "They're value-added items to the car. Jack, we won't spend a dime more than we need."

"Okay, but focus on it," Smith insisted. "That's how companies get into trouble."

That was how General Motors, under the other Smith, had gotten into trouble. Jack Smith had no interest in making the same mistakes.

The only red item on C5's list was engines for the first eighteen alpha cars. "Dick Donnelley assures us that we'll get them," Dave Hill said. "If we don't get them for testing this summer, we're in trouble."

"What about purchasing?" J.T. Battenberg wasn't willing to let that one rest.

"We consider that yellow," McLean answered. And he proceeded to put the board on the spot. "We feel we have met the requirements to go into Phase One. Now it's up to the Strategy Board to accept us, or not." He stood there looking around the big horseshoe table.

He only got part of what he wanted. After a two-minute discussion, the board asked him to come back in a month with a fresh look at when to shut down C4 production. "Balance," Jack Smith said. "I want to know that you've got some balance in your plan."

Mike Mutchler put the question: "Are we agreed that the program is approved conditionally with a report-back next month?"

It had been a rancorous session and the yeses were desultory. The Corvette people walked away without much jubilation. They were out of Phase Zero and into Phase One. That much was official. But instead of plunging full speed ahead, they faced the necessity of reevaluating the entire plan for closing down C4 and starting up C5. It meant putting together yet another package of facts that had nothing to do with their primary chore for the summer—building alpha cars.

Before they could take a deep breath and get started, a new threat was thrown at C5 that would have to be resolved at the same session with the Strategy Board in June. As usual, it came from inside General Motors.

THE memo went to Mike Mutchler and Joe Spielman, with a copy to Russ McLean. When it didn't trigger major changes in the C5 program after five days, Ron Haas faxed a copy directly to General Motors president Jack Smith. It was the second Haas memo in three weeks. The first one went only to the platform and merely caused consternation. The new one, sent out of channels to Smith just fifty-four hours before McLean and Dave Hill were to be back in front of the Strategy Board, tried to break their backs.

"After again reviewing the C5 program content and development status with Russ McLean," Haas began his explosive memo, "the C5 project still appears to be an extremely high risk program."

Those were fighting words. Haas's title was vice president for quality. But it was a position inside General Motors Research and the Technical Center that dealt more with theory and studies than with day-to-day car operations. He recommended stopping C5 dead in its tracks until his objections were addressed. He'd tossed a bomb on Jack Smith's desk and it had to be defused before it exploded.

The first memo arrived in mid-May. Haas had a reputation for putting his faith in statistics. Now he was listing a series of new data-filled reports he wanted on quality, safety, and other items. They were due on June 8. "Here we go again," said systems engineer Tadge Juechter, "new requirements coming in late and being enforced on the team."

"Anybody here for seceding from Midsize Car Division and starting our own Corvette company?" Dave Hill asked in a C5 engineering meeting. He wasn't surprised when most of the people in the conference room raised their hands.

"We asked that question in the decision risk analysis sessions a couple of years ago," added Fred Gallasch from Chevrolet. "We decided we could take it private and have no problem getting investors to put up two hundred million dollars to do the car."

The new Haas reports were just the tip of his iceberg. Haas had the idea that Corvette hadn't done its homework on C5. The car had substantial engineering risks. Even worse to Haas, there was no backup design to be plugged in if it failed. He took his concerns to McLean, listened to all the reasons why C5 was on the right track, and went away unconvinced. After brooding for more than a week, he drafted the memo to Mutchler and Spielman.

Among his criticisms:

"The C5 is a revolutionary all new design.

"• GM has never developed a rear transaxle/torque tube powertrain.

"• The vehicle is virtually all new—far beyond a 'major.'

"• Probably eighty-five–to–ninety-five percent new.

"• Compared to fifty percent new for typical majors."

Then he complained that a "design intent" demonstration vehicle had not been built and evaluated, and that Corvette planned an "inadequate number of P.G. [proving ground] validation vehicles. Five alpha vehicles planned [NAO Validation Center recommended eight], four proto vehicles planned [NAO Validation Center recommended fourteen]."

He hedged his criticism just a bit. "It is difficult to predict the future. We may, in fact, hit a home run and have no major surprises from the all new C5 technologies and powertrain. However, everything will have to go perfectly for a very complex all new vehicle."

Then he recommended that C5 do more work before passing through the gate into Phase One. In effect, he wanted the program stopped until it met his conditions.

Mutchler and Spielman brushed off the memo, and Haas with it. That's when the rankled VP, waiting until the last moment, faxed his memo to Jack Smith. It was all news to the GM president. He scribbled a note and sent it over to Mike Mutchler the next day: "I think the Corvette team needs to address these concerns with a demonstration vehicle."

Now it was Mutchler's turn to be rankled. His reaction paled next to those of Russ McLean and Dave Hill. They were furious. By the time word filtered down to them, they had less than a day to counter the threat to their program. "It's too bad we didn't know Ron Haas would be such a snake in the grass or we'd have done some politicking with him," Hill said.

Instead they were forced to take their case directly to the Strategy Board. Suddenly it seemed that C5 was in an all-or-nothing position. Joe Spielman conferred with McLean and Hill about how to proceed. Should it be Spielman against Haas, an *our vice president against your vice president* dogfight? Spielman was bigger by five inches and fifty pounds. In a back alley, he could take Haas without breathing hard. But this was civilization. People even wore jackets and ties when they addressed the Strategy Board.

Anyway, McLean wanted to lead the charge with Hill as his cornerman. They got their facts together and laid out the plan.

The meeting was in a small conference room at the Manufacturing A building on the west side of the Tech Center. Spielman, McLean, and Hill arrived almost together a little after 2:30 P.M. Ron Haas was already there, standing in the hallway looking uncomfortable. Hill turned away, still too angry even to nod hello. It was *his* engineering expertise and *his* plan that Haas was criticizing. To do it out of channels and in front of Jack Smith and all the rest was unforgivable. Spielman and McLean approached Haas for one last attempt to get him on their side. It didn't work.

McLean led off when Corvette was called in. Haas took the last chair at the rear of the room and sat straight-backed and knees together. It didn't take long for things to get rough. McLean had just shown a revised plan for rolling out three Corvette models, with new features to the cars each year out to Corvette's fiftieth anniversary in 2003.

"But there have been questions raised about our alpha build," he said, and flashed a slide of the CERV-4a test car on the screen. "This is CERV-a, which most of you have driven. We consider *this* to be our first alpha and we had it a year ago."

In the back of the room, Ron Haas moved to the edge of his seat, his feet tapping on the carpeted floor.

"In fact," McLean continued, "Bill Marriott [an outside director of the corporation] was really pleased with it when he drove it at the desert."

"We couldn't get him out of it," Mike Mutchler added.

Jack Smith rubbed his chin. "Ron Haas had some concerns about this." He turned to face Corvette's accuser. "Ron, are you comfortable with what you're hearing now?"

Haas jumped to his feet. "No, I'm not," he said. "This is a very advanced car, with a lot of technology."

That got the attention of everyone in the room. Haas spoke firmly and eloquently, without notes and without hesitation. He brushed his hand through thinning hair before he continued.

"This is an all-new vehicle and it's the first GM car ever with the transmission in the rear. [He didn't know that Pontiac had one in 1961.] I think we're facing all kinds of problems that we can't even guess. Noise is one. Nobody knows what kind of noise transmission paths this car will have, getting noise to the passenger. And there's a lot more to be worried about. I think we should be careful about committing major money here.

"And the validation vehicles are another point, a second point. I think they should have more than they have in the program. So this is an open issue."

McLean began his defense, laying out the plan already in place to deal with the issues. He barely got started before Mike Mutchler had heard enough.

"I'm willing to listen to the platform on this," he said with more than his normal force, "and I'm not willing to increase the engineering budget here."

McLean turned and spoke directly to Jack Smith, and to the money. "We're judiciously spending our money and we're designing and validating the car to the best engineering and business case."

That brought Joe Spielman into the discussion. "Remember, Jack, these alphas and betas cost about seven hundred fifty thousand dollars each. We're going to be watching this all the way and I say right now that if we need more cars, we will add more. But I'm not willing to sit here today and say arbitrarily that I'm going to add more cars."

McLean turned his words to Ron Haas. "There's another point here, too. The typical GM way has been to build validation cars for each user. Then somebody says, 'Nobody else can touch my car. Even if I only need it for two months, I'm keeping it for twelve.' But we're not doing that. We have a plan that says we are swapping cars through various users, moving them around in the test plan to get maximum use out of each vehicle. We're working with Powertrain and sharing data, making use of their vehicles to retrieve information that we need. So we're getting a much bigger impact out of our program."

That was the cue for Dick Donnelley, head of the Powertrain Division, to speak up. He was sitting directly across the table from Jack Smith. "Our high-volume programs might learn something here," he said. "I think what they've come up with has lessons for all of us."

There were nods and assenting murmurs around the table. In no more than three minutes, the Haas agenda had been put to rest. Its author sat gripping his chair tightly, knuckles white, but saying nothing.

Russ McLean's demeanor changed in the other direction. The tension visible in his face and the set of his shoulders disappeared. He smiled and called up another slide. "We've looked at the plant changeover and we've got a new plan for selling additional 1996 models," he said. The plan had been worked out with Chevrolet in the past week and looked feasible. It shortened the plant downtime and added $40 million in cash flow. But it cost $6.2 million.

It was a reminder that plants could be converted faster, but time saved equaled money spent. "We'll be coming to you to ask for that six million," McLean said, and was gratified to see Jack Smith nod a yes. C4s would now be built until June 21, 1996, but plant conversion would still begin in April, with new equipment being installed around, under, and over the old assembly line while it continued to run. McLean was proud of the plan and was convinced that it would work.

He called up his last slide. It showed that Corvette being buried with its owner in Pennsylvania.

"I'm asking for your full approval on this program," he said. "Joe Spiel-man says that if I don't deliver, he's going to give me a premature burial in a Corvette."

"Well, we can't have that," Jack Smith said. "I'm ready to go forward."

"It's a good program," Mutchler added, and the word "provisional" was removed from C5's passage through the Concept Approval gate.

McLean passed around blow-ups of the approval sheet for each Strategy Board member to sign. One copy would go to the new National Corvette Museum opening in Bowling Green, Kentucky, on Labor Day weekend.

This crisis was history, but nobody expected it to be the last.

50

T H E test car schedule was optimistic, ambitious, impossible. When Russ McLean told the Strategy Board that the status of the alpha build was red, even he didn't know how deep and dark a red he was facing.

The first drivable alpha car was only three weeks late.

Later on, that kind of timing would have looked good. Part of the delay was unavoidable. The United Auto Workers at the General Motors Technical Center went out on strike, shutting down the Bumper-to-Bumper operation for about five days. When the union did come back to work, it took a day or two to get rolling again. That was when the other problems reared up.

Parts were late in arriving. To the mounting frustration of McLean and Dave Hill, the General Motors purchasing system couldn't keep up with the demands of multiple programs, all clamoring at the same time for new parts. Orders for parts languished as overworked purchasing agents were flooded by paper from Corvette, the new van program, and several new midsize sedan programs simultaneously.

When parts did show up at the build site, they were often not quite right. Design mismatches were common—holes not lining up between two parts that were to be bolted or otherwise fastened together was a typical flaw. The problems frequently could be traced to an inexcusable conflict inside GM itself. That was the company's long-recognized failure to adopt a common computer design system for its various organizations and groups. Two systems existed inside the Midsize Car Division. Some commodity groups used one, some the other. The body group used a computer design system called CGS (Computer Graphics System). The chassis group used CATIA (Computer-Aided Three-dimensional Interactive Application). CGS and CATIA didn't work with each other. Data couldn't be passed back and forth without going through a conversion process that sometimes introduced errors. Even the basic frames of reference between CGS and CATIA differed. They looked at the car from different angles. Unless special care was taken to integrate the data before parts were ordered, a body part that was to attach to a chassis part often didn't quite fit.

The mismatch forced workers in Bumper-to-Bumper to stop the assembly process and figure out a solution. Sometimes it meant drilling new holes. Sometimes it meant trimming a part or bending it to make the attachment. Sometimes it even meant sending the part elsewhere for rework and waiting for it to come back. One thing it always meant was lost time. It would take more than a year for the technical people to get their acts together and come up with ways to integrate parts efficiently. By then, Corvette was beyond the alphas and struggling to make up for months of lost time.

The first C5, an alpha car destined for grueling tests by the heating-ventilation-air-conditioning engineers, and to be shared initially by other teams at the Milford Proving Ground, rolled out of the guarded assembly room at 2:55 P.M. on a Sunday afternoon, June 26, 1994. Build chief John Fehlberg watched the almost-last pieces (the inside door panels would be installed the next day) being put into place and the hoist being lowered until the car's tires touched the concrete floor. He looked around and didn't see any bosses waiting for the honor of being the first C5 driver. After a moment, he got in, started the engine, and drove the first C5 slowly down a wide aisle to a wheel alignment bay. "Zero to six in forty-eight seconds," he enthused. "It felt great."

They rolled it out again Monday morning, after the first C5 flat tire was repaired. Run-flats wouldn't be available until later in the testing program. The flat was a fallout from the absent hood hinges, deleted from the alpha design but incorporated into later test cars. Instead the engineers opted for a temporary fix borrowed from race cars. The hood was lifted into place by hand and held down by pins slipped into slotted studs. One of the pins came loose and Fehlberg drove over it.

Alpha 1 was flat black, a color chosen to make it more difficult for automotive photojournalists—called "spy photographers" in the business—to get a good picture that could be sold to the car magazines. It had the beginnings of a camouflage scheme, too. A BMW-type grille made of tape and stick-on appliqués was centered where a front license plate would normally be mounted. Fake patches designed to look like exhaust pipes were attached to the left and right ends of the rear bumper and the real exhaust pipes in the center were blackened to make them less obvious. Finally a silver slash was painted on the passenger door, giving the appearance of a large air scoop going in the opposite direction from the real air scoop that started just behind the fender and extended into the door.

The driver's door was left flat black while the camouflage scheme was tested to determined its degree of sneakiness. Later the camo packages would become much more extensive as the Corvette people learned new ways to hide their car from prying eyes. For now, they wanted it out in sunlight to photograph the camoed and uncamoed sides, and to do a group photo of engineers and UAW workers around the car. A double-height door rolled up, Fehlberg revved the engine, and at a stately five miles per hour, the first-ever fifth-generation Corvette moved into daylight, turned right down a ramp, and descended into position in a below-ground-level court-yard. It was wide and low, hugging the ground with a slope-nosed stance that looked fast even at a crawl. John Cafaro's chief studio engineer, Ron Nowicki, was there by happenstance to pick up a brake caliper he needed to measure for the new C5 wheels being designed. He'd seen the car in all its manifestations, from sketches on Cafaro's desk through clown-suit clay models to a dozen variations of full-size clays to the fiberglass car shown to the Strategy Board.

"Nothing does it justice like a real Corvette that moves across your field of vision," he said. "Whew! I'm impressed."

By sundown that Monday, the HVAC car was gone to testing. Wringing the bugs out of a car, and fine-tuning the hundreds of things that needed fine-tuning, is a process that never truly ends. But it does have its way stations. The biggest and most important one seemed to be both a long way off and coming up all too soon. It was that September 3 date in 1996, Russ McLean's birthday, when the assembly line in Bowling Green was to begin assembling its first pilot car, also known as the first salable vehicle. There was a lot still to do in only twenty-six months.

The elite test drivers assigned to Corvette pored over the HVAC car at Milford Proving Ground. They worked for Dave Wickman, who worked for Dave Hill, and they were some of GM's most skilled drivers. More formally, they were development engineers. They were tireless and hard-working, coming into two years of their lives that would demand sixty-, seventy-, and even eighty-hour weeks. They were mostly men in their thirties and their wives and kids would see too little of them from mid-1994 to mid-1996. They put C5 through countless hours of driving followed by eight or ten times that many hours on hoists as they personally tore down vehicles and found ways to fix flaws, improve systems, and fight a never-ending battle to reduce mass.

"The relentless pursuit of grams," Jeff Yanssens called it. The development group normally left that pursuit to the engineers who designed the parts. But Wickman's people had a special dedication to Corvette. Finding grams that the release engineers had overlooked became a mission to them and before C5 went to production, they had four or five kilograms of mass reduction to their credit.

Bumper-to-Bumper worked through the two-week July shutdown, now a corporate-wide edict on its way to becoming a tradition. They delivered their second running car to the engineers responsible for underhood thermal studies and exhaust system work on July 13. It was a month late. Reworking parts, or just waiting for parts to be delivered, was putting the schedule farther and farther behind. Three partial cars, bucks, destined for crash testing, were finally finished at one-week intervals, instead of the three-day intervals in the original plan. The build team was feeling its way and learning but getting later and later in the process.

Powertrain got its first running car in mid-August. It was partly Powertrain's own fault that it was two full months behind schedule. The first aluminum test engines had been recalled when faulty math data resulted in bad internal parts. Until the problem was corrected, GM's Powertrain Division delivered iron-block engines to be installed in alpha cars. They were about a hundred pounds heavier than the aluminum engines, but for most purposes, they'd do the job the test drivers needed.

A comedy of errors made things worse. When they shipped the first car to the desert, the hauler failed to tie it down properly in the truck. It was shaken so badly that it was unusable when drivers inspected it in Arizona, and they shipped it immediately back to Michigan for rework. It was returned to the desert in a week, but the hot-weather testing schedule was now in ruins. By the time they could get multiple cars to the desert, the hottest days of 1994 would be gone.

More problems turned up at Alcoa Aluminum, which was casting prototype blocks for the Gen III engine with a proprietary method that wasn't meeting specifications. The process worked for thin-section military castings, but not for big pieces like engine blocks. Powertrain's Ed Koerner took Alcoa to the limit, then called in the supplier that would do the volume production of aluminum blocks. The Montupet Company of Ontario wasn't ready to produce quality blocks yet, but agreed to use a temporary mold that would give Corvette enough blocks for its test program. Koerner had the blank engine blocks sent to GM's plant in Romulus, Michigan, for milling. If was a short-term solution and expensive. But it worked.

Other C5 news was better. The first alpha car was put into the GM wind tunnel and came back with a drag coefficient of 0.309. "Surprisingly good," system engineer Tadge Juechter said, "considering that it's a rough build and doesn't have the latest refinements."

But one event was worrying Dave Hill more than any other. C5's steering knuckles, big angular castings that connected the wheels to the frame and let them move, had failed in laboratory testing. Their metallurgy was in question and so was the basic design of the part. It was another flaw in the commodity system where Hill and his people set the standards and somebody else did the design. "It looks like a design that was phoned in," Hill said later, when the part was being redesigned.

Meanwhile, the few running cars that had been delivered were restricted to low speeds until a way could be found to brace or strengthen their knuckles and thus keep the program moving while a new knuckle was designed and delivered. A high-speed failure of a steering knuckle could throw a car completely out of control. A few days later a knuckle broke in a low-speed test run at Milford Proving Ground. The damage to the car was minor. But the testing delays brought on by the bad knuckle were major.

By the end of August, they all needed a change of pace. An outpouring of Corvette love gave it to them.

51 I T was supposed to be a joyride, just a few thousand miles across the country with a few thousand other Corvettes.

It was supposed to be an adventure, a high-speed rock 'n roll danced to the music of the Cult of Corvette.

It was supposed to be a gathering of the clan, Corvette builders, Corvette owners, and Corvette wanna-bes converging on Bowling Green, Kentucky, for the opening of the privately funded National Corvette Museum.

It was all that, and much more.

The museum had been in the works for more than five years. The $15 million it took to design and build it came from donations and a local bond issue that would be repaid from museum revenues. It was built in a large field across the road from the Corvette plant and when it was completed, its eye-catching roofline and spire won architectural acclaim. Chevrolet and General Motors provided exhibits, advice, and moral support.

Corvettes began making their way to their Kentucky home for a Labor Day weekend grand opening and celebration. The Beach Boys would be there for open-air concerts. The television networks covered it on their morning shows and on the evening news. The Corvette legends would be there, too. Zora Arkus-Duntov and Dave McLellan, the first two chief engineers, would be there to walk through the exhibits and to talk with the people who loved their cars. Dave Hill, not yet a legend, would be there with them. Russ McLean was there, too. He stood back and enjoyed it all.

On the morning that the ribbon would be cut, nine Corvette caravans from distant starting places in the United States would roll onto the museum site and fill it with cars of every Corvette generation. There were eighty Corvettes in the original Los Angeles pack, some of them more than thirty years old, driven by their owners.

Los Angeles was caravan number nine. Others started from Seattle, San Francisco, Minneapolis, San Antonio, Detroit, and points on the East Coast. But the L.A. crowd had the plum—driving east on Route 66. It only took ninety minutes before a Chevy public relations guy shoved drivers in front of a TV camera at the first stop in Barstow, California.

In 100-degree heat, as a two-mile-long chain of Corvettes rolled by, they talked about a car that inspires thousands of people to join Corvette clubs, that has at least a half-dozen magazines dedicated to it, that draws people every weekend of the year to a Corvette rally somewhere, and that had all of them heading for a party two thousand miles away.

They repeated the interviews in Kingman, Arizona, where the chief of police escorted them through town in a perfectly restored 1953 Chevy cop car, and in Albuquerque, where the guy from the ABC affiliate couldn't believe what he was seeing as the caravan, grown to more than 120 cars, poured into the parking lot of the Route 66 Diner.

Along the way, they saw America. Old Route 66, replaced by Interstate 40, was forlorn. Corvettes in a long line raced past boarded-up motels and closed gas stations straight out of the fifties. Somebody's hopes had lived there, and died there.

Now and then, a row of road-dusted cabins still courted travelers with an "Open" sign, and people ran outdoors to wave at the caravan commemorating America's legendary sports car.

In the overnight towns of Flagstaff, Tucumcari, and Fort Smith, Chevy dealers set up their showrooms with tables full of soft drinks and food. While some drivers had their cars tended in the service bays, which stayed open until all hours of the night for the once-in-a-lifetime visitors, the rest talked with crowds of local people who flooded in to see Corvette history stopping momentarily in their towns.

Car owners put wide-eyed kids into driver's seats and left them chattering about the day they'd own a Corvette.

They shook hands and shared Cokes with working parents who knew they'd never have one themselves, but came anyway because Corvette isn't a car, it's a dream.

They talked to old guys who remembered when the first Corvette came out in 1953 and whispered about wishing they'd just bought one and tucked it away.

They got their lines down with each succeeding interview. "It's just a car," the Channel 7 guy said in Albuquerque. "Why are all these people here?"

"It's not a car," they said. "It's a Superman suit. You don't drive it, you wear it. And when you're wearing a Corvette, you feel invincible."

Thursday was a blur of preliminaries for a few drivers running ahead of the pack. More than a thousand guests showed up for the museum preview and party, complete with a private George Jones concert. *Good Morning America* was filming. So were CNN and all the other networks. One documentary team had even brought its own satellite uplink.

Dawn Friday was misty in the Opryland parking lot in Nashville. When the parade of cars finally began to roll just before 8 A.M., there were more than eighteen hundred Corvettes in the giant lot, the confluence of four caravans west and south.

Up north in Louisville, another two thousand Corvettes staged. They, too, were aimed at Bowling Green.

The Tennessee Highway Patrol shut down Interstate 65 at their end and the Kentucky Highway Patrol did the same up north. One moment the northbound interstate out of Nashville was clogged with eighteen-wheelers and morning travelers; the next, it was empty as far as the eye could see.

Empty until an endless flood of Corvettes rolled out under escort. More Corvettes joined from side roads and the Opryland caravan grew to more than two thousand cars, too. Every overpass along the way was lined with people, two and three deep, all waving and cheering at a symbol of something America does right. Some of them brought flags to wave, and at one overpass, two boys in Scout uniforms saluted as the Corvettes passed by.

Closer to Bowling Green, the crowds overflowed onto the roadside and some hearty fools even ran out to the median with cameras and grins.

On the other side of the interstate, a steady stream of trucks who'd beaten the southbound closure out of Louisville crawled along with horns blaring and lights flashing. Their schedules be damned, the truckers slowed to watch the spectacle. Corvettes old and new, brightly colored and prancing, owned the road that morning.

Three truckloads of new C4 Corvettes sat on museum property close to the interstate. On one truck, the Corvettes were all red. On the second, all white. On the third, all blue. Sky divers streaming smoke carried the American flag into the middle of the crowd as the National Anthem played and the dedication speakers had their say.

Then the doors opened and the luckiest of 118,000 people to enter the museum on its first weekend crowded inside. A half hour later, Paul Zazarine, editor of *Corvette Fever* magazine and one of the museum's directors, stood with a stunned look on his face as he watched the crush of cultists clogging the exhibit-lined halls.

"A proud day, Paul," one the early visitors said.

"Yeah," Zazarine answered, "but it's not what I expected. For five years, this has been our dream, just a few of us. Now it's not ours anymore. It belongs to them."

A teenager jostled him and yelled out. "Hey, Dad, look at this. It's the one-millionth Corvette!"

The look of sadness went away and Paul Zazarine grinned. "Yeah, it belongs to them. I guess we did good."

The National Corvette Museum's gift shop did nearly a million dollars in business that weekend. The 118,000 people who went through the turnstiles was a Kentucky crowd only exceeded by the derby. Within months, the museum was second only to Mammoth Cave among Kentucky's daily tourist attractions.

The General Motors assembly plant that displays a large "Home of Corvette" sign on its manicured front lawn also attracts large crowds. More than seventy thousand visitors a year take a free self-guided tour through the plant, just to see Corvettes being born.

Scores of Corvette people from the team back in Michigan, along with spouses and children, drove to Bowling Green for that Labor Day weekend in 1994. What they saw and heard was an adrenaline jolt to their spirits after the long, difficult years they'd endured. Back home, C5 alpha cars were being built. In Bowling Green, the whole history and passion of Corvette reminded them of why they were doing it.

They drove north at weekend's end remembering the truth of the Corvette team's motto, chosen by Russ McLean from entries submitted by his people:

"The legend lives."

52 I T seemed to Dave Hill that a lot was going wrong. But when he walked through the Bumper-to-Bumper Shop and saw five hoists with alpha cars in various states of completion, or visited the design verification area to look at a full-size model of C5—interior and exterior—being pieced together, or heard that the various mass-reduction initiatives had given him cars that were now underweight by ten to fifteen kilos (twenty-two to thirty-three pounds) across the board, he thought that a lot was going right, too.

He flew to Arizona in mid-September to get into the first two thermal cars and they put a smile on his face. "I'd be scared to death to let Russ McLean or Fred Gallasch close to them, though," he said. "They're rough, lots of stupid little noises and rough and tough.

"But if you do the kind of editing a chief engineer does, trying to be sensitive and factual, but not too optimistic, they were really very good."

Hill was surprised at the feel of the car the first time he was in it. The current Corvette gave driver and passenger a feeling of confinement, with a pinch here and a tightness there. He found none of that in C5. "It was intimate, but it was roomy," he said. "It had the right balance."

He lingered at the Desert Proving Ground until everyone else had gone home. Then just after 9 P.M., with the temperature still 85 degrees, he took the targa roof off, got into a C5, and rolled out into the maze of roads and test tracks. His thinning hair whipped in the wind as he put *his* Corvette through twists and turns, around corners, and down long straightaways at speeds up to 120 mph.

"It was something I worked pretty hard to get to and I wanted to savor it," he said afterward, sighing and grinning in the same contented movement. "Under that moon with infinite headroom, it was like going to heaven."

Instead he went to the airport and caught a red-eye back to Detroit. As he settled in for the overnight flight, he remembered the broken steering linkage on the car at Milford and felt a chill on the back of his neck. He thought about his moonlight drive in the desert. *If that had happened to me at one hundred twenty . . .*

Hill restricted the remaining alpha cars to low speeds until the knuckle problem was solved. They quickly became hoist queens, cars that spent most of their time in the shop instead of on the track. It would be six to eight weeks before even early versions of a new knuckle could be delivered. At the same time, Powertrain was running far behind on delivering aluminum engines as it switched the prototype process from Alcoa to Montupet. Hill asked Wickman to analyze the test-driving program.

Wickman quickly saw that the entire plan had to be adjusted. Once they had new knuckles for their cars, he and his team of driver-engineers could live with iron engines for the first round of tests. Much of that work involved finding and fixing vibrations in the car, locating air leaks and wind and road noise that intruded into the cabin, and plotting out the initial ride and handling parameters. The HVAC people could do their early work on cabin heating and air-conditioning with iron-engine cars, too, but they needed aluminum engines to study engine and transmission coolants. The differences between iron and aluminum were too great to get started on the wrong engine.

Eventually Wickman's drivers would need aluminum engines, too. The heavier iron engine impacted the choice of shock absorbers and springs, and their final tuning. And the added front-end weight changed how the car handled. The drivers were expert enough to make solidly educated guesses on the handling differences, but guesses would only put them in the ballpark. The real setups had to be done on C5s with the correct engines.

So Wickman saw ways to work around his part of the driving schedule. His engineers could do air-leak and noise analyses by using the hoist queen cars in laboratory environments. Pumping one full of smoke to spot the air leaks or rattling it on a shaker plate could be as valuable as running it on the track.

But as the drive schedule got further and further behind, they'd need more cars in the future to make up for lost time. Dave Hill gave Russ McLean credit for always pushing to have a recovery plan and for raising enough hell inside the system to keep Corvette from being shunted aside by bigger programs. McLean responded to the test-drive dilemma by getting additional budget to increase the number of vehicles to be built from 84 to 112. That included running cars, partial cars or bucks, and partial sled cars for crash testing.

The extra cars would help Hill's development drivers, but they did nothing for Powertrain and its lagging test schedule. Engines could be run in static tests on dynamometer stands, hooked up to all sorts of sensors and instruments that would tell engineers what was happening. That was a good start. But engines needed to be run in the real world, on streets and highways in the full range of weather conditions, to find the bugs that didn't show up on a test stand.

Another recovery plan worked out between McLean, Hill, and engine chief engineer Ed Koerner was a beauty.

Twenty thousand driving miles or more on the Gen III engine had been planned for late 1994, followed by several hundred thousand miles in 1995–96. Most of the 1994 miles wouldn't happen. They'd need more cars to play catch-up and do the job right in the time remaining. But Bumper-to-Bumper couldn't possibly build enough alpha and beta cars to meet all the driving demands Powertrain now faced.

They decided to do "Cormaros." They started with eleven in the plan, then went to twenty. Powertrain bought new 1995 Chevrolet Camaros through GM's internal purchasing system. The cars were delivered to a large garage across the road from the Tech Center. Engines, transmissions, and chassis were removed and later donated to a local college. C5 side rails and the central tunnel were provided by Corvette. Mechanics modified the structure to fit under a Camaro body, then installed Gen III engines—some iron engines at first, but eventually every Cormaro had an aluminum engine —and rear-mounted transmissions.

The rear floor of the Camaro was raised to accommodate the Corvette's transaxle and gas tanks and the Camaro's rear seat disappeared. The fuel filler door on C5 was on the left side, behind the driver. A hole was cut into the Camaro body to match it and the body was reinstalled over the Corvette chassis, engine, and transmission. The front seats, instrument panel, steering wheel, pedals, and other Camaro parts would go back into place.

The result was a Cormaro, the perfectly camouflaged C5. A Cormaro could be driven anywhere without raising the interest of spy photographers or anyone else. It took until spring 1995 to get them built and delivered. When they were, engine testing got almost back on schedule.

Another set of disguised Powertrain cars was built using C4 Corvette bodies. Those cars were used in Michigan and in Ontario's frigid mid-north in cold-start tests and in developing the software for the braking system and traction control. Without them, C5 would have slipped again and been a 1998 Corvette.

"Without the Cormaros and C4 mules, they had no way to do two winter tests on the engines," McLean said. "Now they'll get two seasons of Kapuskasing [Ontario] testing. But they still only get one desert season."

That situation would be faced in another year. When the American Southwest cooled at the end of summer, deserts in other places would be just heating up. The Powertrain test drivers would find themselves finishing up their hot-weather work at the bottom of the world.

Joe Spielman told Russ McLean and Dave Hill to put three months in

Australia into their contingency plans for early 1996. The odds on completing all the necessary hot-weather testing, by both the engine people and the HVAC people, were too long to ignore. He didn't know that someone else would be running the Midsize Car Division when the plan was dusted off and put into effect.

T H E change came swiftly and unexpectedly. The slow start-up in producing Chevrolet Monte Carlos at the Oshawa, Ontario, plant may have been a factor, and the engineering delays in getting new midsize models through the system didn't help. Or it may have been a case of General Motors putting two of its senior executive talents in the jobs where they were needed the most.

For all but three of his thirty-one years at GM, Joe Spielman was a plant guy and he was recognized as one of the most knowledgeable managers in the company in the areas of manufacturing, tool and die work, and heavy-duty machinery.

"My alarm goes off every morning at four-thirty and I'm on the road at five-fifteen," he liked to tell the people who worked for him. "On a weekend, it might be six o'clock before I'm in the kitchen making coffee.

"Plant start-up time. That's what rings my bell."

Russ McLean knew it was true because the two often ran into each other getting coffee in the predawn hallways. Some mornings they'd have their first chat of the day about Corvette and be off to other meetings or be wading through stacks of paper on their desks before 6 A.M. In October 1994, Spielman was given another assignment and McLean got a new boss.

In the two years since the boardroom rebellion had shaken up GM, president Jack Smith and chairman of the board John Smale had tackled one devilish problem after another. The car-making divisions had been reorganized and the car-marketing divisions had been reoriented toward the business of selling cars and at least partly away from the business of influencing the making of cars. The components group had become an umbrella organization called Delphi that swept together a myriad of GM divisions involved in making parts.

But a big internal organization remained in trouble. If it wasn't in disarray, it was at least unfocused. Spielman was sent to the west side of the GM Technical Center to become vice president and general manager of the North American Operations Metal Fabricating Division and Manufacturing Centers. He'd have more than thirty-five thousand people under his charge and he was told to bring all of GM's metal-benders and advanced manufacturing processes into the new world of efficiency and economy.

It was the kind of challenge he relished. But leaving the Midsize Car Division and especially Corvette wasn't easy. In two years at MCD, he'd brought the division from a billion and a half dollars in the hole to $150 million in the black. Some of the most improved auto plants in the country, according to J. D. Powers ratings, were his. Once the Monte Carlo went into production, it was a superior car with few flaws, and buyers loved it. But after all that, the only new car in the MCD pipeline that was on time and on budget was Corvette. The high-volume sedan and van programs were in trouble. "I was too process-oriented," Joe Spielman said in retrospect. "The division needed a better balance between cars, people, and process." He'd stayed loyal to his engineering director, and to the Juras Vision, too long.

Whether the new boss at MCD would follow along was the question of the day. The answer wouldn't be known for six months. Don Hackworth didn't just take over the head office at Midsize. He added it to his duties as general manager of the Cadillac/Luxury Car Division (CLCD) headquartered in Flint, Michigan, and eventually oversaw an internal marriage that created a new GM group called the Midsize and Luxury Car group.

Hackworth came in with a reputation as a no-nonsense boss. Russ McLean came away from briefing him on Corvette, both C4, which was producing 1995s and still had the 1996 model year to go, and the new C5, with a feeling of quiet reassurance. He heard nothing in Hackworth's questions or comments that worried him about Corvette's standing. After Hackworth met several times with his top engineering staff, including the platform chief engineers, Dave Hill felt the same way. Hackworth demanded quality cars and Hill's impression was that quality counted more than strict adherence to the rules.

Hill's Corvette engineering staff was ready to break out the red and black flags of rebellion when he shared his feelings in late October.

"I want to do the kind of car Hackworth wants, but I can't do it the way Juras says," Hill said bluntly. "I've decided that I don't care if I'm not doing the engineering management process. I'm willing to withstand any attempt by Juras to fire me if I can do the kind of car Hackworth wants."

"Are you looking for volunteers to cross the line with you?" Dennis Sheridan, the lead HVAC engineer asked instantly.

"We're with you one hundred percent," added manufacturing engineer Pete Liccardello.

"Thank god," breathed Steve Mackin, lead engineer for the interior of C5. "Now we can get some work done."

Systems engineer Tadge Juechter looked up and down the conference table and around the room. "We're ready," he said. "It looks like it's unanimous."

The frustrations of the past eighteen months at trying to do a job in spite of the system instead of with the system bubbled over. Hill told them more. Mike Juras had called his engineering people together the day before for an off-site session to examine the state of the new Midsize programs.

"There were long arguments about whether and who will address the problems," Hill said. "There are major major major problems on the [new Midsize] cars, forty no-builds, more than sixty parts missing, all kinds of trouble. And people are arguing about needing the right paperwork, who does the paperwork, instead of starting without paperwork. It was all finger-pointing and blaming someone else."

Listening to the other programs' troubles catalyzed his thinking, he said. "These people haven't earned the right to tell me how to do a program, and I'm not going to go down the road that ninety-six-point-five programs are going down."

Hill's senior engineers listened with stunned and happy expressions. Rebellion was unheard of in the ranks of GM management. But if this was a sign of the new GM that was trickling down from Jack Smith and the people around him, they were all for it. And if it wasn't, they were still for it.

One question put it all in perspective: "Do we solve the problems before the customer sees them or do we let the customer be our test driver?" Hill asked. "I want to solve the problems first."

It was the right question and the right answer.

The way to get the job done, he told them, "is don't write down assignments that are outside the Juras Vision. The risk is that word will get around not to do these things the Corvette group is asking." Once again, Corvette was doing an end-run around the system. Getting the job done was more important than following procedure.

With that, Hill and his staff seized control of the remaining design work on C5 parts, particularly redesigns to fix problems such as the too weak steering knuckles. They'd ride herd on designers from homerooms, looking over shoulders, recruiting them to the cause, and avoiding direct confrontations with homeroom bosses. They were already doing some of that anyway. Hill just gave them permission.

The first part to get special attention was that steering knuckle. A redesign had been done and the first alpha-2 knuckles cast in just twenty days. One of those broke, too, when an alpha car was taken over a test road marked with potholes. Chassis engineer Jim Lloyd pushed the design for an alpha-3 knuckle through the commodity group this time, making sure it was right.

"When you look at a C4 knuckle," Hill said, "you see something that's streamlined with gentle transitions from one section to another. When you see C5, it's a bunch of sharp angles and abrupt intersections. It wasn't designed. It was drawn."

Cars with the alpha-2 knuckles were being run at Milford on smooth roads only. And the durability testing, in which cars would be run on grueling schedules of 10,000, 24,000, 45,000, and 100,000 miles over every kind of road surface and maneuver, had not been started at all. "It's going to be twenty-four hours a day for the durability people, once we get cars for them," Hill said. "But we can't run durability without alpha-3 knuckles."

They got their first alpha-3 knuckles just before Thanksgiving—another twenty-day miracle—and they were rushed into the lab for metallurgy and stress testing. They passed. But they were virtually handmade and it would be early December before two more sets could be delivered. Hill had those shipped to the desert, where they were immediately installed on two alpha cars and put to work. This time they didn't break, even under the hardest jolts and stresses. Hill scheduled another trip to the desert on December 15 for himself and his key engineers. They'd all get time in the cars and could see the good and the bad for themselves. Driving the cars, Hill said, is the best time an engineer can spend.

Jim Lloyd breathed a sigh of relief and ordered enough knuckles for all alpha and beta cars, plus spares. They could be produced at the rate of two sets a week, but by mid-January, knuckles were arriving in enough quantity to get the test-drive program started again. It was months behind schedule, but with long weeks to be put in by Dave Wickman and his development engineers, and with durability drivers working three shifts, seven days a week, at both Milford and the desert, they could catch up.

At about the same time, John Cafaro got a new job. Chevrolet general manager Jim Perkins asked for him to head up styling of a car they were calling the high-mid, a midsize sedan of modest luxury for the late nineties. Cafaro took the assignment on one condition: He would retain control over all C5 styling issues through the 1999 model year. Design vice president Wayne Cherry, with the happy concurrence of Perkins, Russ McLean and Dave Hill, made it official. The assignment erased the last trace of the young and rebellious Cafaro from the corporate memory. He was still a brilliant and intuitive designer. But Perkins, Cherry, and the rest made it official that he also was a smart executive still on the rise.

"John's been a giant on this car," Hill told his staff when the announcement was made. "He has really been one of us."

What it meant for Chevrolet was unique in the history of the name. By 1999, a single design chief would have been responsible for four new Chevys introduced over a six-year span: Camaro, Cavalier, Corvette, and the yet-to-be-named high-mid.

"The only thing that counts is doing a good car," Cafaro said, "and doing it right."

Doing it right in the design studio was one kind of difficult. Doing it right on the test track was another. The day before they were to leave for Arizona, Dave Wickman got an urgent call from one of his engineers in the desert. The Gen III engines had developed severe lubrication problems. In one engine, oil had completely stopped flowing.

By that afternoon, Powertrain's Greg Cockerill had a report for Dave Hill's staff meeting. "The engines have coolant in the crankcases," he said. "The problem may be porosity in the head bolts or maybe some bolts are cracking."

Either way, antifreeze and oil were mixing. The result was a sludge. Tearing the engines down and cleaning out the sludge was an irritation, but not a showstopper. But the cars couldn't run again until the head bolts were examined and replaced. Hill canceled the trip to Arizona. They would try again in January.

"Time is now our most precious commodity," he told them. Running cars were mandatory to get the preliminary tests and adjustments completed before hot-weather work could even be considered. A chill north wind was bringing the first winter cold to Detroit. But Dave Hill was thinking six months down the road.

"If we lose the summer of '95," he said, "we lose the program."

I T wasn't just the summer, Dave Hill realized later. They needed to be driving test cars in the winter, spring, summer, and fall of 1995 to have a prayer. Then they'd need the winter and spring of 1996 to finish up, and even that would be cutting it close.

At the end of 1993, Hill had looked back at the turmoil of the year and forecast that 1994 would be easier. He may have been a skilled chief engineer, but he was a lousy prognosticator. The year had been filled with one problem or setback after another.

Engineering is the art of making mechanical things work. It is beyond rare for anything, from a can opener to a Corvette to a corporate jet, to work perfectly the first time out. But the number of problems thrown at Hill's engineering team in 1994 was over the top. They expected to find parts that had missed the mark in the design process. That's why they were building and testing cars. But that seemingly straightforward task was compounded and recompounded by the internal problems of just getting parts ordered, or getting the assembly work done, or even finding a name to go with a responsibility at the engineering commodity groups.

They did build some cars, not enough, but it still was a big plus. Every time Corvette engineers saw an alpha car rolling along under its own power, the sheer beauty and magic of the machine pumped up their pulse rates. This was what it was all about. It didn't hurt that the number of people privileged to see a C5 in motion was very small. They managed to come to work in the morning excited and they fell into bed at night exhausted. Being part of Corvette was more than special. It was a unique time in all of their lives, *doing a new Corvette,* and most of them knew that it would be a once-in-a-lifetime experience.

But getting the alpha cars built took more energy than anyone expected. It was energy spent fighting the system to get early parts designed, then ordered and delivered. It was energy spent resolving the mismatches when parts engineered under one computer drafting system didn't line up with parts designed under another system. It was energy spent getting a few flawed, but critically important, parts redesigned.

Russ McLean and Dave Hill looked at each other and were silently thankful that the other guy had somehow gotten into his fifties without burning out. They were type A personalities who could still sit in a meeting and crack a joke, or remember to thank an engineer for a good report. McLean's aphorisms—nobody knew how many were original and how many were borrowed—were jotted down in meetings and then posted around the Corvette area:

"If you walk like you talk, the rest of the team will walk with you. If you're all talk, they will eventually quit listening."

"Success or failure is a matter of attitude by those responsible."

"Any good general has a fallback plan."

"You gotta know where you've been to know where you wanna go."

They'd lost almost all of the test driving scheduled for 1994. That was where they'd been. Where they had to go in 1995 was the rest of the way. It was a very long way.

Corvette test drivers fell into two broad categories. Development engineers were one. They worked for Dave Wickman and shuttled back and forth between the two proving grounds in Arizona and Michigan.

If there was glamour as a Corvette test driver, it fell on the development engineers. They drove the cars with every sense, including the seat-of-their-pants feeling for how to improve it. They were the drivers who tuned the shock absorbers, the springs, and the other suspension parts for the best ride and handling. They listened to wind and road noise, then pulled into the garage to try different kinds of insulation or sound-absorbing material on the next run. They felt how the electronic throttle reacted to their right foot and asked for this adjustment or that. When Goodyear sent tires with varying tread patterns, they mounted them on test cars and ran them through turns and skids and wet slides and more to gauge how C5 reacted.

When development engineers felt unfriendly vibrations through their feet or their backs, they looked for the source and fixed it. Sometimes that meant working with other engineers to get a part redesigned or the material changed or perhaps just a rubber bumper added to eliminate a little buzz. The development engineers got the fun stuff, too—the high-speed runs around tracks and the off-site drives that could come later through mountains and deserts and hidden forests.

The price they paid was twelve-hour days with no overtime, and weeks away from home and family. It looked glamorous and sometimes it was. It looked grueling, too, and it always was.

Other development drivers were specialists in air-conditioning and heating, and engine cooling. They worked for Dennis Sheridan and their jobs were seldom glamorous. In the winter, they were freezing while sitting in cars to see how soon the heater made things comfortable, and in the summer, one terrible test would have a Corvette sitting under the desert sun for three hours, then the engineers would get in, close the doors, start the car and air-conditioning, then monitor the system until they stopped sweating and could draw a cool breath.

Still others worked for the Powertrain Division and would be running cars in cold weather and hot and everything in between, refining the engine until it would work as it should no matter where the new Corvette's owner lived or drove.

All that had to be done in 1995 and the first months of 1996.

The other group of test drivers were not engineers. They were United Auto Workers union people and their job was to drive new Corvettes almost to death. When something broke, engineers would evaluate the problem and fix it. Durability driving was not glamorous.

Part of the logjam broke in the final days of 1994, when enough new steering knuckles arrived to get three cars started on the durability schedules that eventually would pile on thousands of miles of rough treatment. They got one day of durability on December 23, took a three-day Christmas break, then got two more days in before water pumps failed and the cars went down over the New Year holiday. Even the few driving days were not problem free. One day a left muffler bracket broke and on another day the right bracket failed. Glass in the driver's door broke. Each incident was logged and investigated by engineers. And each took the car out of service for an hour or five while repairs were made. On a good day early in durability testing, drivers put about fifty miles on the odometer in an eight-hour shift. Later in the year, when many problems were history, they might log two hundred miles per shift.

The durability cars were taken over test roads designed to inflict damage. A car running through several hundred yards of Twist Ditches was subjected to steep trenches angling across the road and alternating from right to left and back to right. That set up a swaying motion up-down-left-right that put more stress on a Corvette in one pass than it would get in a month of normal driving. A driver might make three to five passes in a single shift. The Belgian Blocks were large cobblestones raised to varying heights that jerked and jarred the car over a mile-long course. The Ride-and-Handling course was nearly two miles of uphill, downhill, and straightaways, with curves and turns ranging from gentle to sharp. The road surface changed, too. One moment it was smooth, the next rough and ratchety.

Along one looping road, the plan required a driver to sweep through a 180-degree constant radius turn at 35 mph, then accelerate to 80 in third gear, hold the speed through gear shifts into fourth and fifth, then brake to 45, accelerate hard back to 65 in third gear, and drop back to 35 for another 180-degree turn at the other end. The accelerations called for wide-open throttle. The first couple of full-throttle runs in a new Corvette were fun. After that, it was work.

Another course was the 5-mph Serpentine. Lanes were painted on a concrete surface the size of a huge parking lot. Every turn was hard left or hard right and they came so fast that maintaining 5 mph was a demanding chore. A good durability driver could manage the course in five minutes. But then he had to do it twice more. A durability car would see the Serpentine hundreds of times over the months of testing.

One unpopular test involved driving into a car-wash building. But the wash was a corrosive salt and chemical solution sprayed from above and below. The first chore after leaving the wash was to clean the windows. On cold winter nights it ranked as a driver's most miserable task. A durability car experienced the equivalent of ten years' corrosion through the test program.

The driveway test required a driver to pull up a short and steep slope, set the parking brake, turn off the engine, wait a few moments, then start up and back down. At the bottom, the driver had to maneuver around, then repeat the test four more times. On Bamber Road inside the Milford Proving Ground, drivers raced over loose gravel that clattered and banged against the underside of the car and in the wheel wells. Running over the Chatter Bumps was teeth jarring to a driver and shook the car and its parts unmercifully.

Engineers sometimes rode with durability drivers to get a feel for what their parts or systems were doing. Almost none could last a full shift as a passenger. Even an hour or two was enough to send some of them off with queasy stomachs and a new respect for the UAW drivers.

When a day went well at the proving grounds, something else would happen. One January morning Dave Hill left home at 5:45 A.M. hoping to get to Milford early enough to spend a half hour looking over cars before a 7 A.M. meeting with his development engineers. That was the morning an eighteen-wheeler rolled over on Interstate 96, spilling a load of red brick dye across the road. With traffic backed up for miles, snow began to fall, triggering more accidents. Hill reached Milford at 9:40 A.M. His engineers had run most of the meeting without him.

Hill and McLean had some hard-and-fast rules about security. They wanted no leaks about what the new Corvette looked like, or how it performed. When the car was unveiled to the press in late 1996, they wanted it to be a surprise. The alpha cars could not be driven outside of a General Motors facility. Even inside the Milford Proving Ground, no alpha car could be taken on the long back straightaway during daylight. There was rising ground beyond the fence where passersby might catch a glimpse of C5 or an enterprising photographer might lurk to get a picture.

All cars were camouflaged. Their true body styles were hidden from the eyes of other GM employees and from the occasional authorized visitor being escorted around the proving grounds. When C5 test cars were moved from one facility to another, they went inside closed transport trucks. No C5 would be moved on one of the open transports used to carry new cars to dealers or to move less-secret GM models.

The Desert Proving Ground was in flat terrain. It was surrounded by high fences and rows of oleander so that almost nowhere could anyone see inside. There was one short stretch near the main gate where the fence was low and there was no oleander. Just behind the fence, test cars sometimes flashed past on their way to the garage area. Russ McLean asked that the fence there be raised, or oleanders be planted, or something be done to shield the cars.

It didn't happen. And when the news media breached C5 security, that was the spot.

55

JIM Dunne ordered a dark beer on draft at the Old Mill, one of his favorite lunch haunts on the border of Detroit and Hamtramck. The ethnic suburb, nicknamed Poletown, was home to a huge Cadillac assembly plant and bordered by other giant General Motors and Chrysler plants.

Until it moved north to Auburn Hills, Chrysler headquarters was only a mile away from the Old Mill and the joint was packed for lunch. General Motors' headquarters was three miles to the southwest and the GM Technical Center was eight miles northeast. The Old Mill crowd thinned after Chrysler left but still included a few GM and Chrysler people from the plants, the occasional executive returning to an old haunt, and a handful of Detroit's best-known automotive journalists.

While he waited for his beer, Dunne leaned just a little to catch the conversation at a nearby table packed with Chrysler engineers. It was nothing that interested him, so he scanned the room checking faces. Nothing again. He relaxed, accepted the beer, and ordered a fish sandwich. Except to the fivesome at his table, he was invisible. That was how he wanted it.

Jim Dunne was a spy.

He brought car companies grief and forced them to spend thousands of dollars on camouflage and subterfuge. "Wanted" posters bearing his face appeared on walls. Long meetings dealt with the "Dunne problem." The security department at General Motors was even rumored to have a short video called *How Jim Dunne Does His Job*.

Jim Dunne was sixtyish and balding, of medium height and weight. His twinkling Irish eyes were set in a grandfatherly face. His friendly manner and casual conversation masked the raison d'être that made him the beloved scourge of U.S. and foreign car makers.

He may be the best-known and most liked spy in the history of industrial espionage. Results of his exploits appeared regularly in daily newspapers and car magazines, to the thrill and delight of every company in the auto business except the one being skewered. And even that one knows that next month the shoe will be on some other company's foot and they'll get a peek at what the competition has coming.

"Spy photos," they called them, and the car magazines paid well. A future family sedan or sport utility might be worth a few hundred dollars to an editor, but a photo of a hot car like a secret new Corvette could bring ten times that much just for one-time rights to a single fuzzy picture. More than any other leak in the secrecy surrounding a new design, spy photos were the most pervasive way for cars lovers and the competition alike to get a quick look at what's coming down the road. Within the industry, the love-hate relationship with spies like Jim Dunne was more love than hate.

Another of Dunne's jobs made him hard for auto companies to ignore. He was Detroit editor for *Popular Mechanics* magazine and his editors in New York got first choice of his pictures.

Dunne invented, or nearly so, the automobile spy photo. He brought it to both high art and science, and thereby created a profitable trade eventually shared by a handful of rivals. If that picture in *Car and Driver* of a Ford or Chevy still two years from a dealer's showroom wasn't taken by Jim Dunne, it was taken by Hans Lehmann of Germany or Brenda Priddy of Phoenix or, more rarely, by some amateur who was in the right place at the right time. Amateurs frequently called Dunne—he was listed in the book—to tell him what they had. Sometimes, if it was good, he bought from the amateur and resold to the editors he knew so well.

He latched onto the spy business when he realized in the 1960s that the game was both fun and profitable. He scouted all the proving grounds. He knew every chink in the fences at the tracks used by Chrysler, Ford, and GM. He knew the tall trees and sometimes carried a ladder on his spy runs. He was chased away by Ford, Chrysler, or GM security guards so many times that he and the guards often knew each other by their first names.

When he couldn't get what he wanted by standing on a hill at Milford or climbing a tree across the road from the Ford or Chrysler tracks, Dunne took to the public roads. Sooner or later, every new car has to get out on real roads in all kinds of weather so that test drivers can find the real-world bugs and fine-tune the car to the roads and the weather where car buyers drive.

In 1982, Jim Dunne got a photo of a C4 being run on a public road in Michigan. It was almost two years before the car would be in dealerships and interest in the secret fourth-generation Corvette was high. The photo, Dunne said not altogether facetiously, put one of his daughters through two years at Michigan State.

Dunne's sources in the industry occasionally tipped him to a scheduled drive. Or he would simply get on a plane to Phoenix, where both GM and Chrysler have large proving grounds in the desert, to see what he could find. He showed up at Death Valley every August, and in January he prowled through the Sault Sainte Marie region of Michigan's Upper Peninsula, drove to Bemidji, Minnesota, or made the long trek to Kapuskasing, Ontario. He rarely returned empty-handed.

But Hans Lehmann beat him to C5. Lehmann got the first C5 spy photo on January 3, 1995. They know that was the day because development engineer Rex Stump's distinctive profile was clearly visible in the driver's seat and that was when he drove the car. The angle of the shot and the surrounding terrain, even though it may have been modified on a computer, convinced Hill, McLean, Wickman, and GM security that somehow Lehmann had gotten a shot over that short fence and escaped without being detected by guards at the D.P.G.

The photo of the heavily disguised alpha car ran in *Automotive News* and its sister publication, *AutoWeek*. Readers saw a Corvette with a long padded bra—a Naugahyde cover—up front to make the nose look longer and a misshapen Naugahyde-and-plastic-foam diaper on the rear to mask the stylish curves that John Cafaro and his studio people had worked so hard to get just right. The flat black paint job, with a white two-tone effect on the lower part of the car from the rear wheel to the front, obscured every styling feature. Even the air scoop running from the front fender into the door looked like just another molding strip intended to prevent parking lot dings.

The disguised car was, almost everybody who saw it up close agreed, somewhere between "just homely" and "really butt-ugly." It was the duckling hiding the swan.

That didn't stop Dave Hill and Russ McLean from being upset. They ordered more camouflage to be designed, particularly for the hood and the doors. By early February, it would be ready.

Jim Dunne was not happy that his rival Hans Lehmann got the first C5 spy photo. Nor that amateurs in Texas, Oregon, and even Australia caught camouflaged C5s on film. He intensified his own efforts to track the elusive new Corvette. But the extraordinary lengths to which McLean and Hill went to protect their car from outside eyes would pay off. Hans Lehmann was the first pro to get a C5 shot, a grainy side view shot over the top of the fence at GM's Desert Proving Ground. There were a few others, mostly by lucky amateurs.

Dunne finally got his C5 shot, courtesy of Oldsmobile. He was invited to Phoenix to drive a new Olds model in March 1996 and saw executive vice president Don Hackworth on the plane. If Hackworth was going to Phoenix, Dunne reasoned, something was happening with the cars in his division. There was. Hackworth and the executives building his new van, sedans, and Corvette were taking a road tour to try out the products. With a morning to spare, Dunne gambled and set up close to the Desert Proving Ground entrance.

Just before noon, he spotted a caravan of camouflaged cars coming home to roost. Dunne raced past them just before they reached the proving ground, skidding to a stop and snapping pictures as each car turned into the main gate. One of them was a C5. Its camo pack still masked its true lines, but Dunne sold the photo to editors eager for anything on the new Corvette.

Another kind of spy photo allowed *Motor Trend* magazine to recover from its erroneous story about C5 in 1994. Someone delivered a mysterious set of Polaroid photos of the car, taken inside a GM facility, to the magazine. The pictures showed the uncamouflaged side of a C5, with its canvas cover hurriedly tossed onto the roof. A magazine artist used them to do a color rendering of the car that came close enough to give Russ McLean heartburn, but still overstated the tailpipe configuration and included the scalloped rear-end design that had been dropped.

Armed with that peek at C5, writer Don Sherman did a piece that got it closer to right in a 1995 story, then followed with a look at C5 that was dead-on in 1996. Sherman used a source he told editors was his Corvette Deep Throat. A retired Corvette engineer helped by checking a first draft of the 1995 story. But Sherman got the timing wrong. Nobody told him that the car had started out to be a 1993 model, and Sherman forecast that C5 would finally be designated as a '98. Inside the program, 1998 was never considered. C5 was a '97 all the way.

It was still enough to send McLean complaining to the public relations department, demanding that Sherman be banned from General Motors. The PR folks demurred.

Sherman delivered more good details about the car and the Gen III engine in 1996. The *Motor Trend* editors put a mostly accurate drawing of C5 on the September 1996 cover, using confidential General Motors information somehow acquired by Sherman, and showed both the targa and convertible cars inside the magazine. They even had the new Corvette logo in perfect detail. It was a coup that made *Motor Trend* the clear winner in the race to reveal C5 to the curious and the faithful alike.

5 6   M O S T of Dave Hill's key engineers got their first chance
to drive a C5 alpha car in late January 1995. They left
Detroit's icy winds and subzero windchills for winter
warmth in Arizona and caught the last of a line of winter
rainstorms drenching the desert before blue skies and
sunshine broke through.

Three alpha cars were pulled into service bays in Corvette's corner of
a large garage that housed other future GM vehicles. None of the vans
and sedans held any interest to the Corvette team. They surrounded their
cars, poking under the lift-off alpha hood, looking up at the exposed bottom of a car on a hoist, and sitting in driver's and passengers' seats to get
their first real feel of what they'd been working on now for more than six
years.

The slow accumulation of miles on the cars still disturbed Hill. "Time is
the one commodity we can never get back," he told them. But more important, he wanted his engineers to experience the cars on the track and
test roads, then to carry their firsthand knowledge back to Detroit. The
deadline was looming for locking in design changes for the beta cars that
the Bumper-to-Bumper Shop would begin building on April 10. The betas
would be vastly improved cars with parts that fit better or had been redesigned to correct flaws found in the alpha testing.

"It's taken millions of dollars and lots of perspiration on the part of
everybody in this room to get to today," Hill said. To more than half of the
people there, *today* translated into *I finally get to drive one*. Bob Applegate
of Chevrolet's Sporty Car group was grinning in anticipation. He was about
to be the first Chevy guy in the car and he could hardly wait.

"We're making progress toward the beta drop-dead date," Hill went on,
"but we've lost a lot of time. Today is the day to size up our accomplishments and see where we are."

He also wanted to make sure that everyone understood where Dave Hill
was. The tone of his voice was a coach's before the big game.

"I want to nail the design so we can deliver a robust Corvette to the
customer," he said. "Nothing is better for acceptance of the car and for
conquesting people out of import cars and into Corvette than if we give

early buyers a trouble-free experience. I want them to say that they have no squeaks and rattles, no recalls, no reason to go back to visit their dealer.

"What the owners say will determine the prestige of the car far more than anything we put into ads or say on TV or put into an Indy pace car." He reached for a flip chart on an easel and exposed the first page. He'd handwritten his questions.

"Is the car good enough? Can we make up lost time in B2B? Is beta design representative for durability work?"

Finally he flipped the page to his most important question of all. "Is the car good enough to get a production car [the prototype cars that would come after the beta build] started on July 1?" He glanced at his watch. "That's only minutes from now and we're the only ones who can answer that question." He paused and looked at his team. Then the tone of his voice turned dead serious.

"If it isn't good enough, we have to adjust the entire schedule, put the plant down [in 1996], and delay start of production. And if we say the car is good enough, then we have to ask ourselves what we should be doing in the next few weeks to maximize the goodness of the prototypes.

"We are in a race against time. All the theory has to be set aside. Now we have to do the things for proto that will make the car great. We're at the racetrack now and the green flag is dropping.

"Let's go drive."

Hill led the caravan out onto the Desert Proving Ground road network in an alpha car. Two more alphas followed, then the now old and familiar CERV-4b. The tail-end Charlies were a Toyota Supra and a 1995 C4 Corvette. Most of the passengers were development engineers, the test drivers who had already put some miles on the alpha cars. Hill, Applegate, and four of Hill's senior engineers were the primary drivers. They planned to make fifteen-minute runs through the proving ground, then pull into the garage area for quick conversation and a car swap. They'd each drive all the cars and note their reactions.

The route they followed put the cars to a rugged test. Many of the road surfaces were exact replicas of real-world roads, scouted and measured by GM surveyors before being painstakingly duplicated in the desert. Long runs of three-lane road had a different surface in each lane, and within lanes, the surfaces changed suddenly, from smooth to blocky, to swales and dips still filled with water from the overnight rain, to spalled concrete with chunks and slivers of cement loose and flying around. One stretch dubbed I-80 was a replica of the interstate highway across Nebraska and Wyoming, where endless parades of heavily loaded eighteen-wheelers had turned the right lane into a bone-jarring fright. Hill took it at 70 mph, sending water spraying from his alpha car.

Slamming over a pothole stretch at 50 mph, Hill slowed to 30 for Val Vista with its bump-a-second surface and major cracks running laterally across the lane. The cracks had been built into the road, then repaired to the standards of a city road crew. The C4 shook and rattled. Radio calls from the three C5s and CERV talked about stability and freedom from vibration. The Toyota radio stayed silent.

Hill accelerated again to 60 mph as he swerved into the left lane called Apache Trail. The C4 wobbled a bit, the C5 didn't. He cut to the Pontiac Trail center lane, then quickly darted right onto the lane labeled Henry Hudson Parkway. The transition was jarring, from Pontiac Trail's relatively smooth surface to the rough asphalt and harsh bumps of Hudson Parkway. Moments later, he pulled up to the garage and stepped out of the alpha car smiling.

"It's not time for euphoria," he said, trying to mask his delight, "but I'm definitely feeling better."

At midafternoon they gathered to discuss the drive. Chevy's Bob Applegate gave his approval. "We're getting there," he said. "The cars are rough, but that's what you expect at this stage. The important thing is that you can feel just how good C5 really is."

John Heinricy nodded. His evaluation of the alpha cars was important to Dave Hill. Heinricy was as close to being deputy chief engineer as the organization charts allowed. He was spending most of his time ramrodding the last years of C4 through a series of upgrades and changes, then getting the cars into production. He had a topflight engineer's critical eye, but more important, he combined engineering with the driving skills of a superior racer. Many weekends found him away from home, at Sebring or Road Atlanta or some other track, running a Corvette against some of the nation's best drivers. Heinricy rolled into the winner's circle his share of the time, and more. In 1990, he was part of a team that set ten international records in a Corvette ZR-1, including an average speed of more than 175 mph over a 5,000-mile course and a twenty-four-hour average speed of 173 mph.

Hill waited while Heinricy chose his words. "I agree with what the others are saying," Heinricy began. "The dynamics were there and the sport-car character was there. I thought it felt pretty good. That doesn't mean it was great yet. I want to get more time in the car, try a few things we didn't do today."

It was what Hill wanted to hear. Heinricy was looking beyond the alpha's imperfection and he liked what he was seeing. With its more powerful engine, stiff rail-and-tunnel structure, and sleek aerodynamic body, C5 was promising to be the best Corvette ever.

"I can't wait to get it out on the road," systems engineer Tadge Juechter added. Driving on the grounds was a good start. But some long days on streets and highways were needed. The question in Juechter's mind was how soon Hill would relax his security restrictions and turn them loose. More Desert Proving Ground rides were planned for February and March. Hill surprised them all with his response.

"We need to take it out in the real world," he said. "We can't do all our work on the proving ground. So maybe next time, or the time after that. Maybe taking the car on roads after dark is something, too. Soon. But not yet."

John Heinricy ended the day at sundown, back in an alpha car, trying some of those things that test drivers don't do when cars are bunched up in a caravan. He took the alpha to a long three-lane straightaway in the center of the proving ground, took command of the middle lane, and pegged the C5's speedometer needle at 55. Then he did his own personal stability test. There was nothing gentle about it.

Heinricy jerked the steering wheel hard left, sending the alpha squealing toward the shoulder. Just as the front wheels left the hard surface, he swerved back to the right. The C5 careened toward the opposite shoulder, its speedometer needle holding 55 as if it were nailed in place. The front wheels touched gravel and he yanked back to the left, across three lanes to the shoulder, then again to the right, the left, the right. At each violent change in direction, the alpha's rear end felt like it might tear loose and send the car into a high-speed spin.

It held.

The body swayed and tilted. The rear end held. Tires tracked through the maneuver on invisible rails, shrieking in complaint. They held. Rough as a cob, noisy, imperfect, and newborn, C5 held in a series of twists that would have spun out almost any other car. Including C4.

Heinricy flowed the car back into the center lane. He let a touch of smile crease the corners of his mouth. At the end of the straightaway, a tight 180-degree curve loomed. A warning sign cautioned drivers to reduce speed to 35.

Heinricy tipped in the accelerator. He put the alpha into the turn at 65, accelerated smoothly through the apex, swooped into the far side, and came back out onto the straight with a stable, in-control C5 hugging the road.

The speedometer said 85.

"Yeah!" Heinricy said. "Yeah!"

5 7 THE meeting between Russ McLean, Dave Hill, and Dennis Sheridan at midafternoon on February 2 didn't take long. Hill proved again that he knew when to break his own rules. McLean concurred.

"We're letting a C5 out into the world," Hill told a few key people. "The HVAC people need to run on real roads, in really cold weather. I've approved a trip next week, on condition that the new camouflage panels are ready and that the guys can install them in the field. The new security rule is that no C5 runs on public roads anywhere near a GM facility."

"Where are they going?"

"A town you probably never heard of. It's cold there. Grand Forks, North Dakota."

Four days later a team of heating–ventilation–air conditioning experts headed by veteran Virgil Finney drove their instrument-laden van and a blue-green 1995 Corvette into Grand Forks, ninety miles from Canada and just across the frozen Red River from Minnesota. It was 3 degrees above zero and the radio weather predicted a cold spell, an Alberta Clipper, later in the week. A closed transport truck met Finney and his engineers on the north side of town, near a secluded warehouse they'd rented and would convert into a garage. The transport held a single C5 alpha car, driven across Canada from GM's cold-weather test site at Kapuskasing, Ontario, over the weekend, then south into North Dakota.

By Tuesday night they had the alpha interior torn down and were devising patches, temporary vents, and flow restrictors that would direct warm air into the passenger compartment.

"It's black magic, trial and error," muttered engineer Jim Fox. "It's easy to make the interior comfortable for a thermocouple [temperature sensor]. It's hard to make it comfortable for a person."

Finney had been out scouting roads. Grand Forks was an ideal location for secret testing of the new Corvette. It sat on the eastern edge of the Great Plains. From southwest through northwest, there wasn't much but flatland, wind, and cold. The trees that were there, mostly in straight-line windbreaks, had been planted by farmers. When the pioneers arrived in the late 1800s, there were no trees at all, except along the river.

A snowbank separated the C5 garage from Interstate 29 sixty yards away. Getting to the garage was not easy. It was hidden in a warren of side streets in a part of town populated by a National Guard storage area, a mustard factory, and a few small industrial companies. Finney found a route away from the garage that avoided any built-up area. The only dangerous part, where they might be seen by a smart amateur with a camera, was a two-mile stretch of Old State Mill Road. But then they'd turn onto a frozen county road and be off into the sparsely populated countryside. It was a reasonable risk, Finney figured.

The new camouflage panels arrived from the Milford Proving Ground Wednesday morning in a plain white pine box. They set to work installing them, gluing, taping, even using pop rivets through the panels and into the alpha's plastic skin. There was already a full padded bra up front, giving the alpha nose a ponderous, stubby character. The new panels included a shield-shaped fiberglass plate to be taped and riveted onto the hood. It was plain and flat, and masked the hood's styling lines and bulges.

Other pieces went over the left and right air scoops and a panel was fastened over the alpha's rear-facing fascia. They cut triangular holes over just one taillight on each side. The distinctive four rounded Corvette taillights were completely masked. More pieces added bulk to the fenders. Finally the engineers ran black masking tape around the rear-deck glass, cutting it from a huge backlight to a narrow transparent trapezoid.

In a matter of hours, the alpha car had gained almost a foot in width and at least that much in overall length. Its rear wheels were sunken deep inside phony fender shapes. It had gone from sleek to fat, an overweight track star with a sprinter hiding inside.

Finney and his men turned to the task of hooking up the air conditioner and heater, replacing the instrument panel cover, and setting flow controls on air vents. Instruments and sensors with wires trailed to black boxes and computers that would record temperatures and air-flow volumes. But it was the human feel that would be the deciding factor.

By afternoon they were ready to take C5 out for its public debut. The test-drive plan had evolved through years of experience. Once on the long and straight Grand Forks County road—it was that part of the world where the roads run north-south and east-west and the roads carve the farmland into precise one-mile sections—they would run thirty minutes at 30 mph, then twenty minutes at 50 mph, then pull over and let it idle for ten minutes. Driver and passenger would record their impressions and their comfort levels. They'd time how long it took for the heater to warm up the cabin and they'd feel for air flow around their heads and necks, at their feet, and across their bodies. They'd try for subjective analysis of how things varied between driver's side and passenger's side. The C5 would have a dual-zone control system, so it should be possible for the two sides to maintain themselves at different temperatures.

All that was left was formal permission from Dave Hill to open the garage door and go.

"We're on hold," Finney announced, returning from his phone check-in. The problem was the software in the engine's main computer. The latest version would run perfectly for a while, then suddenly go to sleep. When it happened, the car stopped dead where it was. The engine-software people had come up with a workaround that could be used in the field to reactivate the computer, but it took thirty-five minutes to implement and still hadn't been proven.

"We don't leave the garage," Finney said, adding, "Hill's concern is that the car would stall out there and be exposed. Stranded. They're running a car all night in the desert to verify the workaround. We should know by seven A.M."

They didn't, so they spent most of the next morning tweaking air flows in the Corvette cabin. In previous tests, confined to driving around inside the Milford Proving Ground or circling a one-mile track at Kapuskasing, there wasn't enough air moving along the passenger's left leg. There was no room in the center pedestal for an air vent, so they cut a tiny opening through the carpet and into the air tube. It brought some air, almost a leak, along the carpet line. Whether it would be enough required getting out on a road and running west into the cold.

It was late morning Thursday when the next word came from Detroit. The software experts still couldn't prove that their workaround worked. An emergency meeting at the GM Technical Center would decide the fate of the North Dakota trip.

"We're all dressed up with no place to go," moaned engineer Guy LaFalce. Then he went back to his motel room to wait for a call. He was back before noon with no news at all. Outside the temperature was dropping, already 2 below as the leading edge of the Alberta Clipper reached Grand Forks. The team trekked to their motel rooms through the first silver bits of snow slanting sideways on a north wind. LaFalce sat by his phone staring.

By 12:20 P.M. the silver snow was thickening. The temperature had dropped to −4 and the windchill was 20 degrees colder. Then LaFalce burst into Finney's room.

"It's a go!" he shouted. "They've gone all the way up the line and gotten approval for us to run. A letter's being drafted right now to make it official, but we don't have to wait. We can run on the road and in daylight, starting right now."

Finney grabbed his coat and charged for the door. "What are we waiting for? Let's go!"

The blue-green '95 Corvette led the way. Then the ugly alpha car rolled out of the garage and into a slowly strengthening winter storm at exactly 1 P.M., Thursday, February 9, 1995. Guy LaFalce drove, with Virgil Finney riding shotgun. The instrument van was third, ready to move forward and shield the C5 if it had to pull off the road. A locally rented van came next, with still another rented chase car at the back door.

The caravan that finally put a C5 on a public street slipped around the edge of Grand Forks. A Pontiac rolled by on Old State Mill Road. Its driver paid no attention to the five vehicles heading north. At County Road 11, they turned left into snow-blown farmland toward Meckinock, North Dakota. The pace was a steady 30 mph and the alpha car threw up a soft rooster tail of dry snow.

C5 was in the world.

All that was left for Finney and his crew was three more days of numbing cold, trying this or that to tweak up the cabin heating to whatever comfort level they felt was best. They'd take their data and their experiments back to Michigan for months of analysis and examination by other engineers who would have to modify their parts or design new ones to be incorporated into the beta cars and the prototypes yet to be built.

And while that was under way, the Finney crowd would be off fiddling with the air-conditioning along the Texas Gulf Coast, at the Desert Proving Ground, in Oregon forests, and on long summer drives through the Midwest, the Rockies, and the salt deserts of western Utah.

They were back in Grand Forks, too, almost exactly a year after the first trip. That time they brought a prototype car with all the latest fixes and they got to town just ahead of the 1996 all-time record cold snap. While they were there, proving that C5 could keep up with whatever nature offered, the morning temperatures ran around 35 below. Two days after they left, the thermometer dropped below −40.

It didn't matter. Thirty-five, 40 below. Only a few things about the winter endgame concerned Virgil Finney. That C5 started on a frigid winter morning was the first one. It wasn't his field, but cold-starts had never been a problem for the Gen III engine anyway. Beyond that, Finney wanted to know that the car delivered warm air to its occupants in a matter of minutes; that if one side or the other wanted it warmer or cooler, the system responded; and that it all worked in real-world driving.

After Grand Forks II, Finney stopped worrying. C5 and winter had become friends.

58 THREE hundred fifty miles north of Toronto there's a sign by the road: "Arctic Watershed. From this point, all streams flow north to the Arctic." It's another two hundred miles north by northwest to reach the place where General Motors runs a cold-weather facility from November through March. In the military, it would be called a winter survival school, and that's what it is for GM cars. No car reaches production without graduating from the Cold Weather Development Centre at Kapuskasing, Ontario. The alpha car came back from Grand Forks on a February day with the temperature hovering around the 10-degree mark. It was too warm to get any outdoor work done.

Kap in winter could be a Hollywood stand-in for a Siberian gulag. The few figures moving after sundown are bundled against the cold. Parkas with hoods, often fur-lined, are the accepted outerwear. General Motors' facility is on the western edge of Kap in a huddle of blue metal buildings, standing out from the mounds of snow, along Highway 11, the Trans-Canada Highway. After GM, there isn't much. The terrain is flat with broad snowfields broken only by lines of trees.

Kapuskasing is a lumber area. Behind the snowfields, heavy forest stretches past the horizon. The most common vehicle on Highway 11 is not a big pickup or sport utility owned by a local, or a GM test car skulking down the road. It is a logging truck loaded with seventy-foot tree trunks heading toward the mill.

They put the alpha car in the nineteen-stall garage, next to the stall where a couple of Powertrain experts were working on another alpha. Like many of those working problems with the Gen III engine package, Mike Polom and Lucius Allen didn't push around carts loaded with wrenches and screwdrivers and they didn't have grease under their fingernails. Polom and Allen were software guys who understood in minute detail how engines worked. Their tools were computers and when three or four engineers surrounded a car and plugged in, the scene wasn't dueling banjos. It was dueling laptops.

The pair, along with a small of team of engineers from GM's Powertrain Division and the Delco Electronics Division, spent weeks on end at Kap in midwinter. They had a C4 mule with the Gen III engine package and an alpha car of their own to occupy their time. At times they shared another alpha car with the HVAC team, but it came and went at odd intervals. Whether or not the heaters worked in their cars was immaterial. When Polom and Allen worked, the engine was cold and so were they. That was the point.

They were trying to pin down the Gen III's cold-start characteristics. No matter what the owner's manual or common sense said, people mistreated engines. They'd start them up, if they started, on cold mornings and drive off without proper warm-up. At 20 below zero on the Fahrenheit scale, engine oil is thicker than syrup. At 40 below, it's almost sludge. Neither syrup nor sludge flows through an engine with the speed it takes to lubricate its parts and let it run smoothly.

Then there's the gasoline. On a warm day, it vaporizes easily, combines with air when it's injected into a cylinder, and ignites under absolute control. On a frigid morning, gasoline doesn't want to turn from liquid to vapor. It might inject into a cylinder as part gaseous, part liquid. The liquid part may be in the form of microscopic drops. But they still don't combine with air and ignite as predictably as a pure-vapor mixture.

Those factors all impact on how quickly an engine starts and how smoothly it runs in the first minute or two before it generates enough heat to reach the next plateau of efficiency. But that's just the beginning of an engine expert's worries. It isn't enough to get the engine running. It has to run cleanly, within all the limits set by federal and state agencies for emissions of nitrous oxide, ozone, carbon monoxide, carbon particulates, sulfurous compounds, and more. And it has to meet the standard whether the engine is cold or hot, running efficiently or just warming up. Excess emissions at cold-start are not allowed.

The computer makes it happen. The driver turns the ignition key to start the engine. The signal does not go directly to the starter motor. It goes to the computer, which makes a quick check of the engine's immediate world. What's the outside temperature? What's the position of the camshaft? Inside each of the eight cylinders, where exactly is the piston sitting—high, low, somewhere in between? Based on that information, which cylinder should be first to get a squirt of fuel and air? It's cold outside, so what's the best mix of fuel and air? How long after that squirt should the ignition system wait before firing the spark plug? Are the emissions controls and devices set properly?

Polling the various sensors, analyzing the data, and making a decision takes no more than a few milliseconds. The driver's fingers are still tight on the ignition key when the computer turns on the starter, sends fuel in the right fuel/air mix to the proper cylinder, fires the first spark plug, and then soaks up an enormous flow of new data as it all comes together and the engine starts.

For the next several minutes, the computer makes constant adjustments. Some drivers immediately put the car in gear and head out. The stresses on a cold engine change all the data and the computer reacts immediately. Other drivers let the car warm up for a minute or two. The computer slowly adjusts the engine to its warmest and smoothest best.

The driver who thinks he or she has much to do with the process doesn't understand modern automobile engines.

Mike Polom and Lucius Allen did understand how it was all supposed to work. What they didn't understand on that chill Monday evening was why it wouldn't. They ran their C5 into the garage. "We've got a new engine and a new electronic throttle control," Polom said, plugging cables from his laptop into the instrument packs filling the C5 cargo area. "We've got new engine software, new transmission software, even new instruments to test it all."

The newness of the Gen III engine, Polom said, was driving them crazy. But it was a good crazy, the kind of crazy that comes with a heavy-duty technical challenge. They wanted to make it work and they wanted it bad. Nothing else explained the schedule they kept in GM's private gulag.

The trouble that day was with the electronic throttle control, which would become a nagging pest in the development process. No other car used the ETC technology, introduced a few years earlier on a diesel-powered GM truck. Problems kept cropping up as they did in any sophisticated engineering program. It was the job of people like Polom to find them and fix them. The electronic throttle control was particularly important. On C5, it was not a piece of optional equipment.

"The driver thinks his foot is the god of speed," Polom said. "But it's just another input device and a crude one at that. The computer gives his foot the value it thinks it deserves. The foot only sets the goal. The computer does all the rest.

"Within the limits set by us electrical engineers, of course."

Isolating that day's problem in the software was keeping Polom and Allen from dinner. The signals being received by the computer from various sensors at full throttle didn't agree. The computer responded by doing what another section of the software code demanded in such cases: It shut the engine off. The conflicting readings from engine sensors might be caused by grease contamination. At least, that was one suggestion. Polom didn't think so. He couldn't duplicate the data on the computer.

"This new instrumentation is full of bugs, too," Allen said. "If it's not the car, maybe it's the instruments." Aerospace engineers had learned that lesson through decades of troubleshooting problems during spaceflights. If an instrument reading shows that something is wrong, make sure that the instrument is working properly. In the heated garage, Polom and Allen replayed the critical signal on a laptop computer. It came and went erratically.

Polom thought about it for a moment, then tugged on his parka and trotted across the parking lot to an old and drafty trailer assigned to the C5 people. Night had come quickly. On the way back, Polom saw through the cloud of his breath that the big decimal thermometer mounted high on the outside garage wall registered −3. It would be cold enough to do some testing in the morning. But barely.

"Let's try this," Polom said, handing Lucius Allen a new cable. Allen felt for a plug, pulled out one cable, and replaced it with the new one. The erratic signal stabilized and at full throttle the engine ran on with a healthy roar. It wasn't an ETC problem, it was a faulty cable in the test instrumentation. "Let's run it a bit to be sure, then put it out for the cold-soak," Polom grunted.

By 10 P.M. they'd had dinner in one of Kapuskasing's restaurant-taverns and were back in their motel. Most of the crowd didn't drink. Those that did had a single beer, at most two. The hours were too long and morning came too soon to risk a fuzzy head.

Their wake-up calls began at 5:30 A.M. By 6:15, there were a half-dozen of them in the lobby ready to pile into the van or the Chevy Lumina they'd been assigned. It was Valentine's Day, 1995, and they were alone together in the gulag. Spouses and lovers down south in Michigan, or in the case of the Delco people, Indiana, would have to make do with the presents left for them and the phone calls that would come late in the day.

The overnight low was 7 below. At 6:15 A.M., the northern sky was an inky black dotted with bright stars. A huge yellow moon hung over the western horizon. The moon seemed bigger and more colorful than the same moon seen in the lower forty-eight. Polom and Allen hardly noticed. They had two cars sitting out overnight, the C4 mule and the alpha.

"I don't know if we can make it for start-of-production," Polom grumbled. "There's too much to do. And these are early iron engines. We can get the calibrations in the ballpark, but we'll be back here next winter to redo them for the aluminum engines.

"If we run into trouble then, we'll be up against the wall."

In the trailer, parkas still on against the indoor chill, they fired up their laptops and looked at yesterday's data. The engines were running rich at cold-start, too much fuel to too little air. Polom scrolled through the computer code to the section he needed, found one line out of thousands, and changed a single number. "That took a tenth out of the leanness parameter," he said. "They won't run so rich."

A few more changes took only minutes. Polom set his cursor to a line of code here and there, tapped in a small numerical change, and saved his actions. In the computer, he had a record of where the software had been, of what had happened, and now of the slightly changed software they were about to try. He and Allen tucked their laptops under their arms, pulled parka hoods up, and walked out to the cars. They didn't wear gloves. It took bare hands to plug and unplug cables, and to use the keyboard.

But they had the moves down pat. In 7-below air, they had the rear-deck lids open, their laptops plugged into the instrument packs, and newly modified software ready to control start-up. Thick cables running from the cars to an instrument van parked one slot over were connected and verified by a technician. All that was left was to turn the key. They did the C4 mule and its iron Gen III engine first.

"Ready?"

"Ready."

In the next one hundred milliseconds, one-tenth of a second, fifteen separate computer chips in the car came to life and sent their data on to the master processor. The result was, to human senses, instantaneous. The engine started with a throaty roar and settled into a midrange hum. It didn't kick, cough, or hesitate. It just started.

So did the alpha car with its iron engine a few moments later. "Really good," Polom said. "Running well, smooth and easy, except for a bit of leanness on acceleration."

If he'd taken too much out of the leanness parameter, it would show in the data and he could add a little back in with a simple software nudge. He disconnected from the instrument van, settled into the icy leather driver's seat, and drove off to the little one-mile track in the northwest corner of the facility. He did a lap, running quickly, then slowly, then gliding to a stop before starting up again. The stresses and strains on the cold but warming engine would show in the data. Polom wasn't happy with the acceleration. The software needed more work to smooth it out and get rid of the tiny hesitation he'd felt.

First though, he put the car back into the lot for another five or six hours of cold-soak. Then after a discussion of his impressions and a quick look at the data, the C5 team went back to town for breakfast. Winter life for GM people at Kapuskasing fell into that kind of a routine: predawn cold-starts and a lap around the track, sample the data, then breakfast at 9:30 A.M. They'd work the rest of the day, in the chilly trailer or outside on the car, bringing in fast-food sandwiches between 3 and 4 P.M. They'd keep working until hours after dark, get a late supper, then be off to the motel, and up again the next morning. It was a seven-day-a-week life for two to three weeks at a time. Each day brought new problems to be solved, new software bugs to be found and killed.

The found the accelerator bug in a few hours. "When you accelerate a cold engine, it wants a bunch of little squirts of fuel on the intake," Polom said. "They vaporize faster than one big squirt and the engine runs smoother. But the software was delivering that big squirt."

The question was why. The answer, buried deep in lines of code, was that a tiny piece of the software was turned off. A one-bit change, changing a zero to a one, turned it back on. Polom loaded the software into his again frigid alpha car and raced off to the track. He was back in fifteen minutes, grinning widely. "What a difference," he announced. "Now we're getting somewhere."

The other question, the one on the minds of Russ McLean, Dave Hill, and the rest of the Corvette team, was whether the Powertrain people would get somewhere fast enough.

The Corvette team would still be asking questions about the engine up to early March 1996, when C5 would face a critical go–no go decision.

59 THE other cold-weather test site was in Michigan's Upper Peninsula, in an area called the Soo, for the twin border towns of Sault Sainte Marie, Michigan and Ontario. It was at Kinchloe Air Force Base, once home to a cold war squadron of Strategic Air Command B-52s. The base was closed in the late seventies. A few years later, General Motors came in. So did a few manufacturing companies, a maximum-security state prison, and a county jail unit.

The nearest town was Kinross and that's what GM people called their test site. "Going to Kinross" didn't have the same barren connotation as "going to Kap," but it didn't rank among anybody's top ten.

Mike Rizzo, a development engineer who usually worked at Milford Proving Ground on Dave Wickman's staff of test drivers, was in Kinross at the same time that Virgil Finney was in Grand Forks and Mike Polom was in Kapuskasing. It was that kind of winter for everyone.

Rizzo's job was getting the software right for the antilock brake system (ABS) and the traction control system that helped prevent skids on slick road surfaces. He and a team of a half-dozen engineers and software specialists from Corvette and from Delco had only a short time to get the first calibrations on the systems completed. The winter had been warmer than usual in the U.P. and the number of test days they'd accumulated was far below the plan.

Cold weather and Kinchloe's tarmac, taxiways, and runways made the perfect combination for testing brakes and other aspects of a car's handling and maneuvering abilities. The key to it all was ice.

A run-up area that once shook with the roar of multiple B-52s ready for takeoff had been painted with white epoxy strips, then coated with ice anywhere from a quarter to three-eighths inch thick. Water trucks and workers with hand wands refreshed the ice coat several times a day.

Other areas of taxiway or runway were painted with epoxy checkerboards, semicircular curves the width of two road lanes, other curves that matched freeway on-ramps, and a variety of shapes that represented road conditions winter drivers might encounter. Another stretch was allowed to build up with snow early in the season, then was bulldozed, carved, and tamped to create a long rectangular snowfield. It wasn't ice, but it was what northern drivers often found themselves on after a heavy snowfall or when the plows missed their neighborhood streets.

General Motors used the abandoned Kinchloe control tower for another purpose. Construction crews built a perfectly circular track, nine-tenths of a mile in circumference, around it. The track was watered until it became an ice-circle, thick, solid, and slick enough to skate on.

On any given cold day in January or February, a steady stream of future GM cars rolled in and out of the test areas. Now and then a convict walking the fence inside his prison unit would catch a glimpse of a car that a spy photographer like Jim Dunne would pay dearly to see. The joke among GM engineers was that the cars would be old before the convict got out and tried to steal one.

Mike Rizzo was waiting for Dave Hill and some of his people to drive up from Detroit. He remembered Hill's Cadillac days and likened them to the work he was doing to get the brake and traction systems tuned just right for the new Corvette. "With Cadillac, it's stability-stability-stability," he quipped. "With Corvette, it's stability-*fun*-stability. Hill knows both sides of that coin."

The goal for C5 was to write software and to tune the car's suspension so that a driver could take it out on a slippery road and drive safely. "Corvette drivers want to know that they can have their fun without losing that last little bit of stability that keeps them out of trouble," Rizzo said.

They had two alpha cars and two 1996 C4 prototypes with the latest antilock brake and traction control systems. The alpha build was nearly done at the Bumper-to-Bumper Shop back at the GM Technical Center and as the winter of 1995 neared its end, there were almost enough cars to go around. But the software wasn't there yet.

When the Detroit group arrived, they loaded up and headed out to the ice. Dave Hill was in an alpha car. He hit the hi-lo ice strip and braked to a stop. On a hi-lo strip, one set of tires was on dry concrete, the other on ice. Concrete friction was high; ice was low. For the first hi-lo run, Hill stopped with the front tires on concrete, the rear on ice. Then he tipped in the foot pedal and accelerated rapidly. The purpose was to see what happened when the computer got a mixed message—front wheels grabbing and the rear wheels trying to spin on ice. Without traction control, a car could spin out as the rear end swung right from the spinning torque. Hill's alpha car lurched, almost broke loose, then caught and ran straight. It shouldn't have lurched.

He tried again, doing a side-by-side hi-lo. The left side of the car was on concrete and the right side was on ice. It was a different mixed message to the computer. The alpha car wiggled and wobbled, but only a little. It held and went straight. Hill wasn't happy with the wiggle and wobble. There was more movement than he expected or wanted.

Drivers switched between cars and repeated runs on the ice strips, through the snowfield, and around the control tower ice track. On the checkerboard, they ran from ice to concrete to ice, wheels catching, slipping, catching, as the computer tried to compensate by alternately braking or letting wheels run free. After a series of runs, traction control began to fail in the alpha being driven by Chevy's Bob Applegate and shotgun-seated by chassis engineer Jim Lloyd. It fishtailed wildly on the hi-lo strip when Applegate tried an ABS-to-traction transition, hitting the brakes at full throttle with half the tires on ice, half on concrete.

"It's a software problem," Rizzo answered to Lloyd's radio call. "We know about it and we're working it."

After nearly three hours in the cars, they trekked back to a barren conference room—a remnant of Kinchloe's heyday—to talk about it.

"If there's any car in the world that ought to be able to pull out of a snowy driveway onto a slick street and go away like a bat out of hell, it's a Corvette," Hill said. His voice was stern. "But we're not seeing that yet on these cars. So what are we missing here?"

The complaints and responses were quick to come:

"Wide-open throttle yields a slip on ice or gravel."

"Brake dive is too noticeable."

"The sensors know when the rear wheels are on a slippery surface and when they aren't. The question is, how long should the delay be before something kicks in? Twenty milliseconds? Seven hundred milliseconds? That has to be settled."

"Whatever is in there now is too long. The car isn't responding fast enough when the driver asks for power."

"Are we writing software for the guy who's comfortable being the human driver or the guy who wants the computer to have more control?"

Hill settled that one immediately. "We should trust the driver. When the throttle is wide open, the chances are that he's not looking at another ice patch, he's looking in his mirror at the truck that's bearing down on him. That's the point where we ought to give him what he's asking for."

That provoked more conversation and a conclusion that had become obvious as winter waned.

"We're not going to get everything perfect this winter," Hill said.

"That means Alaska," Mike Rizzo answered quietly. He and a few of the team had already made preliminary plans to spend the end of October and half of November in Nama, near Fairbanks, where early winter always brought the kind of cold they needed to make outdoor ice.

"What about an ice rink?"

"There are a couple around Detroit where we can do some work this summer. And we will. But you know the size of those things. We can calibrate for low-speed stuff and launch traction. But we need wide-open spaces for the whole package."

Hill sighed. "I'm reticent about Alaska because of the costs," he said. "But I suppose we'll be stuck with it."

60 FIVE days later they were back in the desert. C5 development was going to warp speed. When they looked at the calendar in mid-March, they saw the year 1995 almost a quarter over and they saw March 1996, with its intractable deadline, only an eye-blink away. That was the month when engineering changes would stop and the production pieces of the all-new 1997 Corvette had to be settled once and for all. If they weren't, the assembly line couldn't start up on schedule.

The way to make sure it happened was to drive cars, find the flaws, fix them, and drive some more. This time they were going off the grounds, finally taking a caravan of secret Corvettes across the desert floor and into the Superstition Mountains east of Phoenix.

"The good news is that the route is isolated," announced trip captain Jim Ingle. "The bad news is there are no bathrooms except at Jake's Corner." Whatever Jingles said about any route, they automatically believed. He was a fabled test driver who collected roads and scenery the way kids collect stamps. He knew where to go in any state to put cars to the perfect test, and when he planned a trip, it ran almost exactly on schedule.

He was the kind of driver who got the most from his vehicle. When they needed someone to take a Corvette from zero to one hundred and back to zero in the shortest possible time, it was Jingles at the wheel. But it was a stunt, not a legitimate test. He did it in a Corvette ZR-1 in just over fifteen seconds for an audience of reporters in France. "It's an unnatural act and it really takes screwing your head on right," he said. "You make a panic stop in the middle of a drag race."

But it was a demonstration that gave people a good feeling about Corvette's ability to go to the outer limit of stress with a highly skilled driver and come back safely. It was not something to try at home, unless Jim Ingle was driving.

Before C5 development ran its course, some of the test drivers wanted to see Jingles take it one step further—zero to one hundred to zero and back to one hundred. "Too unnatural," Jingles said. "I'll pass."

Jingles led the way in a Chevrolet Caprice station wagon on the desert trip. He and three other development drivers had spirited four black alpha cars out of the Desert Proving Ground in the predawn darkness, leaving them under car covers at an irrigation district office near a desert intersection. A Pinkerton guard stayed with the cars to make sure that nobody with a camera tried anything funny. One of the alphas was the first of the new C5 convertibles. Only a few people had yet seen it.

Just after 7 A.M. the crew gathered for their driver's briefing. Russ McLean had made the trip, his first time ever to get into an alpha. They had three comparison cars for the ride, a white Nisssan 300ZX, a red Toyota Supra, and a white 1996 C4. At Dave Hill's direction, there would be only seven drivers that day, himself and McLean, John Heinricy, Bob Applegate, and three development engineers. The drivers would swap cars along the 373-mile route laid out by Jingles. Passengers would stay put and record comments. Jingles would lead in the station wagon and a maintenance van carrying parts, tools, extra gas, and box lunches would guard the back door.

"I've been waiting with a lot of anticipation for this day," Hill said. "It's like fine wine that's finally ready. You're making history today. When the articles are written, this is where the game is won. It's this kind of drive that makes the difference, that pulls the coals out of the fire. We have to make sure that this car is the greatest when it's shown to the world for the first time."

He turned to Jingles. "Anything I shouldn't do, Jim?"

"Yeah, don't corner real hard and don't run into anything."

The early part of the drive ran through flat agricultural desert land, miles of crops in every direction, a monument to man's ability to bring water to a parched land and make it flower. The alpha cars ran eastbound on empty roads, playing S-turns across the center line like a warm-up lap at an Indy-car race while the drivers got the feel for their vehicles.

The ag land quickly fell behind as Jingles led the way into scrub desert, with a few stately saguaro cactus peering toward the road. The radio chatter that would build as the drivers passed comments back and forth started when the parade passed a javelina dead by the road. "A little roadkill for lunch, guys?"

Climbing toward the mountains, the saguaro became battalions of cactus marching up the hills and across the desert in picket formation. The green hills were a welcome sight after the snowfields of Kinross and the grayness of Detroit. "Never see 'em any greener," Jingles radioed. "You caught Arizona in the springtime. There are a lot of little wildflowers all over."

The car critiques interrupted his travelogue:

". . . torque converter locking up the long upgrade."

". . . exhaust boom's not a pleasant noise."

". . . arm-rest comfort could be better. Great thing about these trips is that you get enough time in the car to start feeling things like that. It's not like a quick turn around the track."

Dave Wickman's car, one of two with an automatic transmission, faltered at a stoplight in the mining town of Miami. "It just fell down when we pulled away from the light. Then it picked up, fell down again, and now it's all right."

One of Wickman's engineers took that one. "That car has an intermittent fuel glitch. It happens when the tank is just down from full." It was a fuel system problem that would recur often in the coming year and would require reworking the connecting lines between the dual gas tanks straddling the transaxle.

They were on the third driver change, high in the mountains, when Jingles got on the radio. "Guy with a camera up here. I don't know what he's doing."

It was too late to do anything but roll on by.

"Look at that," marveled Scott Leon in the back-door van. "He has four secret Corvettes go by, including a convertible, and he's taking pictures of the scenery."

Russ McLean got on the radio as they approached a deserted campground for lunch. "You're breaking a helluva lot of new ground and I'm really pleased with these alphas. I want you guys to jot down your own report card on what we have and what we're comparing it to. That will give us something to deliver to the writers when we launch the car. They'll know what we were aiming for and can evaluate us on the basis of what we think we achieved, as well as what they see for themselves."

Dave Hill offered a quick point. "The Lexus squeak and rattle was our aiming point, but with this sports car, and with a removable roof, it's beyond our wildest hopes."

"It takes wild people to have wild hopes," McLean said.

A few minutes later Hill was more critical. His car's automatic transmission was shifting in and out of fourth gear on a steep upslope toward seven thousand feet. "This car ought to take this grade in fourth gear, but it isn't. I can't maintain seventy-five. We should plan on working with the transmission people to benchmark this hill."

The day wore on with a list of problems growing, but none of them generating major concern. It was what they were out there to find and for every gripe, somebody responded with a solution or the name of an engineer who could make it right.

Making their way back through the town of Miami in late afternoon, a slow train blocked traffic. The fantasy cars were caught stopped on a busy street, fair game for anyone with a camera.

"Do you see all those people getting out of their cars to look at us?" development engineer Chris Fulton joked on the radio.

"Totally oblivious," Jeff Yanssens answered. "It's like we aren't even here."

"Everybody learned a tremendous amount today," Dave Hill said to begin the debriefing back at the proving ground. "The inherent goodness is in the car. The ability to outshine the competition is there. We have the makings of a good package to go into the betas and I think the betas will be surprisingly good.

"I want to encourage you development engineers to be frequent visitors to the beta build site, to make observations, and to help guide the process. We have to be part of beta evolution and not just wait for the cars to show up at Milford."

Russ McLean wrapped up the day with one of his patented pep talks.

"That was my first alpha ride and I'm impressed. In fact, the whole concept of alphas is something fairly new to the company and it's proving itself. But the other truth is, we are blessed by having Dave Hill here." Hill blushed and put on one of his patented thousand-yard stares. He wanted to hear about alphas, not himself. But McLean didn't let up.

"Because of him my management style has changed. It's hard for me and sometimes I have to be pulled back, but we can only have one person giving direction about the car. That has to be Dave.

"Remember this. In December we were six months late—four months late from the build and two months from the knuckles. But a helluva lot has happened in the last four months and you guys ought to be proud.

"We're making technical history on this car."

He talked about the hours they were putting in, many of them away from home and family. "You're a special breed of cat and you've got that feeling in your gut."

Then, whether it was an off-the-cuff remark or an unexplained sense of things to come, McLean's voice dropped a notch in timbre and he looked again at Hill. "Dave will be taking more leadership in the future," he said. "We're at game time for the next six months and there's only one quarterback deciding what we're going to do."

He was quiet for a moment and the only noise in the room was the faint rumble of a car on the proving ground track. "I wish my career had made me a development engineer, but it didn't," he said. "I'm just lucky to be working with development engineers like you.

"Let's give 'er hell!"

61 THE last Friday in March 1995 was good to Corvette and the rest of the Midsize platforms, too.

At 4 P.M. on that afternoon, engineering director Mike Juras, wearing one of his usual pullover sweaters, was in the Concept Approval meeting for the C5 convertible. He fingered the car's top, talked about design, made it unanimous that the car could continue ahead as planned.

An hour later, Midsize Car Division vice president and general manager Don Hackworth called him to his office. He handed Juras an early retirement package with the suggestion that he consider it seriously. Juras did.

Sunday afternoon Juras left a voice mail for his staff, most of them the commodity group chiefs who had tried to carry off the Juras Vision with so little success. The Juras Message had a bitter tinge.

"I'll be taking unplanned retirement. . . . I won't be in on Monday. I expect our folks to just carry on."

He passed on some administrative assignments to cover the coming days and concluded: "Just wanted to let everyone know, and I'll be kind of continuing on."

The message lasted less than forty-five seconds.

Monday morning in one meeting, a midlevel engineer stood up and removed his pullover sweater. "No more of these," he said, and sat down again.

There were sighs of relief throughout the division, followed by the serious questions and concerns about what would come next.

Good things came. April 10 was the date on the books for Bumper-to-Bumper to start building its first C5 beta car. It did.

Russ McLean was delighted. He had worked around the convoluted Midsize Car Division's engineering system, and the now debunked Juras Vision, to make it happen. He used his authority as Corvette platform manager to call on suppliers personally and let them know that the parts they were manufacturing were important. Most suppliers had never met a platform manager. For the *Corvette* platform manager to show up and give a pep talk was something special.

He lobbied in Bumper-to-Bumper, from the managers to the union work-

ers who did the assembly job, to get priorities for Corvette and to let them
know that he wasn't just a tough taskmaster, he was a tough taskmaster
who cared. He sent down cakes and Cokes and he had photos taken at key
events with the workers gathered around to show off what they'd done.
"You'll get prints when the car isn't a secret anymore," he told them, and
because the idea of working on a secret had value of its own, they were
willing to wait.

"Platforms that don't plan ahead," he said, "gotta make sure they don't
get in our way."

McLean planned ahead. He spent money when he had to, getting parts
delivered earlier than anyone said they could be ready, or agreeing to an
increase here or there on investment costs to push production tooling work
into high gear. He'd figured all along that those kinds of things would be
needed and he'd maintained a budget reserve of almost $30 million that let
him do it.

"You can go over a mountain or around it," he said. "Going around
might add a little in investment and piece cost, but it gets you there. We've
had the luxury of so many platforms being in trouble around here that
nobody paid a lot of attention to us when we did it our way."

One cost that McLean accepted was changing the C5 cockpit floor from
a polyurethane foam sandwiched between plastic composite skins to a
balsa wood core. It was the same balsa that kids use to make model airplanes or those ten-cent gliders. It seemed too fragile for any serious application.

But the foam-core floor wasn't doing the job. It vibrated and jiggled over
rough roads. Noise intruded through it. it didn't like heat and the operating
temperatures of a C5 racing over a hot summer road could exceed its
capacity to endure.

McLean sat in on the engineering decision meeting to hear about balsa's
attributes.

"It sounds like we're talking about a dance floor," McLean said.

"Floors that don't dance," Dave Hill corrected.

But a wood floor in a Corvette? He wanted facts before he signed a
check. What he heard convinced him. Balsa has a natural honeycomb
structure, with hexagonal cells about one-thousandth of an inch across. It
was strong so long as it wasn't bent sharply. It was stiff, it was lightweight
(that brought a smile to Hill's face), and it absorbed sound.

They'd put a balsa-sandwich floor in an alpha car and tested it against
the foam-sandwich floor. It beat the foam in every way, including increasing
the stiffness of the whole car, not just the cockpit. "That floor is a key
element in getting above twenty hertz for the car's stiffness," reported
structures engineer Doug Ego. "We want it."

"Well," McLean mused, "you gotta be creative. Remember the history of Corvette, that famous airplane trip back in 1953 when they went to a supplier and Ed Cole [then chief engineer of Chevrolet, later Chevy general manager, and still later president of General Motors] cleared off a Ping-Pong table and in one night they laid out the whole skin for the first Corvette?"

There were chuckles around the conference table. McLean might have been a plant guy at one time, but he'd been bitten by the Corvette bug and he knew its history. He looked at the money numbers and didn't raise an eyebrow. The balsa floor was more expensive. Balsa had to be imported from a farm in Peru, virtually the only reliable source for the wood in the world. It had to be cut and trimmed on special machines, and for Corvette's purposes, each floor piece would get beveled edges for perimeter protection. Finally it would be sealed between thin sheets of composite plastic. The piece cost broke down to $5.50 more for each car, plus another chunk for tooling investment and the amount they'd have to write off on the earlier floor. It was a total hit that would trim millions from Corvette's long-term profit line.

"Is it the right thing for the car?" McLean asked.

"Yes."

"Then we'll be creative. Do it."

The shake-up in Midsize engineering was looking good, but with their long experience at being left at the altar, Corvette engineers stayed skeptical. "It could be just the first domino," one said, and his cynicism was echoed by the rest.

It was no domino. It was instead the first building block in a better way of doing things at Midsize. And it was a precursor of corporate changes that would shake up Russ McLean and Dave Hill as well.

6 2 THE new engineering director was Frank Colvin. He'd held the same position under Don Hackworth at the Cadillac Luxury Car Division. With CLCD and the Midsize Car Division moving toward a merger, it was logical.

Colvin came in with a reputation as a clear thinker. Hill knew him slightly but came back from his first meeting in their current roles with a sunny disposition. "We'll be enabled to get our job done and there will be places I can go for help when I need it," he announced.

That was all anyone needed to hear. Hackworth's policy had been to leave Corvette on its own. If McLean and Hill cut a few corners to get their jobs done, he looked the other way and focused on programs that were in trouble. Now Colvin would be an active helper for the program. A new vision was taking shape and it would affect not just Corvette and the car programs around it. It would be a new way of doing things for all of General Motors.

"We're going toward something called the vehicle line executive," Hill told his staff. "There will be more platform focus, more authority to perform, more power to the guy who is the VLE."

The power would flow from organizations that had traditionally held it close. Design Staff would give up autonomous control over its studios. A studio chief would report directly to a VLE, while getting support and guidance from Design leaders like Wayne Cherry and Jerry Palmer.

The car and truck divisions—Chevrolet, Pontiac, Buick, Oldsmobile, Cadillac, and GMC—would lose all authority over designing and building cars. They would become pure marketing organizations. It was the direction that had been set for them under Roger Smith in the late 1980s and reinforced by Bob Stempel and Jack Smith in the traumatic early nineties. Now the final step would be taken. Powerful executives like Chevy's Jim Perkins, who had had so much to do with clearing the way for the new Corvette, would have no authority at all over future cars.

They would, however, have influence. In addition to establishing the new position of vehicle line executive to actually engineer and develop new cars, GM would create "brand managers"—one for each car line—

who would be influential interfaces between the engineering side and the sales side. Brand managers would be charged with developing, protecting, and improving the "character" of their car lines.

The vehicle line executives would be chosen from inside GM. But to get some diversity, the company would go outside for a number of brand managers. When all were eventually on board in 1996, they were peppered with people experienced in selling cereals and snack foods, hosiery and other nonautomotive goods, and included a husband-wife combination from the skin-care and pharmaceutical industry. The "brandscape" eventually laid out by GM for Chevrolet positioned the badge as a series of low-priced cars for people who worried about their bills. There was no mention of Corvette in the "brandscape" at all. Along with Camaro, it was left to carve out a market on its own. That was fine with the Corvette and Camaro people and with their brand manager, Dick Almond, who was a Chevy guy through and through. But the many changes at GM didn't sit well with everybody. Jim Perkins would look at the future and take early retirement.

All that was in the distant future when Dave Hill briefed his staff in April 1995. Their questions were to the point: Who will be our VLE? What will happen to Russ McLean? To Dave Hill? To C5? To us?

Hill gave the only answer he could. "I don't know about Russ and me. But C5 will carry on and so will you. The next six months will irreversibly determine the outcome of C5 development. After that, the first two thousand cars we build will establish C5 for the rest of the decade. So we're going to look to the next six months.

"Then we'll see where we are."

Time refused to slow down. By mid-June, the first beta car was nearly done in Bumper-to-Bumper. It hadn't been as easy as they'd hoped and when the body was finally married to the chassis and drivetrain on June 20, the build was three weeks behind schedule and getting worse. Manufacturing engineer Pete Liccardello brought the news to a meeting a few days later.

"We married 'beta one' on Saturday and expect to fire up the engine by this Friday," he said. "It was a true marriage, with many interferences and obstructions to be worked out."

"We're doing some serious counseling," added Ann Baker, one of the managers overseeing the build for Corvette. "We'll have two jobs ready to be shipped to Phoenix by June thirtieth."

"The original schedule was six jobs by June thirtieth and twelve by July fourteenth," Hill pointed out. "So even though we feel good about the quality, we've got some catching up to do."

One by one, Hill talked to his key engineers to let them know that he was counting on them to pull off another minor miracle. John Heinricy would help. He'd finished his work getting the last C4, the 1996 Corvette, into production. The C4 was all but history. Heinricy would focus full-time on C5.

Hill also passed the word quietly that C4 might be resurrected in a real crunch. Nearly three years earlier, the crash engineers had decided that C4 could not be modified to meet the new 1997 side-impact standards. In the spring of 1995, Hill sent them back to look again. This time they were told to take into account advances in materials over the last three years and to factor in some of the lessons they'd learned in designing and doing early crash tests on C5 structures. They came back with the news that C4 was not a lost cause. Its door structure and birdcage frame could be modified to pass the new standards. Hill and Russ McLean put the information in their hip pockets as a hedge against the worries they harbored about the new Gen III engine. If it couldn't be perfected in time for C5, then C5 might be delayed by another six months or even a year. And if that happened, they'd keep right on building C4s.

It wasn't a plan they had any taste for following. But at the moment, both Russ McLean and Dave Hill were getting slightly distracted. The powers inside General Motors had narrowed down their candidates for the thirteen vehicle line executive positions that they would fill in early autumn. There were just forty names on the list. McLean and Hill were among them.

They needed a break from it all. They got it with the late-June gathering of Corvette fanatics in Springfield, Illinois. More than fifty thousand people, and almost six thousand Corvettes, showed up for the long weekend of the event called Bloomington Gold. Cars were judged and awards were given. Cars were sold at auction and in private deals on the infield at the state fairgrounds racetrack. Hill and McLean and their wives walked through the exhibits, talked to Corvette owners, listened to their glowing descriptions of their favorite Corvettes. They fended off questions about C5 without offending. "It's going to be the best yet," they said. "You'll like it."

On Sunday afternoon, Dave and Karen Hill got into a white 1996 Corvette and drove into the countryside with thirteen hundred other Corvettes for the traditional road tour. The Hills were in the fifth car in line. Leading the endless convoy of Corvettes off the fairgrounds was race driver Jeff Nowicki, in his thundering modified Corvette race car. Nowicki's father, Ron, the chief engineer in John Cafaro's old Corvette studio, was there, too.

The Hills waved as Jeff Nowicki pulled off and parked his racer. In the white Corvette, Dave Hill spotted a nine-year-old girl holding up a hand-lettered sign by the roadside: "Vettes Are #1."

He threw her a wave and turned to Karen. His grin gave her the biggest thrill of the day.

"It's all right," he said.

63

D AVE Wickman drove his first beta car in mid-July. He took it over 100 mph at the Milford Proving Ground, then settled back to cruise the roads at around 60. When he pulled into the garage, he grabbed a phone and left a voice mail for Dave Hill.

"It needs work, but it felt really good," he reported. "It was refreshing to hop into a C5 and not have the wind noise and the rattles."

The next day a C5 chassis control arm broke in laboratory testing at the Tech Center. When a second one broke the following morning, Hill knew they had another design problem. Computer analysis verified his conclusion a few hours later. He ordered the beta cars in the desert and at Milford into limited-use mode.

"That means not running betas on durability tests and restricting all betas to mild use," he said. Until a solution was found, they wouldn't be much more than parking lot cars.

The next reports were more discouraging. An engineer named Joe Ryan was putting together a temporary fix with steel splints that could be attached to the control arms already manufactured. That included arms on existing beta cars and on at least a half-dozen betas being assembled already at Bumper-to-Bumper. But a permanent design fix might take eight weeks.

"We're in our last summer," Hill ordered. "I want a solution in one week, not eight. And I want to look at the temporary fix tomorrow morning."

A durability beta car was just completing its first shift at Milford, Hill was told. Maybe it could keep running if it was inspected every four hours.

"No," Hill said, "and here's why. The likelihood of hurting an employee or damaging the car is low, but if it runs off the road, you get the GM proving ground cops taking us through their rigmarole. That can take weeks. Keeping the proving ground cops out of our hair is enough incentive to stop driving. Check the car at the end of its shift and then park it."

Before he could get too depressed at the day's events, Hill got some good news. After months of engineering changes that had driven C5's coefficient of drag back up to nearly 0.31—a change that would slow the car down and increase fuel consumption—Kurt Romberg had finished his last runs in the Tech Center's wind tunnel and come up with a c/D of 0.293, which rounded to 0.29, Hill's target.

Only four production cars in the world were then known to be so aerodynamic: the Audi Quattro, the Lexus LS400, and two Opel Calibras.

"How'd you do it?" Hill asked.

"The underside of the car," Romberg explained. "It really looks good now." In fact, the C5 underside was almost completely smooth and Hill thought it might rank as the best-looking underside of any car in the world.

Hill looked puzzled. The underside hadn't changed that much in months.

"But the earlier clay cars we had available had C4 undersides," Romberg explained. "They're really dirty. We had everything right for the last runs."

"You were using a ringer?" Hill laughed.

"I didn't want to tell you," Romberg said sheepishly, "because I knew it was going to get dramatically better when we had the right underbody." It was the kind of surprise Dave Hill appreciated from his engineers.

"Nice job," Hill said. "It means a lot to the fuel economy. And if we get to one hundred eighty-five miles per hour, we'll remember your name."

The next morning Hill was in the machine shop at Milford Proving Ground looking at a splint for the broken control arm. Joe Ryan had formed a piece of steel by heating it and beating it until it folded over the arm. With a second piece running across the bottom of the arm, it could be epoxied and bolted into place.

"Fast work," Hill said appreciatively. "Get a proof piece to the lab in Warren by the end of the day and have three sets ready by the weekend for air express to the desert."

"Can do," Ryan said.

"After that, plan on doing four sets a week until the beta build doesn't need any more," Hill said. The permanent fix was under way, too. A strengthened design for the arms would be done in a matter of days and new parts would be ordered. Weak spots were eliminated and the new arms would handle stresses beyond any that C5 could inflict. It would be mid-September before they could be delivered, but with the splinted arms on all beta cars, testing could continue on schedule.

Hill breathed a sigh of relief and walked out into misting rain to take a beta car out for himself. He had another decision to make quickly. Near the entrance to the Milford Proving Ground, two large tents had been set up for an event called Chevy Sporty Car Immersion Day. Key Chevrolet executives, along with a group of dealers, would spend the day hearing about Chevrolet's future in the sporty car marketplace and they'd be driving Camaros and Corvettes, along with competing cars from Nissan, Toyota, and Mazda.

Dave Hill was on the agenda. So was a beta car. But if Hill had ordered the cars parked temporarily, how could he justify letting all those people take a spin in a C5 with questionable control arms? He thought about it as he put the car through curve after curve on proving ground roads. When he passed the four-hundred-acre asphalt pad they called Black Lake, he had his answer.

"It was really nice to drive to this meeting in my favorite car," he told them when his turn came. The white beta car already was the hit of the morning. When Hill parked it near the entrance to the largest of the tents, it was surrounded by people who ignored the light rain to get a close-up look. Now he decided to wow them even more.

"We've created, adopted, or expanded low-investment manufacturing technologies.

". . . cut the number of parts by more than 1,400.

". . . simplified body structure with hydroformed rails and a structural tunnel.

". . . sedanlike rocker stepover. No more entry and egress contortions.

". . . open-car torsional frequency better than the best in the world. . . .

". . . a targa roof that detaches with three quick latches. No more tool to get it off."

". . . enhanced the spaciousness and cargo to best in class.

". . . improved the aerodynamics to best in class.

". . . design enables three distinct body styles, a '97 targa roof hatchback, then a convertible with a trunk, a coupe with a trunk."

That brought a roar from the dealers in the tent.

Hill grinned and plunged on. "A unique chassis, suspension, and powertrain shared with no other car; the biggest hydroform piece in the world, a one-piece seamless side rail; a central tunnel that becomes a real structural piece; a cockpit with all electrical already installed when you drop it in; a one-piece tub in back for leak-free, rattle-free driving; a unique balsa-sandwich floor pan . . ."

He told them the beta car outside wasn't perfect, not yet, but it would be ready for production in little more than a year. "Driving the beta car is a marvelous experience," he said, teasing them a bit because they'd already heard that the cars were grounded and they wouldn't get a chance to drive one themselves. "We've got a long punch list, but the car meets my expectations—and they were high."

Barely twenty hours earlier, he'd ordered the beta cars parked. Since then they'd solved the immediate problem of the broken control arms and had a long-term solution in the works. But the car outside had the original arms and it was suspect. As usual, Hill knew when to break his own rules. Even if a control arm broke, the slight swerve it might cause was no problem at all on Black Lake. There was nothing to hit and plenty of room in every direction to slow to a stop. His eyes twinkled and he gave the small crowd what they really came for.

"If anybody wants to give it a spin, I'll be waiting out on Black Lake. You can take it once around. But, please, hold the speed under sixty."

Under sixty? They would have held it under ten just to say they'd done it. Hill himself rode shotgun for the next several hours, sitting there like a proud new father while Chevy's top brass and dealers got their first minutes driving a fifth-generation Corvette. It was something they'd all remember— their first C5 and the chief engineer as their passenger.

"I had too much pride to hold the car out," Hill said later. "I had to let them drive it, not just look at it." And he added the phrase that had guided so much of what C5 had become. "It was the right thing to do."

6 4 DEATH Valley spread left, right, and straight ahead, a golden sub-sea-level blotch of pale sand and white alkali. The sweat on Dave Hill's forehead dried almost as fast as it appeared. He tugged on the bill of his red baseball cap with the GM Delphi logo and glanced at the thermometer in the parking lot of the tourist café at the Furnace Creek campground.

It read 112 degrees.

Hill's yellow pullover had a Corvette logo embroidered on the left breast. Along with his khaki pants, it was rumpled from the day's drive and he looked more like a desert archaeologist than a Detroit engineer. Ed Koerner from Powertrain was next to him on the parking lot, only a little more comfortable in a white shirt and blue shorts. The two men most important to the future of the C5 found a patch of shade under an acacia tree. It was the end of August and time was getting short for Powertrain to get its act, and its Gen III engine, together.

"There's still a flare-up to two thousand rpm at start-up on the car," Hill said. "I want it fixed so that it is at least as good as C4, maybe sixteen hundred rpm. Unless there's a good reason, like you need the revs to get added power."

Koerner shook his head. "No, it's a software thing. We can fix it."

They had eight cars on the Death Valley trip and none of them were C5s. Hill knew the risks of taking cars to Death Valley in the summer, where spy photographers were likely to be hiding around any turn. So they had two Cormaros, those funny rebuilt Camaros with Corvette structures underneath and Gen III engines. They had three more Corvette C4 mules with Gen III engines and three regular Camaros packing the Gen III.

The ride was going only modestly well. Idle control was improving and would get better. The "resume" feature on cruise was still too aggressive. It caught drivers by surprise when it kicked in. There were more issues to be discussed when they drove up from Death Valley to the Nevada hotel where they'd rented a conference room for the evening debriefing.

But first they had to dodge Jim Dunne, or at least neutralize him. There were three Powertrain rides in Death Valley that day, one for trucks, one for Camaros and Firebirds, and one for Corvette. The radio had been crackling all day with warnings that Jim Dunne and his spy camera were in the area; he'd been seen at a Nevada motel the night before and he'd tried to engage one of the Firebird engineers in a conversation.

"We only have one more run, over to Bad Water," Hill said. "We still haven't seen Dunne."

"You have now. There he is."

Jim Dunne pulled into the parking lot in a rented red Chevy Corsica, trolling for action. His brimmed hat was pulled down over his forehead and he cruised past the Cormaros without noticing that the guy in the yellow shirt was Dave Hill. Dunne was focused on hardware, not people. He disappeared to the rear of the tourist camp but was back in minutes wearing a baseball cap backward and holding his hand over his face. He knew something was going on, but the cars parked under the baking sun were only standard Camaros and Corvettes. Nothing special, or so he thought.

Hill chuckled. "I think we've got him fooled."

Dunne pulled out to the main road and parked, hoping for something to appear. One of the Corvette crowd slipped out with his own camera and snapped two pictures of Dunne sitting there, one of the ace spy photographer focusing his own camera on the driveway entrance just in case. "Gotcha," he said, and when the pictures of Jim Dunne, spy, found their way to *AutoWeek* magazine later in the year, the magazine ran them in its special January issue summarizing 1995.

"Spy Photos of the Year," the magazine's editors called them. "Spy Photographer Spied."

It was a bit of playful revenge on the part of the editors. When Dunne finally noticed that there was something strange about two of those Camaros—they had no back seats, the hoods were too high, the rear fenders too wide, and the gas caps were on the wrong side—he took the pictures and sold them to *AutoWeek*. He and the editors concluded that GM was testing a special edition of Camaro, perhaps for release in 1998 as a souped-up high-speed model to counter the five-liter Ford Mustang. So they ran the picture captioned as an experimental Camaro and only later discovered that a C5 Corvette was hiding under the Camaro skin. They graciously explained the GM ruse to their readers a few weeks later. *What the heck,* they seemed to be saying, *the car companies need to win one every now and then.*

Dunne got his own little laugh at Dave Hill's expense that day in Death Valley. Driving up toward Daylight Pass and the Nevada line, Hill's Cormaro ran out of gas. The first car to come along while he was standing there waiting for the maintenance van to turn around and bring a gas can was Jim Dunne's red Corsica. Dunne flashed a grin and almost stopped. Then he kept going. It was just one of those funny Camaros and he already had it on film. But what was Dave Hill doing there?

The debriefing that night didn't go gently for Ed Koerner and his Powertrain engineers.

Traction control still wasn't tuned in and it drew some of its calibration from the engine software, Hill said. "It's going to Alaska at the end of October. We need Powertrain input there, too. Gravel-to-pavement reactions are still a question."

Koerner made a note and added traction-control interfaces to his list of to-dos.

Fuel pressure in hot weather was another issue, Hill said. The manual transmission Cormaro had a ragged start and the fuel pressure wasn't coming up as fast as he'd like.

"It's still marginal in cold weather, too," said Powertrain's Mike Polom, remembering his experiences the previous winter in Kapuskasing, Ontario.

Hill's engineers added to the gripe list. On a ten scale, they gave the Gen III engines in the Cormaros a six for throttle effort, a four on the air-conditioning off-on transitions, a three for surging on wide-open throttle between sixty and eighty miles per hour, and a three for premature detonations at wide-open throttle. Then there were some no-fuel-pressure problems related to running out of gas unexpectedly.

Koerner wasn't bashful about any of the problems. "The Cormaros just didn't live up to my expectations either," the Gen III chief engineer admitted. "In general, the Corvette C4 mules felt better than the Cormaros, though it may just be the environment." By that, he said, he meant that Gen III might be better in any Corvette than in a Cormaro. The Cormaros had done some good for the program, but they weren't as good as everyone had hoped.

Hill held up a three-by-five card. "Here's my list of things I want us to work on before we do the next ride out of Milford in late September," he said. When he saw Koerner's eyebrows raise in mock surprise, he added, "I write small and it's a dozen items."

The list included the power hop—a slight surge in rpm—from the engine, sluggish low-end power response, too much engine noise, unpleasant exhaust noise, and other items already mentioned and discussed.

"Some things are platform, some are Powertrain, but all are customer satisfiers," Hill said.

Koerner thumped the table. "Let's get to it, get it done."

They tried. But Ed Koerner and his Gen III team were still finding out just how hard it was to invent a new engine and get it right.

65 NOBODY was ready for a Milford ride in late September. Dave Hill's development engineers were carrying most of the load now, running cars at Milford and in the desert simultaneously. They were eating their way through the punch list, getting the final tuning on shock absorbers, retrofitting the beta cars with redesigned control arms, tweaking the seats for optimum comfort, replacing the hatchback glass with a new design that eliminated the distortion they'd discovered when looking in the rearview mirror.

Alpha cars were torn down and retrofitted with the latest beta or prototype parts to keep the fleet of test cars growing and active. Bumper-to-Bumper delivered seven betas in one week and Russ McLean ordered in coffee and doughnuts for a celebration with the union people who had done the job. While they munched and shook hands with McLean and Hill, more almost-finished prototypes were in the paint shop and would soon be delivered to their new owners. Two would go to the durability driving team and two to a separate group inside GM that would begin certifying that the new Corvette met its quality goals. Five more prototypes were in various stages of assembly.

The durability cars would begin gathering the final data sets on how well C5 stood up to the rigors of everyday driving. When the prototypes handed over to the durability drivers finished their useful lives in the spring of 1996, they had racked up the equivalent of several hundred thousand miles on the torture trails at Milford and in the desert.

The prototype cars were a sign of new things happening inside General Motors. Once more, Corvette was leading the way. "Prototype parts will be used to totally validate our design," Hill said. "That's encouraging because it's a shift from the old 'it's only a prototype' attitude to 'prototype is the best it ever gets.' "

The final validation would be done on prototype cars that would be built and delivered in early 1996. It wasn't far off and there was still work to be done, Hill cautioned.

At Milford, the development engineers were trying to do it all. Shaky mirrors both outside and inside were fixed with new pads and mounting

brackets. Brake and accelerator pedals were measured for foot force, modified, measured again. The parking brake handle got intense scrutiny. Some
people liked it, others thought it took too much strength to engage. The
engineers tore apart the cable system in the central tunnel and adjusted it
until the complaints went away.

Clutch pressure irritated some drivers. Skilled pros with racing experience like John Heinricy liked it, but when they let novices, particularly
women, drive the cars, the comments weren't good. Clutch pressure was
trimmed. Heinricy still liked it, at least could live with it, and the average
drivers stopped mentioning it.

Development engineer Mike Neal spent half of September under the
baking sun at Goodyear's test track in San Angelo, Texas, running a beta
car with each of the tread patterns that he and the tire people from Akron
had winnowed from suggested designs. Race drivers say that tires make a
car and it was true. The rubber compound in the tire, the stiffness of its
sidewalls, the cut of its tread, all impacted performance. The questions
were important for every car but critical for Corvette. When Neal got down
to one design that he felt came closest to doing it all for the new Corvette,
he ordered up test tires for the beta and prototype fleets. They'd drive them
for several months to get reactions and see how they and C5 fit together on
real roads, not just on the track.

The engineers had other problems, some of them with strange acronyms.
Early in the program they'd wrestled with the CHMSL—the center high-
mounted stoplight—until they found a design that John Cafaro accepted
and the engineers certified would meet federal specs. The CHMSL was
ordered by Transportation Secretary Elizabeth Dole in the mid-eighties as
an alleged safety measure and may have had some effect for a year or two.
Whether or not the "Liddy Light" was still doing much good, it was still
required. The C5 CHMSL was a narrow red strip built into the rear deck. It
was "high-mounted" above the regular brake lights by only a few inches,
just enough to meet the federal spec.

The PRNDL was another problem. It is the device that tells drivers what
automatic transmission gear they are in. It got its name from the gears
themselves: Park, Reverse, Neutral, Drive, Low. The C5 PRNDL was hard to
see. The lettering was too faint, the lighting poor, and the needle that
pointed to the gear being used didn't stand out. It was a problem that had
only come up in recent months, when they were putting miles on the cars.
Dave Hill ordered it redone and new PRNDLs were being readied for the
next drive out of Milford. Then the whole team, including Powertrain people and Chevy's Bob Applegate, could render a verdict.

Through all of those weeks, Russ McLean and Dave Hill were quietly
going through their own durability tests. They were interviewed at length

for the vehicle line executive jobs. None of the forty candidates was told what job he might get. McLean and Hill might both become VLEs and neither of them would be on Corvette. One might get Corvette, the other a sedan. Or neither of them would get a VLE slot and they would be left to wonder what would happen to Corvette.

One weekend they were all taken to Cincinnati, put into a role-playing school run by a consulting firm, and thrust into problem-solving situations that tested their abilities to react under pressure. Other weekends they sat through afternoons of lectures on what VLEs should be and what VLEs should do. They were questioned and probed and watched.

McLean and Hill knew that their own people were being interviewed, too. The questions were tough and the interviewers wanted honest answers. Confidentiality was guaranteed. Do you like the guy? How is he to work for? What does he do when you disagree with him? Do you respect his judgment? Can you trust him?

The interviews lasted several hours and when they were done, the engineers and the admin people who'd been grilled were told to keep their mouths shut and just carry on. But they all knew that their answers would have impact on the final decisions. And they all knew that the one real question, the one the interviewers didn't ask, was this: *Would you follow him into hell?*

For the people working for Russ McLean and Dave Hill, the answer would have been: *We already have.*

Hill's development engineers and Ed Koerner's Gen III engineers at last were ready to drive out of Milford and into north-central Michigan for a three-hundred-mile afternoon ride that would settle a long list of outstanding questions.

The date they picked was October 19. That morning GM issued a news release to the world.

66 D AV E Hill was the Corvette vehicle line executive. He would be the only VLE who was also his program's chief engineer. Hill had it all. Russ McLean was in limbo.

"Life's short," McLean said. "There's a point where you gotta walk away, where it's not your show and you're not the boss anymore.

"The important thing is that leaders need to be in the field, not sitting so far behind the lines that they can't see what's happening. Dave Hill's that kind of leader."

He didn't add that Russ McLean was, too. He did wonder what GM would have in store for him. Twenty-seven of the company's most experienced and skilled executives had been tried, tested, and not chosen. The company wouldn't just forget about them, McLean figured. Meanwhile, Hill would be gone for at least a month, maybe more, with a new series of VLE training classes the company had for its new category of sharpshooters. McLean would continue to run Corvette until the VLE process was officially in place, probably in January.

At Milford, they surrounded Hill and shook his hand. He gave the congratulatory spasm about two minutes, then turned their attention back to work. They had a test ride to take.

It turned out to be a very good day for Dave Hill. The four beta cars, all with aluminum Gen III engines, were the best yet. Everyone came home after dark with few complaints. But one item caught Hill's attention. They'd run over several gravel roads that day and stones were being thrown against the rear rocker panels and wearing off the finish. Under the car, they were scouring the straps that secured the gas tanks—not enough to be dangerous, but more than enough to look ugly. Ugly was not a condition that Corvette owners would accept, even if it existed only on the undersides of their cars.

Fixes to those problems were done within weeks. The gas tank straps were angled up to eliminate impingement and provide even more strength. "It's robust," Hill said when he saw the result. John Cafaro, not relinquishing any control over C5, worked with engineers to design optional stone guards that could be added to the rocker panels. The guards would be recommended to the few C5 owners who would drive often on unpaved roads.

The engine caught some gripes, too. It was getting better, but it wasn't there yet. One big problem was lubrication. In a test called the "skid pad," in which the car is put into a tight, high-acceleration circling turn and measurements of g forces are taken, the oil light was coming on. The car was handling the turn all right and registering maximum lateral g forces of 0.93 or better. That was the minimum spec and the car was hitting it. But in the process, engine oil was being forced into the heads, away from where it was most needed. The skid pad test had only one purpose, to satisfy journalists. It was a standard test the car magazines ran to gauge performance. But it wasn't something that drivers in the real world ever encountered, unless they drove on a racetrack.

Journalists liked to stay on the skid pad for half a minute or more. The oil light was coming on after fifteen seconds. And the C5 spec called for staying on the skid pad for a full minute while maintaining "max lats" of at least 0.93 g and not losing oil pressure. Ed Koerner's Powertrain engineers thought they had a solution, but it wasn't yet ready to try on a real engine.

Their answer was to reshape the Gen III's oil pan to increase its capacity from four quarts of oil to six. It couldn't be done by simply increasing the oil pan's depth. When Dave Hill agreed to let the new Corvette's hood slope at a rakish angle, he forced the engine down more deeply in its compartment. The bottom of the oil pan was only two millimeters—less than one-twelfth inch—from the bottom of the car.

"Gullwings," Koerner said. "That was the solution." His engineers added swoopy side extensions to the oil pan to increase its volume. "The next question was how to test the fix."

Running engines on dynamometers in a lab hadn't found the problem earlier. The test stands were static and the problem occurred only when the engine tilted. Koerner ordered a tilting test stand built. An engine running at full throttle could be suddenly tilted fifty degrees to see if it would survive the journalists' skid pad test. The first engines with gullwing oil pans didn't. Oil was sloshing in the pans, picking up air and turning into a foam as it was sucked through the intakes that pumped it around the engine.

They went back to the drawing board and began devising internal baffles in the gullwing that would keep the oil from churning in skid pad turns. That worked, but now oil wasn't getting pumped to the cylinder bays on top of the engine in sufficient quantities.

Koerner's team wracked their brains to find an answer. It came from an unexpected source during a meeting to analyze ideas for reducing the engine's weight. An engineer suggested that the Gen III's heavy crankshaft be hollowed out. A one-inch rifle-shot drilled down the crank's center would cut 2.5 kilos (5.5 pounds). "There was a moment of silence and then somebody said, 'It'll solve the oil problem, too,' " Koerner told Dave Hill. "We added some windows in the bulkheads and holes in the crotch for breathing, and we were there."

Questions about the electronic throttle control persisted, too. The cruise problem had gone away, but when the test drivers put their foot on the throttle pedal, they weren't always happy with the result. It was a subjective thing. Some drivers wanted a faster throttle response, some didn't. But throttle response is a personal thing; whether the gas pedal is old-fashioned or new-fangled, no adjustment would satisfy every driver. Software writers tweaked the computer code to reduce the complaints. It was all they could do.

Then there was the nagging question of finishing the hot- and cold-weather testing that was mandatory to calibrate the aluminum engine software for every possible climate. The cold tests could be handled at Kapuskasing. But there was nowhere in the hemisphere that was warm enough in the months remaining. Cars would have to go to Australia. Powertrain would foot the bill. Ed Koerner bought into the solution. He didn't have another option.

Traction control was under control. Two beta cars with aluminum engines were already on their way to Alaska. Three weeks on icy surfaces east of Fairbanks would be more than enough to get the traction software finished. And it could be tested and accepted one final time at Kinross, in Michigan's Upper Peninsula, by Dave Hill and the entire engineering team before winter ended in the United States.

Hill looked at his calendar. Dave Wickman had already scheduled another all-day ride in the desert for mid-December, and a two-day trek with beta cars and prototypes over back roads from Phoenix to Salt Lake City at the end of January. Jim Ingle had plotted that one and it promised to take the cars through every kind of terrain from mountain passes to deserts to narrow canyons cut by wild western rivers. If they were lucky, the weather would be good for the first ride and horrid for the second.

New VLE Dave Hill smiled at the scheduling. The December ride would give him time to get his VLE training out of the way and it would give the rest of them another eight weeks to get the latest list of gripes resolved. The January ride would end on a Friday night. Wickman had planned it that way at Hill's request. If the cars were in good enough shape so he didn't have to rush back to work, maybe he could get in a couple of days' skiing in Utah.

He went home that night in a happy haze. He was a VLE. And the C5 gripe list was the shortest ever.

67

T w o major crashes involving 1997 Corvettes happened in October 1994. A speeding car broadsided a C5 on the driver's side at 50 mph. Three weeks later, a station wagon slammed into the rear of a C5.

The first crash was fatal. Neither of the Corvette's occupants survived. The side structure failed, the driver's door punched inward into his body, and the passenger's head and chest suffered massive injuries. In the milliseconds after the impact, tearing metal and plastic ripped a one-inch cut into the fuel filler neck, chopped open the top of the left-side gas tank, and opened a three-inch hole in the crossover pipe between the tanks.

The second crash was a walkaway. The C5 was thrown forward by the rear-ender, its rear bumper crushed and slit open. The fiberglass outer panel of the driver's door cracked as it absorbed energy. So did the hatchback glass. But it didn't shatter. The rear-deck lid was unmarked, but the cargo tub buckled into the luggage area. The fuel system was intact. Nothing ripped, nothing leaked. The beefy structure did its job.

In fact, no one died at all. The occupants in both were crash dummies. The crashes happened inside the cavernous crash laboratory at Milford Proving Ground. High-speed cameras recorded every aspect of both crashes from multiple angles and engineers pored over the cars afterward. They measured, they sampled, they ran data through computers—even spending thousands of Corvette dollars on computer runs so complex that they took three days of time on one of GM's Cray supercomputers. It was a good investment. When they ran the analysis on desktop workstations, it took ten days to complete.

Dorian Tyree, Corvette's lead safety engineer and the man charged with crashing cars, analyzing results, and working with the team to find fixes, looked at the side-impact results and shook his head. He'd hoped for better, but he was never surprised. "It can be fixed," he said. "We just have to add some additional structure to beef up the protection."

It would turn out that part of the problem when a C5 was hit in the side was that it was *too* strong. The door-lock pillars didn't give. There was no energy-absorbing crush that reduced the slam being transmitted through the rest of the car. Forces that should have soaked into the pillar instead radiated into the car and put unexpected stresses on parts and crash dummies.

Part of the fix, worked out in computer analysis and in a series of crash tests with C5 bucks and complete cars, was to weaken the rails through their center sections just enough, and to add some crushable material, so that the structure protected occupants by absorbing shock instead of passing it along.

The twin gas tanks were not production models. Instead they were early samples from a supplier who was still trying to get the shapes and wall thicknesses perfected through a blow-molding process. C5 wouldn't have good samples of the tanks for another five months. Hill told his computer expert, Steve Longo, to get the best data available, then to make runs on GM's Cray supercomputer to predict what would happen.

Meanwhile, he ordered an additional steel wall to be designed and installed between the gas tanks and the Corvette's fenders. The next rear-end crash was everything they'd hoped. "We passed," Tyree said. "We don't have to run it again."

Having enough cars, partial cars, or structures for all the required tests was an ongoing problem. Tyree was earning a reputation for getting cars repaired after one kind of crash so they could be used again in another. "We'll pull the frame on the rear-ender," he told Hill, "to make it usable for another side-angle test."

"Great!" Hill applauded. "We're going to have Dorian Tyree's Used-Car Crash Test Company here."

The tests ran steadily through the months into 1996. In almost every case, the GM rules were half again as strict as federal rules. Many of the tests were engineering trials, not required to make the car salable, but still providing data against the day that a final test would make the difference between officially passing or failing. Air bags were a particular problem. Some bags inflated too fast and could break a neck. Others were too soft and slow to provide real protection. The distance between the steering wheel or passenger-side panel and the human body was vital. Tyree and his people made the measurements, timed the bags in repeated sled tests, saw how the crash dummies bent forward and the air bags inflated toward them. The size of the bags and their materials was sampled, changed, changed again.

Knee bolsters were tested, modified, tested again, until dummies came away from crashes with no serious damage. The shapes of structures were changed, strengthened, and tested until every test was passed with margins to spare.

Iron braces and foam inserts went inside the doors, and occupants survived side impacts. "Congratulations, guys," Hill told them. "You proved it could be done. Now let's prove it can be done smart." They went back to the design tube and refined the braces, lightened the materials, turned three pieces of foam into one for ease of assembly, and passed the test again.

The last tests came in 1996. A C5 ran into a wall at 30 mph. Human occupants would have walked away with only minor scrapes and bruises. In late spring, a prototype C5 with all the right parts was set up in the crash laboratory at Milford. A sedan slammed into it just at the juncture of the driver's door and the fuel filler cap.

Nothing leaked. The crash dummies survived. C5 had passed the tests, exceeding federal standards.

In the real world, an insurance company might have totaled the last Corvette they crashed. Then some lucky restorer would have bought it cheap and spent a few years of garage time making it perfect again.

Dorian Tyree would like that.

68 T H E cafeteria in the training building on the backside of the General Motors Technical Center was empty at night. Dave Hill came out of an all-day session that was supposed to be equipping him to become a vehicle line executive, opened his brief case at one of the lunch tables, and pulled out a handful of reports and memos. He wanted to read them and work out his responses. On the way home in the dark, he'd use his cellular phone to leave voice mail messages and instructions. It was the only way he could keep in touch with the final phases of C5 until he was done with VLE training.

A week earlier, on a chill November afternoon, he'd slipped away to drive a prototype C5 with Dave Wickman. It had the tires that were all but finalized between his engineers and Goodyear, run-flats rated for one hundred miles of airless driving. It had new side windows with heavier glass that dramatically cut wind noise, and the latest body acoustic package of insulation and sound deadeners. It had the latest tuning on the shock absorbers and the latest padding on the leather seats.

He drove the car because he was worried. "People out there are afraid that I'll wreck Corvette because my background was Cadillac and luxury cars," he mused. "They're afraid I'll turn their Corvette into some kind of sporty Lexus."

So he and Wickman ran the roads at Milford—through high-speed turns on a banked oval, flat out on the straightaways, up and down a 15 percent slope steeper than almost anything in the western mountains. They bounced over the Belgian Blocks, slammed through potholes, shimmied and slewed through dips and over corduroy surfaces. Hill took the proto through fifty in first gear, touched ninety in second, blew through one hundred in third. He threw the car into left-right arcs, floored the brake pedal, downshifted and upshifted, until both he and Dave Wickman had had enough.

"That car is exciting," Hill said. "The performance numbers say we're going to exceed everyone's expectations for acceleration, top speed, handling. The car is more agile than C4, more tossable at speed. You drive it and you feel confident because it doesn't bite you like a C4 invariably does when you cross the limits."

One of the notes in his mail package as he sat in the dim cafeteria was from Wickman. It reminded him of the desert ride scheduled just before Christmas and told him that Jim Ingle would be there to lead the way on some interesting roads. He added Wickman to his list for voice mail on the way home. It was going to be a good trip.

They pulled out of the Desert Proving Ground before sunup on December 14, to avoid spies and because they needed the full day for the route Jim Ingle had laid out. It was another ten-vehicle convoy, this time under cloudy skies. Jingles led the way in the black Caprice station wagon, with three white betas and a silver prototype C5 in trail. The C5s were heavily camouflaged with front bras, rear padded diapers, hood and door covers, and excessive masking around the windows. Even a lucky spy photographer wouldn't get much.

A red Mazda RX-7, a red Toyota Supra, a white Nissan 300ZX, and a new silver 1996 C4 followed behind. Scott Leon guarded the back door in the maintenance van, his usual spot when the bosses went for a ride.

The Japanese cars were along because they were all they had to represent the competition. But everyone on the ride knew that they represented nothing at all. In the beginning years, all the way back to 1988, the Japanese cars were the threat. Corvette engineers benchmarked the Japanese sports because they were some of the best in the world for quality. None but a turbocharged Supra that was sold in the United States for a few years could beat a Corvette from zero to sixty, or zero to one hundred, and none at all could maneuver or dance through traffic the way a Corvette could.

But the foreigners looked good. Their bodies were tight. They didn't squeak or rattle. They never leaked water. The ZX was rated as the world-class interior for comfort and ergonomics. Everything was within reach and everything felt right.

When they designed C5, the Corvette team had the Japanese in mind. Toyota and Nissan and Mazda were the cars to beat. Putting those rice burners on the boat back home was the goal.

That was then. The world had changed and the rice burners were all but gone. The new challenge was coming from the land of sauerkraut and dark beer. As the Japanese cars became more and more expensive, while the yen out-valued the dollar, fewer and fewer people bought the hot rice-burners. Corvette sales stayed stable or increased. The Japanese faded. Nissan announced that the 300ZX was being dropped in the United States. Toyota was phasing out the Supra. Mazda ended U.S. imports of the RX-7. It was a clean sweep. Corvette's Japanese competition disappeared.

But the Germans arrived. BMW was getting raves for its little M3 sports car, underpowered but beautiful. Mercedes was bringing in a $40,000 two-seater that aimed at the Corvette price range. But it was a four-cylinder car, too, and was breathing hard before it got close to sixty in an acceleration run. Porsche was coming back, too. A spiffy low-priced sports car they were calling the Boxster would arrive in the States in early 1997. "Low-priced" for Porsche meant a sticker at $39,980. And even that little racer was more of a putter. It handled like a Porsche should, meaning very, very well, but its engine couldn't deliver the power of a C5. And it was a cramped and crowded little car.

None of the German cars was on sale yet in the United States in December 1995. So the comparison would still be made against the Japanese on the run through eastern Arizona. It was just that nobody much cared by then. Corvette and the world economy had ground the Japanese sports cars into oblivion.

With the desert ride, the C5 team was down to its last three chances to find the flaws and fix them. They didn't count the engine. It was still on the bubble. Powertrain continued to promise that it would make the grade, but it needed three months in Australia and much of the first six months of 1996 to finish the software and to test and validate the hardware. It was going to be a close thing. The rest of the car was approaching Dave Hill's definition of goodness. They could make the last little changes in December and check them again in a two-day ride in late January. After that, they'd take cars out for an afternoon in March in Michigan's Upper Peninsula. And then they'd be done making changes. From mid-March on, the job would be to validate, not to change.

The kicker in the back of Dave Hill's mind was whether they'd have final engines. He still had to face a decision in early March. If it went the wrong way, there would be no C5 in 1997.

Between December and March, they had the little problems to settle. John Heinricy was on the radio as they passed Florence Junction. His engine temperature gauges didn't agree. "I've got one hundred ninety on the digital and two hundred twenty on the analog," he said. "Anybody else seeing that?"

Not exactly, but other cars were seeing other differences. Electrical team chief Dennis Gonzales told his passenger, Bob Applegate, to tell them about the problem. "There's only one sensor, according to Dennis," Applegate radioed, "so they should read the same. He's going to look at the calibration."

"Car One has a gas reading of one-quarter full."

"Filled the tanks this morning," Jingles replied. "Another calibration for Dennis."

"Hey, when I open the glove box, the door flops down and dumps stuff in my lap. Is that design intent?"

Interior lead engineer Steve Mackin laughed at the insult. "No, only the silver prototype has the correct glove box door. We moved the detent up about an inch and a half for production."

"This ashtray's hard to get in and out."

"Being fixed," Mackin radioed.

"I see light around the edge of the passenger air bag cover."

"Design intent coming." That was Mackin again. "And the final console lid's not on the cars yet," he added before anyone could complain about that.

Harry Turner, about to leave Chevy's Sporty Car group to take over its motor sports interests, couldn't get the Delco radio to pull in stations with adequate strength. Poor reception in the AM band is a Delco problem that has never been fixed. At one point early in the program, the Corvette team considered dropping the Delco name from its entertainment unit altogether. "These cars have radio antennas?" Turner asked.

"The silver car has a patch antenna on the left rear fender," Jingles answered. "They've been fooling with it on other cars."

"No, the fender patch is for the passive keyless entry antenna," Mike Neal keyed in. "The radio antenna is buried in the backlight. But they are still fooling with tuning it in."

Hill asked the C5 drivers to turn off their traction control and comment on the Off light. "It's much too bright," Chevy's Fred Gallasch answered immediately. "When you have traction control off, it's because you want it off and you don't need this big bright light telling you about it."

"I agree," Hill said. The size and intensity of the Off light would be changed.

In the maintenance van Scott Leon remembered a suggestion he'd made a year earlier, that the ignition software be written to forget the starter motor if a driver accidentally turned the key when the engine was already running. "We did it," Dennis Gonzales radioed back. "It was an easy software thing. Good suggestion."

By late afternoon, they were heading home with a new punch list of problems. But now the items were minor and the mood was relaxed. "Hey," Tadge Juechter radioed, "it takes a lot of pressure to honk the horn."

The electrical guys already knew that. It was a fallout from the mandatory air bags that filled the center of the steering wheel, and car makers around the world were struggling with the problem. An engineering report already existed that said the C5 horn wouldn't activate at all in temperatures below −5 degrees.

"This is a due-care issue that must be addressed," Hill answered. It would be fixed before the winter was over.

They were almost back to the proving ground when a beta car stopped on the freeway, its engine dead. Bob Applegate rolled it to the shoulder. It wouldn't restart. A tow truck from the proving ground hauled it home. It started instantly in the garage. Debris and plastic residue had built up and blocked the crossover line between the two gas tanks. When the tow truck lifted the C5, the debris came loose.

"There should never be debris from the plastic tanks," Hill said later. "That's being worked at the manufacturer end. And the crossover tubes will be shipped to Bowling Green with ends capped. This won't happen on a production car."

At the debriefing, Hill brought up some history. "Three years and twelve days ago, I met Bob Applegate and he offered Chevy's help under the table to do the CERV.

"Well, we've come a long way since then. We have only nine months left until we start the pilot build at Bowling Green. I know we can get the job done."

But first they had another ride from Phoenix to Salt Lake, and they needed a bagful of warm fuzzies from the Powertrain people. The worry nagging Dave Hill was that Powertrain's bag might be empty.

69 WINTER was dumping on Utah with a vengeance. Park City had recorded almost one hundred inches of fresh powder in ten days and it was still coming down. Green and white street signs protruded above snowplow mounds only enough to be barely read, and without four-wheel drive, it was difficult to get around.

Dave Hill looked down on the town, planted his poles, and dropped off the edge into knee-deep powder. The Deer Valley slope was just another challenge to him and he attacked it with aggressive speed. The day before, crossing Utah from southeast to northwest in a blizzard that sometimes reduced visibility to near zero, he and his team had finished their final big drive in C5 development.

They'd arrived south of Salt Lake City at midafternoon, exhausted and exhilarated from the two-day trip. Some of his test drivers had spirited two betas and two prototypes out of the Desert Proving Ground after dark Wednesday night and run them over back roads through the mountains to Flagstaff, Arizona. Hill and the Detroit contingent met them there, mounting up behind Jim Ingle and running northeast into the Four Corners area early the next morning.

The weather started good, turned cloudy during a long run across the desert floor, and changed to snow north of Mexican Hat, Utah. That was when Jingles turned them off onto a narrow side road. "We've got a twenty-mile private road with great conditions," Jingles radioed as he disappeared into the near-whiteout ahead. "Do whatever you need to." The test drivers yipped on the radio and went to work, plowing through drifts and blowing snow until they climbed the cars up slippery steeps to Needles National Monument. Everything seemed to be working. The day's problems—except for the engine and the fuel system—had been trivial.

One more time, Bob Applegate's beta car just stopped dead. It wasn't the car he'd driven to stillness in December, but it was eventually found to be the same problem. Debris in the fuel lines was choking the engine. Adding to the tanks cleaned the line on restart, but the sudden stops would continue to plague them. The usual complaints about Powertrain were the electronic throttle control's feel still wasn't quite right, oil pressure fluctuated, fuel economy was a tenth of a mile per gallon below the spec. But the complaints were subdued. A beta and a prototype were in Australia. Powertrain was double-timing to get the engine right and, fateful words at General Motors, "a fallback plan was in place." There was nothing on this ride that would make the engine better and for a while the other gripes about the car were minor.

Then they hit the last uphill into the Needles. Jingles flowed up the hill in his Caprice wagon, carving foot-deep trenches in the snow, and disappeared over the top. The lead C5 followed. It slowed, it crawled, it stopped halfway up. "It won't go up," John Heinricy radioed. "No traction."

Nothing worked. He revved, skidded, added power slowly, tried it all and the C5 wouldn't climb another inch. "Back it down and take a run at it," Dave Hill radioed. Heinricy did.

"Go! Go! Go!" The catcalls on the radio followed his torturous progress upslope until the C5's nose topped the hill and the car disappeared. The next car up was a C4. It climbed swiftly and smoothly into the snowfall. The three remaining C5s followed Heinricy's pattern. They barely made it. But the remaining C4, the Japanese cars, and even the maintenance van hardly slowed.

It was a puzzle. Why would C5 perform so poorly on upslope snow? The answer wouldn't come until they ran the ice courses at Kinross five weeks later. Then it was all too apparent. The traction control system had been calibrated first for ice and other slippery surfaces. Deep-snow calibration was at the end of the list and was yet to be done.

There were virtually no other serious complaints in the two days between Flagstaff and Salt Lake City. Even driving through a major blizzard and topping mountain passes in trail behind Utah highway department snowplows didn't dampen the enthusiasm they all felt. It was time to relax and have some fun.

At one gas stop, the camouflaged C5s got the attention of a young man and his girlfriend. When several of the drivers went inside for soft drinks, the fellow followed.

"So what are those?" he asked. "New Corvettes?"

"Nope," said Mike Neal with a mischievous grin. "They're Subarus."

"No way."

"Yup."

"You've got real Corvettes out there."

"Competitive cars," Neal said. "We have to run our Subarus against the competition."

At the moment, the girlfriend walked in. "So what'd they say?" she asked. "Are they Corvettes?"

The young man was still perplexed. "No, they're saying Subarus."

She almost jumped for joy. "See!" she laughed. "I told you so!"

Mike Neal slipped away hoping he hadn't wrecked a future marriage when they found out the truth.

The transport truck was ten minutes away when the caravan reached its preplanned ride-and-park lot off Interstate 15 between Provo and Salt Lake City. One more time, a beta car had stopped and wouldn't start. They'd towed it the last mile to the rendezvous, confident that the debris problem, and the possible added problem of a faulty sensor, were already under control for prototypes and production cars. The transport disgorged a big GM van that they drove to Salt Lake airport, while the cars were loaded in the closed truck for delivery back to the desert. Another transport would be in Salt Lake City Monday to take the big van and the maintenance van home. Most of them flew back to Detroit that night, relaxed and thinking about the next January, 1997, when they'd see C5 Corvettes on the streets and the drivers wouldn't be running tests. They'd be the owners and hopefully they'd be smiling.

Jingles took the train to Detroit the next morning. It was one of his loves after a long drive. Scott Leon drove the Caprice to Phoenix and Dave Hill went skiing.

He pulled up in the powder at the bottom of the slope and brushed falling snow from his mustache. "Next year I think I'll come back with Karen for a real vacation," he said. "Two days of this just isn't enough."

70 MARCH 6 was a Wednesday. Decision day.

The previous Monday Dave Hill and his team were up north, putting their C5s through the last feel-good run on the ice courses at Kinross and Kinchloe Air Force Base. Then they went into the deep Kinross snowfields to work on the final traction control calibration and discovered a second problem. The new Goodyear Eagle tires for C5 had treads that were narrower than the treads on C4 tires. Even with an improved traction control calibration, they clogged with snow, and they lost some needed traction. While software experts continued to improve the deep-snow calibration, a flash went out to Goodyear. But it was too late to change the tire design. Goodyear thought it over and decided that for the first time it would make snow tires in Corvette sizes. It was the perfect solution.

The last-minute problems were being solved. Many had gone away completely, including the question of mass. The "relentless pursuit of grams" cited by engineer Jeff Yanssens years earlier had produced a test-loaded C5 that weighed in at 3,546 pounds—more than Hill liked, but well inside the 3,500-pound test weight class.

Now Hill faced the most important moment since he'd been named a vehicle line executive. His staff was meeting with him—his administrative staff as VLE, not his engineering staff—and a decision was needed on parts for the C4 Corvette. It was a decision that only a VLE had the authority to make and it was one of the reasons that General Motors had decided to give such power to a single individual. Hill's job was to do the right thing for the car and for its buyers. He had to decide on the future of Corvette.

If Hill trusted Powertrain to deliver engines for the start of C5 production in September, the decision would be to do nothing. Suppliers would stop making C4 parts as their contracts expired.

Otherwise today was the day that General Motors had to inform C4 suppliers to keep working. They would need parts to build cars beyond June 21, the day the thirteen-year-old C4 assembly line was to shut down. Faxes would go out and C4 suppliers would keep their own lines and machines running.

If that happened, Hill knew, the word would leak immediately. In days, maybe hours, the news media would be trumpeting another General Motors failure, another delay in Corvette.

But if he shut down the C4, and Powertrain didn't deliver, the same result might come in September instead of March and Dave Hill would be the villain for not having C5s rolling down the new assembly line in Bowling Green. Ed Koerner and Powertrain would be criticized, too, but the brunt would fall on the VLE.

Ed Koerner, the Gen III chief engineer, had made his pitch for moving ahead. Production engines already were being built at the Powertrain plant in Romulus, Michigan. The fixes were in. They just weren't proven. The engine hadn't been validated through a long series of rough tests. But the plan was in place. And horsepower was not in question. Tests had rated the new engine at 345 horsepower, slightly more than the original specification and 15 horsepower more than the most powerful engine available in the 1996 C4.

Production-level engines already had completed grueling survival tests on the dynamometer stands. Two engines had finished the GM-required test of running full throttle for 50 hours without a problem. But Koerner wasn't satisfied. He had two more engines run all-out for 260 hours. When they passed the Koerner test, he doubled the requirement and ordered another engine run full throttle for 520 hours. "Every one of those engines looked absolutely new when we tore them down," he reported. "And they all developed between three hundred thirty-eight and three hundred forty-five horsepower for every minute they were running." That would give Gen III the horsepower rating that the Corvette team wanted. Just as good, the fuel economy ratings in tests at 55 mph held steady at 23.5 miles per gallon. C5 would not be tagged with the dreaded federal "gas-guzzler" label.

"Stick with the plan," Koerner urged Dave Hill when they discussed whether or not to proceed toward C5 production. "Give me ten cars with Gen III engines for the last set of tests."

The worst that could happen, Koerner argued, was that they'd find problems that would slow the ramp-up to full assembly line speed beyond the three months already planned from September to December. Maybe somebody would have to go through the back lot at the Bowling Green assembly plant and load updated software into the C5s stored there until shipments to dealers began in mid-December. In the worst of all possible scenarios, some revamped part would have to be retrofitted into those cars before they were shipped. But it was better to plan for success, Koerner said, and be prepared to make minor changes on cars already built, than to not build them at all.

Koerner would take the first cars out of the prepilot build in late August and put them through the final validations. He'd have drivers running them down to Mexico for the end of hot weather and up to Alaska for the first chill of winter. The cars would not be transported to locations. They'd be driven, and driven hard.

Three cars would go on one lap of America. Koerner would fly drivers wherever they were needed, along with maintenance people, to run the C5s around the entire country. They would be in the mountains and forests of the west, across the high plains of Wyoming, and through Montana and the Dakotas. They'd run the cars to the northeast and down to Florida, then back west again until they had lapped the country.

When they ended tests around November 1, Koerner said, his group would have put seventy production-level Gen III engines through the most extensive verification runs in General Motors history. That included three months in Australian heat that would end in April 1996. "This engine is durable," Koerner reported. "They've been taking it on some of those long Outback roads in one hundred-ten degree heat, setting the cruise control at one hundred twenty-five mph and running for ninety to one hundred twenty minutes straight without a problem. They would have gone longer, but they were running out of gas."

At the opposite extreme, Koerner said, winter tests at Kapuskasing, Ontario, in February 1996 yielded better results than expected. In one record cold wave, his engineers tried starting a C5 that had cold-soaked at −43 degrees. The Gen III engine started in 1.5 seconds, faster than any car on the outdoor test lot.

The arguments Koerner presented looked good, but Dave Hill wanted to think it through.

"You let me do it," Koerner told Hill in his closing pitch, "and I'll give you an engine that does everything we promised." He compared Gen III to the first V-8 installed in a Corvette by Zora Arkus-Duntov. "This is 1955 all over again."

Maybe there wouldn't be two thousand Corvettes in the back lot at Bowling Green on December 9. Maybe there would only be six hundred for the first transports to pick up and begin hauling off to dealers. But they'd be good 1997 Corvettes. They'd have engines that met the specs. They'd be validated and their owners might never have to see a dealer for anything more than an oil change.

And there would be shiny new C5s at the Detroit International Auto Show in early January and another at the Los Angeles auto show on the same day to be unveiled to the world. Journalists would have seen it in November, strict rules embargoing their reports until show day. On a January day, their stories and pictures—pictures of the real car, not spy photos of an ugly duckling—would be crisscrossing the globe.

"The engine is the question," Hill told his VLE staff when they convened on March 6. "Now do we call the C4 suppliers or not?"

He walked to the projector screen and pointed to a list. "We've had a lot of interaction with Powertrain on this. They are now building production-level engines at Romulus and we already have three in cars.

"We've been inside their testing and peeled back the onion on their true status."

He pointed to Gen III items still labeled red: the feel of the electronic throttle control, software, shuffles, fuel economy. "Shuffles," he explained, were what happened when the car went over a rough road and the driver's foot bounced on the accelerator pedal. The car shuffled under engine surges. The fix would be to add friction to the electronic throttle control, which itself was still being refined. Some test drivers still complained that it lagged too much when they floored the accelerator. "I think I could beat this thing in a C4," Bowling Green plant manager Wil Cooksey complained after one test drive. "We tried and you can't," answered Jim Ingle. "We'll show you the numbers." Still, the impression of lag was there and would be fixed.

Other items were labeled yellow: oil control, exhaust manifold cracking, bore liner cracking, cylinder head gasket, accessory drive rumble, oil pump relief valve, manifold air pressure sensor. The fixes were in but hadn't been proven in long road tests.

"The red items are readily retrofitable and we can exercise the pilot cars on software and shuffles," Hill said. Retrofit would cost money, but it wouldn't stop production.

"Yellows are retrofitable, too," he said. "Powertrain can verify those items with its one lap of America."

He summed it up in his role as vehicle line executive. "There are relatively few remaining red items, we have availability of pilot engines, we can exercise those engines ourselves in April and May."

Around the conference table, heads were nodding. Hill looked at the screen and made a decision.

"The recommendation is that we end C4 and put all emphasis here. The recommendation is that we stop the '96."

C4's thirteen-year run was irrevocably sealed. The last fourth-generation Corvette would roll off the assembly line on June 21, 1996.

It was seven and a half years since Chuck Jordan sent artists to the basement at Design Staff and John Cafaro opened the Corvette Skunk Works. Dave Hill was a guy at Cadillac and General Motors was minting money. Ronald Reagan was president. Japan ruled the auto world.

Dave Hill wasn't thinking about any of that on March 6. He was focused on the future. C5 was alive.

EPILOGUE

The last C4 Corvette, a white targa-top coupe, moved down the assembly line at Bowling Green, Kentucky, on June 20, 1996, one day ahead of schedule. There was no fanfare. In the eyes of the people who run the General Motors MidLux Car Division, it was just another car and just another day.

Chevrolet saw it differently and asked for some ceremony. They were told no.

But corporate cool couldn't contain the raw emotion of the moment. And it didn't stop Mike Yager, owner of Mid-America Design, a huge Corvette catalog house, from wrangling a film crew into the plant. That last car was his, going on display in his museum in Effingham, Illinois, and he wanted a record of the day. Yager got it, and a bit more.

The line workers were free to leave after installing their own last part. Some of them finished before 9 A.M., then stayed for the rest of the day, following the last C4 they would ever build. Plant managers dropped by hourly to check on the car, then went back to their offices to work and wonder. When the historic car got close to the end, they came and stayed to watch.

Behind the last fourth-generation Corvette, the assembly line that had been in place for nearly fourteen years was disappearing in a yammer of jackhammers and clouds of torch sparks and concrete dust.

Moments after workers at each assembly station finished their tasks, someone was there to unhook the air tools, unplug the electrical cables, and begin cutting the overhead rails. Some workers simply turned to hand a tool to a waiting disassembler, then joined the growing crowd following the car.

Empty parts racks were wheeled away. The concrete floor, and the moving chain that had pulled Corvettes along to completion for so many years, disappeared. Skip loaders rumbled past with bent trolley rails and buckets of rubble.

For the first time since the line was installed in 1982, there was nothing behind a moving Corvette. Nothing but destruction, soon to be followed by resurrection.

Along the way, the men and women of the United Auto Workers signed the last parts they installed. Near the end of the line a worker finished bolting the driver's seat in place, stood up, and handed the keys to Yager. Someone laid a neat sign on the hood: "The Last of a Legend." Yager's expression was somewhere between disconsolate and eager. Then he broke into a broad grin, got into his car, and started it up. The crowd around the car, now several hundred workers who didn't want to leave, cheered and applauded.

It took another hour to get the final checks and alignments. An unfurled banner repeated "The Last of a Legend" and they crowded around for a huge group photo. Finally it was done. They stood around more, even after the quitting horn blared. It would be a summer with most of them on furlough, drawing pay, but not spending their days building a car they really loved. When the noise of destruction—and off in distant corners of the plant the noise of construction—rose to intolerable levels, they drifted off and went home.

Mike Yager had his car. It would be displayed the next day at the National Corvette Museum across the road, just after an interment ceremony for the ashes of Zora Arkus-Duntov. Then it was loaded into a carrier and hauled north to Illinois.

Through the summer Dave Hill wrestled with the last few problems on the C5 Corvette. His drivers broke a brake lining and crashed during a twenty-four-hour endurance run at the Gratten Raceway in Grand Rapids. No one was hurt, but the engineers spent their summer verifying that the part was designed well.

At Bowling Green, a new assembly line rapidly replaced the old. By early August, test parts were arriving at the loading docks along with the first pieces of pre-pilot cars—seventeen cars that would be built to help train assembly workers, and to give Hill and Ed Koerner at Powertrain a final few cars to put through tests.

The last of the pre-pilots were still on the general assembly line on September 3. That was the date forecast nearly four years earlier, in November 1992, for the plant to begin assembling pilot cars, the first salable C5 Corvettes. Most of the parts for the pilots had arrived. Thirty feet from a short line of white pre-pilot cars creeping along, Bennie Bradley put the silvery half of a central tunnel into a welding jig. That tunnel would go into the all-new Corvette whose long vehicle identification number (VIN) would begin "97Y" and end "00001."

At 6:49 A.M. sparks flew as Bradley tack-welded additional pieces to the tunnel. A moment later, as he lifted the sheet metal to place it in a jig for a robot welder to finish the job, sparks flew across the way where another worker began assembling his half of the tunnel.

Job One on the first production C5 was supposed to be over. It wasn't. It was the beginning of a frantic four weeks that threatened to throw years of preparation into the trash. On the loading dock and in the parts bins, plant workers were rejecting fenders, hoods, wheelhouses, and rear decks. The parts for the pilot cars coming in from suppliers didn't meet Corvette's new standards and plant management refused to certify them.

It would take a week to get new and improved parts shipped to Kentucky. The tunnel that should have been part of the first salable vehicle became part of a test body structure instead. Three were built. Three were rejected as fatally flawed. When new parts arrived, they were no better. More changes were ordered.

In another part of the plant there were additional problems. The cockpit didn't fit easily into the car; rework on a few parts was needed by the supplier. Then a critical bracket at the cockpit team failed—the supplier had changed manufacturing procedures and the new bracket didn't have the strength demonstrated by the pre-pilot cars. New parts, made the old way, were ordered, but it would take another week before they arrived.

Dave Hill and plant manager Wil Cooksey agreed: The first salable C5 would not be built from shabby parts. A handful of test cars was created in mid to late September. To get around the GM bureaucracy that mandated building salable cars at this point, they called the pilot cars Product & Process Verification Vehicles. They were built, checked, tested, and stored away. Slowly, toward the end of September, quality improved. "We're getting there," Hill said when a pilot car finally began coming together. It rolled off the line on October 1. C5 was weeks behind schedule.

But the time could be made up. The first pilot car went from Job One to drivable (and salable) in four days, rather than the thirteen originally planned. What they'd learned in September they now applied to the assembly line.

Dave Hill felt a measure of victory in that first car. Despite the last-minute snags, he'd kept Russ McLean's and Joe Spielman's promises to deliver the car on time and under budget. It wasn't under by much, but it was better than other car programs had managed. Hill believed that these would be the best Corvettes ever built. Some of them would be shown to the automotive press in November, when the writers would have the chance to drive them mercilessly. Hill knew that their verdicts, and the verdicts of buyers like New York Knicks guard John Starks, who had already left a C5 deposit at a Chevy dealer, were the ones that counted.

As the first C5s rolled down the assembly line, Dave Hill saw one additional difference in the new cars. Traditionally at GM the first few hundred cars off the line are all one color, invariably white.

Hill had argued for another color, and he got his way.

"Maybe *all* Corvettes aren't red," he said, as he watched the line. "But these are."

WHERE ARE THEY NOW?

Roger Smith retired from General Motors and lives quietly in the Detroit area.

Bob Stempel retired from General Motors and devotes his time to promoting electric car technology.

Cardy Davis retired from General Motors and became a vice president at Mercury Marine in Chicago.

Dave McLellan retired from General Motors and promotes Corvette products. He has written a history of Corvette.

Chuck Jordan retired from General Motors and consults and writes about design issues. He has mellowed and doesn't miss work.

Mike Juras retired from General Motors and does occasional consulting.

Jim Perkins retired from General Motors and remains active in the automobile business.

Tom Krejcar died April 11, 1994.

Earl Werner became vice president for engineering at Harley-Davidson.

Russ McLean declined the offer to run GM's new-car project in China for personal reasons and became director of all prototype and modeling facilities for General Motors North American Operations.

Zora Arkus-Duntov died April 21, 1996. April is the cruelest month.

The Advanced Concepts Center in California closed in mid-1996. Some artists were reassigned to studios at Design Staff in Warren, Michigan. Others left the company.

General Motors purchased the multitower Renaissance Center on the Detroit River in 1996 and announced that it would move significant operations out of its slum-surrounded headquarters on West Grand Boulevard.

With C5 development complete, the Corvette team was reduced to a small core of people reporting to Dave Hill. Many of its engineers were reassigned to other programs.

INDEX